MY FIRST LIFE

MY FIRST LIFE

Conversations with Ignacio Ramonet

Hugo Chávez

Translated by Ann Wright

VERSO

London • New York

This book was translated with the support of Mémoire des luttes

This English-language edition published by Verso 2016
Originally published in Spanish as *Mi primera vida*
© Penguin Random House Spain 2013
Translation © Ann Wright 2016

1 3 5 7 9 10 8 6 4 2

Verso
UK: 6 Meard Street, London W1F 0EG
US: 20 Jay Street, Suite 1010, Brooklyn, NY 11201
versobooks.com

Verso is the imprint of New Left Books

ISBN-13: 978-1-78478-383-9 (HB)
ISBN-13: 978-1-78478-385-3 (UK EBK)
ISBN-13: 978-1-78478-386-0 (US EBK)

British Library Cataloguing in Publication Data
A catalogue record for this book is available from the British Library

Library of Congress Cataloging-in-Publication Data
Names: Châavez Frâias, Hugo, interviewee. | Ramonet, Ignacio, interviewer. |
Wright, Ann, 1943– translator.
Title: My first life : conversations with Ignacio Ramonet / Hugo Chavez ;
translated by Ann Wright.
Other titles: Mi primera vida. English
Description: Brooklyn, NY : Verso Books, [2016]
Identifiers: LCCN 2016011444 | ISBN 9781784783839 (hardback : alk. paper)
Subjects: LCSH: Châavez Frâias, Hugo – Interviews. |
Presidents – Venezuela – Interviews. | Presidents – Venezuela – Biography. |
Venezuela – Politics and government – 1974–1999.
Classification: LCC F2329.22.C54 A5 2016 | DDC 987.06/42092 – dc23
LC record available at http://lccn.loc.gov/2016011444

Typeset in Adobe Garamond Pro by Hewer Text UK, Ltd, Edinburgh
Printed in the US by Maple Press

To Maximilien Arveláiz

Contents

PART III
The Road to Power (1982–1998)

One Hundred Hours with Chávez

We had arrived the previous evening at a house somewhere in the middle of the Llanos, the seemingly endless central plains of Venezuela. It was nine in the morning and already baking hot. The house had been lent by a friend and was a simple, rustic, one-storey building typical of the Llanos. It had a tiled roof and at the front a wide, open veranda, furnished with low wrought-iron tables, wicker rocking chairs and dozens of lush potted plants. All around, the hard cracked earth was dotted with bright shrubs, some grandiose tall trees, and others laden with blossom. A tenacious breeze stirred up a golden, perfumed dust but, punished by these burning gusts, the surrounding vegetation appeared limp and exhausted.

In a shady part of the garden, a table had been prepared for the interview with documents and books. While I waited for Hugo Chávez, I sat on a wooden fence surrounding the ranch, or *hato* as they are called in Venezuela. The silence was broken only by birdsong, the odd cock crowing, and the distant throb of a generator.

There were no buildings in sight, no noise of traffic. It was an ideal retreat. No Wi-Fi, not even a mobile phone connection, only a few satellite phones, via a military network, for the bodyguards and the president himself.

The previous afternoon, the Falcon light aircraft in which we were travelling had landed at the small airport of Barinas. Before starting our conversations for this book, Chávez wanted to show me the land of his childhood, the roots of his destiny. The 'setting that made me what I am', he said.

He had arrived almost incognito to avoid protocol and ceremony: simply dressed in trainers, black jeans, white shirt and a lightweight blue military-style jacket, accompanied only by Maximilien Arveláiz, his brilliant young foreign affairs adviser, and several bodyguards in olive-green uniforms. At the foot of the aircraft steps, the Saharan heat and two discreet black 4x4s were waiting for us. Chávez got behind the wheel of the first jeep. Maximilien and I jumped in beside him, while the bodyguards boarded the one behind. Night was beginning to fall. We set off for the historic centre of Barinas.

A low, ramshackle city, Barinas had the feel of a 'frontier' town. It was full of battered pick-up trucks and the spanking 4x4s of the new rich. The men all wore wide-brimmed hats and leather boots. The Llanos is cowboy country, a land of adventure, mythical exploits, contraband, rodeos and wide open spaces. And of *corridos* and *joropos*, the typical ballads and dances of the plains, their own unique country music. Seen from Caracas, this is still very much the Wild West, and the heartland of Venezuelan identity.

Barinas, capital of the state of the same name, has mushroomed in recent years. We were surrounded by frantic activity: construction sites, cranes, road works, gridlock . . . On the outskirts, the architectural style of downright ugliness had wreaked havoc, as in so many other cities, but as we approached the old urban centre, the geometric colonial harmony and the odd impressive historic building reappeared.

In his beautiful calm baritone voice, Chávez recounted the history of the city. He showed me where the Liberator, Simon Bolívar, had passed; where the plainsmen of Páez 'the Centaur' had crossed; where Ezequiel Zamora – 'the general of free men' – liberated Barinas, proclaimed the Federation and left for the decisive battle of Santa Inés on 10 December 1859.[1] Not only did Chávez

---

1   See J. E. Ruiz-Guevara, *Zamora en Barinas*, [facsimile re-edition], Fundación Editorial Pervo y Rana, Caracas, 1999.

know Venezuelan history, he expressed it, lived it, with enthusiasm, and illustrated it with a thousand anecdotes, memories, poems and songs. 'I love my country,' he told me. 'Profoundly. Because, as Alí Primera says, "the country is the man".[2] We must connect the present with the past. Our history is our identity. If you don't know it, you don't know who you are. Only history makes a people aware of itself.'

Suddenly the phone peeped. It was a text message from Fidel Castro congratulating him on that afternoon's speech. He showed me: '21h 30. I was listening to you. I thought it was very good. Congratulations. You're taking a gamble. It was terrific. You're brilliant.' He made no comment, but I could see he was happy. He had a deep affection for Fidel.

We reached the historic centre. It was already dark and the city was not well lit, but we saw the striking Palacio del Marqués and the enormous old prison. That was followed by a tour of Chávez's own personal geography. He showed me his old secondary school – the Liceo O'Leary – and the art academy where he had studied painting; where he had lived as a teenager on the Rodríguez Domínguez estate, and where his friends the Ruiz Guevara family had lived; the local baseball pitch; the house of his first girlfriend. 'I used to walk along this avenue with Nancy Colmenares . . . we called this bar "The Faculty" . . . Radio Barinas was in this building – I did my first radio broadcasts from here.'

The dark night and the tinted car windows meant I could hardly see a thing. What's more, in his nostalgic pilgrimage, Chávez was interweaving memories from the two different periods he had lived here: first during his secondary school years (1966–1971), then as a graduate fresh out of the Military Academy (1975–1977). I got somewhat lost in the labyrinth of his past experiences. He realized, and made a disarming apology: 'Forgive me, memories suddenly came flooding back. You know how memories ambush you at every bend in the road.' He patiently started again, reorganizing the chronology.

---

2 Alí Primera (1942–85), a very popular Venezuelan protest singer–songwriter. President Chávez often quoted his songs, a reference for the entire Venezuelan Left.

The son of schoolteachers, Chávez was a natural pedagogue, who knew instinctively how to put himself on the level of the listener. He enjoyed explaining things clearly and deftly. He was never over-bearing. He hated boring his audience. He wanted to be under-stood and tried hard to achieve it. Almost always, when he was with me, he carried a handful of coloured pencils and a notebook. With his left hand – he was left-handed – he would sketch, draw figures, jot down statistics, and explain concepts, ideas, numbers. He tried to make the abstract visible, and had the knack of simplifying quite complex problems.

He'd acquired that passion for teaching when he was very young: 'I even used to accompany my mother. She was a rural school-teacher in a village called Encharaya. I loved the schoolroom, and listening to my mother teaching the class. I helped in some way or other. I always loved education, the classroom, studying.'

As a schoolboy, student and cadet, Chávez was always a bright spark, that is, top of the class, the one who was exempt from end of year exams because his marks throughout the year had been excel-lent. Especially in science. His teachers and lecturers adored him. He was keen to learn, avid for knowledge, curious about every-thing. He also wanted to fit in, to please, to seduce, to be liked and loved.

Two types of learning came together to form his intellectual make-up: the academic, at which he always shone, and the autodi-dact, his favourite, which enabled him to educate himself, and goes some way to explaining his particular temperament. A gifted child with a high IQ, he learned to make good use of everything he read. This included children's educational magazines like *Tricolor*, or encyclopaedias like *Quillet's*, which he'd learned almost by heart. Chávez was a hyperthymesiac, meaning that everything he read remained imprinted on his mind. He absorbed it, processed it, assimilated it, digested it, and incorporated it into his intellectual capital.

He was always reading. He always had two or three books with him – essays rather than novels – which he read simultaneously, and took notes, underlined things, and made comments in the margins.

As an intellectual, he knew how to 'read productively': he picked out concepts, analyses, stories and examples which he engraved on his prodigious memory, and then beamed out to the public at large through his torrent of speeches and talks. His bedside reading varied. There was the period of *The Path of the Warrior*, by Lucas Estrella, which he quoted hundreds of times and which the whole of Venezuela ended up reading. Then came, among others, *The Open Veins of Latin America* by Eduardo Galeano, and *Hegemony or Survival* by Noam Chomsky, essays which became the indispensable handbook of every good Bolivarian. There was also, more recently, Victor Hugo's *Les Misérables*, 'a wonderful book which I recommend, about people who lived in poverty all their lives. You must read it.' It was astonishing; every book he recommended became an immediate best-seller nationally and, sometimes, internationally.

He could also do anything with his hands, from growing corn to repairing a tank, driving a Belorussian tractor or painting a canvas. He owed this trait, like many others, to his deceased grandmother Rosa Inés, a very intelligent, humble, hard-working woman, with a good education and exceptional common sense. She brought him up, educated him and transmitted to him, from a very early age, a whole philosophy of life. She explained the history of Venezuela as experienced by the common people, the example of solidarity, the secrets of agriculture, how to cook, and how to clean and tidy the modest house, with its thatched roof, earth floor and adobe walls, in which they lived with his brother Adán.

As a boy, Huguito Chávez was very poor – a poverty alleviated by the enormous love of his grandmother, his 'old mum' as he called her. 'I wouldn't swap my childhood for any other,' he told me. 'I was the happiest child on earth.' From the age of six or seven, he used to sell *arañas* in the streets of his small town, Sabaneta; they were spider-like sweets his grandmother made from the fruit picked in her garden. The revenue from his street vending was almost their only income, although he also made *papagayos*, colourful kites made out of straw and paper, and they brought in a bit more money.

So, very soon this third way of learning joined the other two in the brain of the young Chávez, and gave him skills he retained all his life: school, or the theoretical; the instinctive, or self-taught; and the manual, or practical. Combining these three sources of knowledge – with none being considered superior to the other two – is one of the keys to understanding his personality.

His mental make-up, though, was also determined by other qualities.

First was the incredible ease with which he formed relationships and communicated his ideas. He controlled and manipulated his own image with great skill. And he had an admirable facility with words, acquired no doubt during his years as a sweet-seller, a street kid, chatting and haggling with potential clients as they came out of cinemas, shops, games of bowls or cockfights. He was an exceptional communicator, skills honed in senior school and at the Military Academy, where he showed promise as a party organizer and master of ceremonies. He was especially adept at beauty pageants . . .

An exceptional orator, his speeches were entertaining and easy on the ear, colloquial, illustrated by anecdotes, jokes and even songs. However, contrary perhaps to appearances, they were also real didactic compositions: highly structured, with concrete objectives, and prepared with seriousness and professionalism. They generally aimed at transmitting one central idea, pursuing one main avenue of thought within a roundabout discourse, so that nothing was boring or laboured. Chávez would stray from this main avenue of thought and make detours into related themes, memories, anecdotes, jokes, poems, or ballads which did not appear to have any direct connection to his main subject. Then, after seemingly having abandoned his central theme for quite some time, he would swing back to the exact point at which he had left it, creating an awesome subliminal impact on the admiring audience.

This rhetorical technique allowed him to make immensely long speeches. He once asked me, 'How long do speeches by political leaders in France generally last?' I replied that in electoral campaigns they rarely lasted longer than an hour. He pondered for a while and confessed, 'I would just be warming up, I need to speak for about four hours.'

His second quality was his competitive nature. He was a born winner. From very young he had been obsessed by sport; a baseball player of an almost professional standard, a terrible loser, known for giving his all in order to win, within the boundaries of sportsmanship. 'I was a really good pitcher,' he recalled. 'Baseball was my obsession. It taught me to be tough, to endure, to give my best, to show character. It's Venezuela's main sporting passion. We have about 30 million inhabitants, and the same number of baseball experts.'

Third: his enthusiastic enjoyment of popular culture. He loved the tales and ballads of the Llanos, reams of which he could recite by heart; traditional Mexican *rancheras*; protest songs by Alí Primera; the unforgettable box office hits of Mexican cinema of the 1950s and 60s, and the films of popular Hollywood tough guys like Charles Bronson and Clint Eastwood. He was also a fan of television, well versed in the programmes and personalities of all the Venezuelan channels. All these symbolic reference points of mass culture, which he shared with the Venezuelan public, meant he could immediately connect with the majority of the population.

Fourth: his popular religion. 'I'm more of a Christian than a Catholic,' he admitted, 'and more than a Christian, let's say I'm a "Christist", that is, a fervent follower of the teachings of Jesus as told in the Gospels.' He saw Jesus as the 'first revolutionary'. He clearly did not go to mass every Sunday, nor did he particularly respect the Church hierarchy, with a few exceptions. But he believed in magic and the miraculous power of the saints – canonized or not – and, like his grandmother, he was particularly devoted to the Virgin of the Rosary, patron saint of Sabaneta. His popular faith was sincere, and extended to other beliefs, whether indigenous, Afro-Caribbean or Evangelical. In this he felt an empathy with the vast majority of Venezuelans too.

Fifth: his military leadership. In the Military Academy, he learned to give orders and be obeyed. He was taught to behave like a leader, a chief. He never forgot it. Chávez knew how to command. And woe to any who did not know it; the full force of his wrath could fall on them! Although he was generally recognized to be a good-natured man, his temper and bouts of anger were legendary. He had been the best cadet of his generation. He had undergone a strict military training – theoretical and practical – the harshness of which sprang from the Prussian tradition of the Venezuelan Army. He was a military man to the core. And this had forged the distinctive intellectual quality he had, of thinking strategically. He got used to forward thinking, to setting ambitious objectives, and finding a way to achieve them. He put it this way: 'From the very first moment, I liked being a soldier. In the Academy I learned what Napoleon called the "arrow of time". When a strategist plans a battle, he has to think in advance of the "historic moment", then of the "strategic hour", then of the "tactical minute", and finally of the "second of victory". I never forgot that pattern of thinking.'

Sixth: his ability to make people underestimate him. His adversaries – and even some of his friends – regularly tended to do so. Perhaps because of his simplicity, or his physical appearance, or because he talked a lot, or liked making jokes, whatever . . . The fact is that many people fell into the trap of not appreciating his true worth. A very serious mistake. Those who did, bitterly regretted it, and ended up biting the dust.

Seventh: his dedication and diligence. He was an indefatigable worker, willing and tenacious. He didn't know what a weekend was, nor Sundays or holidays. He laboured far into the night, slept for a mere four hours, and was up again at six in the morning. 'It's not a sacrifice,' he often told me. 'There's not enough time in the day to do everything that needs doing. The people expect a lot from us, and we can't let them down. They've been waiting for centuries.' He had no problem subjecting his ministers and colleagues to his tempo. They all knew he could consult them at any time of the night or day. And if they had fallen short in anything, at the drop of a hat he would give them a terrible dressing down. Successive ministers in the President's Office, who looked after cabinet matters and were in the front line, were certainly the most stressed-out people in Venezuela. The burnout rate was so rapid that it had the highest turnover of any government department.

And lastly: his solidarity with the poor, the social group with which he identified. He would often comment, 'I'm always reminded of what Gramsci said: "You don't go to the people, you have to be the people." ' He lived his childhood and adolescence among the have-nots, and his 'old mum' inculcated in him a respect for the poor. 'With her,' he said, 'I learned the value of the forgotten people, those who have never had anything and who are the soul of Venezuela. Among them I could see the injustices of this world and the pain of sometimes having nothing to eat. She taught me solidarity, by sharing the little she had with families who had even less. I'll always remember what she taught me. I'll never forget my roots.'

We had left Barinas and were heading for Sabaneta, his birthplace, some sixty kilometres away. It was past ten o'clock and we were driving in the dark. From time to time, as he drove, the president would ask for a cup of black coffee. Chávez was a coffee addict, drinking over thirty cups a day. I've seen him smoke a cigarette in private, too. Never in public.

Halfway to Sabaneta, we came across a roadblock. A military patrol had closed the road and was inspecting car boots and checking drivers' documents. They were looking for smuggled drugs and weapons, common enough in those parts near the border with Colombia. The soldiers had laid a sort of metal rake with iron spikes on the road. The 4x4 carrying the bodyguards drove on alongside the waiting cars. They talked to the officer in charge. There was a sudden flurry of activity. But Chávez didn't expect special treatment, he was content to wait his turn. The inspection of the three or four vehicles in front of us was done in double time. We reached the officer. He stood to attention. Two bodyguards approached. Chávez lowered the window and greeted the soldier seriously and affectionately. He fired questions at him: what was his name, where was he from, what regiment, his commanding officer, was he married, children, wife, family? After this friendly chat he adopted a more military tone, and asked about his mission. What were they doing, why, what was the purpose, and with what results?

As we were driving off, he said, 'They've detected groups of armed men, mostly paramilitaries and hired killers. They come to cause mayhem with a very clear political objective, that is, to destabilize and spread the idea that in Bolivarian Venezuela there is insecurity and disorder. Some have even infiltrated as far as Caracas, where they control the drug traffic in certain violent neighbourhoods. Others have a more precise mission: to kill me. Once, we captured a commando of almost 150 men with Venezuelan Army weapons and uniforms.[3] I still get death threats, but now our Military Intelligence works. It's not like in 2002. If they try another coup d'état like the one on 11 April 2002, they'll regret it. We're going to make this revolution stronger.'

We were nearing Sabaneta. Before driving into town Chávez took a detour, turning off the paved road down a stony track full of potholes and bends. Soon we were enveloped by thick vegetation. It was dark as the inside of an ocelot's mouth. The 4×4s advanced carefully, guided by the headlights. Chávez wanted to show me the ford on the Boconó River, where Sabaneta was founded. 'This ford is called the Baronero Pass,' he told me. 'It was the only pass from the Llanos to central Venezuela. All the roads converged at this point, so hostels and inns were built in the surrounding country-side. That's how Sabaneta was born: founded on a "sabaneta", a large meseta on the right bank of the Boconó.'

We reached a small esplanade. We parked the car and got out. By the light of a couple of torches, we crept towards the wooded banks of the river. The waters flowed black and slow, with the dying roar of a wounded animal. I found the place gloomy and disquieting. Chávez, however, was happy, relaxed, smiling. He walked around without a torch, as if he knew every stone. He breathed in deeply, the air was heavy with nocturnal aromas: 'Here I feel like a fish in water. I came to this place thousands of times, to play with my brothers and my friends, to swim, to fish with my father, to enjoy this oasis of nature, a haven of freshness in the baking summer of the Llanos.'

We retraced the road back to the asphalt. The phone didn't stop ringing the whole journey. From Mauricio Funes, newly elected president of El Salvador; from his minister of education about the

---

3   See Luis Britto García and Miguel Ángel Pérez, *La invasión paramilitar. Operación Daktari*, Ediciones Correo del Orinoco, Caracas, 2012.

University of the Armed Forces (UNEFA); from the health minister ('there's no swine flu'); from several governors.[4]

Chávez talked and dealt with things extremely seriously as he drove. He was brief and to the point, he listened and took decisions. Suddenly a text message from the vice president worried him.[5] He showed me: 'We've found a cache of FAL weapons. Five with telescopic sights, two pistols, six revolvers, three rifles. Foreign. Dominican.' He texted something back and immediately received the following reply: 'Half a kilo of C-4 explosives, 20,000 cartridges. 6 military uniforms. Symbols. Jackets. Number plates. 3 walkie-talkies. 3 Dominicans. 2 men, 1 woman. Young. Woman 28. Both men 36. In the apartment of a European.' We later learned the names of the Dominicans (Luini Omar Campusano de la Cruz, Edgar Floirán Sánchez and Diomedis Campusano Pérez). The European was a Frenchman, Frédéric Laurent Bouquet. And what at first seemed to be more related to drugs- and arms-smuggling mafias, eventually turned out to be more political and connected to an attempted magnicide.[6]

It was getting late. We reached Sabaneta and drove straight to the old town.[7] 'It has grown a lot: when I was a boy, this was a village with four dirt roads. In winter, it was all mud, cars couldn't pass. Yet for me, it was the whole world . . . a microcosm of the complexities of the planet.' First, he showed me, at the Camoruco roundabout, a hundred-year-old tree. 'Bolívar rested at the foot of this tree.

---

4   Mauricio Funes, candidate of the *Frente Farabundo Martí de Liberación Nacional* (FMLN), was elected president of El Salvador on 15 March 2009; he took office on 1 June 2009.

5   Ramón Carrizales, vice president of Venezuela from January 2008 to January 2009.

6   Arrested on 18 June 2009, Laurent Bouquet was tried in August of the same year, and sentenced to four years in prison. He was freed on 29 December 2012, and deported from Venezuela. At that time, the Venezuelan minister for prisons, Iris Varela, revealed, 'An agent of the French intelligence services who finished his prison sentence for his part in an attempt to assassinate President Hugo Chávez, after having confessed to his involvement, has been deported from Venezuela.' (Cable Ria Novosti, 29 December 2012).

7   Sabaneta (state of Barinas) is now the capital of the municipality of Alberto Arvelo Torrealba and has 40,000 inhabitants.

There's no historic record, but popular memory has passed the tale down from generation to generation.' We then went to see the church, an unprepossessing modern building: 'My childhood church where I was an altar boy was a more humble wooden affair, with more authenticity and charm. It burnt down and they erected this one.'

At that time of the night, the streets were almost empty. They were clean, well-lit and arranged in a grid pattern; the houses mostly single-storey. In those days Sabaneta had the feel of a quiet, unpretentious rural town.[8] The heat was still asphyxiating. Windows and doors were wide open. As we drove by, we could see families inside with the lights on watching television. Others had put chairs in front of their doors and were chatting outside. Several children were playing on their bikes. Here and there, like in the old days in Castile, groups of women were sitting outside their front doors on stools, with their backs towards the street.

Ours were the only cars around at that time of night. Swiping at mosquitoes, people watched us pass with mistrustful faces. 'I know almost all of them,' said Chávez, 'but if we stop to say hello, the whole town will come tumbling out to greet us, and we won't get out of here till dawn.'

He went on to show me his favourite childhood haunts: 'This is where the cinema was, this is the ice cream parlour where they sold fruit from my grandmother's garden; and in this shop Adán and I got our Mexican cartoons and comics like *The Silver Mask*, *The Golden Cowboy* and other superheroes of our childhood. I sold my spider sweets in all these streets, and on that corner I bought chicha from Timoleón Escalona; that's where the Italians lived, there the Russians, further on the Arabs, and over there the Canary Islanders; this is the Calle Real, that's where I fell over and almost broke my nose; and over there was my school, the only one

---

8   About Sabaneta in the first part of the twentieth century, see: Ricardo Aro Durán, *Sabaneta, Vivencias y recuerdos*, Ediciones Fondo Cultural Sabaneta, Mérida, 2008; and Pedro Mazzei G., *Sabaneta de Barinas, Historias para una historia*, Editorial Nemesio Martínez, Caracas, 1992.

in the village in those days; I was, I think, a good pupil, very spoilt by my teachers.'[9]

We went up to where his grandmother used to live, the house where he was born and raised. He did not stop, as if not wanting to contaminate his happy memories: 'We were very poor, "the bottom of the heap". The house was demolished, and nothing is left of our quarter-acre garden either. Only a few of those mango trees are the same as fifty years ago. Time has taken the others. But the past is engraved on my memory forever.'

We drove away from Sabaneta, his own intimate Macondo, and plunged into the heat of the night on the Llanos. Concentrating on the road, the president drove in silence, lost in thought, submerged in his memories. After a while he said, 'It's so important never to lose the sense of where you came from.'

I first met Hugo Chávez in 1999. I talked to him in Caracas, a few months after he became president. His image then was of a *golpista*, a soldier who'd staged a military coup. And that, in Latin America where for decades so many people had been tormented by the brutality of army '*gorilas*', is the worst thing you can possibly say.

I was not a stranger to Venezuela. First, for professional reasons. In the 1970s and 80s, I'd been head of the Sociology of Latin America Department of the Université Paris-VII. And for years I had run the Latin American Geopolitics section of the monthly *Le Monde diplomatique*, which meant that in Paris I met, among others, the veteran former guerrilla leader Douglas Bravo and his then partner Argelia Melet, and had long conversations with them.

Venezuela was also one of the South American countries I knew best, because of the vagaries of my personal life. During the 1980s, I'd had a close relationship with Mariana Otero, daughter of the great writer and intellectual of the Venezuelan Left, Miguel Otero Silva, and of the progressive activist María Teresa Castillo, and sister of Miguel Henrique Otero, current director of *El Nacional* newspaper.

---

9   Chicha is a soft drink made from milk and rice, very popular in Venezuela. Cinnamon and condensed milk are added and it is served over ice.

Thanks to them, to their warm hospitality in their holiday home in Macuto and their unforgettable house 'Macondo' in Caracas, full of beautiful works of art and souvenirs from many of the famous people who visited them (Alejo Carpentier, Pablo Neruda, Gabriel García Márquez, François Mitterrand, Jacques Lacan, etc.), I was able to meet well-known Venezuelan journalists, writers, artists and intellectuals. From the unforgettable Margot Benacerraf to the well-loved Arturo Uslar Pietri, and including José Vicente Rangel, Moisés Naím, Teodoro Petkoff, Oswaldo Barreto, Tomás Borge, Tulio Hernández, Antonio Pasquali, Isaac Chocrón, Ignacio Quintana, Juan Barreto, Ibsen Martínez, José Ignacio Cabrujas, Haydée Chavero, among many others.

In this way, I was lucky enough to find myself in Venezuela at key moments of its recent history. For instance, invited to give various seminars, I went there just after the Caracazo of 27 February 1989. I remember finding a country traumatized by the outbreak of so much violence. I saw how a sector of the terrified bourgeoisie bought weapons to defend themselves; I even took part in a collective training course on how to use the weapons.

I also found myself in Caracas, giving a seminar at CELARG, in the weeks following the rebellion of 4 February 1992, during the demise of the Acción Democrática (AD) government of President Carlos Andrés Pérez, whom I interviewed several times.[10] In the articles that I wrote then about this 'military insurrection' led by 'Lieutenant Colonel Hugo Chávez', I said that 'not only did the population not oppose him, in many places they enthusiastically supported him'.[11] I added that in the Venezuela of the social democrat Carlos Andrés Pérez, 'more than half the population lived below the poverty line. Inequality was on the rise; the richest 5 per cent possessed 20 per cent of the nation's wealth, while 40 per cent of children still do not go to school.' And this in 'one of the world's major oil-exporting countries'. In ten years, sales of hydrocarbons had brought Venezuela a foreign exchange revenue 'equivalent to

---

10   CELARG, Centro de Estudios Latinoamericanos Rómulo Gallegos, Caracas.

11   Ignacio Ramonet, 'Les rébellions à venir', *Le Monde diplomatique*, Paris, March 1992 and 'Derniers carnavals', *Le Monde diplomatique*, Paris, November 1992.

twenty-five Marshall Plans'. A sum 'squandered by a corrupt and incompetent political class'.

I also stated that 'Comandante Hugo Chávez, leader of the Revolutionary Bolivarian Movement (MBR-200), has become the most popular man in Venezuela, and is glorified on its city walls.' And I reproduced an extract from a television interview which Chávez gave secretly from the Yare prison, which the authorities had banned but which circulated throughout the country on videocassettes. 'We do not believe', declared Chávez, 'in the false dichotomy between dictatorship and democracy which the ideologues of pseudo-democratic regimes in Latin America expound in order to manipulate public opinion and hide the grave defects and degeneration of their phoney democratic systems ... Either profound changes radically modify the current situation, or there will be a huge outbreak of violence.'

When the majority of political forces, both in Venezuela and abroad – and particularly the social democratic parties which supported Carlos Andrés Pérez – called this insurrection 'a coup d'état', my 1992 articles flagged up the opinion of analysts who pointed out that 'this is not a classic Latin American coup d'état. The Nasser-type conspiracy of 4 February was led by progressive army officers.'

I tried to emphasise a different, geopolitical, view. In an international context characterized by three important aspects – the rise of neoliberalism, the defeat of an authoritarian concept of State socialism, and the collapse of the Soviet Union – the two Venezuelan bombshells (the Caracazo of February 1989 and the uprising of 1992) marked the beginning of a new cycle of international resistance to the insolence of the financial markets. While some people hailed the 'end of history', the Venezuelan people showed that in Latin America history was on the march again.

I went back to Caracas in May 1995, invited this time by President Rafael Caldera, to take part in a seminar about communication.[12] The historic leader of Copei, the Christian Democratic

---

12   Ignacio Ramonet, 'Le Vénézuela vers la guerre sociale?' *Le Monde diplomatique*, Paris, July 1995.

party, Caldera had abandoned it to stand – after Pérez had been removed from office because of corruption – in the December 1993 elections, supported by, among others, the Venezuelan Communist Party (PCV) and the Movement Towards Socialism (MAS). He won and took office in February 1994.

Caldera immediately had to face a serious financial crisis caused by the collapse of the Banco Latino and a dozen big Venezuelan financial institutions. When I interviewed him, he was still in his critical phase of standing up to the pressure of the IMF and neoliberal hegemonic forces. Several of his ministers, like former guerrilla leaders Pompeyo Márquez and Teodoro Petkoff, came from the historic Left. His government, implementing a Keynesian-style interventionist economic policy, had re-established exchange controls and fixed prices for basic necessities. 'That is indispensable,' Caldera told me, 'in order to preserve the purchasing power of Venezuela's poorest citizens. I prefer to defend the workers and social justice than obey macroeconomic indicators. I radically oppose the new economic totalitarianism of the fanatics who favour imposing the same norms on every country just to satisfy the interests of the big financial markets.'[13] However, in April of 1996, Caldera and his ministers from a Left in disarray ended up kowtowing to the IMF, and embracing that selfsame neoliberal dogma.[14]

In my article of July1995, I stressed the unprecedented levels of violent crime reached during those decades of corruption and social decomposition. The article began with the incident being discussed at the time by the entire media:

> Three delinquents, masked and armed, broke into a house in a residential suburb of Caracas where two families were having dinner. They looted the house, stole all valuables and destroyed with particular ferocity all signs of opulence. They then raped the women, granddaughters and grandmothers alike. And went on to rape the menfolk.

---

13   Ibid.
14   See Ignacio Quintana, *Caldera ilegítimo*, Ediciones Paedica, Caracas, 1999.

The sociologist Tulio Hernández told me, 'There are more deaths here per week than during the war in Bosnia. And the violence has reached such heights of madness that the delinquents don't stop at burgling a house. They want to humiliate, inflict pain, kill. Every month, dozens of adolescents are murdered by other youngsters just for their trainers. Dying for a pair of trainers has become tragically banal.'

This was confirmed by two other sociologists, Carmen Scotto and Anabel Castillo. 'They beat people for the pleasure of it, they kill people for the pleasure of it; without considering the value of their lives. They are drunk on cruelty, with a hatred akin to delirium; and this tells us the state of decomposition of a society without values.' In those days, about fifty people were murdered in Caracas every day, and at the weekend between twenty and thirty youngsters. And not only in the shanty towns:

> In one week near the end of May [1995] several well-known personalities – among them a surgeon, a lawyer, and the famous baseball player Gustavo Polidor – were murdered on their doorsteps, in front of their families, by delinquents who had come to steal their cars . . . Nowhere is safe. Some fifty bus drivers were killed in the capital between January and May of 1995, and in the interior, 'motorway pirates' ambush lorries, steal their cargoes, and slaughter the drivers. The overcrowded militarized prisons are absolute hell. Last year [1995], over 600 prisoners were murdered.

If I reproduce these extracts, it is to remind people that violence, insecurity and criminality in Venezuela are not new. And also to contextualize the non-stop accusations that the dominant press throws at Bolivarian governments on this subject today.

One of the first measures President Rafael Caldera took was to free from prison, on 24 March 1994, the popular hero adored in the shanty towns – Hugo Chávez. And one of the first trips abroad Chávez took, in December 1994, was to Cuba. Fidel Castro received him with full honours. This demonstrated, to those who still

doubted the Venezuelan lieutenant colonel's political orientation –
golpista or progressive – that the seasoned comandante placed him,
very clearly, on the Left.

Chávez then proceeded to tour his country with a handful of
compañeros (among them Nicolás Maduro), immersing themselves
in the depths of rural Venezuela, talking to the poor and the forgotten. He put forward one simple idea: in order to drag the country
out of the mire, radical constitutional change and a new republic
were needed. He believed that the 'pseudo-democracy' in Venezuela,
instituted by the Pact of Punto Fijo, was due for an overhaul;
prolonging its agony by participating in elections of any kind was
pointless. This abstention option was in no way shared by the main
parties on the Left (the Communist Party, the MAS, La Causa
R[adical]), which were either part of President Caldera's government, or participating in the elections themselves, in the belief that
the system could be reformed 'from within'.

Isolated, delegitimized, attacked, persecuted, Chávez maintained
this position. A charismatic leader and magnificent speaker, he felt
a rapport with the people. In the wilder provinces of the interior,
and in shanty towns round the periphery of the urban centres, ordinary people identified with him. They saw him as one of them: for
the way he talked, for the solidarity in his words, for his shared
cultural references, for his sensitivity to the misfortunes of others,
for his way of being, even for the way he looked. Chávez was a
mixture of native Indian, European and African. Tricontinental.
The three roots of Venezuelan identity. In this sense, he was always
an exception among the predominantly white Venezuelan elites.
The people shared his rejection of a political elite that was distant,
wealthy, and more often than not, corrupt. Chávez's organization
– MBR-200 – was becoming an irresistible force.

That was when Hugo Chávez changed his strategy. He had
carried out a series of opinion polls which showed two things:
one, that the majority of Venezuelans wanted him to stand in the
presidential elections on 6 December 1998; and two, that if he
stood in the elections, he would win. Being a pragmatist, he
promptly abandoned both the abstention option he had defended

for so long and the military path to power, and decided to run for office. He had trouble convincing his own friends. But he managed. 'The important thing is the Constituent Assembly,' he said. So he founded the Fifth Republic Movement (MVR). And after a spectacular campaign, he won the elections with an unusually high turnout, sweeping away the two main parties (Copei and AD) which had dominated political life for decades.[15] At the age of forty-five, he became one of the youngest presidents in Venezuelan history.

His investiture was held on 2 February 1999. And less than two months later, on 25 April, he called as promised a referendum for a Constituent Assembly. He got 88 per cent of the votes. The Bolivarian Revolution was on the march. In July, members were elected to the Assembly. The Polo Patriótico, the president's coalition, swept the board again, with 121 of the 128 seats. The new Assembly began work on the Fifth Republic's Constitution, the text of which had to be ratified by a national referendum on 15 December 1999.

That was the political context in Venezuela when the possibility of my interviewing Hugo Chávez first came up. The president had read some of my articles and several of my books, and wanted to talk to me. The meeting was arranged through the president's press office, run then by Carmen Rania, the wife of Miguel Henrique Otero. I knew this couple very well, as I already mentioned. When I arrived in Caracas at the beginning of September 1999, I visited them. Although today they are – especially Miguel Henrique – among the strongest opponents of Bolivarian policies, in those days they were sincere and enthusiastic Chávez supporters. The newspaper *El Nacional*, of which Miguel Henrique was the editor, had played an important role in bringing about the resignation of Carlos Andrés Pérez, and had campaigned for Chávez, contributing to his electoral victory in 1998. The couple had nothing but praise for the

---

15 The result was as follows: Hugo Chávez (MVR) 56.20 per cent; Henrique Salas Römer (Project Venezuela) 39.97 per cent; Irene Sáez (IRENE) 2.82 per cent. There was no need for a second round.

president, his 'peaceful democratic revolution', his political skill, his tactical and strategic genius, and the breath of fresh air that the Fifth Republic and the new Constitution represented.

Such was their enthusiasm that, before talking to the president, it seemed only normal and professional to also seek out critical opinions and analyses. For several days I listened to the views of various businessmen, economists, intellectuals and academics who were radically opposed to the policies of the new government. They had good arguments for expecting 'certain failure', namely that it was impossible for a Bolivarian Venezuela to go against the current of economic globalization, and they were wary of the Chávez brand of *caudillismo*. Some were betting on foreign pressure: 'The United States will never allow a political adventure in this region, let alone in a country on which it depends for its oil supply.'

It was in this climate that I went to my interview with Hugo Chávez in the Miraflores Palace. I remember that first meeting very well. It was Saturday, 18 September 1999. He received me in his office. I noticed two conspicuous black-and-white photographs on his desk: one was of his great-grandfather Pedro Pérez Delgado, alias Maisanta, one of the 'last rebels on horseback' who rose up against the dictator Juan Vicente Gómez and died in prison in 1924; the other was of his grandmother, Rosa Inés. There were other framed photos of his parents, Hugo de los Reyes and Elena, and his four children, Rosa Virginia, María Gabriela, Hugo and Rosinés. Also a pile of books, documents, a rough draft of a speech, and a big map of Latin America.

I was seeing him in person for the first time. It was immediately obvious that his reputation as a warm, spontaneous, good-humoured man was no fantasy. He gave me the traditional Latin American handshake and bear hug. With a big smile, he said he had read my articles on Venezuela, particularly my analysis of the rebellion of 4 February 1992. He was taller than I had imagined, at least one metre eighty, athletic and muscular. He looked elegant; his thick black hair was meticulously groomed; he had smooth cinnamon-coloured skin, a mole on the right side of his forehead, prominent cheekbones and closely shaven, lotion-scented cheeks; an impeccable set of teeth, with an endearing gap between the bottom ones; small, penetrating, slanted eyes; manicured hands with a gold wedding ring on his right hand; casually dressed for the weekend, without a tie, a gold and brown tartan shirt under a grey V-necked sleeveless jumper, and grey jeans. Being smart and well-groomed was clearly important to him.

Naturally enough for a connoisseur of the philosophy of history, he began by talking about the heroic founders of the Venezuelan *Patria*. I asked who, apart from Bolívar himself, were the three other heroes represented on the giant murals decorating the presidential office. He explained, 'When I arrived, my desk was over there, with my back to Bolívar and facing Urdaneta.[16] I changed it around. The other two are Sucre and Páez.[17] One of the four should not be there, whereas Zamora is missing.'[18]

During that first conversation, I tried to decipher the famous 'enigma of the two faces of Chávez' which Gabriel García Márquez wrote about.[19] I was surprised by his excellent knowledge of Gramsci. He quoted, 'We're experiencing, at the same time, a death and a birth. The death of an old model, worn out, hated; and the birth of a new, different political movement, which brings the people hope. The old one is dying, and the new cannot be born, but this crisis is giving birth to a revolution.'

I asked him what he understood by revolution.

'Look,' he replied, 'we're inventing here. Revolution is a state of continual invention. After the economic crisis, Venezuela went primarily through a moral and ethical crisis because of the social

---

16 Rafael Urdaneta (1788–1845), Venezuelan statesman and general, the last president of Gran Colombia.

17 Antonio José de Sucre (1790–1830), Bolívar's comrade in arms, victor at the decisive battles of Junín and Ayacucho (1824). José Antonio Páez (1770–1873), general in the Venezuelan Independence War, 'the Centaur of the Plains', three times president. He is considered the archetypal Venezuelan *caudillo,* or strongman.

18 Ezequiel Zamora (1817–1860), soldier and statesman, one of the heroes of the Federal War (1859–63), who championed agrarian reform for peasant farmers.

19 See Ignacio Ramonet, 'Chávez', *Le Monde diplomatique*, Paris, October 1999; Gabriel García Márquez, 'Los dos Chávez', *La Nación,* Buenos Aires, 31 January 1999.

insensitivity of its leaders. Democracy is not only political equality. It is also, and actually most importantly, social, economic and cultural equality; all within political freedom. These are the aims of the Bolivarian Revolution. I want to be president of the poor. I love the people. But we need to learn the lessons of the failures of other revolutions which, even while espousing these aims, betrayed them; and even when they achieved them, they did it by eliminating democracy and freedom. You need creativity to make a revolution. And one of the worst aspects of the current crisis is the crisis of ideas. Our objective is for the people to live with humanity, dignity and decency. Happiness is the ultimate aim of politics. We have to make the Kingdom of Heaven reality here on earth. Our aim is not only to live better but to "live well".'

And he added, 'Our project is simply to establish the "most perfect system of government", along the lines which the Liberator set out in his Address to the Congress at Angostura: "The most perfect system of government is the one which creates the greatest possible happiness, the greatest social well-being and the greatest political stability." '[20]

Although he had been in office for barely six months, some international media outlets were accusing him of 'authoritarian Jacobinism', 'autocratic tendencies' and 'preparing a modern form of coup d'état'.[21] Absurd. There was a series of democratic elections. And despite the atmosphere of heightened passions in Venezuela at the time – when the excitement of political discussion and debate were reminiscent of France in May 1968 – there was no serious violence, nor any form of censorship of the opposition, journalists or the media, many of whom, on the contrary, did not balk at ferocious criticism of the new president.

'These accusations sadden me,' confessed Chávez, 'because what we want to do is move from a representative democracy to a participative, more direct, democracy. With the people playing a greater

---

20   Bolívar speech, February 1819.

21   See, for example, *New York Times*, 21 August 1999, and *International Herald Tribune*, 1 September 1999.

role at every level of decision-making. That is, we want more democracy, not less. This will enable us to fight human rights abuses of all kinds.' He explained that the text of the new Constitution, then being debated in the Assembly, would give greater autonomy to local authorities. It would introduce the popular initiative referendum, and the 'power-to-revoke' referendum, which would force all elected representatives, including the president of the Republic, once they had completed half their mandate, to stand for their office again, if that were the will of the people.

The new Constitution would also envisage, among other things, the right to conscientious objection; gender equality; explicit prohibition of the practice of 'disappearing' people, carried out in the past by the forces of law and order; the appointment of an ombudsman; recognition of the rights of the indigenous or original peoples of Venezuela; and the introduction of a 'moral authority' charged with combating corruption and abuse.

On the subject of corruption, he gave me a typically witty account of how, during his first months in office, he had been courted by big business leaders and the rich elite, those who saw themselves as Venezuela's 'natural owners', and offered all kinds of tempting gifts – expensive cars, apartments, business opportunities – just as they had done with numerous presidents in the past. They thought Chávez would be just another politician with a dual discourse and a dual morality. But Chávez had driven them from the Miraflores Palace, like, as he put it, 'Christ driving the moneylenders from the Temple'. From then on, those oligarchs began to conspire against him. 'We can't buy him, so we'll get rid of him.' That's when they launched the conspiracies, the attacks, the sabotage, the media campaigns of demonization, and the preparations for the coup of 2002.

And what was his economic policy? Chávez explained very clearly that he wanted to move away from the neoliberal economic model and resist globalization. 'We want to build a more horizontal state,' he said. 'Work, and not capital, will be what really creates wealth. We will prioritize the human. We want to put the economy at the service of the people. Our people deserve better. We need to find

the balance between the market, the state and society. We need to
bring together the "invisible hand" of the market and the "visible
hand" of the state, in an economic space within which the market
exists as far as possible and the state as much as necessary.'

He reminded me that 'a hundred years ago, imperialism assigned
to Venezuela one single task in the international division of labour:
that of oil producer. It paid a very low price for that oil, and everything else – food, industrial goods – we had to import. Now, one of
our objectives is economic independence and alimentary sovereignty within, of course, the context of protecting the environment
and ecological imperatives.' Private property and foreign investment were guaranteed, within the limits required by the greater
interests of the state, which would retain under its control (or take
over) strategic sectors whose sale would mean the loss of part of
national sovereignty. That is, exactly what the National Council of
the Resistance (CNR) in France proposed at the end of the Second
World War, or what General de Gaulle did when he established the
Fifth Republic in France in 1958. In the context of neoliberal
globalization and the fever of privatization, these measures seem
even more revolutionary.

Listening to him discuss those objectives, I asked myself, 'What
else can the main protagonists of globalization, owners of so much
of the mass media, do but demonize Chávez and his Bolivarian
Revolution?'

We spent hours talking. I asked whether he would define himself
as a nationalist, and he said he considered himself a 'patriot'.
Quoting de Gaulle, he explained, 'Being a patriot is loving your
country. Being a nationalist is hating everyone else's.' In a typical
gesture of a chief of staff, he opened the big map of Latin America
on his desk and commented that Venezuela's 'backbone was in the
wrong place', a consequence of 'past colonial planning'. He showed
me how, in an ideal geography, the capital city would be situated in
the centre of the country, and described the huge infrastructural
projects that were indispensable to the creation of a cohesive state:
railways, motorways, gas pipelines, oil pipelines, bridges, ports,
dams, tunnels, airports.

He spoke of how imperative South American integration was, an integration announced and desired by Simón Bolívar, and 'dreamed of by all Latin American revolutionaries'. He pointed out on the map how the Liberator had chosen to free South America via the 'Andean axis' of Colombia, Ecuador, Peru and Bolivia, and declared that to liberate it from neoliberal influence today, they could opt for an alliance of the 'Atlantic axis' of Brazil, Uruguay and Paraguay. I was impressed by his acute understanding of Brazil, its history and economy, something that was not very common among Spanish-speaking Latin American leaders. He also revealed his intention to free the continent of vertical, North–South relationships, and establish 'horizontal links' with Africa, Asia and the Muslim Arab world.

The unusual way he reasoned, always mixing theory and praxis, history and society, and also the international scope of his thinking, to me made his political perspective unique. I was seduced by his original thought processes, always factual, never dogmatic, and often bolstered by quotations from progressive thinkers, chiefly Latin Americans. There was no doubt he thought like a man of the Left, structurally Marxist, but – mercifully – free of the academic references to the 'obligatory pantheon' of Marx, Engels, Lenin, Trotsky, etc. Chávez thought for himself, he had an original mind. He was nobody's clone, nor the sequel to any existing system.

As I listened to him talk so passionately about such a plethora and range of projects, I became convinced that this man had not arrived at the presidency by accident. He was not just passing through the Miraflores Palace. There was no doubt he was going to create a discipline and a doctrine. He seemed driven by a burning and ambitious mission: to turn Venezuela upside down, stand it firmly on its feet at last, transform it from top to toe, make it a Latin America leader again as it had been in the days of Bolívar, liberate it from poverty and ignorance, give poor people back their dignity, and restore their pride in patriotism. In a nutshell, make Venezuela, as he said, 'a great country'. At no time did I sense any personal ambition or greed. He hated caudillismo. But his desire to create a *patria*, a motherland, was boundless.

It seemed to me that the 'enigma of the two faces of Chávez' was resolved by simply observing that in his personality two temperaments existed side by side: a rational, logical, Cartesian, pragmatic mind cohabiting with an altruistic, affectionate, enthusiastic, chaotic, sentimental nature. Because of his social background, Chávez understood early on that the world gives you nothing for free, and that each individual has to deal with his circumstances. He realized that material conditions determine social consciousness. He had to overcome the weight of history and the powerful forces ranged against him. He discovered power relations and the different forms of violence, both material and symbolic. That could have made him bitter, spiteful or resentful. But he was not at all, because he had very soon decided not to accept society's inequalities. In this sense, Chávez was always an '*indignado*' – a rebel who throughout his life sought freedom, fighting coercion and refusing to comply with demands that seemed absurd or unjust. The one constant trait of his personality was his rejection of resignation. Hence his great spirit of resistance and his denunciation of an intolerable economic and social system under the hegemony of the relationships of power.

I came out of that first meeting convinced that something new was happening in Latin America. This man was bound to create a new current and doctrine. And it would not be long, I felt, before the Chávez 'hurricane' swept through the continent raising polemic and controversy; but also enthusiasm, passion and supporters. I contacted friends among journalists and intellectuals in Europe and Latin America, progressives all, to share my positive impression, and invite them to visit Caracas, to see with their own eyes this democratic revolution on the march. With few exceptions, they all replied the same thing: 'Soldiers no! *Golpistas* never!' They were wrong. But their reaction showed that it would be an uphill struggle for the leader of Bolivarianism to win them round.

I met Chávez again in Paris in October 2001, one month after the terrible attacks of 11 September in Manhattan and Washington. Invited by René Blanc, rector of the Académie de Paris, he came to the Sorbonne to give a lecture entitled 'Transforming Venezuela, a

Possible Utopia?'[22] in the prestigious amphitheatre of the venerable Paris university. The organizers had also asked me to speak, together with three other well-known intellectuals, Viviane Forrester, Richard Gott and James Petras.

In his unique metaphorical style, Chávez began by conjuring up the young Bolívar in the French capital.[23] 'Walking these Paris streets two hundred years ago was a young man who had crossed the Atlantic; as he walked, aflame with passion, he set everywhere he passed on fire, like Nietzsche's Zarathustra when he climbed the mountain.' He spoke of his political project: 'We are not improvising. From way back we have had clear ideas and a clearly defined path.' He spoke in solidarity with the victims of the 9/11 attacks: 'The twenty-first century must be the century of peace; we must destroy the cannons and silence the drums of war.' He described how the campaign of demonization against him had ramped up a notch: 'They keep telling lies about me. I would not be surprised if, any minute now, they didn't accuse me of hiding Osama bin Laden in Venezuela. They also told lies about Bolívar and he died a poor man, alone, almost crucified. He once said, "Jesus Christ, Don Quixote and I are the three greatest scoundrels that ever lived, for having dreamed of a better world."'

Sophisticated and well argued, his speech was a triumph. It positively impressed many of those who had swallowed the idiotic notion of Chávez the *gorila*, or uniformed thug. Many French people who were interested in Latin America began to change their mind about him and to think of him in a more constructive way.

I met Chávez again on various occasions. Most importantly, a few days before the coup d'état of April 2002, when the whole of Caracas was talking about an imminent pronunciamento. The dominant press was relentless in its portrayal of the president as a

---

22   See *Foro en el Gran Anfiteatro de La Sorbonne, París, Octubre 2001. Transformar a Venezuela, ¿una utopía posible?*, document edited by the President's Office, Miraflores Palace, Caracas, 2001, with an introduction by Maximilien Arveláiz, colour photos of the event and texts of all the papers.

23   See Gustavo Pereira, *El joven Bolívar*, Fundación Defensoría del Pueblo, Caracas, 2007.

'dictator', even a 'Hitler', and calling for him to be overthrown. Chávez, as the peaceful and affable man he was, appeared serene.[24] To persuade me that everything was under control, he invited me for a spin round Caracas that evening in a customized car he drove himself. He had no bodyguards or security, but kept several weapons in the car. On two or three occasions, he stopped and got out to talk with groups of street traders, who couldn't believe their eyes. They hugged and cheered him. Not without a certain naivety, he revealed that the very same afternoon he had spoken to the US ambassador, Charles Shapiro, who had assured him that his country 'would never get involved in an adventure like a coup' against Venezuelan democracy.[25]

Less than a week later, of course, a coup by the military and the media, backed by Washington, tried to overthrow Chávez. He was a whisker away from being shot by the coup leaders. He was very nearly assassinated. But, brimming with indignation, the people came out into the streets to defend him, and rescued him. He returned to power in less than forty-eight hours, and instead of seeking revenge, provided an impressive example of generosity and responsibility.

This was followed by the 'oil coup', several assassination attempts, and numerous international defamatory campaigns. Chávez – who often quoted Trotsky's 'the revolution needs the lash of a counter-revolution' – took advantage of each one of these attacks to radicalize his political project, always within a democratic framework, putting each new idea to the popular vote. As of 1999, Chávez submitted his ideas for approval at the ballot box about fifteen times – doubtless a world record – with the democratic nature of these consultations confirmed by respected international bodies.

When in 2001, my friend Bernard Cassen and I created the first World Social Forum in Porto Alegre, Brazil (under the slogan

---

24   See the editorial of the monthly magazine *Exceso*, April 2002.

25   Known in Washington for his experience at coups d'état, Charles S. Shapiro (b. 1949) had been applauded for his work as military attaché in Chile during the planning of the overthrow of Salvador Allende in September 1973. He also excelled during the 'dirty war' against the guerrillas in El Salvador and Nicaragua in the 1980s.

'Another World Is Possible'), we invited Chávez. He came two years later, in January 2003, for the Third Forum. We wanted him to explain in person, to the thousands of social activists and intellectuals gathered there, his concept of the Bolivarian Revolution. His rousing rhetoric and political clarity generated enormous enthusiasm. The youth of Latin America discovered a confident, optimistic discourse. The notion of political will was revived as he proposed lifting the continent out of the inertia and suffering of neoliberalism, while at the same time respecting all the freedoms. Another Left was possible! At that time Chávez was the only neo-progressive leader in power in Latin America, aside from Luiz Inácio Lula da Silva who had just become president of Brazil.

In January 2005 we invited Chávez to the Fifth World Social Forum, held once again in Porto Alegre. His plane landed in the early morning, just as the sun was coming up. Maximilien Arveláiz, Bernard Cassen and I went to meet him at the steps to the plane. The first thing he did was take us to Lagoa do Junco, an agrarian settlement of the Landless Peasants' Movement (MST) situated in the municipality of Tapes, over 130 kilometres away. Once there we were escorted by João Pedro Stedile, leader of the MST. Chávez met producers and peasant farmers, and in an improvised speech to an audience of several hundred, declared for the first time that this experience of agricultural self-management showed that 'socialism is not dead'.

In the afternoon we went back to Porto Alegre, where he was scheduled to appear at the Gigantinho stadium before about 50,000 'another world' youngsters. It fell to me to introduce him and I began as follows: 'It took many people time to be convinced; some doubted for a long time; and others won't yet admit, that in Latin America, this Latin America so battered by neoliberalism and globalization, a new kind of political leader had emerged: President Hugo Chávez. Some people justified their doubts and mistrust because he was a military man, one that had even led a military uprising. In a continent where so many uniformed thugs have acted as their people's executioners, we have to admit that, to a certain extent, such mistrust was understandable.'

Then Chávez took centre stage and, continually interrupted by an audience that applauded him deliriously, gave one of the best speeches I can remember him making.[26] He declared that the Forum was 'the most important political event in the world. There is no other event of comparable significance. Over the last five years, it has become a rich platform where the excluded of the world have a voice, can say what they feel, and where they can reach a consensus on many things.' He went on to say that he came to Porto Alegre 'to learn, to soak up more passion and more knowledge'. He then enumerated the reforms that the Bolivarian Revolution was carrying out: distributing land to poor peasant farmers; recognizing the languages and the rights of Venezuela's indigenous peoples; introducing literacy programmes for children and adults; providing a health service for all; creating Misiones Barrio Adentro (social programmes in the shanty towns); supplying micro-credits; creating a Women's Bank and promoting women's rights; introducing a Fishing Law, building solidarity with Cuba, and much more.

For the second time in a speech that day, he declared his commitment to 'socialism' – a word that had fallen into disuse, that not even the Left believed in. But he, right there and then, committed himself to 'transcending capitalism via the democratic road to socialism'.

Over the years that followed, I saw Chávez again several times, on some visit of his to Paris or Galicia, or when I went to Caracas for a conference or to appear on his famous television show, *Aló Presidente*. In those days I was deeply engaged in the conversations with Fidel Castro that became our book *Fidel Castro: My Life*.[27] While preparing this work I travelled with the Cuban comandante to Quito, in January 2003, to attend the inauguration ceremony for the new Ecuadorian president, Lucio Gutiérrez. Chance had it that we were staying at the Swiss Hotel, the same hotel as Chávez.

---

26 See *Lula y Chávez en el foro de Porto Alegre. Discursos y resoluciones*, Colección Le Monde diplomatique, Editorial Capital Intelectual, Buenos Aires, 2005.

27 Fidel Castro with Ignacio Ramonet, *Fidel Castro: My Life*, Simon & Schuster, 2007.

Those were the months when the Venezuelan president was facing the harshest assaults of the 'oil strike', promoted by the Venezuelan chamber of commerce and supported by the board of directors and lower echelons of the Venezuelan Oil Company (PVDSA) as well as by the dominant right-wing media. That piece of sabotage lasted from December 2002 until February 2003.

I attended an informal meeting in Fidel's suite between the two comandantes, Cuban and Venezuelan, in which they expressed their surprise at the initiative launched a few weeks earlier by Lula (before he had become president of Brazil) to create a 'Friends of Venezuela Support Group' made up of Ricardo Lagos's Chile, José María Aznar's Spain, George W. Bush's US and José Manuel Barroso's Portugal, as well as Brazil.[28] I remember Fidel commenting 'with friends like these, who needs enemies,' while Chávez confirmed he had no intention of 'internationalizing' that particular social conflict: 'it's exactly the pretext Washington is looking for to control our oil.'

About Lucio Gutiérrez they were also very frank and clear. I must confess that, rather naively, I had myself been taken in by the apparently progressive positions of the Ecuadorian colonel, which seemed confirmed in his inaugural speech.[29] Fidel looked at me almost pityingly, and exclaimed with a laugh, 'Lucio is a coward!' According to the Cuban comandante, it would take no longer than six months for the Ecuadorians to see he was an imposter and get rid of him. He was not wrong. It took a mere three months for Gutiérrez to drop his mask: he broke with his left wing and joined the North American Free Trade Area (NAFTA), before the angry Ecuadorians threw him out in April 2005.

Chávez told me that both he and Fidel had thought for a moment that Colonel Gutiérrez might belong to the progressive tradition of

---

28   Luiz Inácio Lula da Silva was elected president of Brazil on 27 October 2002, but did not take office until 1 January 2003. Meanwhile Fernando Henrique Cardoso was still the acting president.

29   See Ignacio Ramonet, 'Lucio', *La Voz de Galicia*, La Coruña, 3 December 2003.

Latin American army officers, which he himself adhered to, and which included officers like Velasco Alvarado, Luis Carlos Prestes, Jacobo Árbenz, Omar Torrijos, Juan José Torres and Francisco Caamaño. 'To find out,' Chávez told me, 'Fidel and I decided to come to Quito after Lucio was elected but before he took office. To see his reaction. The pretext was the inauguration of the Chapel of Man by the late painter Oswaldo Guayasamín. This was on 29 November 2002. We thought the two of us – Fidel and I – would meet Lucio and talk, to see who he really was. But we found out soon enough. Barely had he got wind that we were coming, than he speedily announced he was off to Colombia to see Álvaro Uribe. He fled. The idea of being in a photo with us terrified him. He was shit-scared.'

Hugo Chávez's great achievement was the refounding of the Venezuelan nation – '*¡Tenemos Patria!*' (We have a *Patria*!) was a favourite slogan – as a truly democratic political model serving the interests of the majority. Indeed, the Bolivarian Revolution reorganized all the structures of Venezuelan society.

Since Fidel Castro, no leader in Latin America had made such an impact as Hugo Chávez. In his fourteen years at the helm, not only did he change Venezuela in Copernican fashion from top to bottom, but all of Latin America. Never in the two centuries of independent history had Latin America known such a long period of democracy, social justice and development. Never had so many progressive governments been in power at the same time in so many Latin American countries. It was unprecedented. For decades, the mere idea that a progressive, democratically elected government might bring about structural change in order to reduce inequality and injustice, was enough for it to be overthrown. Examples abound: Guatemala 1954, Brazil 1964, Dominican Republic 1965, Chile 1973, Peru 1975, etc. As a result, in many Latin American countries the only way left open to those wanting to bring about social justice was armed struggle and guerrilla warfare.

Hugo Chávez, who with other officers took part in the military uprising of 4 February 1992, has been the first great progressive leader since Salvador Allende to choose the democratic road to power, and the first to succeed. This is fundamentally important. It is impossible to understand Chávez if we don't recognize the profoundly democratic nature of his progressive alternative: his determination to submit every one of the advances of the Bolivarian Revolution – regularly, periodically – to the will of the people. Chávez's gamble was on democratic socialism. His political resolve and his faith in the collective intelligence of the Venezuelans led him to include the people in all the big decisions of his government. In this, and in his concept of the 'civilian–military alliance' (the union of the people and the armed forces), Chávez revolutionized the Latin American revolution. And his example has caught on. In Latin America, neo-progressive governments are consolidating the welfare state, the very welfare state that neoliberal governments are destroying in Europe. Thanks to these redistributive policies, which the Bolivarian Revolution was the first to set in motion, some 50 million Latin Americans were lifted out of poverty between 1999 and 2013. Progress of this kind had never been seen before.

That is why Chávez was never afraid of democracy. On the contrary, he stressed that democratic elections can only consolidate policies that aim to give the people 'the greatest possible happiness'. And it is also why it is no surprise that Chávez has enjoyed such wide popular support, and has won almost all his electoral battles.

Chávez's speeches and the gains of the Bolivarian Revolution hit Latin America like a hurricane. The inability of the traditional political classes to channel the revolt of '*los de abajo*', the 'underdogs', opened the door to new leaders with different backgrounds – trade unionists, social activists, military men, and even former guerrillas. Never before has there been such a wave of exceptional leaders as the current one, producing the likes of Lula and Dilma in Brazil, Evo Morales in Bolivia, Rafael Correa in Ecuador, Néstor Kirchner and Cristina Fernández in Argentina, and Tabaré Vázquez and Pepe Mujica in Uruguay.

This might upset any Marxists who cling to the dictum which says, 'There is no God, nor Caesar, nor tribune.' Nevertheless, in exceptional circumstances the role of the 'charismatic leader' is self-evident, because it acts as a catalyst for the will of millions of people who participate in the 'processes of change'. Cuba could not have withstood US aggression for sixty years had it not been for Fidel. And in Venezuela, it is clear that the Bolivarian Revolution would not be what it is without Hugo Chávez. Fidel himself said as much when he declared. 'I have long believed that when the crisis erupts, leaders emerge. Bolívar emerged when Napoleon occupied Spain and the imposition of a foreign king created favourable conditions for independence in the Spanish colonies of the southern hemisphere. José Martí emerged when the time was ripe for the Cuban War of Independence. Similarly, Chávez emerged when the terrible human and social situation in Venezuela and Latin America determined that the moment for a second independence had come.'

During Chávez's fourteen years as president (1999–2013), the Bolivarian Revolution achieved considerable progress in the field of regional integration: the creation of Petrocaribe, Petrosur, the Banco del Sur, ALBA (Boliviarian Alliance for the Peoples of Our America), SUCRE (Unified System of Regional Compensation), Unasur and Celac, alongside Venezuela's entrance into Mercosur, and many other policies, turned the Venezuela of Hugo Chávez into a source of innovation for moving towards the definitive independence of Latin America.

Although aggressive propaganda campaigns claim that in Bolivarian Venezuela the media is controlled by the state, the fact is – ask any independent observer – that the majority of the media is in private hands. The two main newspapers, *El Nacional* and *El Universal*, criticize the government in systematic fashion.

Chávez's great strength was that his policies were directed towards the whole range of social sectors – health, food, education, housing – that most affect poor Venezuelans, 75 per cent of the population. He refounded the Venezuelan nation, he decolonized it, he gave citizen status to millions of undocumented poor people, he made the 'invisibles' visible. He allocated over 42 per cent of the state budget to investment in social projects. He halved the rate of infant mortality; eradicated illiteracy; and increased five-fold the number of teachers in state schools (from 65,000 to 350,000). In 2012,

Venezuela had the continent's second highest number of students in higher education (83 per cent), behind Cuba but ahead of Argentina, Uruguay and Chile; it even came fifth worldwide, higher than the US, Japan, China, UK, France and Spain.

The Venezuelan government shrank the foreign debt; extended free health and education to all; increased the number of houses built; raised the minimum wage (making it the highest in Latin America); introduced pensions for all workers, including those in the informal sector, and senior citizens; improved hospital infrastructure; subsidized food for poor families through the Mercal system, cheaper than private supermarkets; limited land monopoly while doubling food production; provided technical training to millions of workers; reduced inequalities; more than tripled the number of people above the poverty line; outlawed trawl-fishing, and introduced eco-socialism. All these measures, uninterruptedly carried out, explain the popular support Chávez has always enjoyed.

I have witnessed more than once the incredible passion Chávez could provoke. I was lucky enough to accompany him on trips all round Venezuela, to mass meetings, small Bolivarian fiestas, cadre meetings, military parades, press conferences, and gatherings of students, *campesinos*, women, indigenous people, workers . . . encounters with the Venezuelan people in all its diversity.

Once, for instance, he invited me to join him in a surprise operation on the shore of Lake Maracaibo. The occasion was the expropriation by the state of some forty merchant marine companies that provided services for the oil platforms on the lake, using a fleet of 300 large motor boats based at terminals along the shoreline. Planned with almost military precision, the operation relied on the element of surprise to prevent the owners sabotaging their installations and sinking the boats. Eight thousand workers on short-term contracts were being exploited by these companies; they received very low wages, but had to pay for their own food, medicine and even repairs to equipment.

Chávez announced that the Revolution was taking over the terminals and the speedboats, worker exploitation would end and they would become permanent employees on the PDVSA payroll.

The surprise of the workers at the sudden nationalization turned into enthusiasm. And when the President added that the $500 million profits these companies had made would be re-invested in schools, clinics, ecological projects, workers' housing, etc., and that these resources would be administered by the workers themselves through community power, the explosion of joy was indescribable.

'The Revolution is here! Long live Chávez!' they shouted. 'PDVSA will pay you everything you're owed,' added the president. Some veteran workers, their faces lined from long years of hard labour, shed tears of emotion. Surrounded by a noisy throng, Chávez climbed onto the tugboat *Canaima*. He started talking to the captain, Simón, a man with twenty years' experience navigating the lake. 'Until today,' he said, 'this boat belonged to a capitalist; now it belongs to the people, and the Revolution entrusts it to you.'

Later, under a red awning, he spoke to hundreds of the men who operated the boats, some with their wives and children: 'My soul,' he confessed, 'is the soul of the people. Those who want a *Patria*, join me! Christ said, "Render unto Caesar that which is Caesar's and render unto God that which is God's." And I say, "Render unto the people what is the people's." Step by step, we are breathing life into the transition to socialism. Every day the people will have more power. Every day we will have more freedom. This is an act of independence.' When he finished speaking, the audience leapt to its feet, shouting, 'That's it! That's it! That's the way to govern!'

One woman stood out for her energetic cheering for the Revolution. The president noticed her, and invited her to speak. He asked her name, and whether she had a family. She made her way to the front. She was young and well-dressed. She introduced herself: 'Nancy Williams, twenty-nine years old, I have one son and I'm married, but if you want I'll get divorced . . .' Everybody laughed.

On another occasion, I went with Chávez to the inauguration of some work being done to modernize the Dr José María Vargas hospital in the state of Vargas. 'Our commitment is human,' he told me, 'not only political.' He walked round the hospital corridors with unassuming simplicity, talking to the doctors, the patients and the orderlies, asking questions, delving into things, finding out about the type of care, the technology, the treatments, the medicine, the food.

He talked to one old man of eighty-six, a former soldier and stevedore at the nearby port of La Guaira who had no pension. Chávez was shocked: 'The bourgeois state and capitalism exploited this man for years, and when they could no longer profit from his labour they threw him away like a used toy.' He promised him compensation, and said, 'We will never be able to do enough to honour this country's martyrs. We are the descendants of those martyrs. This is a heroic people.'

Afterwards, we went out to a courtyard full of people in white coats sitting on rows of chairs. A white tent with red pillars had been erected. Chávez proceeded to distribute the keys of apartments in a medical residence for young doctors. 'This year,' he explained, '638 new doctors have graduated. They will go to work in people's clinics. The day will come when the Cuban doctors go back to Cuba, and we'll have to replace them in remote places in Venezuela and around the world.'

In front of this appreciative audience, he thanked health professionals. 'You represent the best of Venezuela. Twenty years ago, infantile mortality stood at twenty per thousand. Today it is down to ten per thousand.' He assured them the aim of the Bolivarian Revolution was 'to guarantee a quality, integrated health service to all Venezuelans. The day must come when private health centres are irrelevant.'

Amid the cheering, a middle-aged lady spoke up: 'My name is Inocencia Pérez,' she said, overcome by emotion. 'I bless you and commend you to the Archangel Michael. The day of the coup [11 April 2002], I went all the way to Caracas to defend you. I walked so much my feet bled.'

There are myriad testimonies like this. Millions of poor people worshipped him like a saint. Chávez would often calmly say, 'I will wear myself out serving the poor.' And he did. The writer Alba de Céspedes once asked Fidel Castro how he could have done so much for his people – education, health, agrarian reform and the rest.

And Fidel replied quite simply, 'With a lot of love.' Chávez might have said the same.

Farruco Sesto, the poet and architect who served several times as Venezuela's minister of culture, told me the following anecdote:

'One afternoon in Caracas, we were going back to the Miraflores Palace after some event. We were in a 4x4 with Chávez at the wheel, driving slowly, looking around. There were three or four of us in the car. Going down a street in El Silencio [a neighbourhood in the centre of Caracas], he noticed a beggar in rags, half naked, sleeping on a piece of cardboard. Without stopping, he asked, "And that man?" Someone answered, "He's crazy." Chávez responded sharply, "How do you know?" And he immediately stopped the car. He got out, telling his bodyguards to leave him alone, and went up to the beggar. He kneeled down and began to talk to him, even embraced him. He stood him up and had a conversation with him that lasted a quarter of an hour. We had no idea what they were talking about. That's what he was like, compassionate, he wanted to help the needy. And it turned out that under the piece of cardboard lay another homeless person, a young man who was also a drug addict, a crack victim. He embraced him too, and they went on talking. From the instructions he later gave his assistant, we guessed that he'd convinced them to accept his help. Sure enough, next day they joined a voluntary drug rehabilitation programme. "I think we saved them," commented Chávez.'

When I finished my book of conversations with Fidel, it seemed natural to suggest a similar project to the Venezuelan comandante, so as to show people the less public aspects of his personality. Chávez had become one of the most important leaders in Latin America; the power behind the neo-progressive wave then sweeping across the subcontinent, embodied in a new generation of leaders. In his very different context, Chávez could be seen as a kind of 'successor' to the veteran Cuban comandante.

I suggested we do a book of interviews about the less well-known part of his biography: the 'Chávez before Chávez'. 'Aha! You want to talk about my early life,' he said, 'my first life, because I've had several.' Yes, that was the idea; to provide answers to the questions so many people are asking. People wonder, who was Chávez before he became the public figure everybody knows? What was his childhood like? Where did he grow up, in what circumstances? What kind of a teenager was he? How was he educated? When did he become interested in politics? What did he read? What influences was he exposed to? What was he like as a soldier? What was his geopolitical vision? What ideological tendency did he follow? What strategies won him the elections and took him to power in 1999?

Besides answering those and many other questions that arose during some 200 hours of conversations with Hugo Chávez, this book also aims to be a work of history. Removed from contemporary controversies, it looks at a stage of his life than ended in 1999, one that can now be assessed with a certain tranquillity. Hence it is an intimate history that aims to acquaint us with the *person* of Hugo Rafael Chávez Frías; not just the politician, but the human being that he was, his temperament, his character, his humanity, his sensitivity, his complexity.

We did not touch on his illness, the cancerous tumour in the pelvis, which was announced in June 2011. This is simply because this health problem came up when we had already finished the recordings and I, working on the book, had not seen him for months. On 1 June 2011, a day after announcing his illness publicly, Chávez explained how it had been detected. It happened in Havana. Exhausted by his extraordinary workload, the Venezuelan president confided to his friend Fidel Castro that he was in constant pain and that he felt the effects of this pain most strongly in one of his legs.

The Cuban leader took the information very seriously. 'There was no way I could avoid Fidel's eagle eyes,' Chávez told me. 'He asked "What's wrong? What kind of pain?" and started quizzing me like a father does with a son. Then he began calling doctors, getting opinions. He took charge.' As a result, Chávez underwent two urgent operations, one for a pelvic abscess and the other to cut out a tumour which was, in his words, was 'almost the size of a baseball'. And everything seemed to have been fixed. On 20 October 2011, after rigorous tests, Chávez declared that it had been 'scientifically verified there were no active malignant cells in my body; I am free of the illness.'

In January 2012, I sent the finished draft of the manuscript for him to read and revise his answers, as we had agreed. But a few weeks later his problems reappeared, and he announced on 22 February 2012 that a fresh lesion had been detected, 'about two centimetres in diameter in the same place as the extracted tumour, and this means a new surgical intervention to remove it.' The operation took place in Havana on 27 February 2012. It was followed by several courses of radiotherapy that forced him to spend long weeks in Havana, maintaining active contact with his followers on Twitter. In April 2012, during Easter Week, he went back to the city of Barinas and at a mass that was broadcast live, surrounded by his family, he moved Venezuelans with his emotional prayer:

'Christ, give me life. Even though it be a life of pain and suffering, I don't mind. Give me your crown of thorns, Christ, that I may bleed. Give me your cross, a hundred crosses, that I may carry them. But give me life. Do not take me away just yet. Give me your thorns, give me your blood, I am ready to bear them, but let me live.'

Ten months later, on 8 December 2012, when he had won the presidential elections of 7 October by a wide margin, Chávez made a dramatic speech to the nation in which he revealed that his cancer had returned, that he would be having a fourth operation in Cuba, and that there was a risk that he would not return to Venezuela to take office. He went on to express his desire that the then vice president, Nicolás Maduro, be named the candidate of Chavismo in the event of elections to replace him:

'If any circumstances prevent me from continuing this presidency,' declared Hugo Chávez, 'Maduro must complete it for me. My last absolute, unqualified wish, whole as the full moon, irrevocable, is that in those circumstances, which would necessitate calling new presidential elections, as the Constitution requires, you elect Nicolás Maduro as president of the Bolivarian Republic of Venezuela. I ask this of you with all my heart.'

He added, 'Maduro is a man with a great capacity for hard work, group management, and handling difficult situations. He is one of the young leaders best equipped to continue – if I cannot – with his firm hand, his firm gaze, his heart of a man of the people, his way with people, his intelligence, the international recognition he has achieved, his skill as a leader, as president of the Republic, and to guide – always subordinate to the interests of the Venezuelan people – the destiny of this *Patria*.'

The news of another operation, that Chávez had announced so dramatically, took me by surprise. I'd had the privilege of being with him a couple of months earlier for the presidential election of 7 October 2012, and more frequently during the previous July, in the first two weeks of the electoral campaign. To me he had seemed in fine physical shape.

It was to be his fourteenth encounter with the Venezuelan electorate.[30] The official campaign kicked off on 1 July, with two notable differences from previous elections. First, President Chávez was coming out of thirteen months of cancer treatment. The main conservative opposition parties had decided this time not to split the vote, and formed the Mesa de la Unidad Democrática (MUD, Democratic Unity Roundtable). Their candidate, selected via primaries, was Henrique Capriles Radonski, a forty-year-old lawyer and governor of the state of Miranda, who was betting on President Chávez's physical deterioration.[31]

But that was a mistake – because at the time Chávez thought he had beaten his illness. In fact, he'd had a complete check-up in June to see if he was in good enough shape to stand the exhausting electoral campaign. The results had been conclusive: there was no sign of any malignant cell in his body. Certain that he was cured, Chávez threw himself into the electoral battle with the energy of a centaur.

---

30   As well as Chávez, there were six other candidates at the 7 October 2012 elections: Henrique Capriles Radonski, for Mesa de la Unidad Democrática (MUD); Orlando Chirinos, for the Partido Socialismo y Libertad (PSL, Socialism and Freedom Party); Yoel Acosta Chirinos, for the Partido Vanguardia Bicentenaria Republicana (VBR, Bicentenary Republican Vanguard Party); Luis Reyes Castillo, for Organización Renovadora Auténtica (ORA, Authentic Renovating Organization); María Bolívar, for the Partido Democrático Unidos por la Paz y la Libertad (PDUPL, Democrats United for Peace and Freedom); and Reina Sequera for the Partido Poder Popular (PP, Popular People's Power). Chávez won in the first round with more than 55 per cent of the vote.

31   In mid-July 2012, the main opinion polls gave Chávez a lead of between fifteen and twenty points over the candidate of the right, Henrique Capriles.

On 9 July 2012, he declared publicly, 'I am absolutely clear of any illness, I feel better by the day.' Those who had counted on the merely 'virtual' presence of the Venezuelan leader during the campaign were surprised by his decision 'to reclaim the streets' and begin to criss-cross the length and breadth of Venezuela to obtain a third term. He declared, 'They said, "He'll be confined to the Miraflores Palace, running a virtual campaign on Twitter and YouTube." They made fun of me. Well, here I am again, on my way back, with the indomitable force of the Bolivarian hurricane. I missed the smell of the masses and the roar of the people in the streets.'

I have rarely heard as powerful and exultant a roar as that which greeted Chávez in the streets of Barcelona (Anzoátegui state) and Barquisimeto (Lara state) on 12 and 14 July 2012, respectively. A scarlet torrent of red flags, banners and t-shirts. A tsunami of shouting, singing and cheering. For miles and miles, on a red lorry wending through the multitude, a tireless Chávez greeted the hundreds of thousands of supporters who had come to see him in person for the first time since his illness. They came with tears of joy and kisses of gratitude towards a man and a government which, respecting democracy and the rule of law, had kept faith with the poor, paid the social debt and, finally, promised free education, employment, social security and housing, for everyone.

To deprive the opposition of the least sliver of hope, he would begin his electoral speeches (delivered with no sign of fatigue) by saying, 'I am like Nietzsche's eternal return, because in fact I've come back from various deaths. Make no mistake, as long as God gives me life, I will be fighting for justice for the poor and, when I leave you physically, I will be with you in these streets and under this sky. Because I am no longer myself, I feel I am the incarnation of the people. Chávez is the people, and now we are millions. Chávez is you, *señora*. Chávez is you, young man. Chávez is you, little boy. You, soldier. You, fishermen, farmers, labourers and shopkeepers. Whatever happens to me, they can't get rid of Chávez, because Chávez is now an invincible people.'

He invited me to accompany him on his tour. I had several

conversations with him, and I could see how well he was. He was back to his old self, the same enthusiasm, dynamism, sense of humour, charm. We talked about the book. He had obviously read and reread the manuscript, which he thought 'very good, but a bit long, isn't it?' He had also given it to Castro.

'Do you know what Fidel said? We talked about the book, I told him you were coming, and he said, "Chávez, don't do what I did, let Ramonet put what he wants, because I know you, you're not going to have time for it. If they give you the manuscript, you're going to write another book, so leave the creativity to him." Fidel respects you very much and says he made too many corrections to *One Hundred Hours with Fidel*.[32] So I'm going to take his wise advice, because it's true, I don't have time. You have done a splendid job, you write very well, but I am so finicky that if I start correcting, I'll start crossing things out. And I don't have time now.'

I felt he was happy to have been able to set down in this book, for generations to come, the truth about his early life.

After his fourth, and last, operation in Cuba in December 2012, Chávez suffered a post-operative lung infection, which developed into a respiratory failure that he was not able to survive. It is well known that, after treatment, the Bolivarian leader was breathing through a tracheal cannula for several weeks, which made it diffi-cult for him to speak. His return to Venezuela to be cared for in the Military Hospital in Caracas was interpreted as a sign of improve-ment. A few days earlier, in fact, Nicolás Maduro had assured people, 'The comandante is the best we have seen him in these days of fight and struggle.'

But complications kept arising. On 22 February, Maduro admit-ted, 'He has a problem with his breathing and is in intensive care; he is still on an iron lung.' And on 4 March, Ernesto Villegas, the minister of communication, informed that the Venezuelan presi-dent's health had worsened considerably: 'There is a deterioration in the respiratory system. There is also a new severe infection. The

---

32   *Cien horas con Fidel* is the title of the Cuban edition of Ramonet and Castro, *Fidel Castro: My Life*.

President has been receiving high doses of chemotherapy. His general state of health is delicate.'

Now everyone feared the worst. And only a few hours later, on 5 March 2013, a shocked Nicolás Maduro announced the distressing news to the world: 'Comandante President Chávez has died, after a two-year battle with his illness.' And so ended, prematurely, one of the most important political journeys of our time.

I remembered that moment five years earlier when Hugo Chávez agreed to my suggestion to record our conversations. From that day on, with his characteristic seriousness, the Bolivarian leader committed himself to finding time in his crazy diary to devote to our interviews. He always kept his word. He sent me documents, books, pamphlets, and photos to properly document the story of his early life.

Begun in April 2008 in the heart of the Llanos, on that small ranch which served him as a retreat, our work sessions had gone on for three years in different parts of Venezuela and particularly in his modest quarters in the Miraflores Palace in Caracas.

There, on a small terrace, this affectionate, nostalgic, sentimental president had tried to replicate the sights, sounds and smells of that house and garden of his childhood in Sabaneta: there were tropical plants, whistling parrots, noisy cocks and hens, a typical *llanero* hammock, and even a wooden hut with a palm thatched roof.

A sign of eternal loyalty to his unforgettable childhood with his grandmother Rosa Inés, in some sense the 'Rosebud' of Citizen Chávez. He was the driving force of 'Twenty-First-Century Socialism', but he never lost sight of his roots among the people. And he never forgot 'his first life'.

Ignacio Ramonet
Barinas, 15 April 2008
Paris, 5 March 2013

PART I

CHILDHOOD
AND ADOLESCENCE

(1954–1971)

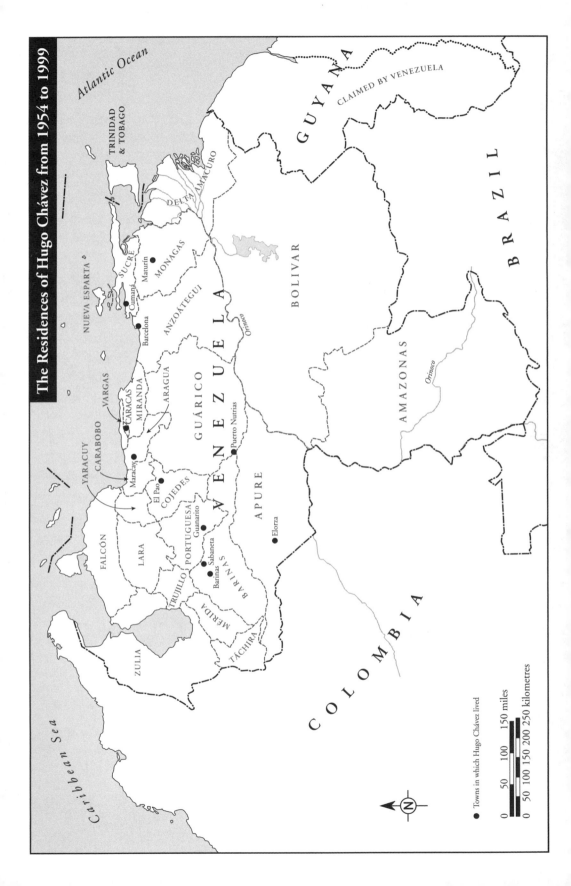

The Residences of Hugo Chávez from 1954 to 1999

Atlantic Ocean

Caribbean Sea

GUYANA

CLAIMED BY VENEZUELA

BRAZIL

COLOMBIA

TRINIDAD & TOBAGO

DELTA AMACURO

SUCRE

NUEVA ESPARTA

MONAGAS

Maturín

Cumaná

Barcelona

ANZOATEGUI

BOLIVAR

Orinoco

AMAZONAS

Orinoco

VENEZUELA

GUÁRICO

MIRANDA

CARACAS

VARGAS

CARABOBO

YARACUY

ARAGUA

Maracay

El Pao

COJEDES

Puerto Nutrias

APURE

Guanarito

PORTUGUESA

Elorza

FALCÓN

LARA

TRUJILLO

Sabaneta

Barinas

BARINAS

MÉRIDA

TÁCHIRA

ZULIA

N

● Towns in which Hugo Chávez lived

0   50   100   150 miles

0 50 100 150 200 250 kilometres

1

'History will absorb me'

28 July 1954 – Historical context – Uslar Pietri
The Third World rises – The Cold War
Dictators in Latin America – Sabaneta – El Boconó
Los Llanos, 'magic land' – Being a llanero – Anecdotes
Anti-Indian racism – Grandmother Rosa Inés – Black blood
Christ, the first revolutionary

Mr President, you were born on 28 July 1954, in a historical context which saw the birth of the so-called Third World and the beginning of the end of colonialism. I'd like to look back at a few other important dates around that time. Almost exactly a year earlier, on 26 July 1953, Fidel Castro led the attack on the Moncada Barracks in Santiago de Cuba. And a month before your birth, on 27 June 1954, there was a coup d'état against Jacobo Árbenz in Guatemala. Almost a month after that, on 15 August 1954, Alfredo Stroessner's dictatorship took power in Paraguay. This was followed, on 24 August, by the coup d'état in Brazil and the suicide of Getulio Vargas. A few months earlier, on 7 May 1954, the French Army surrendered at Dien Bien Phu, Indochina. And just a few days before your birth, the war in Indochina ended in victory for the newly decolonized country of Vietnam. A few months later, however, on 1 November 1954, war would break out in Algeria. And we were only a year away from the famous Bandung Conference which heralded the concept of the Third World and Non-aligned Countries.

So, there was a discernible political and historical context in which one period died and another was born. And you, too, were born. What inspires you about this constellation of events surrounding the date of your birth?

Yes, I came into the world in this historical context, that's true. The morning I was born was, I believe, the day Fidel Castro planned his escape from the Modelo prison on the Isle of Pines. Lots of things were happening all around the world. We were just halfway through the twentieth century. And when you list all those events, you're talking about real history. That naturally leaves its mark. Our lives are influenced and determined by the conditions into which we are born, the circumstances we grow up in. Marx said, 'Men make history with the conditions reality imposes on them.' I realized this as I went through life, and from reading Marc Bloch.

A great French historian, a member of the anti-Fascist resistance. He was Jewish and was shot by the Nazis in 1944. A huge intellect.

I admire him very much. I've had his short book *The Historian's Craft* beside me for a long time.[1] Between adolescence and maturity, at the stage you start to become aware of life, I used to ask myself, as Marc Bloch does, 'What is the use of history?' History can arouse your curiosity, and it can also be a seductive narrative. Because the spectacle of human activity is seductive. And Bloch classifies actions as 'historical' or 'unhistorical'. Seeking a more exact definition of history and asking himself what use it is, he says 'History is like the ogre in fairy tales; wherever he smells meat, there lies his prey.' Because the object of history is mankind, human beings.

Of course, we come into the world an empty vessel, born like a calf on these plains, like a cristofué in the branches of those trees.[2]

---

1   Marc Bloch, *The Historian's Craft* (1954), Manchester University Press, Manchester, 1992.

2   A bird of the *Tyrannidae* family which catches insects. Its scientific name is *Pitangus sulphuratus* and it is called *cristofué* because its song sounds like '*Cristo fue*' (Christ was).

Unconscious. But then, slowly we become aware, we acquire consciousness. Or not. In my case – with a nod to Fidel's famous phrase 'History will absolve me' – if as a boy I had thought about history and life, if I'd been aware, I might have said, 'History will absorb me.'[3]

You plunged into history, like Achilles into the River Scamander or Siegfried in the dragon's blood . . .

Thinking 'history will absorb me' was simply intuitive on my part. I am, as Bloch says, human flesh. I was dragged along by the ogre of history and torn to pieces by him. The teeth of history, or – not to make history aggressive or malevolent – the arms of history enveloped me, the hurricane of history swept me up. Bolívar said, 'I am a mere wisp of straw swept up by the force of a hurricane.' I am submerged in a hurricane, or an invisible river. I see that history in the wind of the Llanos, in the breeze that sways the trees, in the heat of this savannah, I touch it, feel it. Because into that history, I was born.

Arturo Uslar Pietri said, 'The Venezuelan is thirsty for history.' Do you share that idea?

Yes, I think I do. Uslar was upper-class – you knew him, I think – but he was a great patriot.[4] He wrote the novel *The Red Lances*, about the exploits of the llaneros, the men of the Venezuelan plains, and *Robinson's Island*, a marvellous novel about Simón Rodríguez.[5]

---

3 Translator's note: To paraphrase Fidel, it is literally 'History will absorb me'. The sense is 'I will one day become part of history.'

4 Arturo Uslar Pietri (1906–2001), one of Venezuela's most eminent twentieth-century writers and intellectuals. Author of novels like *Las lanzas coloradas* (1931) (The Red Lances), *El camino de El Dorado* (1947) (The Road to El Dorado), *Oficio de difuntos* (1976) (Profession for Dead Men), *La Isla de Robinson* (1981) (Robinson's Island) and *La visita en el tiempo* (1990) (The Visit in Time). (Titles translation AW.)

5 Simon Rodríguez (1769–1854), Venezuelan philosopher, teacher and mentor of Simón Bolívar. During his long exile in Europe (1801–1823) he called himself Samuel Robinson.

Dr Uslar Pietri was a highly respected man, and is greatly missed. In the 1940s, when General Isaías Medina Angarita was in power, he talked about the need to 'sow oil'.[6] I knew him too, first because I used to read a lot, and then after our uprising of 4 February 1992, when I was in jail, there was speculation about its 'intellectual authors', as if we couldn't think for ourselves. And they tried to implicate Uslar. It's true he made a few statements justifying our action, and they raided his house.[7] So, after that, Uslar opposed the government of Carlos Andrés Pérez even more fiercely, and declared, 'I said it was going to rain . . . and it rained.'[8]

Two years later, in 1994, when I came out of prison, I contacted him and he invited me to his house in the Caracas suburb of La Florida. He received me in his library and we talked for a long time. He was recently widowed. I'll never forget what he said when I asked him why he was no longer writing the column he'd had in *El Nacional* for fifty years. He replied, 'You know, Commander, you have to leave before they throw you out.'

He had light blue eyes and a hoarse, warmly modulated voice. The tone of his voice, the clarity with which he spoke and the way he expressed himself made an enormous impression on me. I was bowled over. I had seen him on television; he had a weekly programme on Radio Caracas Televisión called *Human Value* which was excellent. Personally I was moved by his intelligence and the warmth with which he received me. I remember him saying, 'Comandante, life is like a play, some actors are at the front of the stage, others stand at the back; some write plays, others direct them; and others are spectators. When you're a theatre actor, you have to

6 Isaías Medina Angarita (1897–1953), elected constitutional president for the period 1941–1946, governed with the support of the Communist Party, and was ousted on 18 October 1945 in a coup d'état headed by Marcos Pérez Jiménez and leaders of the Acción Democrática Party, among them Rómulo Betancourt.

7 See Arturo Uslar Pietri, *Golpe y Estado en Venezuela*, Grupo editorial Norma, Caracas, 1992.

8 Carlos Andrés Pérez (1922–2010), nicknamed CAP, leader of Acción Democrática (affiliated to the Socialist International). He was Venezuelan president twice, 1974–1979 and 1989–1993, but stripped of his office by the senate in May 1993 for misuse of funds and fraud.

be careful at two particular moments: when you come on stage and when you exit.' He added, 'I watched you come on with a red beret and a gun, now it's up to you how you get off.'

What was that phrase he told you?

'The Venezuelan is thirsty for history.'

I think Arturo Uslar Pietri summed up the essence of Venezuela in a nutshell; there is enormous truth in that phrase. He wasn't talking about an individual but about the Venezuelan people as a whole. And it is that thirst that they have been partially able to quench in the last few years, after a long drought. They have found a source, a spring. The Bolivarian Revolution has given Venezuelans back their history. They were thirsty for a *Patria*, and that thirst has been quenched.

I myself began gorging on history a long time ago. Probably looking for the key to our future. It was Heidegger who said, 'There is nothing so full of the future as the past.'[9]

And when did you become aware that the reality enveloping you was the product of history?

What was happening at that particular moment of the century I was born into? More or less what you were saying before, except I wouldn't say that I came into the world when the Third World was being born, because the Third World already existed, though it wasn't called that then. So perhaps what was emerging was the awareness that a Third World existed, don't you think?

Yes, the concept of the Third World emerged at that time. The French economist Alfred Sauvy gave it to us in 1952. Just as before the French Revolution in 1789, there were three social categories in France: the aristocracy, the clergy or Church, and ordinary people. Using this model, Sauvy says that, during the Cold War, there was a First World – the capitalist world; a Second World

---

9   Martin Heidegger (1889–1976), German philosopher, one the most important of the twentieth century. Author of *Being and Time* (1927).

— the Communist one; and a Third World which was neither capitalist nor communist but a 'colonized, exploited and despised, world'. But then, at the Bandung Conference in 1955, when, as you said, a political awareness of developing countries emerged, the press referred to them collectively as the Third World.

Just as 500 years earlier they called us the New World.

That's right.

There was no first, second or third then, just two worlds: the Old World was Europe and the New, which appeared in 1492, was the New World. Then this idea of the Third World emerged. When I was born, of course, we were already halfway through the century; the Soviet Union was already forty years old. And Mao Zedong's China was five.

The era of the Cold War.

The Communist camp had come into being; the Soviet Union and all its allies. We now had a bi-polar world dominated by two hegemonies: the United States and the Soviet Union. The Second World War had been over for almost a decade, the conflicts in Vietnam and Algeria had started, as well as many other less chronicled wars in Africa and Latin America. You talked about coups d'état: Juan Domingo Perón was ousted by a coup in Argentina about then.[10]

September 1955, to be exact.

Who ousted Perón? The United States. By the time I was born, the Americans had bombed Guatemala, and were engaged in a full-blown invasion of that country.

---

10   Juan Domingo Perón (1896–1974), an Argentine army colonel, was minister of labour in 1943. He was very popular because of his pro-working-class policies, which got him removed from his post and jailed. This only increased his popularity and he was elected president of Argentina in 1946. His policies – called '*justicialistas*' because they addressed social demands, and sought to modernize Argentina and gain economic independence from the United States and the United Kingdom – turned him and his Evita into real popular idols, but they were ousted in September 1955. After decades in exile, he returned to power in October 1973 but died on 1 July 1974.

*You'd arrived one month earlier, on 27 June 1954. Jacobo Árbenz
had already been forced into exile . . .*[11]

That's right. The US invaded Guatemala, toppled Perón, overthrew Juan Bosch,[12] backed a coup in Brazil[13] . . . A few years
before that, in October 1948, they had supported a coup d'état in
Peru led by General Manuel Odría.[14] And even before that, on 9
April 1948, they had assassinated Jorge Eliécer Gaitán in Bogotá.[15]
Imagine, six years before I was born, they had killed Gaitán, right
on our doorstep in Colombia. That caused the *Bogotazo*, and
started the conflict that is destroying Colombia to this day and
affecting several other South American countries. Coincidentally,
our friend Fidel Castro actually witnessed the assassination of
Gaitán and the *Bogotazo*.[16]

We're talking about hugely significant events all over Latin America:
Guatemala, the Caribbean, Peru, Colombia, Brazil, Argentina,

---

11   Jacobo Árbenz (1913–1971), army officer and democratically elected president
of Guatemala from 1951 to 1954. His policies aimed to bring Guatemala out of the colonial era, gain independence from the United States and introduce agrarian reform.
Washington opposed these policies, and the CIA organized a coup led by Colonel Carlos
Castillo which deposed Árbenz in June 1954.

12   Juan Bosch (1909–2001), first democratically elected President of the Dominican
Republican. He took office in December 1962, following the dictatorship of Trujillo
(1930–1961), and introduced a series of socialist reforms. He was deposed in 1963 by a
US-backed coup d'état. In 1965, Bosch was reinstated in a counter-coup by a group of
army officers, but the United States sent 20,000 troops to invade the country to 'prevent
it becoming another Cuba'.

13   The left-wing president of Brazil, João Goulart (1919–1976), was ousted by a
CIA-backed military coup in April 1964.

14   General Manuel A. Odría (1898–1974) led a coup d'état in October 1948
against the legitimate president of Peru, José Luis Bustamante. He ruled Peru from 1948
to 1956.

15   Jorge Eliécer Gaitán (1898–1948), Colombian political leader popular with the
working class. In the 1948 elections, he was standing as presidential candidate for the
Colombian Liberal Party on a platform of revolutionary socialist reforms. He was assassinated on 9 April 1948.

16   Fidel Castro recounted his experience of the *Bogotazo* in our book of conversations, *Fidel Castro: My Life*. There is also a long account of this event by Fidel Castro in an
interview with him by Arturo Alape published under *El Bogotazo: Memorias del olvido*
(Casa de las Américas, Havana, 1983). For another description of this important event,
see Gabriel García Márquez, *Living to Tell the Tale*, Vintage, 2003.

Stroessner's dictatorship in Paraguay, and here in Venezuela, by 1954, the Pérez Jiménez dictatorship was in full swing.[17]

And actually, four years earlier in Venezuela, in November 1950, they had also assassinated Colonel Carlos Delgado Chalbaud, a progressive army officer who had studied in France. He was the son of the political leader Román Delgado Chalbaud, former head of the Venezuelan Navy, who had spent fourteen years in jail during the long dictatorship of Juan Vicente Gómez.[18] Gómez eventually released him and he went to France to be reunited with his young son, Carlos, who had been sent there while his father was in jail. Carlos Delgado Chalbaud studied in France, graduated as an engineer and married a French student called Lucía Devine, an active member of the French Communist Party. He returned to Venezuela after Gómez's death in 1935 and, even though he was an engineer, he joined the army. He was a man of great prestige. When the gringos got rid of President Rómulo Gallegos, author of that brilliant novel *Doña Bárbara*, in November 1948 . . .[19]

Rómulo Gallegos was from this region, the Llanos, wasn't he?
No, Gallegos was from Caracas, but he based *Doña Bárbara* on the history, geography and myths of the Llanos. It's interesting to note that *Doña Bárbara* is the quintessential Venezuelan novel, doubtless

---

17   Alfredo Stroessner (1912–2006), Paraguayan general who authored the coup d'état of 4 May 1954. He installed a dictatorship allied to the United States and subsequently supported Operation Condor, the US-led military project against Latin American democracies. He was deposed on 3 February 1989. Marcos Pérez Jiménez (1914–2001), Venezuelan general who installed a dictatorship from 1952 to 1958. He was deposed on 23 January 1958, by a civilian–military uprising.

18   Juan Vicente Gómez (1908–1935), Venezuelan general who as vice president ousted General President Cipriano Castro while he was away in Europe for health reasons, and was dictator for twenty-seven years until his death. Gómez was the inspiration for the dictator protagonist of García Márquez's 1982 novel, *The Autumn of the Patriarch*.

19   Rómulo Gallegos (1884–1969), writer and statesman, author of *Doña Bárbara* (1929), considered the finest Venezuelan novel of the twentieth century, which earned him a period in exile during the dictatorship of Juan Vicente Gómez. Minister of education in 1936, he was elected president of Venezuela in February 1948, as the candidate for Acción Democrática. He was deposed eight months later in a military coup led by General Marcos Pérez Jiménez.

because of the writer's enormous talent, but also because the Llanos are the essence of Venezuela. In this boundless savannah, in the freewheeling winds that caress it, in its audacious nature and in its indomitable people, lies the very heart of Venezuelan identity.

That would be what attracted Gallegos. You were saying that they ousted him as well . . .
Yes, Rómulo Gallegos was overthrown on 24 November 1948. I met a man who worked with him in the presidential palace. He died not long ago, he was extremely old. His name was José Giacopini Zárraga, and he was an historian, researcher, oil expert. He was an exceptional witness to a great many events in Venezuela, having always been in the corridors of power and close to governments.

Apparently Giacopini was one of the most important oral sources of contemporary Venezuelan history.
Yes. I became very fond of him. He was an exceptional storyteller. One day he told me that when Gallegos was overthrown, the authors of the coup – Pérez Jiménez and his cronies – broke into the White Palace in Caracas. This was across the street from the Miraflores Palace where President Gallegos had his office, and Giacopini was toing and froing across Urdaneta Avenue, negotiating between the two buildings. Suddenly Gallegos stood up and declared, 'Tell those traitors that they are Doña Bárbara and I am Santos Luzardo.[20] And Santos Luzardo does not negotiate with Doña Bárbara.' Two hours later he was put on a plane and sent off to exile in Havana. He said in a speech on arrival in Havana, 'The United States has removed me from power.'[21] He was an admirable man and a progressive thinker.

---

20   In the Gallegos novel, Santos Luzardo embodies the ideal of Civilization against the Barbarity of Doña Bárbara, i.e., the rule of law versus the cruelty and violence of the caciques (minor strongmen) of the Llanos.

21   Rómulo Gallegos arrived in Havana on Sunday, 5 December 1948. Carlos Prío Socarrás had recently become president of Cuba, on 10 October 1948. His Partido Auténtico belonged to the same Social Democratic International as Gallegos's party, Acción Democrática. Prío Socarrás was himself deposed by the military coup led by Fulgencio Batista on 10 March 1952.

Let's get back to Carlos Delgado Chalbaud.

Yes, because after that, after they deposed Gallegos, in November 1948, the prestigious figure of Colonel Carlos Delgado Chalbaud took a leading role. He was respected for both his experience and his ability. He had been minister of defence in the Gallegos government; a brilliant man. As head of the military Junta, he proceeded to give it a progressive turn, something that was not in Washington's plans. Venezuela was by now an important oil-producing power.[22] And so, Delgado Chalbaud was kidnapped in Caracas in murky circumstances and assassinated on 13 November 1953. A magnicide, in fact. Remember that a few months earlier, in another oil-producing country – Iran – they had ousted Mossadegh.[23]

That's right. It's very important. Mossadegh, the Iranian prime minister, was toppled by the United States and the United Kingdom in 1953.

Yes, they toppled Mossadegh because he nationalized the oil industry; he was an important symbol of anti-imperialism. There were huge global repercussions. A few months later, in February 1954, in Egypt (where two years earlier the Free Officers' Movement had rebelled and deposed King Farouk), Colonel Nasser became prime minister and shortly afterwards he, in turn, nationalized the Suez Canal.[24] Nasser was subsequently defeated militarily in 1956 by a

---

22 Oil was discovered in Venezuela in 1914; the first well was the Zumaquel, in the Mene Grande oilfield on the west bank of Lake Maracaibo. By 1929, Venezuela was the world's second-largest producer, after the United States. When the Second World War broke out in 1939, Venezuela took on a huge geopolitical importance because it would provide almost 60 per cent of the Allied Forces' petrol, a major factor in their eventual victory in 1945.

23 The prime minister of Iran, Mohammed Mossadegh (1882–1967), was deposed on 18 August 1953, in a joint operation by the US and the UK – Operation Ajax. Mossadegh had been elected in 1951 with a good parliamentary majority and proceeded to nationalize the Anglo-Iranian Oil Company, the only one operating in Iran at the time. The coup restored the shah; it gave him absolute power, and initiated a period of repression and torture lasting twenty-five years.

24 Colonel Gamal Abdel Nasser (1918–1970), leader of the Free Officers' Movement that brought down the monarchy in July 1952 and proclaimed Egypt a republic. He nationalized the Suez Canal in 1956 and constructed the Aswan Dam. He is thought of as one of the most important and popular leaders in contemporary Arab history.

coalition of the United Kingdom, France and Israel. So, all these changes occurring were acts of liberation, and resistance to the neo-colonial and imperialist powers.

With all these transformations, liberation from over a century of colonization, especially in Africa and Asia, it was obviously a very powerful historical moment, the cusp of two different eras. So I'm going to ask you again: How do you interpret this histori-cal configuration that presided over your birth? Do you see it as heralding your political destiny?

No, no, not at all. What I believe is that there are certain objective historical conditions. As the philosopher José Ortega y Gasset said, 'I am I and my circumstances.'[25] We are part of that rebellious river of history and human events. We come into this world purely by chance. And then there are our circumstances . . . Karl Marx said in one of his writings, 'Men make their own history, but they don't make it of their own free will, under circumstances they choose themselves, but under the circumstances they find, which exist, bequeathed to them by the past.'[26] One of the most arbitrary of all arbitrary circumstances is where and when a human being is born. I was born by pure chance: the union of a black man, Hugo Chávez – a nineteen-year-old rural schoolteacher, who spent his days on horseback or on a mule – and a young girl of seventeen, Elena Frías. I was born more than a year after my brother Adán, who arrived on 11 April 1953.

You were born fifteen months after your brother, on 28 July 1954: under the Western horoscope's star sign Leo, like Simón Bolívar who was born on 24 July, and Fidel Castro on 13 August; and under the sign of the horse in the Chinese calendar. Two strong signs for those who believe in astrology . . .

---

25   José Ortega y Gasset (1882–1955), Spanish philosopher. His most famous book is *The Revolt of the Masses* (1929); the quote is from *Meditations on Quixote* (1914).

26   Karl Marx, *The 18th Brumaire of Louis Bonaparte*, Chapter 1, New York, 1852.

I don't. I came into the world that winter, on a rainy night according to my mother. 'From midnight towards daybreak', as they say in the Llanos.[27] I was born in Sabaneta, state of Barinas, in the house of my grandmother Rosa Inés, on a street now named after Antonio María Bayón. In the rainy season, the street would be one huge puddle. My mother remembers that by midnight on the 27th her labour pains were unbearable. She was about twenty at the time. The midwife arrived. There was no electric light then, just lots of water, lots of rain. My birth certificate states I arrived 'at two in the morning', but my mother said it could have been a little later. There was no moon, no crowing cock, it was the kind of dark night the poet Alberto Arvelo describes at the beginning of his epic poem *Florentino y el Diablo*: 'Night of a fearsome cloudburst over the black-garbed plain'.[28]

Beautiful.
So, I was born on a 'night of a fearsome cloudburst over the black-garbed plain: candles burning in rough holders, lighting a humble domain'. I was born by chance, on that night of the fearsome cloudburst.

On these plains that surround us now.
Yes, we're in Arvelo Torrealba's '*ancho-terraplén*', the flood plains on the wide open spaces of the Llanos. I suggested we talk here, in my *ancho-terraplén*. On that map of Venezuela [he points to the wall], you see the Cordillera of the Andes to the West, and the flood plains are all this part over here: the Llanos.

---

27   In tropical zones there are only two seasons, rainy and dry. In Venezuela, the rainy season, from May to October, is called 'winter' although it roughly coincides with summer in the temperate zones of the Northern hemisphere.

28   One of the most popular legends of the Venezuelan plains recounts the struggle between Good and Evil, between a feisty troubadour who wanders the immense savannah and Mandinga, as the devil is called. The myth was turned into an epic poem – *Florentino y el Diablo* (1945) – by Alberto Arvelo Torrealba (1905–1971). Florentino, the quintessential hero, represents the image of the strong, indomitable man who manages to defeat the devil in a long poetic duel. Evil retires with the arrival of the dawn light; but after the duel the cantor loses his voice for ever.

You can feel the powerful presence of nature.

Yes, here nature is palpable, immediate and diverse. In ecological terms, it hasn't been too badly damaged yet, and the aim of the Revolution is to protect and preserve its exceptional biodiversity. These plains are criss-crossed by an enormous number of rivers, home to hundreds of species of wildlife which we want to conserve: ocelot, puma, jaguar, giant beaver, capybara [a type of giant rat], anaconda, caiman, Terecay tortoise; beautiful birds like the yellow-headed caracara or bicoloured hawk, red-tailed hawk, widgeon, and the beautiful Venezuelan troupial which is our national bird; and typical plants and trees of the Llano like mahogany, rain tree, cedar, chaparro, cockspur coral tree and Venezuela's national tree, the araguaney [tabebuia chrysantha]. This incomparable nature – in all its variety, authenticity and sometimes cruelty – has been forcibly tamed and controlled by the men of the plains; and that struggle has left its indelible mark on the personality and culture of the llanero.

What is it to be a llanero? Do you feel a llanero?

Various attempts have been made to study the llanero. Being a llanero is being like the savannah itself. Larger than life, with huge aims, big goals. Rómulo Gallegos used to say, 'The llanero is always in the centre of a moving circle.' You move, you look around and there is another circle, and you are always in the centre of that huge circle. It is a land, not only of exceptional flora and fauna, but also of skilled horsemen, thoroughbred steeds, cattle, history and wars.

Many wars?

Countless wars. If you follow the most dramatic events in Venezuelan history, politics and wars, you'll find llaneros there. The Llanos is a land of legends. There is magic here. Of course, I feel Venezuelan in all plenitude, but on another spiritual level, I feel llanero. Paradoxically, I discovered the essence of what it is to be a llanero when I was gone thirty: not in my childhood, nor my adolescence, but when I was an army officer. The feeling of being a llanero blossomed inside me when I commanded a troop of cavalry in the central plains. Seeking an answer to the enigma of my great-grand-father Maisanta, I began to take on the llanero identity.[29]

It's a culture, as well.

Yes, of course. Being a llanero is also a culture: the music, the harp, the poetry, the ballad . . . a way of getting closer to life, work, nature, love, the magnitude of the journey. The Llanos is a land of Quixotes, because the savannah is La Mancha and Castile writ large. *Doña Bárbara* ends with an extraordinary sentence: 'Venezuelan llanos! Land of hard work and heroic exploits, wide open spaces, infinite horizons, where a good people loves, suffers and waits.'[30] Today we can add that this 'good people' not only waits but is fighting, developing, building – alongside the whole of Venezuela – a path to a better future.

You say the Llano is a 'magical land'. For its legends and superstitions?

Obviously, most of us know they're only superstitions and don't exist. It's hard for me to imagine any llanero in this day and age

---

29   Pedro Rafael Pérez Delgado, 'Maisanta' (1880–1924). Revolutionary general, son of Colonel Pedro Pérez, hero of the Federal War (1859–1863). In the mid-1870s Pérez married a woman from Ospina, Bárbara Delgado, with whom he had two children, Petra in 1878 and Pedro, the future Maisanta, in 1880. The boy lived his early life in Ospina. At the end of the century he moved to Sabaneta. He took part in several insurrections and came back to Sabaneta between 1904 and 1907 before going off to the wars again. He had a reputation for being audacious, a friend to those in need and defender of the rights of the poor. In the Llanos, he was the last of the popular *caudillos* to sway crowds. In Sabaneta he met Claudina Infante who bore him two children: Pedro (1903) and Rafael (1904). Rafael Infante lived with Benita Frías but did not marry her. They had two children: Elena Frías (1935) and Edilia Frías (1937). Elena married the schoolteacher Hugo de los Reyes Chávez in 1952. Their son Adán Chávez Frías was born in 1953, followed by Hugo Chávez Frías on 28 July 1954. Then came Narciso, Aníbal, Argenis, Enzo and Adelis Chávez Frías, younger brothers and sister of President Chávez. Maisanta's physical features were apparently 'tall, thin, smooth white skin, green eyes, drooping moustache, curly brown hair'. He was also known as the 'American'. He died in prison aged forty-four, on 8 November 1924.

30   Translator's note: This translation by AW.

believing in *El Silbón*[31] or some other wandering ghost, or the *Tuerto Bramador*,[32] or the *Jinete sin cabeza*,[33] or the *Caimán patrullero*.[34]

But you yourself mentioned in some speeches that you once saw this Patrolman Caiman.

Well, it's true that once when I was living in Elorza, between 1985 and 1988, I came face to face with a caiman so huge it seemed the stuff of legends.

How do you mean?

I was an army captain going down the Arauca River with some fellow officers; we were on the Venezuela–Colombia border somewhere between Elorza and Puerto Infante. It was a pitch-black night. We reached a lagoon they call *Encantada del Término* where there were sand banks and dunes in very shallow water. Suddenly, our boat hit something we thought was an island. But it was a giant caiman, like the legendary patrolman. We nearly capsized. That caiman was about forty metres long. Nobody believes me when I tell them. It was so enormous it looked like an actual island, even had a palm tree growing on its back.

Amazing. So some of the legends of the plains may be based on real life?

Undoubtedly, and at one time people even believed in *La Sayona*, in

---

31 The Whistler is a lost soul wandering the Llanos who, according to legend, killed his father in order to eat his liver, heart and intestines. His mother put a curse on him and he fled, but a dog was let loose to bite his heels until the end of time while his grandfather rubbed chilli on his wounds. The Whistler is afraid of dogs and chilli. He emits a hair-raising whistle as he wanders the plains carrying a sack of his father's bones, which rattle like a maraca at Easter.

32 A man-eating one-eyed caiman in the Bramador canal.

33 A headless horseman who gallops the plains at night; we can hear the ghostly whinny of his bolting horse.

34 Legend has it that an enormous caiman patrols the Arauca River, protecting the flora and fauna from depredation.

souls in Purgatory, in wandering spirits.[35] And those beliefs are still there. But I think there is something else. All this savannah is also – as Rafael Alberti might put it – 'one great steppe for fighting in'.[36] It has seen 500 years of epics, heroic battles, thousands of Odysseys and Iliads. Homer and his poems pall in comparison with the epic accounts of the savannah and the countless legends of these Llanos. Stories based on real events, distorted by mythology and turned into legend. These lands originally belonged to tribes of plains Indians, very warlike people. Remember that in Venezuela there were numerous uprisings against the colonial power.[37] But during our wars of independence, even if the Republic lost several battles in the Centre [Caracas], the Spanish were never able to dominate these plains.

Wasn't Boves a llanero?

José Boves was a Spaniard, from Asturias. He came to Venezuela when he was very young and lived here in the Llanos. He did indeed become a llanero, and the llaneros followed him.

Against Bolívar, wasn't it?

It wasn't exactly against Bolívar. Using the banner of racial hatred, Boves waged what we could call a very Manichean class war, the war

---

35   A jealous woman who killed her mother and her husband because she thought they were having a romance. On her deathbed, her mother put a curse on her. Ever since, *La Sayona*, with her long white petticoat and long black hair, has wandered the earth in pursuit of unfaithful husbands, to seduce and kill them.

36   Rafael Alberti (1902–1999), Spanish poet of the Generation of 1927. A militant communist, he sided with the Republic in the Spanish Civil War (1936–1939). The quote is from the poem 'The Lover' (1926).

37   Mutinies, military coups, uprisings and insurrections, both individual and collective, dominated the history of Venezuela from the sixteenth century on. To mention only those in the eighteenth century: the uprising of Andrés López de Rosario 'Andesote' in the Yaracuy valley (1730–1733); the mutiny of San Felipe el Fuerte (1741); the uprising of El Tocuyo (1744); the insurrection of Juan Francisco de León (1749–1751); the Comuneros de los Andes movement (1781). There were also rebellions that proposed political changes: the movement lead by José Leonardo Chirino and José Caridad González (1795) at the head of 350 blacks, *zambos* and Indians; the conspiracy of Manuel Gual and José María España (1797); the attempted uprising of Francisco Javier Pirela (1799); and finally the invasions of Francisco de Miranda, 'The Precursor' (1806).

of the poor against the rich. Every white person was an enemy, every rich person was an enemy.

Apparently Bolívar, at the beginning, didn't pay much attention to the question of racial discrimination, or the subject of slavery.

Bolívar was an enlightened man who defended the French Revolution's Declaration of the Rights of Man, which rejected discrimination of any kind between human beings. The proof is that, in 1815, he sought asylum in Haiti, which was then a pariah state, marginalized by the great powers for having declared independence from France after the world's first black revolution. He received help from President Alexandre Pétion, and promised in return to free the slaves in Venezuela. He passed several decrees to that effect. The Liberator's attitude towards Venezuelans of African descent was always one of absolute equality. There is a wonderful anecdote which shows how true this was. It occurred in Lima, in December 1824 where, after the battle of Ayacucho, a celebratory ball had been organized. None of the ladies in racist Peruvian society would accept a dance with one of Venezuela's greatest army officers, the black general José Laurencio Silva, hero of a hundred battles. Bolívar noticed and, ordering the orchestra to stop, went up to the officer amid an impressive silence, and said, 'General Silva, shall we dance?' And the two of them danced for a long time. That's what Bolívar was like. Although initially, perhaps, he may not have given the matter much thought. And Boves took advantage of that.

The llaneros who fought with Boves were coloured, weren't they?

Yes, blacks, Indians, mestizos, mulattos, *pardos*, *zambos*, former slaves.[38] Poor people, that is. It was a class and race struggle. Boves gave the llaneros land he took from *criollo* [white] patriots. But after

---

38 Translator's note: There are many names all over South America for people of mixed race. In Venezuela, the main names are mulatto, white and black African; mestizo, white and Indian; *zambo*, black Africa and Indian; *pardo*, mix of black African, Indian and white.

Boves died, those same fearsome llaneros, led by José Antonio Páez, joined Bolívar, and their support was decisive in his victory over the Spanish. They were exceptional fighters.

There is an immense thirst for freedom and equality here, a historical rebelliousness that has been unleashed once again for the Bolivarian Revolution. That's what being a llanero is. Roaming the boundless savannah like Florentino, battling demons. Always ready to accept the challenges these great lands might represent.

It's like an ocean of land . . .
Yes, an ocean . . . Gallegos says, 'The Llano is exquisite and terrible at the same time; it contains beautiful life and atrocious death.' To be a llanero, in any case, is to be a poet. Every llanero has a lot of poet in him; some develop it, others keep it in their souls, or show it in their songs, or in the way they live.

You can see that immensity of the Llanos on the map.
Yes, all this [pointing on the map] is the Llanos: Barinas, Apure, Portuguesa towards the north; Cojedes, Guárico over here to the east; and down here the flood plains extend as far as the Orinoco River. Over there are the Colombian Llanos, a continuation of the same flood plains.

Those Colombian Llanos used to be Venezuelan territory, so they say.
Only one part. We're very near Santa Inés; this here is the capital of Barinas state. And here is Sabaneta, where I was born.

Is there a river at Sabaneta?
Yes, to the east of the town, the Boconó, it's very long with wooded banks, full of myths about canoes and fishermen. Sabaneta is on the left bank. From a reservoir, the Boconó flows slowly down around the edge of town, then joins the Guanare, and together they flow into the Apure which carries their waters on into the vast father-river Orinoco, before finally reaching the immensity of the ocean. The Boconó comes down from the Andes, flattens out onto the plains and courses through the

Llanos. It then flows into another river, loses its name and branches out. Here [he points to the map] it becomes the Guanare Viejo, then the Guanare and the Guanarito. And finally, they all flow into the Apure, and from there into the magnificent Orinoco.

Why was Sabaneta founded in that particular place?

The town was founded on the large plain at the foot of the Andes, on a bank of the Boconó, near a ford which connects the high Llanos to the low Llanos. That ford is the main reason Sabaneta exists. The Spaniards built a settlement a short distance from the ford on an important route to Apure and Colombia.

A strategic route called the Baronesa route, or something like that, wasn't it?

The Baronero Crossing. Yes, that's the ford over the Boconó. This colonial royal road passed through Sabaneta, it's the 'old road'. Nowadays it's the main highway to Ciudad de Nutrias and Puerto de Nutrias. The plains in the state of Apure, and its capital San Fernando, are very low-lying; the whole of this area is irrigated by an enormous number of rivers.

It must get flooded very often.

It's like a basin, flooded for a good part of the year, very hard to reach in the rainy season. You can only get to it from the north. So, geography shaped Sabaneta as an obligatory staging post for business and trade. And armies passed through there, too, on their way to the military supply centre at Barinas, the western depot which stored gunpowder, weapons and munitions.

This was a very prosperous region with a lot of cattle, tobacco, coffee and cacao. In colonial times, the tobacco grown here was considered 'the best in the Indies'.[39] And Barinas cacao and coffee were world-famous; the coffee particularly was appreciated all over Europe. They

---

39 Fray Antonio Vázquez de Espinosa, in *Compendio y descripción de las Indias Occidentales* (1628, re-edited by Ediciones Atlas, Madrid, 1969) mentions 'Varinas tobacco ' as 'the best brought from the Indies'.

used to call it 'Varinas' coffee, with a V for Venezuela, which was the name of the indigenous tribes in these parts. Barinas was indeed a great province; it rose against Spain, and was honoured with one of the eight stars on the Venezuelan flag. So, the ford at Sabaneta was the obligatory aperture in the royal road from Guanare to Nueva Granada [Colombia] through the Andes. It was a vital, strategic access route.

And that's precisely where you were born?
And in what circumstances? It's like a seed. You throw a seed on stony ground or on sandy ground, and the chances of its sprouting are not great. But it would seem I was born on ground fertilized for something to grow. Not just a man, but an historic time; so he could play a part in it. Nevertheless, I don't believe in predestination, which was the question you asked me. I don't believe the course of history is plotted by star signs when someone is born.

You were born into a poor family. One couldn't say you had anything but modest means.
No, we had hardly any money. We were the poorest of the poor. Of course, like all families, we had our own history. My father was black, but his mother was more Indian than anything.

When you say 'black', do you mean skin colour?
Black, yes. My father's skin colour.

Is your father of African descent?
Yes, but the son of a woman who was mostly Indian, from an ethnic point of view. She looked very indigenous, my grandmother Rosa Inés.

Are there indigenous communities in the Llanos?
Yes, a lot of them. Well, actually . . . not very many now, unfortunately.

But there are indigenous people?
There are native peoples – Yaruros, Guahibos, Guamos, Cuivas – towards the south, towards the Apure, around the most remote

rivers. They retreated there, hounded by so-called civilization, which was actually barbarity . . .

Are you talking about the Spanish Conquest, or more recent times?

We know the Conquest was a monstrous genocide, but I'm talking about more recent times, much more recent. The Indians have had their rights trampled on forever. Look, in the mid-1970s, when I was an army officer, a priest told me that near the Colombian border, landowners went out hunting Indians as if they were hunting deer. To terrorize them and chase them off their lands. They killed them, cut them up with machetes and burned their corpses.

Only a few decades ago?

Yes. In the Apure region, I myself witnessed a scene I'll never forget. I've told the story often. We were out on patrol, looking for a group of Indians because a woman had accused them of stealing some pigs. We had a guide with us, a good tracker who knew all the short-cuts, and also – as I found out – an expert in hunting Indians. We located the group, and they greeted us with a shower of arrows. One nearly grazed my head. Fortunately none of my soldiers was hurt. I gave the order not to shoot. The Indians fled. Then through the undergrowth I heard an Indian woman screaming. We made our way to the bank of a fast-flowing torrent. And there I saw, in the middle of the current, almost drowning, a woman carrying a baby. She was terrified. She watched us with eyes full of fear and hatred. Because we were wearing uniforms. And because many governments used soldiers to defend the landowners' interests and decimate the Indian population. I can't forget those eyes.

The woman was having trouble swimming, sinking lower and lower. I was wondering how to get her out, when our guide said, 'Captain, shoot her!' I was shocked: 'What?' He insisted, 'Shoot her, Captain! They're not people, they're animals. Kill them!' It gives me gooseflesh to this day. That guide wasn't a bad person, he wasn't a monster, I knew him well. He was expressing the racist anti-Indian sentiment that was the norm around there.

Is there still racism towards indigenous people?
Much less, because we're really fighting it. But there are still some uneducated people, peasants, poor folks, even good Christians, who say, 'Ten Indians went by, with two reasoning people.'[40] They use that expression. As if Indians were not rational beings. Our indigenous brothers are still excluded in some sectors of society in rural Venezuela. We have to give no quarter in the fight against social exclusion.

Your grandmother Rosa Inés was indigenous?
My grandmother Rosa Inés, who brought up my brother Adán and me, told us that her own grandmother was a pure savannah Indian. From her ancestors she inherited a special relationship with nature and even with meteorology. She would suddenly say, 'Huguito, bring the washing in, it's going to rain.' I was surprised because I could see the sun shining. 'Grandma, it's not going to rain. It's brilliantly sunny.' She'd insist, 'There's a smell of water in the air.' And not long afterwards, it would rain. Sometimes it was the opposite, I'd see a sky black with rainclouds and I'd say, 'Grandma, I'll bring the washing in, it's going to rain.' And she'd say, 'No it isn't, son.' And it didn't rain. My grandmother said her grandfather had come from beyond Apure, near Barranco Yopal, and was an ethnic Yarura. So I am proud to have Indian roots. I'm Indian through my roots and my consciousness.

But your surname, Chávez, which comes from your grandmother Rosa Inés, is not an indigenous name.
No, it's Spanish, because there has been a lot of racial mixing in Venezuela and also because it was the custom, in colonial times, to give black slaves the surname of their master – the plantation or ranch owner.[41] Indigenous people were usually baptized with the

---

40　Translator's note: I use 'reasoning' for the Spanish word '*racional*', which means someone with the ability to reason.

41　Chávez is originally a Basque name; it comes from *Etxabe* (Echave) which means 'the house below'.

name and surname of the priest carrying out the ceremony, or the godfather, who was almost always the local Spanish cacique or landowner. Apparently they baptized indigenous people with just one surname and one forename.

She remembered her grandmother as being pure Indian?
Yes, she remembered it well, her ancestors were pure Indians. I never met her mother, the beautiful, black Inés Chávez, who was the daughter of a black man and an Indian woman. She died young. Life expectancy here was only fifty in those days. At that age, a person was already very old, with not long to live, according to the statistics. My father was the son of grandmother Rosa Inés and a black man whom I only found out about later. I never knew him. He died while my father was still a boy. He lived on horseback, he sang ballads and he loved cockfighting and the *coleo*.[42]

A pure llanero?
A pure llanero from Guanarito. Passing the island of the Boconó, you follow that road until you get to Guanarito. My grandmother often told us about Guanarito. Of course, only later did I understand why she talked about Guanarito with such affection. She used to say, 'Sing *Guanarito*' to me. I liked singing. And she loved that ballad. [Chávez sings] 'Guanarito, beautiful land / land of ballads and love / with sandy banks to fish from / when I gaze at your savannahs / your aroma and your heartbeat / the girls who are calling me / while the herons bathe /on the banks of the spring.' 'Go on, sing,' my grandmother would say. And I'd sing, '*Va el solitario bonguero . . .*' Do you know what a *bonguero* is?

A musician who plays the bongos, I suppose.
No! [Laughter.] In the llanos, a *bongo* is a dugout canoe. *Doña Bárbara* begins, 'A large dugout was making its way up the Arauca.'

---

42   The *coleo* or *toros coleados* is now the main sport of the llaneros. The word comes from *cola*, Spanish for tail, and dates back to the huge cattle drives when cowboys would catch escaping steers by grabbing their tails and bringing them down.

As the ballad says, 'The solitary *bonguero* goes by / with the moon and his song / and in the night he dreams / longing for his home town.' My black grandfather, the *coleo* horseman, was from Guanarito, José Rafael Saavedra was his name. I learned about him by investigating myself, because no one in my family talked about him.

Your grandmother Rosa Inés never talked about your black grandfather.
Not a word. Absolutely nothing.

Because he was black, do you think?
No. It was obviously a short relationship, it didn't last very long. He left, and had a family in Guanarito.

Ah! He abandoned your grandmother?
She was a single mother, both mother and father. That Mr Saavedra never came back, and he died a few years later. He's buried in Guanarito. I found all that out much later. My father never knew him.

So your father has his mother's surname?
Yes, my grandmother's. She was called Rosa Inés Chávez.

Was this the family secret? They say every family has a secret, something nobody talks about.
Yes, nobody mentioned it, and no one dared ask. I didn't know much about grandfathers. I grew up with my mother and grandmother. I learned love and respect as a boy from the strength and the passion of women. I saw how women bear the cross. Instead of *Cristo* [Christ], it should have been *Crista*.

You also said Christ was the 'first revolutionary'.
He was a man and also a rebel. He fought for the poor, confronted the established political power – the Empire. He refused to conform, and for that he was crucified. He was born in Bethlehem,

and walked the paths of Galilee preaching social justice and equality. He challenged the Roman Empire that had enslaved the Hebrew people. His punishment was to die, taunted, humiliated, crucified.

Some reproach him for not having been more political.

Jesus was a true socialist thinker, a committed fighter for justice. In a recent article, I remembered something I had read in an old encyclopaedia I'd had with me since I was a lieutenant.[43] It said, 'In times of extreme tension, internal and external, great prophets will appear to demand a reversion of the growing misery of the poor and the maximum concentration of wealth in the hands of the few. In 765 BC, the oldest and perhaps the greatest of those prophets, Amos, appeared and, in the name of Jehovah, cursed the rich, saying "I will send fire upon Judah that will consume the fortresses of Jerusalem . . . they sell the righteous for silver, and the needy for a pair of sandals." '[44]

In that same encyclopaedia, it said, 'We find the same in Hosea, and especially in Isaiah: "Woe to you who add house to house and join field to field till no space is left and you live alone in the land."'[45]

Then Jesus came and condemned the rich in his Sermon on the Mount: 'Blessed are you who are poor, for yours is the kingdom of God. Blessed are you who hunger now, for you will be satisfied. Blessed are you who weep now, for you will laugh. But woe unto you who are rich, for you have already received your comfort. Woe unto you who are well fed now, for you will go hungry. Woe unto you who laugh now, for you will mourn and weep.'[46]

Christ was a rebel. A revolutionary, in fact. That's why he came into the world, to fight with the poor and for the poor, against those who have trampled the poor underfoot for centuries. He

---

43   See *Las líneas de Chávez*, a compilation of the president's articles and commentaries, Caracas, 2010, 1 June 2009.

44   Amos 2: 5–7.

45   Isaiah 5: 8.

46   Luke 6: 20–25.

came to give his blood for the wretched of the earth. I learned about Christ as a child. And our upbringing shapes us. All those things you mentioned, those historic events that happened in 1954, have an impact, in some form or other, directly or indirectly, sooner rather than later.

2

Family Secrets

Hidden grandfathers – Maisanta a murderer?
Popular memory – 'Bolívar passed through here'
Ezequiel Zamora – The Federal War – The scapular
The 'American' – Aunt Ana
The 'last man on horseback' – Cleansing family honour
Cipriano Castro – Juan Vicente Gómez
Wartime trickery – The last centaurs
Awareness of roots

Tell me about your family.
My family was, as I said, very poor. We lived in a house with a thatched palm roof, an earth floor, adobe walls of straw and mud [he draws it in an exercise book], in what was then a very small rural town. Sabaneta.

On my father's side, I'm a mix of Indian and black. A mixture, that is, of the wisdom of the Indians and the rebelliousness of the blacks; indigenous resistance and the spirit of negritude. And in both cases, the love of liberty. We must never forget the horror of Africa's colonies.

The slave trade, slavery.
Genocide. Slavery and negritude filling these plains with their drums and songs. With their pain, 'their moans and sighs', as the

poet Arvelo says. You carry that whole legacy with you, inside you. I received all that from my father's side. And from my mother's side I got the white, the European part. When my mother was a girl in Sabaneta, they called her the 'American', and that's a long story I was determined to uncover when I was in my teens.

To find out about your own background?
Yes, and because there was also a mystery in that family.

The Frías family, another family secret?
And the Chávez family too. I wanted to know more. More than about the surnames, I wanted to know where the two currents, the two rivers, that met in me came from. On my father's side, no one had ever talked to me about my grandfather, the black *coleo* rider José Rafael Saavedra, because my grandmother kept that secret hidden. Hardly anybody knows who my father's father was. They don't even ask. It's never occurred to them. Like you say, it was a family secret. I discovered it years later. My grandmother Rosa Inés died without anyone asking her a thing. And she didn't tell anyone either.

She herself, as I told you, was the daughter of a black woman called Inés, who was famous for her beauty. Imagine, the poets of the Llano still remember her. They say Inés was the daughter of an African from the Mandinga tribe, and an Indian woman from the savannah. Inés was Rosa Inés's mother, and her father – my great-grandfather – was Italian. They loved each other passionately for a while and had two children, Rosa Inés and my great-uncle Ramón Chávez, whom I knew very well. I was there the day he died of 'an attack', as they used to say in those days.

On your mother's side, there was another family secret, because she kept her mother's surname too.
Yes, on my mother's side; it was common knowledge that my mother was the daughter of one of the sons of Pedro Pérez Delgado, the 'last man on horseback'.

The famous Maisanta.

Maisanta, indeed.

Why did they call him Maisanta?

Because when he was fighting the dictator Juan Vicente Gómez, just as battle was about to commence he'd hold high his machete and, before setting off at a gallop, would hurl his war-cry at the heavens: '*¡Madre Santa!* [Holy Mother!]', invoking the protection of the Virgin. But he pronounced it 'Mai'santa!' 'Mai'santa!' Hence his nickname.

He was a white man born in Venezuela?

Yes, Pedro Pérez Delgado – Maisanta – was *criollo*, fair-skinned, a pure llanero, although he too had indigenous blood, his father was Indian. Apparently he was tall, very tall, handsome, suntanned, with big Colombian boots and a short sabre.[1]

Are there any photos of him?

Very few. I managed to get hold of the two now best-known portraits. One of his daughters had them. She lent me the originals, I photocopied them and distributed them. Nobody knew these photos existed. In one of them, Maisanta is with an Arab companion called Dáger, whom they called *El Turco*, father of Kurt Dáger, who was with Copei for many years.[2] *Turco* Dáger was Maisanta's lieutenant, his bodyguard; he had been a guerrilla with him. Maisanta lived in Sabaneta around 1904, over a hundred years ago.

That same Sabaneta where you were born.

Yes, the very same Sabaneta. It was a thousand-to-one chance, or a million to one, that I was born there because that gentleman, Pedro

---

1 A short sword, sabre, or machete is called a *terciado* because the end third is missing.

2 Copei (Independent Electoral Politics Organizing Committee), a political party created on 13 January 1946 by leaders of the Catholic student movement, affiliated to the Christian Democratic International. Its historical leader was Rafael Caldera (1916–2009).

Pérez Delgado, Maisanta, came to Sabaneta as the civil and military authority of a revolutionary government, during the revolution of Cipriano Castro.[3]

Was he a soldier?
Yes, he was. He eventually rose to the rank of general, but in those days he was a colonel. Of course, they were horsemen, warriors, forged in the school of war, product of the vortex, the maelstrom of war.

Not out of a military academy.
His school was the battlefield. His training was facing the enemy, in war.

Like Napoleon's field marshals, who were forged in the heat of battle.
Military history is full of those field marshals and generals who earned their spurs on the battlefield. Pedro Pérez Delgado was very young, merely a boy, when he was reluctantly swept up in the whirl-wind of the Venezuelan conflicts, the maelstrom of those confrontations between caudillos, who favoured central power, and the Federalists.

You're named Rafael after your two grandfathers.
After my mother's grandfather, Pedro Rafael Pérez Delgado, Maisanta, and, of course, after his son, my mother's father, who was also called Rafael, although he no longer had the surname Pérez but Infante, his mother's name. Once again, mothers, grandmothers, women.

---

3   José Cipriano Castro (1856–1924). Victorious in the civil war at the head of a Revolutionary Committee, he was president of Venezuela from 1899 to 1908. During his mandate, from December 1902 to February 1903, the fleets of several foreign powers (Germany, Great Britain, Italy) blockaded the Venezuelan coasts to demand payment of the foreign debt. In 1908 he broke off diplomatic relations with the United States. Also during his mandate, divorce was legalized in 1904. Then, on 19 December 1908, while away in Germany for health reasons, he was deposed by Juan Vicente Gómez.

And after your other grandfather, the* coleo *horseman whose name was Rafael too.

Yes, by strange coincidence my father's father was also called Rafael, José Rafael. My father, however, is called Hugo de los Reyes. He was born on 6 January and my grandmother called him 'de los Reyes' because that's the day the Three Kings came to visit Baby Jesus in his manger in Bethlehem. And, of course, I'm called Hugo like my father.[4] Although my mother thought I was going to be a girl – because she already had a little boy, my brother Adán – and had my name ready, Eva, because of Adam and Eve [laughter].

According to the Bible, Adam and Eve were expelled from paradise for seeking answers.

Like me. I was a very curious little boy. They used to call me the *Bachaco*.

What does it mean?

Bachaco because I'm mixed-race – indigenous, white and black.

I see. A synthesis of South America, with your indigenous, European and African components.

Yes, the three ethnic roots of the Venezuelan people. My grandmother had a kind of locket in which she kept strands of my infant hair, she kept it all her life. It's lost now. There was some fair crinkly *bachaco* hair, a cross between black and white. There's a photo of me looking very *bachaco*, I was about three, and there I was, a little reddish-haired boy – I looked like my mother – in a smock sitting on a rustic wooden chair. It's the only photo of me as a child, someone must have taken it, because we didn't have a camera. I was a teenager before I watched any television. I even think it was an advantage.

---

4   Hugo is a name of German origin which means 'man of character' or 'man of clear intelligence'. The saint's day is 1 April.

It meant you read books.

I read books and listened to the radio. My grandmother had an old wireless. I loved listening to the news, Radio France Internationale and Radio Sutatenza, a Colombian educational station. I did a lot of listening, to everything going on around me. I was very curious, always wondering about things, and I found creative ways of seeking answers to questions, to mysteries. One them had to do with my search for this scapular I wear round my neck [he takes it off and shows it to me].

The one Maisanta wore. Did you know about Maisanta when you were a boy?

Yes, of course. I was born in 1954, almost exactly thirty years after Maisanta died in prison, in November 1924. The thirtieth anniversary of his death in prison was 1954. And it was forty years since he took up arms in these plains in 1914, and fifty years since he arrived in Sabaneta in 1904.

As mayor.

Yes, as I said, he was the civil authority in Sabaneta. He had been born further north, in the savannahs of the province of Portuguesa, near Curpa, where José Antonio Páez was also from.[5] Maisanta grew up there, the son of a former Zamorista general.[6]

Who'd fought with Ezequiel Zamora?

Yes, with Zamora, the 'general of the sovereign people'. His name was Pedro Pérez Pérez. I once saw a photo of him, a very old one; he

---

5   José Antonio Páez (1790–1873). General in chief of Venezuelan Independence, and thrice president of Venezuela, 1830–1835, 1839–1843 and 1861–1863. He was known as the 'Centaur of the Llanos'. He was accused of having betrayed Simón Bolívar. Páez dominated the Venezuelan political scene from the battle of Carabobo (1821) to the Treaty of Coche in 1863, when the Federal War ended.

6   Ezequiel Zamora (1817–1860). As a general, he led the peasant revolt with the cry, 'Land and free men! General elections! Hatred of the oligarchy!' He fought in the Federal War. He was assassinated a month after his victory at the Battle of Santa Inés de Barinas, on 10 December 1859. A genius at warfare and a revolutionary politician, he was both a military and popular leader: he wore a straw hat with an army beret on top. He said it was the symbol of the unity of the people and their army.

was an Indian from the plains of Guárico. Pedro Pérez Pérez joined Zamora as a guerrilla fighter; we're talking about the years 1840 to 1845.

Zamora left a deep imprint on the Llanos, didn't he?

Sure, because he was a revolutionary. He is without a doubt the most important popular leader of our century. Zamora had one principle: talk to the people, listen to the people. He wanted to change Venezuela and make it a fairer, more just country. A country 'where there will be no rich and poor,' he said, 'no landowners and slaves, no powerful and humiliated, only brothers, all equal'. He was a visionary. He proposed abolishing the death penalty, total freedom of expression and universal suffrage. When slavery was finally abolished on 3 March 1854 (Bolívar had abolished it in 1816, but his decision was not respected), Zamora opposed the bill to force freedmen to pay compensation to their former owners.[7]

You've described Zamora as a socialist, on what grounds?

I have no doubt that he had pre-socialist ideas. Remember that in those days [1850–1860], socialism was starting to take root in Europe in the wake of the Industrial Revolution. The first workers' unions had been created. Proudhon's ideas of social revolution were circulating.[8] Karl Marx and Frederick Engels had published the *Communist Manifesto* in the year that France and other countries in Europe had experienced 'the people's spring' – the 1848 Revolution. The First International was also emerging.[9] The impact of those

---

7   On 6 July 1816, Bolívar decreed, 'This wretched portion of our brothers who have groaned under the misery of slavery is now free. Nature, justice and politics beg for the emancipation of the slaves: from henceforth in Venezuela there will only be one class of men, all will be citizens.'

8   Pierre-Joseph Proudhon (1809–1865), French philosopher and economist, one of the first socialist theoreticians, and the 'father of anarchism'. His main work is *What Is Property?* (1840). A question which was answered by 'property is theft'.

9   The International Workers' Association (IWA), also called the 'First International', was founded in London on 28 September 1864, by workers' delegates from all over Europe with the aim of coordinating union and popular struggles worldwide. The statutes were written by Karl Marx.

ideas and movements was felt in our America. Zamora demanded fair wages for agricultural labourers and wanted every town and village to set aside a piece of land several leagues across for the collective use of landless labourers. He also envisaged an embryonic social security, asking the owners of large herds of cattle to give each community ten cows whose milk would go to feed children and the poorest families.

The germ of the welfare state.

Yes, a desire for social protection. That's why Zamora and his revolutionary project left such an indelible mark on the Llanos. Remember that the state of Barinas was once called Zamora state. Later on, the oligarchy tried to destroy his positive image in the popular memory by inventing a black legend, turning him into an 'exterminator'. But the poor people of the Llanos still retain a fond memory of Ezequiel Zamora, leader of the peasant revolt.

And that's why your great-great-grandfather, Maisanta's father, joined his army?

Yes, and when I discovered all this, I understood that I come from a lineage of guerrillas on horseback. That is, I'm not a missing link in history. Maisanta's father, Colonel Pedro Pérez Pérez, the Indian guerrilla, was one of General Zamora's officers, and Zamora's father had been a captain under the command of the Liberator Simón Bolívar himself. So we form a continuous chain: our grandfathers and we, their sons and grandsons, are one blood, one spirit; the same battles, the same flag, the same cause. We are freedom fighters. I also discovered that my grandfathers never sat on their backsides, they never spent time at home; they were always in the saddle, lance in hand. For a long time, these grandfathers were hidden from me. I didn't know what grandfathers were, the wars took almost all of them.

And did your great-great-grandfather, Pedro Pérez Pérez, take part in the battle of Santa Inés?

Zamora, the 'general of free men', came here over a century ago, and I imagine Pedro Pérez Pérez was with him in the Santa Inés jungle, at that important battle on 10 December 1859, and at the victory, though there's no record of it. Zamora was killed in 1860. The bullet which killed him did not come from the ranks of the oligarchy, but from Federal ranks, from the revolutionary army. The Federal War [1859–1863] continued for another three years after his death.

A war which destroyed the country?

It was a conflict that originated in the search for equality in Venezuelan society. Its aim was to eliminate colonial privileges and to resolve once and for all the social problems facing the country. In reality, it was a civil war between, on the one hand, the conservatives in power in Caracas who represented the urban bourgeoisie and the landowning partisans of centralism, and on the other, the Liberals or Federals, who stood for an end to the privileges of the oligarchy and greater autonomy for the provinces, in the name of the principles of liberty and equality. Zamora led the Federal army, until his assassination in 1860.

That war, the longest in Venezuela's history, ended with the Treaty of Coche [23 April 1863] signed by José Antonio Páez, president of the Republic and Juan Crisóstomo Falcón, the new leader of the Federals, elected president [1863–1866]. He was to betray Zamora's revolutionary ideals.

Some of Zamora's former comrades in arms from the Federal High Command subsequently became presidents, like Joaquín Crespo [1884–1886 and 1892–1898] and General Antonio Guzmán Blanco [1870–1877, 1879–1884 and 1886–1887]. But they also turned their backs on Zamora's revolutionary drive.

That Federal War left its mark on Venezuela's collective memory, didn't it?

Yes, first because it was very long – it's known as the Five Year War – and second because the cost in human lives was enormous. Over one hundred thousand people died, out of a population of barely 2 million. Whole towns were razed, crops burned, populations massacred. The entire agricultural economy was wrecked. Livestock production, one of nineteenth-century Venezuela's main sources of wealth, was decimated. Of 12 million head of cattle, only 2 million survived. Exports plummeted, and the country's foreign debt rose.

Zamora passed through Sabaneta, I imagine.

He passed through, of course, in March 1859, on his way to Barinas. He took that city, liberated it, set up his government, proclaimed the Federation and hoisted the Federation flag with twenty stars on the yellow band. The Federal anthem was sung: 'The overcast sky / heralds a storm / oligarchs, tremble / long live freedom.' The revolution inundated that land. When Zamora rode through Sabaneta, with trumpets sounding and horses' hooves churning up clouds of dust, the crowds cheered, following him on foot or on horseback: 'Bolívar is back!' cried old veterans. My grandmother Rosa Inés used to tell us, 'Zamora passed through here . . .' She hadn't witnessed it herself, but her grandmother had seen that centaur and his army of horsemen pass through the streets of Sabaneta. She had described it thousands of times. And, you know, I heard the same expression from my godfather, Eligio Piña, and other elders in town, like Eduardo Alí Rangel, a poet, writer, town chronicler, who was also poor but a notch above us. He had a brick house in the lower part of Sabaneta, the middle-class area. I liked going there to listen to him; he had been a good friend of my grandmother's mother, *la negra* Inés Chávez.

They also said, 'Bolívar passed through here'?

Yes, they said that too. The liberating army came through Sabaneta via the Baronero pass we mentioned before. What's more, the people of Sabaneta cherish the tradition that Simón Bolívar camped in the middle of town, at the foot of a hundred-year-old tree about forty metres high at the Camoruco roundabout.[10] They also say that José Antonio Páez and his troops passed through on their way to Carabobo in 1821. All this became part of the town's collective memory. 'Bolívar passed through here.' 'Zamora passed through

---

10   Typical tree of the Venezuelan plains which grows near rivers. Its scientific name is *Sterculia apetala.*

here.' Later I found poems, and works by historians that confirmed this refrain that had been passed down through the generations.

'Zamora passed through here . . .'
The very expression picked up from the people by the writer José León Tapia, author of *Maisanta, the Last Man on Horseback.*[11]

You said Maisanta was the product of a vortex. What did you mean by vortex?
The violent, convulsive times at the end of the nineteenth century. Maisanta is a product of that maelstrom. His father was beaten in the Federal War. Then came the pact between the Liberal and Conservative oligarchies, and he came to the Llanos, to Ospina, a town in the state of Portuguesa. He lived there with a woman and had two children, Petra and Pedro. Petra was the elder. Maisanta also had another daughter, Ana Domínguez de Lombano, born in 1913 from another relationship. She's still alive and still sewing on buttons, remembering her father.[12] She lives in Villa de Cura, in the state of Aragua, near Maracay. I phone her from time to time.

Does she remember her father?
She does. She told me he was a giant. She met him in Ospina when she was about eleven. She had not seen him much because he didn't live with her mother, but once he turned up and took her out for the day, the same day one of the few remaining photos of Maisanta was taken. Ana remembered very clearly how smartly he was got up for that photo in a professional studio. I found out a great many things from her.

You were telling me about the scapular of the Virgin of Mount Carmel that Maisanta wore.
It was Ana who gave it to me, actually.

---

11   José León Tapia, *Por aquí pasó Zamora*, Ediciones Centauro, Caracas, 1979; José León Tapia, *Maisanta. El último hombre a caballo*, Centro Editor, Caracas, 1974.
12   This was in 2009.

Did he always wear it?

Always, till the day he died.

And how did it come into his daughter Ana's hands?

Ana inherited it. Maisanta was thrown in the dungeon of the Puerto Cabello fortress, the Liberator's castle, in leg irons weighing seventy pounds each. And when he died [8 November 1924], poisoned by ground glass in his food, because he was an irredentist, an authentic Quixote, his fellow inmates sent all his belongings to Ana's mother in a box: a few photos, keepsakes.

Her whole inheritance.

Among those belongings was the scapular of the Virgin of Mount Carmel.[13] He always wore it around his neck, and died with it on. This scapular is over 150 years old, because his father, Colonel Pedro Pérez Pérez, had it before him. Maisanta had it from the age of fifteen, when he went off to war. And now I wear it, close to my heart and with all my love for the people. Look there . . .

There's a cross. Of red gold.

And on the other side is the emblem of the Virgin of Mount Carmel, who is also the Virgin of Succour, that is, the virgin of warriors.[14] A bishop, Monsignor Mario Moronta, explained the symbolism to me when I was in Yare prison [1992–1994].

---

13   According to Catholic tradition, in the thirteenth century, facing serious difficulties in the Carmelite Order, the prior general Simon Stock begged for the protection of the Virgin Mary. His prayer was answered when on 16 July 1251, the Virgin of Carmen appeared to him in Aylesford, Kent, accompanied by a host of angels, holding the medallion of the Order and saying, 'This is your right, for you and all Carmelites; whosoever dies with it will not suffer.' The medallion's prayer says: 'Be a shield for our warriors, a lighthouse for our sailors, a shelter for our absent ones and travellers.'

14   On 5 January 1817, the Argentine Liberator José de San Martín officially declared the Virgin of Mount Carmel 'Patron Saint of the Army of the Andes', placing the baton of command in the right hand of the religious image. On the eve of the Battle of Chacabuco on 12 February 1817, Bernardo O'Higgins, Liberator of Chile, proclaimed her 'Patron Saint and General of the Chilean Forces'.

Does it represent a crescent moon.
No, they're like laurel wreaths. But look how intricately embroidered they are . . .

Very fine work.
It represents cross and sword. Look, there's a sword in the shape of a cross, and forming another cross, three dots that, according to the bishop, symbolize the Holy Trinity: Father, Son and Holy Spirit. This scapular was worn by that warrior, caught up in the wars caused by the devastating collapse of Bolívar's independence project, and which brought an orgy of violence to all these parts; a vortex, no less.

Battles which were to last almost the entire nineteenth century.
For Venezuela, and also for Colombia, the nineteenth century was a vortex. In 1811, we had a republic which only lasted a short time; and at the head of this First Republic [1810–1812] was that universal native of Caracas, Generalísimo Francisco de Miranda. That republic fell. Simón Bolívar came back to help it to its feet, but it fell again. The Second Republic [1813–1814] lasted less than two years. The Third Republic [1817–1818], so long in coming to fruition, did not last long either. And when Bolívar died, in 1830, all hell broke loose: the *Patria* disintegrated, thanks to the bad government of all sides.

Who ruled after that?
For the first fifteen years [1830–1846], the Conservative oligarchy; then came a Liberal period dominated by what we could call a dynasty, the Monagas brothers [1847–1858]; then the Federal War broke out and, as we've seen, it lasted almost five terrible years involving over 350 battles and two thousand guerrilla skirmishes, and a death toll of one hundred thousand. There was the dictatorship of General José Antonio Páez [1861–1863]; a subsequent period [1863–1870] dominated by General Juan Crisóstomo Falcón, and the return to power of General José Tadeo Monagas; then the dictatorship of Antonio Guzmán Blanco [1870–1888];

following him what we could call a Decade of Transition [1888–1898], dominated by the figure of General Joaquín Crespo; and the century ended with the government of Cipriano Castro, a general who came to power in 1899 with, finally, a truly Bolivarian project. He called it the Restorative Liberal Revolution.

Restorative? That sounds reactionary.
No, because he wanted to restore, to re-establish Bolívar's original liberating project, approaching it in a different way. Cipriano Castro was a nationalist; he refused to surrender the country's riches; he expropriated, nationalized. He refused to pay the foreign debt and, in reprisal, Great Britain, Germany and Italy, aided by the United States, imposed a naval blockade on Venezuela at the end of 1902. Thanks to Castro's firm stance, the Drago Doctrine was adopted. This determines – to this day – that no foreign power can use force against a country in the American hemisphere in order to recover a debt.[15]

But Castro fell ill, and his doctors recommended he go to Europe to recuperate. And while he was away, one cold night in December 1908, his vice president Juan Vicente Gómez proclaimed himself president. A few days after this coup, warships arrived at the port of La Guaira. From where? What for? From the US; to support the new 'transitional government'. And exactly a year later, a new Oil Law granted all manner of concessions to the gringo oil companies, including non-payment of taxes: effectively giving the country away.

All these references to history you heard as a child made an impression on you, I guess.
I was always interested in history. I reckon history is like a path you have to know so you don't get lost. Schopenhauer said, 'A country

---

15   Following this naval blockade, and after Washington's decision not to apply the Monroe Doctrine, this jurisprudence was proposed in 1902 by the Argentine minister of foreign affairs, Luis María Drago, and adopted in 1907 by the Permanent Court of Arbitration in The Hague, which added that negotiation should always be attempted first.

that doesn't know its history can't understand its present, nor build its future.' History is a great teacher, it makes us conscious of what we are. And I, from a very young age, was fascinated by the tales of the Federal Wars, those rebellions, those warriors who rode through Sabaneta, whose memory was still alive in the minds of the town's old people.

And also because those tales were linked to your own personal history.

Yes, they interested me personally. As we know, a child's background and surroundings have an impact; he accumulates experiences which leave their mark, and help to build character. As a child, I used to hear things, mostly in whispers, at home, in the street . . . and I remember my godfather saying on several occasions, 'Huguito, do you know who your great-grandfather was, your mother's grandfather?' And he'd tell me the stories. So much so that it caused a lot of confusion in my young mind. Because he'd tell me about war, or violence; actually more about violence than war.

What kind of violence?

Once – I must have been five or six – in the house of my maternal great-grandmother Marta Frías, behind the bamboo wall of the big kitchen, I heard them scolding my mother Elena, who had always been a rebel. Standing by the stove, my great-grandmother was saying, 'You're headstrong as you are because Benita [Marta's daughter, Elena's mother] was descended, curse the day, from that murderer who killed Palacio, tied him to the foot of a mango tree and shot him in front of his children; and in Puerto de Nutrias cut off Lord knows how many heads, chopped up about twenty with a machete . . .'[16]

---

16 Hugo Chávez's mother, Elena Frías, confirmed, 'My grandmother Marta, who brought me up, used to tell me, "I don't know why that girl – 'that girl' was my mother, Benita – got the seed of that murderer." She would say that my grandfather, my father's father [Maisanta] had been a murderer, that he killed people, that he'd cut their throat and stick the head on the back of the chair.' (Interview with the author, Barinas, 11 May 2009.)

My brother Adán and I, listening through the wall, were scared stiff.[17]

They depicted Maisanta as a murderer.
A monster who had killed a father in front of his children, who cut his head off . . .

Pretty traumatic for you as a boy.
On top of that, my godfather Eligio always insisted, 'Your mother's grandfather was very quick on the draw . . .' But no matter how menacing it seemed back then, I liked talking to the old folk and listening to their stories, especially the town grannies, women who had never been to school themselves but who were a school for us. It seems women are better at preserving historic memory . . .

In Africa they say that every old person is a library.
That's right, they're a library, the memory of a time and place. When I was born, Sabaneta was a small country town with three or four streets: Calle Real, Calle de la Playa, Calle de la Madre Vieja and another that served as the main road out of town. So memories were very vivid. Maisanta passed through and left traces that are alive to this day.

Why did they call him 'the American'?
Because he was tall, fair, pale-skinned and blue-eyed. Gringos were already coming to that area. The oil was there and they came to exploit it. Saying 'Here comes an American' was like saying 'Here comes a white guy, a blondie.' That's how people saw them. In a poem dedicated to him, Andrés Eloy Blanco wrote, 'Some call him Maisanta / and others the American, / they call him American /

---

17 Adán Chávez remembers, 'The image we had of Pedro Pérez Delgado was of a murderer, a bad guy, a thief, a rustler of the Llanos who killed people. Talking in our family, my maternal great-grandmother Marta and my mother Elena would mention Maisanta and complain that if my mother had a strong character, it came from that murderer's family. It was the kind of thing people said and that we'd hear a few words of, in passing.' (Interview with the author, Barinas, 11 May 2009.)

'cause he's a handsome paleface, / between a grey and a bay' –
between white and black, that is, because a grey is a white horse and
a bay is dark – 'leaving La Chiricoa / with forty men on horseback
/ riding to Menoreño / goes Pedro Pérez Delgado.'

The fact is that a seed of doubt was sown; I was faced with a
mystery. I said to myself, 'My mother's grandfather is a murderer.'
And it made me ashamed. I had a sort of complex.

**Because you heard the things they were saying about Maisanta
being violent; and what your great-grandmother said?**
Yes. Within the family, we weren't allowed to talk about it, we couldn't
even mention him. It was like a stain on the family, a stigma, positively a curse. As if we came from a bad seed, the lineage of a murderer.

But, on the other hand, I'd hear different things in town. On one
occasion, I heard, 'No, Maisanta was not a murderer.' In conversations my godfather had with his father, and also in the house of
another, let's say, progressive family, closer to the social democratic
government.[18] Because I went to houses all over town.

So young, your parents let you roam round town alone?
Of course, like I said, it was a very small town, quiet and safe.
Besides, I sold sweets to rich and poor kids alike, in the street or at
front doors or at cockfights, and I also went to the baseball pitch, El
Bolo, and that way I'd hear loads of things. So I knew there was a
mystery surrounding my mother, and therefore me. Who was that
forebear I only knew of as 'Maisanta', 'the American', the 'murderer'?
As I grew up, my urge to discover the truth grew too.

What was that truth?
I had this nagging doubt inside of me. It was always there. Until
one day, when I was a second lieutenant [in 1975], I came across

---

18   Hugo Chávez would have been between six and ten in those days, and Rómulo
Betancourt's social democratic Acción Democrática party was in power in Venezuela for
the second time. Betancourt was elected in December of 1958, in the first free elections
after the fall of dictator Marcos Pérez Jiménez, and was in power until 1964.

the book *Maisanta, the Last Man on Horseback* by José León Tapia, a writer who collected legends of the Llano and delved deep into its culture. He had travelled the Llanos, asking people about Maisanta. I downed the book in one night, easy as a glass of water. I was amazed. It was a revelation. And some time later, in 1978 when I was a lieutenant with an armoured unit in Maracay, we went on manoeuvres in El Pao, state of Guárico. When I got back, a fellow officer Hernández Borgos said, 'Here, I kept this for you.' He handed me a cutting from a Maracay newspaper with the headline, 'Maisanta, the Guerrilla General'. Some officers even started calling me Maisanta.

Why?

Because I was always declaiming that poem, 'Some call him Maisanta and others the American'. The name became popular among the soldiers. But no one knew much about the historical figure; they knew the poem, and that the protagonist was a guerrilla fighter. Some even thought he lived in Bolívar's time. So I started doing some research.

And what did you discover?

Maisanta's father, Pedro Pérez Pérez, that guerrilla colonel and Zamora supporter we talked about before, had spent the last years of his life in Ospino. There he married Bárbara Delgado, a very pretty woman from the state of Portuguesa and, like I said, they had two children, Petra and Pedro. The veteran colonel died when they were still children. Petra, fair-skinned like him, was renowned for her beauty even as an adolescent. She caught the eye of a local cacique, Colonel Pedro Macías, the type of abusive macho who was very common on those savannahs. Disregarding the fact that she was still a child, he got her pregnant but wouldn't admit to being the father. In the Llanos, that had to paid for in blood.

But her father wasn't around to avenge the affront . . .

Exactly, so despite being just a lad, it fell to Maisanta, the only man in the house, to avenge his sister, and in those days debts of honour were redeemed with blood. One night, with his father's old shotgun his mother had given him, he waited at a fork in the road for the powerful cacique Pancho Macías, who they say was returning from a night out on the town. He confronted Macías, who fell on his face from the impact of a single bullet. He had cleansed his family's honour.

He fled that same morning in 1895, after his mother had hung the scapular of the Virgin of Succour from Valencia round his neck, and set off to see what life had in store for him.[19] He was barely fifteen. That was the start of the legend.

What did he do then?

He went to war, swept up in the revolutionary currents of the time. He enlisted first, in 1898, with General José Manuel Hernández, known as *Mocho* Hernández because he'd lost two fingers of his right hand in some battle. Hernández gave ordinary people hope. He travelled the country and was immensely popular; they say women venerated his portrait as if he were a saint, and threw flowers as he passed. But he had been robbed of an electoral victory in 1897, so he took up arms, and started a revolution.

And so began the revolutionary fortunes of Pedro Pérez Delgado.

You mentioned a newspaper article one of your fellow officers gave you. What did the article reveal?

Its author, Oldman Botello, talked about 'a daughter of his, actually living in Villa de Cura, who is the spitting image of him'. Maisanta's daughter! My mother's aunt! I knew Maisanta had had two children, Pedro and Rafael Infante. My mother and my Aunt Edilia, wife of Ubaldino – who used to leave his pick-up with the *topochos* for me to keep an eye on – are both daughters of one of Maisanta's sons, Rafael Infante, my grandfather. So, I asked my mother, 'Where's your uncle Pedro Infante?' And she replied, 'Your Aunt

---

19   Valencia, capital of the state of Carabobo in Venezuela. Not to be confused with the equally revered Virgin of Succour from Valencia in Spain. They are two different images. See, in Spanish, folkloreando.com.

Edilia in Guanare may know.' That's how I arrived at the house of
Pedro Infante, Maisanta's other son. When a man two metres tall
came out, he looked just like the portrait of Maisanta. Pedro is dead
now as well. He was reaching the end of his life, but he remembered
things, he told me, 'After my dad went off to war in the Apure area,
he sent letters, saying, "You can sign yourselves Pérez, I give you my
name." But we were never registered. My mum started living with
another man, and . . .' Well, those are private stories. So, I had
already met his son Pedro, but I didn't know Maisanta had a daughter still living.

Were you able to speak to the author of the article?
Yes, I went straight to Maracay to ask about Oldman Botello. I
found out he was a left-wing regional deputy, from the Movement
towards Socialism (MAS). I went to the Legislative Assembly and
introduced myself. I was in uniform. I explained, 'I'm a descendant
of Maisanta. Can you give me any information about his daughter,
the one living in Villa de Cura?' 'Of course,' he said. 'Señora
Lombano, Ana'. He scribbled the address on a bit of paper. He had
been doing research too; he would publish a book about Maisanta.[20]
I asked my commanding officer for some leave and off I went. I
arrived in a small town and found my way to Villa Las Palmas, a big
colonial house. I knocked on the door, it was almost dark, a sweet
little girl came out, I asked her, 'Is Señora Ana at home?' But I was
in uniform, and the girl ran off, squealing, 'Grandma, a policeman's
looking for you!' [Laughter.]

She was scared.
Yes, so then the lady of the house came out. She still looked sprightly.
Now she's over ninety-five. But she wasn't yet seventy then, she was
a seamstress, she made trousers. She still sews. She came to Caracas
in April 2009, when we organized an event with the daughter of

---

20 Oldman Botello, *Historia documentada del legendario Pedro Pérez Delgado
'Maisanta'*, El Centauro, Caracas, 2005.

Emiliano Zapata.[21] I invited her. Zapata, Maisanta and their two daughters, two little old ladies, it was wonderful! So, anyway, the lady came out, I took off my beret – we wore black berets in the armoured division, the parachute division wore red ones and the light infantry wore green – and, know what she said?

No.
'Who are you, young man, you look so like my sons?'

She saw an immediate likeness.
More than a likeness, a certain air ... She's a very intelligent lady, creative, always making jokes. I said, 'You're my mother's aunt.' She was surprised: 'How come?' I explained. 'I had heard,' she said, 'that I had family in the Llanos, my Auntie Petra told me ...' I interrupted her: 'Petra who?' 'Petra Pérez, who used to live here with me.' 'It can't be! But did she pass away?' 'Yes, a bicycle knocked her down. She was very old.' I spent the best part of the night talking to Ana.

Did she have any of her father's papers?
She started to bring things out, photos, the scapular ... After 14 February [1992], she gave them to me. She had a little coconut with a photo of herself set in it and some words. 'My dad made it when he was in prison,' she said. 'Those things prisoners do.' I realized that she knew her father well, she saw him just before he died, she went to his funeral, and took the box with his personal effects back to her mother.

He died in prison.
Yes, I told you, in the Castillo Libertador in Puerto Cabello. Meeting Ana encouraged me to dig deeper into Maisanta's life. She began to tell me more things, and at weekends I'd go round asking questions of people who knew the story. She gave me lots of pointers. I'd take maps, a tape recorder, a camera, and look for old people. I went as far as Arauca looking for traces of Maisanta.

---

21 Emiliano Zapata (1879–1919), one of the main leaders of the Mexican Revolution of 1910.

Did you put any of these people in contact with your mother?
Yes, I once took Ana to Barinas where she met my mother and my grandmother Rosa Inés. I took Ana to meet Pedro Infante as well, I said, 'Why don't we go and meet your brother before one of you dies?' He didn't know we were coming, he didn't have a phone. We just turned up at his house. His wife was younger and didn't seem to like him very much; he was pretty old and she mistreated him, verbally that is, or she despised him and didn't look after him. I introduced them: 'You're both children of Pedro Pérez Delgado.' When she saw Pedro, Ana began to cry, 'You're the image of my father!'

Did she remember her father well?
Yes, although she didn't see him when she was very small. She was born in Villa de Cura in 1913. The older children, Petra and Pedro, were born around 1904, and remembered him better. She met her father when he made a pact with the government in 1921, after the battle of Guasdualito. Those were the days of the last cavalry charges with lances and machetes led by guerrilla leaders like Arévalo Cedeño, *Mocho* Hernández, José Manuel Hernández and Pedro Pérez Delgado, Maisanta. These 'last men on horseback' waged several wars against the dictator Juan Vicente Gómez – the repression has been masterfully described by José Rafael Pocaterra in his book.[22] By 1921 the dictatorship's troops were equipped with repeating rifles, motorboats and even planes. For the first time since 1810 Venezuela had a modern army, while the guerrillas were still on horseback, just as they had been in the wars of Independence.

And under these conditions, Maisanta made a pact with the government?
Yes. First, Pedro Pérez Delgado quarrelled with other revolutionary leaders, then he made a pact, in Elorza, with the Gómez government. They gave him guarantees and he went to live in San

---

22   José Rafael Pocaterra, *The Shame of America: Memoirs of a Citizen of the Republic of Venezuela in the Days of Decadence*, A. Delpeuch, Paris, 1929.

Fernando. He was a very dynamic man, and immediately made friends and began dealing in cattle. Being temporarily retired during those months in 1922, he returned to Villa de Cura. Ana would have been about nine. She remembers her dad arriving, and thought he looked like a giant. Maisanta was already a popular legend.

Were you able to verify if he was 'quick on the draw' like they said?

Look, Maisanta was terrifying. I got hold of a book by José Garbi Sánchez, an old soldier from Apure who wrote his battlefield memoirs and devoted a chapter to Pedro Pérez Delgado.[23] At the end he says, 'I knew him in wartime, in peacetime and in prison. As a friend he was terrific, but as an enemy he was terrifying.' He lived through tough times and was an outsize, excessive character. I'll give you an example. Once, in Guasdualito, Maisanta was commanding a cavalry brigade. He had been assigned the most difficult mission, and the enemy had killed nearly all his men. The story goes that he wanted to take revenge by storming the barracks in Guasdualito, setting fire to it and burning all his adversaries alive. His enemies were petrified of him. He had spent so many years in combat – battles, skirmishes, guerrilla warfare. Always on a horse with his lance, machete and ancient musket.

So the thing about him being a fearsome man was true, then?

Well . . . fearsome to his enemies. Death was his travelling companion. But many testimonies describe him as a very generous person, not self-interested, and even Quixotic towards poor people. When I arrived in Elorza in 1986 as an army captain, I decided to go and visit the local people. I asked a soldier who knew the town to take me to the poorer areas. We rode over to a place called Flor Amarillo. We tied our horses under some *samán* trees and found a lady sitting nearby. I introduced myself as the new captain. I sat down, and she

---

23 José Garbi Sánchez, *Alzamientos, cárceles y experiencias*, Editora Venegráfica, Caracas, 1977.

sent for coffee. I could see she was old and liked to chat, so I asked her, 'Señora, might you have heard talk of an old warrior around here?' 'Which one?' 'Maisanta.' 'Of course! No one my age doesn't know who that man was. Why do you ask?' 'He was my mother's grandfather, and I'm wondering what memories there might be of him.'

'Ah, if you're Maisanta's grandson, you're welcome in this house,' she said. It made me feel proud of my blood.

She went on: 'When I was a little girl, the war came through here; my grandfather was a friend of that great-grandfather of yours, both revolutionaries fighting the government. One day a colonel and his troops came asking for my grandfather. "He's not here," replied my grandmother and her two daughters. My mother was a young girl, and I was just a baby. The colonel took a fancy to my aunt, arrested her and forced her up onto his horse, saying, "When your husband appears, I'll give you back the girl," and took her away. The next day Pedro Pérez came by and asked, "*Comadre*, why are you in mourning?" My grandmother and my mother, in tears, told him, "They took the girl away." "Who did?" "Some govern-ment soldiers, a colonel." And he asked, "Where's my *compadre*?" "No one knows, he's in hiding." "Where did they go?" "In that direction." "I'll be right back." And he galloped off with about forty men. Three or four days went by, then one morning they saw him coming back with my aunt riding pillion behind him. He had killed that colonel and his henchmen!

He also fought under Cipriano Castro, didn't he?
Yes, he rose to colonel in the revolutionary forces supporting Cipriano Castro and his Restorative Liberal Revolution. They arrived in Caracas victorious. These were new times, new men, new ideas and new ways of doing things. And those rural fighters had to face, in the words of the poet, 'with lead, blood and flames' the armed opposition of the richest families in the land, and the bank-ers with international support. Maisanta and his centaurs went into battle against the oligarchy. Once again, Venezuela was awash with blood. But the counter-revolution was defeated.

And how did he react when Cipriano Castro was ousted?

When Juan Vicente Gómez toppled Castro, Maisanta was very bitter. As a colonel, living in San Fernando, he was the military and civil authority there. So he pretended to support the new Gómez government. But very soon, officers loyal to Castro started plotting against the corrupt autocrat who had become the richest man in Venezuela and its biggest landowner. Maisanta decided to join this conspiracy. Unfortunately, the plot was discovered; an order went out for his arrest, and a friend of his was hacked to death by a river. So, to avenge this, he in turn took a machete to the colonel who was pursuing him; he hacked his face so badly he completely disfigured him. The colonel's name was Colmenares.

Five years later, Maisanta was in Arauca with his guerrilla army, near Elorza. As a border town, Elorza was ideal for guerrilla warfare; half in Colombia, half in Venezuela, it was the last remnant of the republic of Gran Colombia. One day, he was warned that a certain Colonel Colmenares was looking for him. He heard the 'disfigured' colonel was bringing a patrol upriver in a boat, and decided to take a few of his own men and meet him. They left the previous evening, slept on the riverbank, and waited. As day broke, they saw the boat approaching. As it pulled into the shore, in the half light, Maisanta came out of hiding, shouting, 'Who goes there?' 'Colonel Colmenares,' replied the officer. 'Are you looking for me?' asked Maisanta. 'I'm looking for Pedro Pérez Delgado,' replied Colmenares, surprised. 'I'm waiting for you,' cried Maisanta, as he shot him between the eyes. Colmenares fell into the water. His body was never found.

Looking at Maisanta from this perspective, you learned that he was not just a common rustler, nor a bandit, nor a murderer as some of your own family thought, but a political rebel, a revolutionary of those times.

The bourgeoisie called him a 'murderer' because he took up arms. For the rich, that's what he became, simply a murderer. In the same way, Daniel Ortega, the president of Nicaragua, told me that when he was a boy, the schoolbooks branded Augusto César Sandino a bandit, cattle rustler, highwayman and murderer. We had to wait until the 1960s for the Cuban Revolution to give Sandino his rightful place in history.

The work of José Léon Tapia was essential in rescuing Maisanta from disgrace, was it?

Absolutely crucial. Tapia's book *Maisanta, the Last Man on Horseback* opened my eyes, as I already told you. I uncovered many other things myself, poking around, digging up stories, researching, asking questions, collecting seeds and growing them within my heart . . . I wanted to write a more comprehensive book, but I never did. I made notes, set up files, even bought a book on research methodology, to do more rigorous work.

An old man once told me that Maisanta would arrive, take a town, shoot people like they did in wars in those days, open all the storehouses and shops, and let the people go in and loot. Nothing would be left, not even a candle. He told me, 'We'd take everything. Whenever Maisanta arrived, it was like a fiesta in the town. He'd take cattle from the rich, and share it out among the poor.'

Maisanta belonged to that class of men – men and women, of course – who were rising up against injustice all over Latin America at that time. Those were the years of Pancho Villa and Emiliano Zapata in Mexico; Charlemagne Péralte in Haiti; Luis Carlos Prestes in the south of Brazil, Lampião the *cangaceiro* [bandit] in the North East of Brazil, Augusto César Sandino in Nicaragua, Farabundo Martí in El Salvador, etc. They were the last men on horseback, the last centaurs, who charged the forces of the criollo oligarchs and imperialism with lances and machetes. These savannahs bore witness to the cry of revolution raised aloft by Maisanta.

All these discoveries about the real Maisanta were fundamental for you?

They were indeed. Because they helped me understand his political motivations. I also began to understand Juan Vicente Gómez and his time better, when I studied the historical context. I realized I couldn't look at the figure of Maisanta in isolation. It led me to wonder why all those men rose up against Gómez; and I discovered that Gómez took power in 1908, when President Cipriano Castro was ill and went to Europe for treatment. And that a few months later, Gómez signed into law concessions to foreign oil companies which covered more than half the country, while exempting them from paying tax for fifty years, that is, a practically unlimited period. Gómez sold Venezuela – and very cheaply, too – in return for foreign support for his dictatorship. He betrayed the Restorative Liberal Revolution, and betrayed the army as well. He turned the army into his personal pawn, using it for assassination and persecution. Those were dark years. That was Gómez's legacy: he kept the country back, while the winds of change were pushing the rest of the world forwards.

So, I began putting two and two together. I read books, documents, historical analyses of what was happening here between 1900 and 1905. I began to study the economics of it all: how the question of oil became so important, how Venezuela became the world's foremost oil exporter in 1922 and 1923. And I realized that the long years of Gómez's dictatorship were also years of insurrections and uprisings. I understood how and why so many leaders and generals joined the struggle – including my great-grandfather Maisanta. And to me this confirmed something very important. You must never lose sight of where you come from, never forget your roots.

3

Hard-Working Boy

The wise grandmother – The world in a backyard – Crops
Animals – 'Spiders' – Kites – Three mums
Canary Islanders, Arabs, Italians, Russians
Cinema – Mexican films
Three schools of life – Cartoons – First love
Tricolor magazine – Work, study, create – A good lesson
Young rebel – Street vendor – The *coleo*
Streetwise

Let's go back for a moment to your memories of everyday life in Sabaneta during your childhood. You said a man came every day and got a generator going. Was there no mains electricity?
There was a small generator that ran on diesel. Don Mauricio Herrera Navas was the man who got it started in the morning and shut it down at night. The ancient power plant was housed in a small shed with a corrugated-iron roof, a hundred metres from our door. In the late afternoon, after sundown, at eight on the dot, Don Mauricio shut down the motor and the lights in Sabaneta went off. First he'd do a short sharp cut-off, as a warning; then two more short periods, so people could take precautions, and finally he cut it off for good. That was when I was a child, but it apparently went on until 1972 when mains electricity was brought by CADAFE

[Compañía Anónima de Administración y Fomento Eléctrico], the state electricity company created in 1958.

You were from a very poor family. Did you have an unhappy childhood?

Absolutely not. Poverty is not the same as destitution. I was certainly a poor child. One of my aunts, Joaquina, my mother's sister, remembers that I wasn't allowed into school at first because I was wearing old rope-soled shoes. My grandmother had to find some proper shoes – heaven knows where – before they'd let me in. But I never went hungry. I was a very happy child. There have been newspaper articles claiming that deep down I must feel resentful socially, and want to take revenge because I was poor and wretched. Absolutely wrong. I repeat, I was poor, but if I had to relive my childhood, I'd want it exactly the way it was! Living modestly, with dignity, studying, working, selling fruit, flying kites made of old newspapers, fishing in the river with my father, playing ball in the Calle Real.

I was happy in that humble house with my brother Adán and my grandmother, Rosa Inés Chávez, my 'old mama', so full of love. The love for a man which she never had – because I never saw her with a man – she gave to us. She was born in 1913, so when I was born she was forty-one. A dark, pretty woman, with very long black hair, who devoted herself entirely to bringing us up, my elder brother Adán and me. Absolutely dedicated. I shall pay homage to her all my life, because she gave us everything.

Why didn't you and Adán live with your parents?

They lived out in the sticks, in mountainous countryside where things were more difficult. They didn't have a house of their own. My dad was a schoolteacher in a hamlet called San Hipólito, in Los Rastrojos, where my mother was from. That's where they met, he was the teacher there. She was seventeen and he was about twenty when they got married. They settled there for a while. My mother came to my grandmother's house in Sabaneta to give birth. That's why both Adán and I were born here. My father used to cycle over to see us. We always had the love of father and mother, but really it was my grandmother who brought us up.

You never felt abandoned by your parents?

No, not at all. My parents never abandoned us. We'd go and spend weekends there, or they'd spend time at my grandmother's. And by the time their third child Narciso was born, they had come to live in Sabaneta.

Near your grandmother's house?

Yes, very near; just across the road. We still lived at our grandmother's, but we were like a community, one family spread between two homes.

Your grandmother really brought you up.

For Adán and me, our grandmother was the formative influence as we were growing up.[1] We learned from her example. She taught me solidarity, humility, honesty. She was a very caring woman. She spread her affection, her goodness, and her great love of nature.

She sowed seeds and grew plants.

My grandmother loved gardening. We had a beautiful backyard, with loads of fruit trees, plums, oranges, mangoes, avocados, and a maize plot, and flowers and rosebushes. She'd spend all day in her vegetable garden, tending the plants and fighting pests. I loved going with her, I liked watering the plants.

The water, did you get it from a well?

In the early years there was no mains water. Just well water. But you didn't have to go and fetch it; a tank supplied several houses in our

---

1   Adán Chávez confirmed: 'The influence of my grandmother Rosa Inés is with us to this day. It was a very positive influence, because we learned a lot from her. She was humble and extremely sensitive to other people's pain. She taught us solidarity, and this nurtured our spirit. Now we can say that it was where our revolutionary spirit took shape because it's about solidarity, love for your fellow man, sharing the little you have, trying to alleviate the pain of others, the needs of your neighbours. That's how we were brought up, with humility and honesty.' (Interview with the author, Barinas, 11 May 2009.)

community. Later on, they built the aqueduct. And by the time we moved to the house opposite, made of breezeblocks with a cement floor, we already had tap water. Although before we got drains that took away human waste, we had a privy at the bottom of the garden. The sewage system came years later.

So, you had drinking water.
Yes, my grandmother's house had drinking water. Adán and I shared the chores: we helped water the plants and weed the vegetable patch, sow, pick fruit and maize. My grandmother was respectful that way. Although her education only went as far as primary school, she possessed a natural wisdom. She understood what was fair; the job we wanted to do, without being forced to. She guided me: 'Huguito, give the birds some plantain.' She had several birdcages.

Did you catch those birds yourselves?
Yes, and I learned to make trick-cages to capture them alive: you place two thin bits of stick to hold the door open and fruit inside for the bird to eat. When it steps on the sticks, they break, and the trap closes. Nowadays, with the ecological awareness we've developed, I wouldn't use traps like that, because birds should be free, especially the protected and threatened species. In our yard we also kept tortoises, hens, a cock and doves.

Did you have a dog or cat?
I had a cat, Tribilín, but that was later, in Barinas.[2] In my grandmother's house we had an old dog, Guardián, very faithful, very noble. And a parrot, Loreto, who was not in a cage; my grandmother taught it to speak, it ate with us, flew around the kitchen.

What was the house like?
Nice. On the outside, like I said, adobe walls and a thatched palm roof. Inside, an earth floor and a spacious kitchen where my

---

2   In Latin America, this is the name given to Goofy, the character in Walt Disney's cartoons.

grandmother was always working. The best part was the garden, full of flowers and fruit trees. For me it was the whole world. I learned to walk, got to know trees, plants, the natural world. How flowers opened, how after the flower came the fruit. There were oranges, mandarins, grapefruit, tamarinds, mangoes, plums, another local fruit called *semerucas* – red berries with a sweet-sour taste – and a small patch of pineapples. Avocados, too. I sowed maize, and learned how to harvest it, store it during the winter, and grind it. I knew how to make *cachapas* [sweet corn pancakes]. Everything I needed was there. It was a garden of dreams. A whole universe.

Was it big?
To me it seemed enormous. In fact, it wasn't that big, a quarter of a hectare maximum. But we made the most of it. I grew up in that garden. I liked climbing trees. My grandmother called me 'the orange tree bird', after a Paraguayan song, '*El pájaro chogüí*'. [He sings] 'And so the story goes / at the top of a tree / was an Indian Guaraní . . .' who fell out of the tree, died and turned into an orange tree bird who 'singing, goes flying by / off into the Guaraní sky'. She used to say, 'You're just like that little Indian, careful you don't fall.' I'd spend all day perched in trees, like Tarzan. The higher, the better. My favourite spot was right at the top of the *matapalo* tree.[3] 'Huguito, come down,' she'd shout. 'Don't climb the plum tree, it gets all slimy! Climb the orange tree, at least you can grab hold of it.'

Did your grandmother work?
She worked in the home, doing the housework; she didn't stop for a minute, she cleaned, cooked, made sweets, looked after the garden. I never saw her take a rest.

---

3 The *matapalo* or *higuerote* is the Venezuelan name for a stocky tree of the Ficus family (*Ficus elastica*). It lives in semi-tropical jungle where there is very little light, so it grows fast, like a climbing plant, winding round other trees to reach the light, ultimately strangling the tree it is using as a support. Hence the name 'woodkiller'.

Did she get an old-age pension, or any kind of help?
No, there wasn't any of that. She had two children, who luckily both took responsibility for her.

They helped her?
Her eldest child, my Uncle Marcos, lived in Barinas [in 2009]; he's old now. He had a different father, a white guy from the Andes, a trader.

How much older is he than your father?
About five years. Marcos was always very serious and hard-working, with a strong personality. He lived in Barinas and worked in local government, as an inspector of public works. He'd often come to visit my grandmother in his jeep, and bring her money. I'll always be grateful to him, he was considerate and affectionate with us. Seeing how keen I was on studying, reading and drawing, he used to bring me exercise books and coloured pencils. He liked me showing him my drawings. It was if he was setting me a task. I'd draw anything and everything.

Were you always good at drawing?
Yes, I had a natural aptitude, a kind of gift. When I was little, I made an easel out of rods of cane and painted a picture of my grandmother's house. One of the first things I wanted to be was a painter. As a teenager, I took classes at an art school in Barinas for a year, the Cristóbal Rojas.[4] It was near the Liceo O'Leary, my secondary school in the old colonial centre of Barinas.

Let's go back to Sabaneta. Did your father help your grandmother financially as well?
He helped her too, of course, but my father's salary was very small and he had quite a lot of children.

---

4 Cristóbal Rojas (1857–1890) was one of Venezuela's best nineteenth-century painters.

Before he became a schoolteacher, your father had been a travelling pedlar, hadn't he?

Yes, when he was very young, he'd gone from village to village with a donkey selling meat for a living; he'd also worked as a farm labourer. When his brother Marcos, the white son, went to Barinas, my grandmother kept her black son, Hugo de los Reyes, with her. Then he got married and went away as well, leaving his first two children, Adán and me, with his mother. So the economic constraints were considerable. That's why my grandmother had to make ends meet by selling things.

What did she sell?

Home-made sweets, and fruit.

Did she sell the fruit in the market?

No, we sold them on the street, and to an ice cream parlour that made ices with them. The owners were Italians who'd settled in Sabaneta. When we brought them our fruit, the Italian lady – who was very nice – would pay us and give us an ice cream as well. Thanks to that, my grandmother could buy what she needed for the house.

You say she made sweets with the fruit from the trees in her backyard. And who sold them around town? You?

Yes, she made sweets out of papaya. I helped her with that, as well. I'd look out for ripe papayas and pick them. Then we'd peel them and scoop out the seeds. Adán helped too. But she and I were the entrepreneurs . . .

The businessmen.

Sort of. I liked doing it. We'd slice the papaya into thin strips, and put them on a wooden tray to dry overnight. Early next morning, my grandmother would prepare a big pan of boiling water and sugar, and we'd throw everything in, until it caramelized. Then she'd lift the strips out with a fork, and on a wooden table she'd prepare little piles of them, they looked like *arañas*, spiders.

So you were a street vendor too?
Yes, as a little boy I'd go round the streets hawking my delicious 'spiders'. I was part of what they call the 'informal economy'. I'd keep track of the twenty lochas I earned.[5] What a lot of things I learned in the street! I was the 'spider seller' and, from age six or seven, I learned spider-seller skills: chatting people up, persuading them to buy, convincing them.

Did you call out your wares in the streets?
Yes, I made up some cries: 'Hot spiders good to eat, even for ladies without teeth!' And 'Hot spiders very tasty, even better than a pastry!' This helped me develop my voice, and I learned how to declaim, with a little help from Daniel Viglietti perhaps.[6] It was like a social education. There was nowhere I didn't go, mixing with old folk, women, people with more life experience; listening to grown-up stories, picking up gossip. Rubbing shoulders with the people, in fact.

Did you only sell 'spiders'?
I sold kites, too. I made them myself in different styles; my speciality was the Vulture. I'd fly them myself to demonstrate, then sell them. A capitalist past which sometimes embarrasses me [laughter]. I had a proper industry going. The prettiest and best-quality kites were 'Hugo Chávez's'. I was in competition with a man from a different neighbourhood, a professional. Colombian, I believe. He would make cube-shaped kites and even put a lighted candle inside, to fly them at night. I never managed to do that. But no one ever beat me at the Vulture. My best ones had a skeleton made of *veradas*.

What are 'veradas'?
Veradas come from a special type of bamboo that grows in former river beds. It has a long spike at the top, with a kind of wispy

---

5 A locha was a quarter of a bolívar. A few pennies each.
6 Daniel Viglietti (1939–), Uruguayan singer–songwriter whose songs contain a strong element of social protest.

hair growing out. If you cut that spike you get the *verada*, which has a kind of spongy material in the stalk, it's very light. I'd buy paper, and from one sheet I'd get two big or three small vultures. The skeleton of the kite made from the *verada* looked like a cross. Then I had to add a long tail. So, I was a Vulture-maker too. I did lots of things. It was entertaining, a game and also a job, because we lived off the sale of this stuff. Victor Hugo says in *Les Misérables* that poverty is like a dark room, 'but beyond that is a darker room: destitution'. Poverty is not the same as extreme poverty, wretchedness. I was not an abandoned street kid.

You had your grandmother's love.
Yes, I was much loved as a kid. I recently had a strange experience. During my *Aló Presidente* programme, I remembered a woman called Sara Moreno who was very sweet to me when I was a little boy.[7] I'm talking about age three, four and five, before I started school.

You started school at six.
Let's say I was about four or five. I remember Sara as this very pretty young woman who adored me as much as I adored her. My grandmother used to laugh at the silly things I said. 'Huguito says he's got three mums.' 'And who are your three mums?' They were Mamá Elena, my mother; Mamá Rosa, my grandmother; and Mamá Sara. What a happy boy, having three mums.

Anything but an orphan, then.
Absolutely! I was super-loved by three mums. One day I talked about Sara Moreno publicly on *Aló Presidente*, and just look what the power of remembering can do. Shortly afterwards I received a letter from Sara Moreno's family, with a photo. I still have it. I recognized her at once. I hadn't seen her since those days; I'd never

---

7   Created in 1999, *Aló Presidente* was a programme hosted by President Chávez and broadcast by the public channel Venezolana de Televisión every Sunday at 11 a.m.

had a picture of her. The letter explained various things in response to what I'd said: 'Sara died, but I don't know where, or what she died of, nor where she came from, but she arrived in Sabaneta like an angel, and for me she left as mysteriously as she arrived, leaving me a huge amount of love . . .'

Did you contact her family?
Yes, the letter had some phone numbers. I called and said, 'This is the president speaking . . .' Sometimes people don't believe me, they think it's a prank.

They never thought you'd call them personally.
Right. I said, 'I got your letter.' It was her brother. He gave me the phone number of a cousin in Barinitas, a town in the mountains where the old Spanish town of Barinas originally stood, before people had to move to the new town because the Indians wouldn't leave them in peace. Barinas had quite a few capitals before the current one.

A cousin of Sara's lived in Barinitas.
Yes, a cousin on her sister's side. I spoke to her mother, a very old lady by then, about eighty. The old lady told me that she and Sara's mother had gone to Sabaneta one day to visit her. Sara had come to Sabaneta as a nurse, and rented a house across the street from ours. She lived alone, and worked in the town clinic. I remember her white coat.

You used to go to her house?
I spent a lot of time there; she'd make me oats for breakfast.

And what happened to her?
She suddenly fell sick, and was taken away. It was winter, and they put her in a pick-up truck, one of the few vehicles that could get into town in the rainy season. She hugged me, crying. 'I'll come back, don't cry.' She never came back. Some time afterwards, we heard that Sara had died. I was in floods of tears.

What did Sara's aunt tell you?

Back then, in 1958 or 1959, Sara graduated as a nurse and they sent her to the clinic in Sabaneta. Her mother and aunt came to visit her one summer. The old lady remembered: 'We got to Sara's house and a little boy with frizzy fair hair came running up. Sara told him to go and buy a soft drink, because her mother was there. The boy rushed off and got it from a nearby grocery. That boy was you, she called you Huguito.' They spent several days with Sara, and remembered Huguito being in the house all the time.

Several houses. Several mums. Several women. I had loads of women [laughter]. I grew up among women. That's why I say I was a happy child. And a loving father who taught us things. My father would arrive on his bicycle.

What was Sabaneta like in those days?

Like I said, a small town, two main streets, a newer one, several smaller streets, set a little way back from the river. We lived on the outskirts, ours was the one of the last houses on the way up the hill out of town. Sabaneta was divided into two areas: uphill and downhill, depending on how near the mountains you lived. People would ask, 'Where are you headed?' 'Uphill.' That is, towards the mountain. Or 'Downhill.' The poorer people lived in our part of town. There were lots of thatched adobe huts like ours. But there were some modern houses near the Plaza Bolívar in the lower part of town; some even had two storeys.

Were social differences clear-cut?

There were some great friendships, yes, but there were social divisions. We belonged to the lowest class, the rural poor, with no property or belongings. I never wanted more because I thought I had it all. My grandmother's backyard was my whole universe. As I told you, we didn't lack for anything.

What did people live off? What was the main commercial activity?

In the countryside, it was agriculture and forestry. A lot of men worked as lumberjacks – there were still forests then – while others drove the huge lorries which took the timber to various sawmills. In those days the owners were usually Italian. There was a lot of commercial activity, too. There was a small community of Canary Islanders, some of whom had ranches, cars, and fancier houses. The Arab community owned the biggest shops.

Were they Christians or Muslims?

Jadán Raduán, for instance, belonged to one of those Arab families. I remember them being Muslims. I saw them not long ago. The family owned a general store, most of the Arab families did.

There was also an Italian community. Remember that President Pérez Jiménez [1952–1958] encouraged European immigration, particularly from Portugal, Spain and Italy. Venezuela, a country of almost a million square kilometres, had a population of less than 7 million in those days, and the per capita income was among the highest in the world. Many Europeans, whose countries had been destroyed in the Second World War, saw our country as the Promised Land, a world of opportunities for rebuilding their lives. In Pérez Jiménez's mind – as in that of other Latin American leaders who practised it – this policy of open immigration for Europeans was not without a racist motivation. The hidden agenda was to 'whiten' a population which was thought to be 'too black'. Three hundred thousand Italians arrived during this period and, by 1960, the Italian community was the largest minority in Venezuela, even more numerous than the Spanish.[8] Many of those who had previously worked in agriculture came to settle in the Llanos. In the Sabaneta region, the Italians worked in the forestry sector: cutting trees, working in sawmills, also owning several businesses.

Canary Islanders, Arabs, Italians. Sabaneta was almost a cosmopolitan metropolis . . .

There were Russians too. Well, we called them 'Russians', but, since the Soviet Union still existed, they might have been

---

8   Venezuela has had two presidents of Italian descent: Raúl Leoni (1963–1969) and Jaime Lusinchi (1984–1989).

Ukrainians or other Soviet nationalities. I remember at least two. One, called Samolenka, was a construction engineer. Very hard-working. A group of us kids talked to him once; he gave us some advice. To me he seemed a very noble, respectable person. The other one was called Alejandro Rokitansky, he lived opposite the school with his wife Doña Carmen. Both Russians were married to women from Sabaneta, they had Russian–llanero families, so they put roots down. When the guerrilla armies came to this area at the beginning of the 1960s, the intelligence services watched the Russians carefully, as if they were Soviet agents, infiltrators . . . [laughter].

How do you explain the presence of so many foreign communities?
Like I said before, Sabaneta lies in a strategic position, on an access route. Anyone coming from Caracas, from the Caribbean, wanting to go to Colombia or Apure, to do business, sell goods, or buy cattle, had to go through Sabaneta; especially if he wanted to go to the Andes. It's a strategic point for going to Central Apure and Upper Apure. So it's obvious that armies, traders, mule trains, immigrants, all passed through Sabaneta.

And some of those immigrants stayed.
They certainly did. For example, Arab immigrants heading for Apure, where Arabs have settled in all the towns. Perhaps because these plains look rather like Arabia. When I was in Saudi Arabia [February 2001], I was invited to the desert. There I understood the relationship between the Arabs and ourselves a little better. There are similarities: the singing, the effusiveness.

The majority of those who came to the Llanos were Syrian. Not long ago, I went to Syria and had a meeting with some Venezuelan Arabs, who had returned to Syria, and they talked about Sabaneta.[9]

---

9   In September 2009, on an official visit to Syria, President Chávez met members of the Syrian–Venezuelan community in the city of Swaida, one of the places with most family members living in Venezuela.

What did people do for entertainment in Sabaneta? Was there a cinema, for instance?

Of course, there was the Cine Bolívar which belonged to one of the Italian families, the Toppis. They had the cinema, an ice cream parlour, a tailor's shop and a café. They also sold clothes. My father and my Uncle Marcos were friends of various Italian families, and used to go to the cultural evenings they held. They were educated people.

Did you like the cinema?

A lot. When I was ten, my father used to take us to the Saturday matinees. We would go up in the balcony, which was a bit more expensive, but the stalls were disgusting because people went in with bikes, and threw chewing gum, or stuck it on the seats, or smoked, and pissed, and at Christmas they threw bangers. It was a battlefield. People had fights, like at a boxing match. Women didn't sit downstairs, only in the balcony. I saw almost all the films of Antonio 'Tony' Aguilar.

I haven't heard of him.

He was a great singer of *rancheras* and *corridos*.[10] He was also a star of the Mexican Western, a hero seeking justice for the poor. I remember some of the names of his films: *El rayo justiciero, La rebelión de la sierra, Cuatro contra el imperio, La justicia del Gavilán Vengador, El fin de un imperio*.[11] I spent my childhood at that cinema.

Did you go with your brothers and sisters?

---

10   Translator's note: Like *coplas* in Venezuela, *rancheras* and *corridos* are traditional Mexican folk music usually with a solo singer plus a guitar, about love, patriotism, nature. The corrido is more of a ballad, a popular narrative, with a moral.

11   *Ray of Justice* (1955), dir. Jaime Salvador; *Rebellion in the Hills* (1958), dir. Roberto Gavaldón; *Four Against the Empire* (1957), dir. Jaime Salvador; *Justice of the Avenging Hawk* (1957), dir. Jaime Salvador; *End of an Empire* (1958), dir. Jaime Salvador. All translations by the translator.

My father usually took the three eldest: Adán, Narciso and I. It was like a reward. A custom he kept to religiously. He never let us down; we knew what film was showing on Saturday, and we knew we would be going. Except if you didn't do well at school. But I never missed a Saturday because of not doing well, only once when my father punished me for being disobedient. He didn't take me to see *Neutrón contra los autómatas de la muerte*, I missed it.[12] Neutrón, who fought in a black mask, was unbeatable. I also remember *Santo contra los zombies* and *Santo contra las mujeres vampiro*, some statuesque females.[13] Those films often came to the region.

Mexican films.

All of them. In the Cine Bolívar, they also showed films of Miguel Aceves Mejías starring Alfredo Sadel, a Venezuelan singer with a golden voice.[14] I also remember films like *Chucho el Roto*, and a song called 'Rufino el Forastero' [he sings]: 'Men say "Go away" / Women say "I'll wait for you" / Who is that great horseman? / Rufino the mysterious stranger.'[15]

But the one I liked best, as I said, was Antonio Aguilar. He sang 'Four Candles', for instance, it's a fantastic song [he sings]: 'Lying spread at your feet / four candles await me / four candles after martyrdom / hurting from your cruel love.' My grandmother loved those songs. And when I first arrived in Barinas, the local lads used to call me 'Tony', because I'd sit and sing, one guy would come up with a cuatro, another with a guitar, and I'd imitate Antonio Aguilar singing *rancheras* like the 'Corrido de Mauricio Rosales *El Rayo*' [he

---

12   *Neutron Against the Automatons of Death* (1963), dir. Federico Curiel. The film was the third part of the *Neutron Trilogy*, a hero of the 'masked avenger' type. The first two parts are *Neutron the Black Mask* (1961) and *Neutron Against Dr. Caronte* (1962).

13   *The Saint Against the Zombies* (1961), dir. Benito Alazraki; *The Saint Against the Vampire Women* (1962), dir. Alfonso Corona Blake.

14   Alfredo Sadel (1930–1989), a very popular Venezuelan singer and actor, known as 'Venezuela's favourite tenor'. He was in three films with the Mexican Miguel Aceves Mejías: *You and the Lie* (dir. René Cardona, 1958), *Good Luck* (dir. Rogelio González, 1960) and *Martín Santos, the Llanero* (dir. Mauricio de la Serna, 1962).

15   *Chucho el Roto* (1960), dir. Miguel Delgado.

sings]: 'They call me "Lightning", real name Mauricio Rosales / I raise my hand gladly to toast a gentleman / I go through life to bring justice / to villages and valleys with neither peace nor rest / I never let the powerful humiliate the poor . . .'[16] Or the 'Corrido del Águila Negra' [he sings]: 'I'm Black Eagle / at your service / friend of all men / and of course the ladies.'[17] And the one my grand-mother liked best, 'Ojitos verdes' [he sings]: 'Ay, ayayayay! Where are theeeey? / Green eyes that made me siiiigh / Ay, ayayayay! Where are theeeey? / Green eyes I can't forgeeeet . . .'

You know them all by heart.
Yes, and the songs of Jorge Negrete, Vicente Fernández, Pedro Infante. Another singer–actor was Javier Solís, with his 'Payaso' [he sings]: 'I'm a sad clown / at dead of night / with smiles and tears . . .' I got into singing and poetry through Mexican cinema. I always loved the *rancheras* and *corridos* of the Llanos.[18]

There were films about the Mexican Revolution as well, weren't there?
The films were rather naive, everything was seen in terms of good and evil, but there was a lot of social content. For instance, Mauricio 'Lightning' Rosales was on the side of the poor, he fought for the people against the powerful . . . And some of the films were remi-niscent of the struggles of the Mexican Revolution, the spirit of rebellion.

Did you like that message?
I wasn't really aware of it, in terms of political analysis. I wasn't even in my teens then. But, on a subliminal level, I liked the message.

---

16   A cuatro is a small four-stringed guitar common in Latin America.

17   The singer of the *Corrido of the Black Eagle*, composed by Cuco Sánchez, was Miguel Aceves Mejía (1915–2006). Black Eagle was a character similar to Zorro, who in 1950 gave rise to a series of films starring Fernando Casanova.

18   In October 2007, Hugo Chávez put out a CD entitled *Canciones de Siempre* (Traditional Songs), which includes some of the *rancheras* and Venezuelan folk songs he has sung on his Sunday programme *Aló Presidente*.

The Cine Bolívar was an education for me. Like my grandmother's backyard. Or the streets where I sold my 'spiders'. These three 'schools' were where I learned how to cope with life from a very young age. As I tell you about it, it makes me realize I enrolled in the school of life very young, and I'm still there, learning. I've always tried to learn. That's why I never found it hard to adapt to different environments.

What other forms of entertainment did you have?
I liked the circus. It came every October. I was really happy. My grandmother let me buy a ticket out of the sweets' sales. I loved the trapeze artists.

When was the town carnival?
At Easter. We had an old folk tradition of dancing devils, similar to the Dancing Devils of Yare.[19] We dressed as devils; I was a little devil with a mask made from a *totuma*.

What's a totuma?
It's a big fruit with a very hard skin; you take out the pulp, dry it and you get a very hard gourd. That's a *totuma*; big ones are good for storing water and little ones can be used for beakers. Anyway, I'd cut a big *totuma* in half, make two holes for eyes, paint it red with black stripes and there was my mask. It was tradition that each little devil made his own mask.

Now I understand why some of your opponents say you're a devil.
They mean something else . . . [laughter]. But yes, in my last two years of school, I was an openly declared devil, in the street, with a red mask with black stripes. I stuck bits of rag on it for pretend hair, my costume was a floppy shirt, a red-and-black

---

19   Since the eighteenth century, the town of San Francisco de Yare (state of Miranda) has celebrated Corpus Christi with a ritual called the Dancing Devils in which dancers dress up in bright costumes (usually red), with capes and masks of distinctly African influence.

cape, and striped trousers. I was barefoot or in gym shoes. I carried a whip and scared people by cracking it in the streets: a devil is a devil.

I also remember doing the sebucán, an indigenous dance from Oriente, which we danced in Sabaneta. Twenty coloured ribbons are tied to a vertical pole, each dancer takes a ribbon and spreads out in a circle of colours; half of them go one way and the other half go the other way; they weave over and under around the pole. The challenge is not get the ribbons mixed up, or else it's a disaster. The ballad says it all [he sings]: 'Weaving the sebucán / ribbon over ribbon under / but when unweaving comes / they all can fall asunder.'

Did you do theatre at school?
Yes, I loved drama. The teachers chose me to play the main role in a play called *El Chiriguare*. A *chiriguare* is a kind of tiger, and I was Zamurito, the hunter . . . I had to go very carefully so the *chiriguare* wouldn't eat me. I recited poetry too, the classic romances of the Llano.

Did you read comics?
Yes, I read a lot of comics. I collected them. Adán and I had boxes full of them, almost all from Mexico. They told tales of characters like the Avenging Llanero, a masked man on a motorbike who rode round avenging the poor or Santo, the Silver Mask, he was very famous. In the end, they were all popular heroes, seeking justice for the oppressed. They offered positive values. Good always triumphed over Evil. The one I liked most was *El Charrito de Oro*, about a little cowboy and his horse fighting for justice, overcoming wild animals and bandits. Two or three bookshops in Sabaneta sold these comics, and I didn't miss a single one. I'd buy them, read them, and swap them with friends.

Did you watch television?
No, there was no TV, but I listened to the radio a lot.

Was there a radio station in Sabaneta?

No, but there was one in Barinas. My grandmother had a small radio and we got some Caracas stations – especially Radio Continente. One evening – I was about ten or eleven – they put a radio in the middle of the street and turned the volume up full blast, so we could all hear the boxing match in which *Morocho* Hernández [Carlos Hernández], with his awesome left hook, became world champion and the hero of Venezuela. What a party there was that night [8 January 1965]!

Grandma Marta Frías, my mother's grandmother, had a bigger radio with a wider range. In the evening, we'd listen to Colombian radio stations, news reports and soap operas about love.

Do you remember your first love?

Impossible to forget. I first fell in love, platonically, with Isabel. One very rainy day, there were huge muddy puddles in the street in front of our house. People had put planks across them. Along came Isabel, all elegant, well-dressed, pretty, white skin, blue eyes. I was scared to go near her; I watched her come up, conquered my fear, went up to her, stepped in the water and offered her my hand: 'Allow me . . .' It felt like flying, taking her white porcelain hand, looking into her pretty face . . . I've never forgotten it. Then, when I was about twelve, my first 'utopian' girlfriend was called Hilda Colmenares. She was Spanish from the Canary Islands, a very pretty girl, she lived half a block from me. I thought she was a goddess, I serenaded her with *rancheras*. She was my first puppy love, my first sweetheart. She went back to Spain shortly afterwards.

Before that, when I was in year four, I'd had a great impossible love . . . Our teacher, Lucía, got pregnant and was replaced by Egilda Crespo. I immediately fell madly in love, I was bewitched. She was about eighteen. I'd watch her, enraptured, completely over-come. I never forgot her. She had – she has – beautiful green eyes. She was from Santa Rosa de Barinas, the women there have always been beautiful. I liked all the pretty girls: Ernestina was another, and Telma González, a girl I liked a lot as well.

What other aspects of your childhood do you remember?

One thing made a big impression: a lesson my father taught me. I was in year five, I was about eleven. One day, Adán was going to study at the house of his friend, Lalán Torres, about two blocks away. I went with them and as we passed a shop, I saw a coin on the ground and picked it up. I put it in my pocket and said to Adán, 'I've got a bolívar.' A bolívar was a lot of money in those days. We bought cowboy comics, a drink, some sweets . . . In short, we spent the whole bolívar.

A couple of hours later, a local character, name of Lieutenant Polo, turned up at my grandmother's house. He was drunk, and laid claim to the bolívar. Somebody had told him that Huguito Chávez found a bolívar, and he said it was his. My father was furious; he gave Polo a bolívar and gave me my first whipping. But first he put me in the dock in my grandmother's kitchen. He said, 'Where did you get the bolívar?' I confessed, timidly, 'Well, I found it on the ground and spent it.' 'And why didn't you ask who it belonged to?' That's what I should have done. That was an important lesson for me. I should have asked who the bolívar belonged to, not gone off and spent it.

Why do you think it was a good lesson?

Because I was able to use it. Six years later, I was in my fifth year of secondary school in Barinas, and my father and I were on our way to fill in forms for my place at the Military Academy. We parked the car in front of the Department of Education building. While he went in to sign a certificate of good conduct, I got out of the car, stood on the corner and saw a pretty girl waiting for a taxi. I went up and started talking to her. I was almost seventeen. I noticed the girl because she looked a bit out of place in Barinas. She told me she was a journalist: 'I've come to do some work for El Sol del Llano.' I suggested, 'We can wait for my father then take you to the newspaper, if you like.' And we did. She sat in the back, and we took her. When we got home, my dad got out of the car and as I was getting out, I saw a small wallet on the back seat. There were two or three hundred bolívars in notes inside it.

I didn't say anything to my father, of course. He never knew anything about it. I grabbed the wallet, borrowed a bike from a neighbour, and pedalled off to the newspaper. I arrived, asked for the girl, she was there feeling pretty desperate, as she had all her papers and documents in that wallet. I handed her the wallet. Everyone there said, 'How incredible!' She was very happy; she gave me her journalist's card, but I was just a little nobody and I never saw her again. Deep inside, I told myself that Lieutenant Polo's bolívar had taught me a useful lesson. If today I find a gold bar in the savannah, I'm sure as anything going to find out whose it is, before some Lieutenant Polo turns up to claim it. That lesson cost me a good hiding. I never forgot it.

Did your father often . . . ?
No, he never hit us. My mother would sometimes go too far . . . Once I rebelled. I grabbed the stick she was going to hit me with; I broke it in half and threw it on the floor. My mother never dared touch me again. That time I rebelled against my mother, I was already in the first year of secondary school in Barinas, spending weekends in Sabaneta.

Was it the first time you'd rebelled?
No, that came a few years earlier, in protest at a really stupid ban. Late one afternoon, I went for a bike ride, and riding in Sabaneta's Plaza Bolívar was forbidden. I was arrested and taken to the police station.

Why was it forbidden?
A decision by Pérez Jiménez. He'd decreed that citizens had to wear jackets and 'behave correctly' in all Venezuelan squares and avenues named after Bolívar, out of respect for the Liberator. Walking in front of Bolívar's statue without being dressed like a wealthy person was considered sacrilege. You weren't even allowed to be there in your shirt sleeves. It was a way of turning squares into places for the bourgeoisie. Barefoot Indians, or poor people, or kids not wearing shirts because of the heat, couldn't

go into the Plaza Bolívar, much less on a bicycle. Absurd, unjust. They were sanctifying Bolívar so as to depoliticize him. Pérez Jiménez's decision was actually a way of stopping poor people, workers, from gathering in the main squares of Venezuela's towns and cities, because they were all called Bolívar. In that way they could prevent demonstrations against the dictatorship.

And what did you do?
Well, one afternoon, I decided to ride my bicycle around the square in protest. The police grabbed me and took me, bicycle and all, down to the station. They sent for my 'guardian'. My mother came, then my father, who had a fierce argument with the police chief, they almost came to fisticuffs. In the end, they released me. That was my first protest. And my first spell in 'prison': two hours detained in the Sabaneta police station. It made quite an impact on me.

At that age, what work did you do around the house?
Everything. I'd fetch wood for the kitchen stove, and cut the branches of a yellow-flowered bush that was used to make brooms. You'd take a handful of twigs, put a short stick through the middle, tie them up with twine, and there you had it, a broom! I always liked making things with my hands, sowing maize, cultivating it . . .

In that yard?
Yes, there was room for everything. The yard had a great diversity of plant and animal life. It was a universe. We sowed maize when the rains started, around May. First we cleared the land, then we'd use a wooden tool for making holes to drop the seeds in.

Like indigenous people?
Yes. We'd work together placing the seeds. My grandmother would say, 'Don't put in more than five.' Five little grains of maize. 'And don't press too firmly.' You had to cover the seed gently, so the earth

held it with its own weight. If you pressed too hard, the seed didn't sprout.

It suffocated.

Yes. But when it was planted well, three days later you'd see a shoot. How beautiful it is for the spirit to see a plant being born! And then to tend it. Protect it from the winter, from worms, from birds. And later harvest the corn cobs. I'd do all this with my grandmother.

You didn't mind doing these agricultural jobs.

No, I liked all of them: husking the cobs, scraping them with a knife to get out the last drop of milk; gathering up the diced grains of maize. We had a little wooden mill, with a handle and a wide mouth. We'd put it on a table, throw in the niblets and begin grinding. The ground maize fell on one side, the milk on the other. The milk was then poured over the maize to make the corn dough, which was then thrown onto the *budare*, on the wood stove. *Budare* is an indigenous word for the griddle that the dough is cooked on, to make the *cachapa*. We'd also prepare a big cooking pot and boil ground corn balls wrapped in the maize leaves, which in Venezuelan are called *hallaquitas*. Or we'd make *mazamorra*, a fermented maize drink, like chicha.

Do you know how to make it?

Well, I helped. Not in brewing it.

Your grandmother brewed it.

But I provided the labour. From the very start, collecting the seeds and sowing the maize, right up to the preparation, the cooking . . . and the eating. And I'd take some *cachapas* to a neighbour. My grandmother took pride in sending *cachapas* to her neighbours, or a jug of *mazamorra*. As well as the pleasure of knowing it had been made in our own backyard. All natural, organic, without pesticides, with absolute ecological respect, as we'd say today. Honestly, that backyard provided everything.

Do you think your grandmother instilled the spirit of sacrifice in you?

The spirit of solidarity. And it was Bolívar's idea too, when he said, 'Glory lies in being useful.' As a child, I learned to be useful. To work and live in a 'family commune'. When we harvested the oranges, for instance, I used to put a bag of oranges in a little cart and take them round the houses to sell, and especially to the town's ice cream parlour. I sold oranges, avocados, pineapples.

All harvested in your back yard.

Everything. That yard was a global agricultural powerhouse [laughter].

When my grandmother died, I wrote a poem for the funeral. It was 1982, the year the Bolivarian Revolution was born. She died of tuberculosis at the age of seventy. The poem was a hymn to a rebel, because inside her burned a continual protest . . . against established truths. I inherited that from her. She was always telling us, 'Don't believe in priests. God is everywhere.'

In my poem, I wrote, 'Perhaps one day, my beloved grandma / my steps may lead me to your grave.' And I went on, 'And then / in your old house / your white doves / will spread their wings' (there were always lots of white doves on the roof, at certain times of the year – they came and went – and my grandmother told us to put maize out for them) 'and under the *matapalo* / Guardián will bark / and the almonds will grow / beside the orange tree / and the mandarins / beside your pineapple patch / and the *semeruco* will ripen / beside your rosebush / and the plum tree / beside the *topocho* tree.'[20]

You were self-sufficient.

Yes, we had alimentary independence. Didn't I say we sold fruit and preserves? And in the midst of all that, my grandmother did

---

20 The *semeruco* is a tree with leafy branches and fruit like small red strawberries; the *topocho* is a kind of small plantain.

something great for Adán and me – she taught us to read and write before we went to school.

Apparently your grandmother taught you to read from a magazine called Tricolor, _didn't she?_
Not long ago, I chanced upon a collection of *Tricolor* [he shows it to me]. Early one morning, I started looking through some old books in the library of La Casona [the official private residence of the Venezuelan president]. I came across a collection from 1955. And I saw myself anew in the pages of *Tricolor*, which had been kept in very good hands.

How did your grandmother come by those magazines?
My father brought them. Because he was a teacher, he used *Tricolor* in his classes. So we always saw them too. I'd wait for them eagerly. When my father arrived on his bicycle, the first thing I said was '*¡Papá, Tricolor!*' It came out monthly.

When was it first published?
In March 1955. I was eight months old when it first came out. A great magazine, with an original design, excellent colour. It called itself 'A Venezuelan magazine for children, a monthly publication from the Ministry of Education, Department of Culture and Art'. It was published in the days of Pérez Jiménez, but it came into being – I've looked into its history – when Carlos Delgado Chalbaud was president. The editorial team included people like Rafael Rivero, or draughtsmen like Desiderio Trompiz and Arturo Moreno. All of them Venezuelan. But this patrimony gradually deteriorated; the magazine was privatized. Today we are reclaiming it.

Did you really learn to read with it?
Yes, but it also taught me things; it was a fundamental influence on developing the open mind of that little boy who became a book addict. I can't be without a book. I learned to read and write in a world where television, fortunately, hadn't yet arrived. We had our

Tricolor instead. Magazines, and the wireless, were the first means of communication I came in contact with. I used to draw pictures for exhibitions at school, sometimes they'd pay me half a bolívar, and I gave it to my grandmother.

Did it have an influence on your education?

Very much so. That magazine caught my imagination. It taught me lots of things I still talk about today. It was like a complete study course, and easy to use: history, geography, natural sciences, physics, chemistry, folklore, music, journeys, adventure. It sowed a seed of values, love of our country, our history. I read it incessantly. It inspired me to draw. I was totally devoted to working, studying and playing sports; I wasn't inclined towards anything unethical. It was a very complete education. If only all children could live like that. It was utopia, Arcadia.

Producing, learning, creating . . .

I lived in a utopia. With that grandmother who taught me to read, who read with us. I loved reading the magazine from cover to cover with her. I thank the Lord there was no television in my house. I learned so much from *Tricolor*! My dad had the whole collection. I immersed myself, not only in the current magazine, but in all the back issues. That's how I got interested in history. All that knowledge, rooted deep in the Venezuelan Llanos, have to a large extent made me what I am today.

Did your grandmother go through standard schooling?

She read very well, and had nice handwriting. She'd finished Sabaneta primary school. I remember something that made her laugh a lot. One night I said, 'Grandma, bet you don't know where it says "rolo".' 'Rolo? I can't see it. Where?' 'Here, look,' I said. It was the end of *Tricolor*, read backwards. She laughed a lot, she enjoyed that kind of thing. She told my dad, 'Huguito reads backwards!' The fact is that by the time I got to school, I could read and write.

Did you learn to write with the left hand or the right?
The left.

Was it allowed? In many countries they forced left-handed people to write right-handed.
Look, my brother Adán is only a year older than me, but when he went to school and wrote left-handed, they forced him. He told me, 'They threatened to hit me on the hand.' He had to write with the right. My father, also left-handed, remembers how they made his hand swell up for writing with the left. Not surprisingly, he writes right-handed. But by the time I went to school, they'd changed the law. I was lucky.

Tell me what you remember about hawking in the streets as a child.
Yes, I was a street vendor. But I sold sweets at school to start with. I'd keep my little pot of twenty 'spiders' on the floor, beside my desk, and at break time I'd go into the schoolyard and sell.

To your schoolmates?
To schoolmates and to the teachers.

How much did you earn?
I did my sums, I knew I got twenty lochas every day, unless there were any 'spiders' left over. I could eat one myself, and even give one away. There was one little girl who was very poor, and I always gave her one.

My grandmother was very strict, I had to give her twenty lochas every day, but she'd always give me a couple back. After school, I'd go round town selling my 'spiders' at the baseball ground, the bowling area, the cockpit, the cinema. Fiestas for the town's patron saint were the best for this trade. Sabaneta turned into a street market: there were stalls of every type, the circus came – with elephants, and pretty trapezists . . . There were rides in the Plaza Bolívar: flying chairs, merry-go-rounds, bumper cars. I'd wander around selling my sweets. The fiesta lasted the whole week. There were crowds of people, with the odd drunk. And in the afternoon, the *coleo* – the national sport of bull-tail twisting.

Was there a bullring?

No, the *coleo* took place on a dirt track about one hundred metres long, with guard rails on both sides. They'd bring young bulls in a truck, get them out and line them up behind a solid gate . . .

Are these bulls fierce?

Yes, they have to be. There are ten horsemen. This national sport has very strict rules. The horsemen wait beside the gate. When it opens, the bull shoots out and the riders gallop after it, trying to grab its tail. *Coleo* horses are fast. A good horse can quickly overtake the bull, which is heavier. When the horse catches up with the bull, the rider has to be strong enough to grab the tail, but then it's the strength of the horse that counts for pulling the bull back and flipping it over. It's a technique.

Does the bull get hurt?

Sometimes, of course, some bulls do get hurt, they might break a leg. Even as a kid, in fact, I never liked this sport. Some of the horses get injured as well. I once saw a bull gore a horse, and the poor thing bled to death in seconds. Riders also get injured. Some people are diehard fans, it goes back to the days of the cattle drives.

When the main activity in the Llanos was raising huge herds of cattle?

Yes, it was a way for cowboys to control wayward steers that wanted to escape; they had to chase the fleeing steer on horseback, grab him by the tail, pull him down and tie him up.

Were the coleo shows a big part of patron saint festivals?

They still are. No festival in the Llanos is complete without three days of *coleo*; the whole town comes to watch. There are championships, a trophy for the best horseman and a beauty queen – the

Queen of the Bulls. In my day in Sabaneta, the *coleo* was held in the Calle Real, there was no special bull run. Now there is one, with iron fences and floodlights. The ground is properly prepared, and there are stands so people get a better view. Not back then. It was mayhem, crowds of people from the 1st of October to the 7th, the day of the Virgin of the Rosary, patron saint of Sabaneta, the last day of the festival. Many people came from outside too, from Barinas and Apure.

So, that's when the little street vendor worked overtime, was it?
You bet. I was a street vendor until graduating from year six. I even sold sandwiches when there were no fruit or sweets: I'd buy baguettes, fill them with mortadela and butter, and set off for the streets; I had to sell something to help my grandmother. I'd find a way to sell whatever there was: plantains, kites, sweets, etc. One time, my Uncle Ubaldino Morales – the husband of my mother's sister – came from the Andes with his family. They were very poor and had nowhere to live, so they moved in with my parents.

Ubaldino was a good worker, and soon got hold of a red pick-up truck – a Power Wagon – and went from town to town selling plantains and *topochos*. I'd help him for free, and on occasions he'd take me in his pick-up. We'd go as far as Puerto Nutrias. And I went to Barinas for the first time selling fruit with him. I loved it. Ubaldino would say, 'Sell eight for one real,' or half a bolívar, I can't remember. But I'd give ten for a real, because I could see people were really needy.

So that was a sociology lesson too, wasn't it? Seeing what life was really like?
Yes, the things I observed stayed engraved on my mind, and helped me understand the real world. I learned in the street, seeing life in the raw. I was a working child, not an exploited child, but a 'voluntarily working child'. A street kid, a little Don Quixote of the Llanos, dreaming of righting wrongs.

Do you like reminiscing about your childhood?

I sometimes go to Sabaneta incognito. I can't go during the day, because there would be a big furore and I wouldn't be able to contemplate old times in peace. But at night I can walk around the streets alone, remembering, like making a return to the womb. So many details of my past come tumbling into my mind. I enjoy those memories in silence, with emotion and nostalgia.

4

Politics, Religion and Encyclopaedia

A political child – An 'Adeco' uncle – 'Long live Rómulo!'
Punto Fijo Pact – Wolfgang Larrazábal
Guerrillas in the local bar – Father in jail
Death of Kennedy – Alliance for Progress
Boy literacy teacher – Altar boy – Grandmother's death
Father Velázquez – Church and poor – Visit of the bishop
A good student – *Quillet's Encyclopaedia*
'Getting ahead in life' – Training willpower
Forging a character – Setting a goal

What place did politics occupy in your childhood?
First I must say this: I believe I was a political child. Aristotle said
that 'man is a political animal', so I was a 'little political animal'. Of
course, when Pérez Jiménez was overthrown by the Venezuelan
revolutionary forces [23 January 1958], led by Fabricio Ojeda of
the Junta Patriótica, I was only three and a half, so I had no notion
of its impact on life in Sabaneta. But then came the governing Junta
[23 January 1958–13 February 1959], the elections [7 December
1958], the victory of Rómulo Betancourt, the years from 1960 to
1963 . . . and by then I was eight or nine, so I began to understand
things, and saw how those events affected our home.

And how did they affect it?

Through my father; he was always keen on politics. Even today [2009], he has that same quiet unruliness of my grandmother, his mum. When he was young, he was very energetic and always involved in lots of activities. And when his brother, my Uncle Marcos, came to visit, they'd discuss politics. And I'd listen. It became clear to me that there were two positions: my uncle and his friends, and my father and his friends. I always respected Uncle Marcos, and I still do. For me he represented an authority figure, he was serious yet affectionate. He was an inspector of public works and pro-government, of course. He was an 'Adeco' – supporter of the Acción Democrática party (AD) – and the first person I ever heard talk about the then president, Rómulo Betancourt [1959–1964].[1] He defined himself as a *Romulero*; he admired Betancourt.

Were there a lot of Adecos in Sabaneta?

There were some. I remember that, in 1962, they bussed our school group to attend the inauguration of the new Puente Páez–Cejita–Mijagual–Santa Rosa main road, and someone shouted, 'There goes Rómulo!'[2] That's what the people called him, just Rómulo. I saw him, he had a pipe, and was wearing a traditional *liqui-liqui* suit, white, his party's colour. Some sectors of the public were thrilled to see him.

Your uncle moved in those circles?

Well, he lived in Barinas, but yes, most of the people he saw when he came to Sabaneta were Adecos. People of a certain economic

---

1 Founded in 1941 by Rómulo Gallegos and Rómulo Betancourt, Acción Democrática (Democratic Action) was originally a left-wing socialist party which, alternating with Copei, controlled Venezuelan political life from 1958 to 1998. It also controlled the country's main trade union, the Venezuelan Workers' Confederation (CTV). From 1999, while it continued to be affiliated to the Socialist International, AD was ideologically centrist and maintained a very critical position with regard to the Bolivarian Revolution.

2 On a tour round the state of Barinas, President Rómulo Betancourt inaugurated that main road on 13 May 1962, nine days after the *Carupanazo*.

status: landowners, shopkeepers, Italians who were generally conservative businessmen. Don Timoleón Escalona, who owned the town's biggest hardware store, and sold everything from cement to a little tube for your key. In short, all people who supported that government's policies.

But Acción Democrática wasn't a conservative party; it was social democrat, a member of the Socialist International.

Yes, in theory that's right. And in a region full of Washington-supported dictators like Somoza, Batista, Trujillo or Duvalier, Rómulo Betancourt was even called the leader of the Left. But, international opprobrium against those tyrants was so great that the Empire also used to cosy up to leaders who opposed dictatorships. Among them was Betancourt, who made a pact with the gringos while he was in exile in the US. His mask dropped. He signed the New York Pact in 1957 with Rafael Caldera's Copei.[3] And when Betancourt returned to Caracas after the dictator Pérez Jiménez was ousted [23 January 1958], he won the elections [13 February 1959] and took political power with the approval of the Venezuelan oligarchy. There had been a glimmer of hope for change when the dictatorship fell; especially since a month earlier, on 1 January 1959, not far from Venezuela on the Caribbean island of Cuba, Fidel Castro had toppled the Batista dictatorship despite its US support, and showed that an anti-imperialist victory was possible in Latin America. But Betancourt betrayed that hope, and showed he was in no shape or form left-wing. The oligarchy and the criollo bourgeoisie engulfed him, and the Empire penetrated his government.

And what did the Left do?

The real Left took up arms; many took to the hills; the guerrilla movement emerged; some patriotic soldiers joined them – Colonel Juan de Dios Moncada Vidal, for example, or Lieutenant Nicolás

---

3   The Comité de Organización Política Electoral Independiente (Copei), a Christian Democratic party, was founded in 1946 by Rafael Caldera. It alternated in power in Venezuela with Acción Democrática from 1958 to 1998.

Hurtado Barrios, and other officers and NCOs.[4] Moncada Vidal became a commander in the Armed Forces of National Liberation (FALN). There were also two left-wing military uprisings in 1962: the *Carupanazo*[5] and the *Porteñazo*.[6]

Betancourt retaliated with a heavy hand. His terrible words in a speech to the army and police – 'Shoot first and ask questions later' – showed what a conservative, repressive mentality he had. He unleashed a terrible wave of repression against the country's progressive forces, the political movements of the opposition and even the Armed Forces. Che Guevara had seen it clearly, because it seems he met Betancourt in Costa Rica in 1953 or 1954, and in a letter wrote something like, 'I've met a Venezuelan who says he's a revolutionary but I'm certain he's no revolutionary.'

Was your father active in any party?

My father was active for many years in the Christian Democratic party, Copei. He was a 'Copeyano' because he liked Rafael Caldera and Caldera's ethics . . . But at the same time, a local branch of a left-leaning party – the Unión Democrática Republicana (URD) – was founded in Sabaneta. Luis Miquilena, Fabricio Ojeda and José Vicente Rangel were among the founders at national level. It was the party of Jóvito Villalba [1908–1989], a prominent leader of Venezuelan politics from the 1930s to the 1960s. He had formerly

---

4   See Régis Debray, 'Quinze jours dans les maquis vénézuéliens', in *Essais sur l'Amérique Latine*, François Maspero, Paris, 1967.

5   On 4 May 1962, the city of Carúpano was occupied by a Marine Infantry battalion and a National Guard and put out a manifesto in the name of the Movimiento de Recuperación Democrática (Democratic Recuperation Movement). The following day, forces loyal to the government retook control and detained hundreds of people, among them members of the Venezuelan Communist Party and the Movimiento de Izquierda Revolucionaria (MIR) (Movement of the Revolutionary Left). President Betancourt decided to proscribe these latter two organizations.

6   2 June 1962, in Puerto Cabello, a group of officers and sailors from the naval base supported by armed civilian groups took up arms against the government. The following day loyalist forces quashed the insurrection, with a toll of four hundred dead and seven hundred injured. President Betancourt initiated a purge of the Armed Forces against any officer suspected of sympathy with the extreme Left.

belonged to the Partido Revolucionario Venezolano (PRV), founded [in 1928] by Professor Salvador de la Plaza [1896–1970] and the communist brothers Eduardo and Gustavo Machado. Along with Rómulo Betancourt and Rafael Caldera, Jóvito Villalba formed the 'trio of stars' in political life during that particular quarter-century. Of all of them, Jóvito, like his URD party, was the most left-wing. He had actually won the November 1952 general election, but Marcos Pérez Jiménez proclaimed himself president after a coup.[7] A tireless fighter against dictatorships, from Juan Vicente Gómez to Pérez Jiménez, Jóvito spent countless years in exile or in prison. When Pérez Jiménez fell, he signed the Punto Fijo Pact with Caldera and Betancourt.[8]

What did the Pact consist of?

It was signed in October 1958. Pérez Jiménez had been removed on 23 January of that same year. Democracy had returned, and the elections were approaching. But then what happened? Wolfgang Larrazábal was put up as a candidate by the Communist Party and the Left in general. Larrazábal [1911–2003] was a naval officer, an admiral, who joined the revolutionary movement and took part in the uprising that toppled Pérez Jiménez. At that moment of transition, he held the reins of power as the head of a Military Junta, part of a generation of army officers who belonged to a movement called Trejismo, after its leader Hugo Trejo [1922–1998]. I got to know Colonel Trejo quite well, much later on, and through our many conversations I learned a great deal from him. He called me 'the other Hugo'.

---

7   Acción Democrática and the Venezuelan Communist Party were proscribed and could not take part in the elections.

8   On 31 October 1958, some months after the toppling of Marcos Pérez Jiménez, in a house called Punto Fijo in the Sabana Grande suburb of Caracas, owned by Rafael Caldera, three parties signed a pact 'to assure the stability of the nascent regime'. The parties were Acción Democrática (AD), Copei and the Unión Democratica Républicana (URD). In practice, the Punto Fijo Pact would mean exclusive power-sharing, for forty years, between AD and Copei. The Pact would also include other actors that wielded considerable influence, such as the business sector (Fedecámaras), the trade union sector (CTV), the Armed Forces and the Church.

Those young officers included General Jacinto Pérez Arcay (just a second lieutenant then), who taught me at the Military Academy and was very influential in my political education. But the other leaders began to sideline Trejo for being a 'leftie', eventually neutralizing him by getting him out of the country as ambassador to Costa Rica.

Larrazábal assumed the provisional mandate. He was a young man, well respected, charismatic, a good speaker, in touch with the progressive movements of the day. He sent Fidel Castro's guerrillas, still in the Sierra Maestra but within sight of victory, some 150 American semi-automatic M1 Garand rifles. And to Fidel himself, who has not forgotten, he sent an excellent Belgian FAL automatic rifle.[9]

So, before the elections of December 1958, Larrazábal emerged as the man of the moment.

Yes, he was an educated man with a considerable knowledge of politics, and he was backed by almost all the left-wing parties. But then, AD, Copei and the URD entered into that historic alliance – the Pact of Punto Fijo – in which Betancourt, Caldera and Jóvito Villalba, all bourgeois leaders, decided to share power between them and cut the Left out of any possibility of taking power at the ballot box. In the end, Betancourt won the elections of 7 December 1958 by a handful of votes. But Larrazábal won in Caracas.

That's when your father was active in the Unión Republicana Democrática.

Well, my father founded the local branch of the URD in Sabaneta, but that was before the Pact of Punto Fijo. They were certainly to the left of AD, because, for instance, he founded it with a friend of his, Eduardo Zamudia, who ended up being persecuted by government forces. Another founder was Dr Escobar, who lived next door

---

9 'The provisional government of Admiral Larrazábal gave me a FAL automatic rifle in November 1958, the last month of the war,' confirmed Fidel Castro on 29 November 2009, in a 'reflection' entitled 'Is There No Limit to Hypocrisy and Lying?'

to us, and one night the army raided his house, looking for him. But he'd already left. We found out later that he'd joined the guerrillas.

That was the early 1960s?

Yes, very early. By 1962, the URD had withdrawn from Betancourt's government and left the Punto Fijo Pact. Many of its activists joined Venezuela's nascent guerrilla movement, including Fabricio Ojeda, who had been president of the Junta Patriótica that toppled Pérez Jiménez in 1958. By then the Cuban Revolution had triumphed, and McCarthyism had infected Venezuela. Anything that smacked of protest or social justice was condemned as 'subversive'.

It was the time of the Eisenhower–Nixon duo in the US.

Richard Nixon came to Venezuela in 1958, when he was Eisenhower's vice president, and was greeted by huge anti-imperialist demonstrations.[10] As Republican president after two decades of Democratic domination, staunchly anti-Communist and an advocate of strong military governments in Latin America, Eisenhower had been the ally and protector of Pérez Jiménez, whom he had decorated with the Legion of Merit [25 October 1954]. All this was the talk of the town.

Did you hear what people were saying?

Don't forget I was a street vendor, going up and down the main streets between the Plaza Bolívar, the cinema, the cockpit and the baseball ground. I heard a lot of political discussions, because Sabaneta was a small but politicized town, very politicized. And above all, in my own house, this little political animal began to hear, on the one side, 'Long live Rómulo!' and the one the other, my father replying, 'Down with Rómulo!'

---

10   US Vice President Nixon arrived in Caracas on 13 May 1958. On his way back from seeing Wolfgang Larrazábal, president of the governing junta, his car was besieged during one of the most violent popular protests ever seen in Caracas.

My father abandoned the URD and joined a new party, which was socialist or preached socialism: the Movimiento Electoral del Pueblo (People's Electoral Movement, MEP). It was founded by a teacher, Luis Beltrán Prieto Figueroa [1902–1992], a great educator, socialist, for many years a comrade of Betancourt's, but when Betancourt moved to the right, Prieto assembled the left wing of the AD and founded the MEP. So my father started bringing home books and speeches by Prieto. His symbol was the ear, he had very big ears. He was called '*El Orejón*', Big Ears.

I listened to my father commenting on all these events. And I understood there were opposing forces, and also guerrillas.

Were there guerrillas near Sabaneta?

Yes, and between Sabaneta and Apure, Comandante Arauca's men, rural guerrillas on horseback in the mountains.[11] There was a Llanos guerrilla movement throughout Portuguesa, Barinas, Puerto Nutrias and Apure: and there was a sort of 'guerrilla triangle' between the foothills of the Andes, Portuguesa and the Boconó mountains. The army chief of staff put a centre of military operations at La Marqueseña, from where it controlled all movement towards the mountains or towards the plains. Sabaneta was practically an occupied town in the 60s; it was a red line for Betancourt's anti-subversive campaign. It was a hard campaign. The guerrilla fronts weren't the most powerful, but there were several hubs throughout the savannah.

---

11   Francisco Prada Barazarte, better known as Comandante Arauca or '*El Flaco*' (Skinny) Prada. An anthropologist, he was, together with Douglas Bravo, Alí Rodríguez, José Vicente Scorza and Fabricio Ojeda, a founder member in the 1960s of the Venezuelan Revolutionary Party–Armed Forces of National Liberation (PRV–FALN), an organization which favoured armed struggle. The FALN was formally created on 1 January 1963. It consisted of the José Leonardo Chirino Front (Douglas Bravo, Elías Manuitt Camero), the 2 June Movement (Comandante Manuel Ponte Rodríguez, Captain Pedro Medina Silva), the Civilian–Military Union (Lieutenant Colonel Juan de Dios Moncada Vidal, Comandante Manuel Azuaje), the 4 May Movement (Captain Jesús Teodoro Molina, Comandante Pedro Vargas Castellón), and the National Guerrilla Comando.

The Cuban comandante Arnaldo Ochoa was supporting the Venezuelan guerrillas.

Yes, Ochoa[12] came, but the Cubans landed at Barlovento, in Machurucuto,[13] and then went on to Falcón state, where one of the strongest guerrilla fronts was forming: the José Leonardo Chirino[14] Front led by Douglas Bravo.[15] The MIR organized guerrilla concentrations in Oriente.[16] Sucre and Monagas were also strong. In contrast, it was hard for the guerrillas to get support here, because there was no social base to draw on, the countryside was thinly populated. There were a few attempts but they never flourished.

---

12   Following a request from the Venezuelan Communist Party and the MIR, Cuba organized the *Operación Simón Bolívar* and, in July 1966, sent fourteen guerrilla tactics instructors (including the then Captain Leopoldo Cintra Frías) under Arnaldo Ochoa (1930–1989), who would later become one of the leaders of the Cuban expeditionary forces in Ethiopia and Angola. He was awarded the title of Hero of the Revolution. When he returned to Cuba from Angola, Ochoa was detained in June 1989, accused of corruption and implication in drug trafficking. He was tried, condemned to death and shot in Havana on 13 July 1989.

13   In July 1966, the first group of Cuban soldiers landed, under the command of Arnaldo Ochoa. There was one Venezuelan, Luben Petkoff, among them. In May 1967, the Machurucuto Landing saw another group arrive from Cuba. It was made up of MIR guerrillas and Cuban veterans, one of which was Ulises Rosales del Toro. A few months later, in October, in Bolivia, Ernesto Che Guevara was captured and killed, and his guerrilla group dispersed.

14   José Leonardo Chirino (1754–1796) was a *zambo* Venezuelan revolutionary (son of an indigenous woman and black slave) who led a failed slave uprising in 1795.

15   Douglas Bravo (1932–) is the most famous of Venezuelan guerrillas. In 1962, he founded and led the José Leonardo Chirino Front in the mountains of Falcón, together with Teodoro Petkoff and Alí Rodríguez. From March 1966 he was leader of the Venezuelan Revolutionary Party (PRV), whose armed wing, the Armed Forces of National Liberation (FALN), continued the armed struggle by merging with the MIR and forming the National Liberation Front, abbreviated as FALN–FLN. Nowadays, Douglas Bravo is leader of the 'Third Way Movement'.

16   Founded in 1960, the Movimiento de Izquierda Revolucionaria (MIR) (Movement of the Revolutionary Left), was the result of the first split in AD, when it lost most of its youth sections. The MIR was one of the first groups in Venezuela to opt for the armed struggle. It carried out urban attacks in 1961 and 1962, and set up a guerrilla hub in the east of Venezuela called the Manuel Ponte Rodríguez Front, which was dismantled in 1964 by the army and reformed in 1965 as the Antonio José de Sucre Guerrilla Front.

Did you sense the presence of guerrillas?

Well, I remember once . . . My father was working in Los Rastrojos, several kilometres from town, and on the way out of Sabaneta you were obliged to pass the bar of Francisco Orta. While my father chatted to friends inside, I'd stay outside in the patio, or go in and out, because it was a family-friendly place, not out of bounds to children. Families would sit around in the patio, making chicken stew . . .

So what happened?

One day when we were there playing outside, some armed men appeared, who had come down from the mountains to get food: they were guerrillas.

Did your father have any contact with the guerrillas?

Not directly. But several of his friends who were on the Left, or the extreme Left, like Dr Escobar or Zamudia who I already mentioned, eventually had to join the guerrillas because the government was after them, and not with good intentions. Or like Rodríguez who was 'disappeared'.

Were there any communists in Sabaneta?

Yes, Francisco and Juan Orta from the bar were communists and they joined the guerrillas too. In those days, rumour had it that communists were 'bad' . . . It was psychological warfare. Oddly enough, years later, that same Francisco Orta joined our Bolivarian Movement; and I went back twenty-five years later to Francisco's bar, to that same house, to conspire with those same old guys and their sons. Because, from as early as 1957, the Venezuelan Communist Party they belonged to had decided to foment a civilian–military conspiracy, building bridges with patriotic elements in the Armed Forces.[17]

---

17 'In 1957, the armed wing of the PCV, with Douglas Bravo, Teodoro Petkoff and Eloy Torres as its representatives, met in the house of the then Colonel Rafael Arráez Morales in El Paraíso. They created the Military Front of the Communist Party within the Venezuelan Armed Forces. The aim was to recruit career soldiers to join their

Did they ever come after your father?

My father was never part of a movement that, let's say, 'openly challenged the established order'. And his friends were above all bohemian, anti-conformist, argumentative. My father was like Juan Charrasqueado, he loved a party.[18] Though he was once detained in La Marqueseña, an anti-guerrilla command post. A whole bunch of them were arrested and kept overnight. I went with my mother to take him food and get him out. I remember we were very scared going into that post . . . to which ten years later I returned as commanding officer.

Were there still guerrillas by then?

No. When I went back in 1975 as a graduate of the Military Academy to that army post at La Marqueseña, the guerrilla war was over. The most important job I was given then was protecting some gigantic radio transmitters belonging to the US Embassy. This telecommunications and decoding centre was part of the gringos' Southern Command operational system.

Were US personnel there?

I didn't see any, but obviously if this equipment had been installed, they must have had US technicians on site, they weren't going to hand it over to Venezuelans, were they? At least they installed the equipment and operated it together with Venezuelan technicians.

---

revolutionary project . . . and it was successful inasmuch as as many as 170 officers reported back to the PCV. However, these officers went on to join the Guevarist MIR and were eventually responsible for the 1962 uprising in Carúpano and Puerto Cabello, where these civil–military insurrection forces were defeated. Jesús Teodoro Milina Villegas, Juan de Dios Moncada Vidal, Pedro Medina Silva, Manuel Ponte Rodríguez, Víctor Hugo Morales, were some of the fifty officers who subsequently created the Armed Forces of National Liberation (FALN), and some even commanded guerrilla fronts.' Alberto Garrido, 'Venezuela: De la revolución al gobierno de Hugo Chávez', available online at vcrisis.com.

18 'Juan Charrasqueado' is the title of a famous Mexican *corrido*, composed in 1942 by Víctor Cordero (1914–1983), which tells 'the sad story of a rancher in love, who was a drunk, a party-goer, and liked a bet'. *Charrasqueado* means someone with a knife-scar on his face.

There was a big North American presence in Venezuela until recently: when I was elected president, I got rid of the gringos from the Venezuelan military bases where they had offices.

I imagine they had agreements . . .?

Yes, draconian, abusive agreements, signed with supine, submissive governments who gave the gringos rights to everything, offices, administrative centres and even sites with no access for Venezuelans. There was a massive Green Beret presence.[19]

Those early years of the 1960s were characterized by heavy persecution in Sabaneta and the string of towns down to Apure. And as a child you heard all sorts of things; over there, far away, a certain Che Guevara and a certain Fidel Castro with a beard . . .

You heard about them?

Yes, I heard talk of Cuba, of the revolution there, of Che and Fidel . . . They discussed it in hushed voices, though, in whispers; photos of Fidel circulated secretly. I did glimpse a photo of Fidel and Che somewhere. Sometimes I got hold of a newspaper; *Últimas Noticias* was the most widely read paper. My uncle bought it, and ever so sporadically he'd bring it home, so then I'd see it. For me these were distant, vague, hazy things. I didn't understand. But, yes, I heard those names.

Did you tell Fidel about that?

Of course. And I invited him to Sabaneta. It was a magic moment, when Fidel came to town.

When was that?

In 2001.

---

19   Green Berets are elite troops of the US Army set up at the beginning of the 1950s to carry out clandestine and counter-insurgency operations. From 1987 the Green Berets reported to US Special Operations Command (USSOCOM), based in Fort Bragg, North Carolina. They were split into different groups for special training according to their theatre of operations: the 7th Special Forces Group, with 1,400 men based in Florida, was trained to fight in Latin America.

It was the only time he came, wasn't it?

To the Llanos, yes, but he came to Venezuela seven times in all. The first was in 1948, when Rómulo Gallegos was president. He still remembers the journey from Maiquetía Airport to Caracas along the old highway, there was no motorway then. He says he thought the taxi driver would go over the cliff because he was driving so fast, and at one stage he had to tell him, 'Listen, slow down or I'm getting out.' He was a student leader then, on his way to Bogotá to a university congress, which is when Gaitán was killed.

He came back, on his first foreign visit after the triumph of the revolution, to celebrate the first anniversary of January 23, 1958 [the ousting of Pérez Jiménez]. I was still a small boy at the time. Fidel told me how embarrassed he'd felt when he mentioned President Betancourt in El Silencio [a large square in central Caracas], because people started whistling and catcalling, they were quite incensed . . . Betancourt hadn't dared show up at the square but Fidel referred to him several times, and had to gesture to stop the whistling.[20] The people had already sensed Betancourt's betrayal, which became entrenched over the next forty years.

Apart from the Cuban Revolution, do you remember hearing about any other international political event?

The death of Kennedy.[21]

---

20   Fidel Castro confirmed, 'When, at the end of January 1959, I spoke in the Plaza del Silencio, where hundreds of thousands of people had gathered, and I mentioned Betancourt just out of courtesy, I heard the longest, loudest and most embarrassing whistling I'd ever heard in my life. The radicalized masses of heroic and combative Caracas had voted overwhelmingly against him. For me, it was a good lesson in political realism. I had to visit him because he was the president of a friendly neighbouring country. I found a bitter and resentful man. His was by then the very model of a "democratic and representative" government that the Empire needed. He did all he could to collaborate with the Yankees before the mercenary invasion of the Bay of Pigs. 'Reflections of *Compañero* Fidel', 29 November 2009.

21   John Fitzgerald Kennedy (1917–1963), thirty-fifth president of the United States, a Democrat. He began his term on 30 January 1961 and was assassinated in Dallas, Texas, on 22 November 1963.

The echo of that assassination in Dallas even reached Sabaneta, then.

In 1963, I was starting my fourth year, and they killed President Kennedy on 22 November. Early the following morning, our teacher Lucía Venero came in and told us, 'Boys, I'm afraid there'll be a world war, they've killed President Kennedy!' I went home, very worried, to tell my grandmother there was going to be a world war, and to listen to the news.

Had you heard of Kennedy?

Well, I'd seen Kennedy's photo. Pro-US propaganda presented him as 'the good father'. So I knew he was the president of the United States, and being a little peasant boy, I didn't yet regard the US as a threat, not at all.

Was there any US presence in Sabaneta?

I remember at the beginning of the 1960s, two young Americans, John and David, arriving in Sabaneta. I imagine they were Peace Corps; they distributed bags of provisions, food, oats – especially Quaker oats.[22] I'd be about six or seven. They gave us English lessons on the blackboard in the school hall, they taught me my first words in English: 'How are you?' which I pronounced just like they did. They brought baseball mitts to school, I played with them. They also played basketball. John played the guitar. We planted trees. They stayed in Sabaneta for one or two years. The school was the centre of activity for those North Americans. Then they disappeared.

They must have been part of the Alliance for Progress, the policy of penetration launched by Kennedy to try and counter the influence of the Cuban Revolution and Fidel Castro throughout Latin America.[23]

---

22 Created by President Kennedy in 1961, the Peace Corps was a US government agency whose official mission was to 'defend peace and world friendship'. Some of its members were accused, in some countries, of being CIA agents.

23 The Alliance for Progress was a US economic and social aid programme for Latin America which lasted from 1961 to 1970. Created by President Kennedy in March 1961, it became official the following August with the adoption of the Charter of Punta del Este

John F. Kennedy came to Venezuela in December 1961, and there are still people who remember Kennedy and his wife Jacqueline in La Morita, on the outskirts of Maracay, handing out land titles to peasant farmers, because Rómulo Betancourt had recently signed a decree that was called 'agrarian reform'. US strategy in those days was to drive agrarian reform in Latin America as a whole.

So that peasants would not join the revolution.
Correct. So Rómulo Betancourt embraced agrarian reform and distributed land. Of course, it was a farce because there was no follow-up. Rich landowners ended up buying back for peanuts the land given to poor campesinos who had received no machinery, no credit, no services or anything. Oil-producing Venezuela had no interest in food production.

Did the Alliance for Progress have any other effect in Sabaneta?
Yes, I remember something else. There was this book called *Off with Our Chains!*[24] which was used for the literacy campaign in the countryside. I took part in the campaign. I was in year six, and received a literacy teacher diploma – my grandmother kept it for many years – for having taught two peasant farmers to read and write.

The manual was called Off with Our Chains?
Yes, it's a line from our national anthem, that's what it was called. The basic idea was obviously good, because illiteracy was rife in the countryside, the result of so much neglect by so many governments, and we needed to break the chains of ignorance.[25] But the way that

---

in a meeting of the Inter-American Economic and Social Affairs Council of the Organization of American States (OAS) in Punta del Este, Uruguay. The Alliance for Progress was created to stem the influence of the Cuban Revolution and support more reformist policies.

24   The first verse of the Venezuelan national anthem: 'Off with our chains! / the gentleman cried / and in his hovel the poor man / demanded freedom.'

25   In 1958, the year the Marcos Pérez Jiménez military dictatorship fell, there was over 60 per cent illiteracy in Venezuela. Rómulo Betancourt's AD government created primary schools country-wide and aimed to eradicate illiteracy through a 'method unique to Venezuela, adapted to our circumstances and comprehensible to the popular mind'.

programme was applied was also a farce. Even I could see that, and I was only a boy. Because the criterion used to evaluate the programme was writing your name. If after a few classes you could write your first name and surname, you had learned to write. You were literate.

You didn't think that was enough.

Certainly not. And I began to speak up; I told my father, my mother, my teachers, 'All Señor Juan knows is how to write "Juan", that's not reading and writing.' For that manual, being able to read meant knowing what words with their pictures came next in the book. Without the pictures, the students were lost. It was a farce, a fraud.

Changing the subject, what place did religion occupy in your childhood? For instance, did your grandmother go to mass?

No, I never remember my grandmother going to church, not once in all those years.

But did she talk to you about religion? Did she teach you the Gospels?

It's not that she was an atheist, or a *santera*, or a faith healer, but she wasn't someone who went to mass or talked about religion.[26] She didn't go to church but she certainly had faith, and she prayed a lot.

Were you christened?

Yes, of course I was. I told you about Eligio, my godfather. We were all christened. My grandmother was, I repeat, a believer, but she didn't talk about religion, or about the Bible, or anything like that.

The method had first been mooted during the Rómulo Gallegos presidency (1945–1948), under the influence of education minister Luis Beltrán Prieto Figueroa, and its manual was 'Off with Our Chains!'

26   Santería is the belief in African deities common in the Caribbean.

Were there religious images in the house?
Yes, but only modest ones. What she liked the best was the nativity scene at Christmas, and better still when we sang to the Baby Jesus . . .

Christmas carols and the nativity.
Ah! She loved it, and I helped with the nativity scene each December. Even when I went off to the Military Academy, she wouldn't start making the nativity scene until I'd arrived home for the holidays. She waited for me to arrive and tell her where to put it and help her make it. I'd make the stable and the animals out of cardboard, and paint stars in the sky and the Star of Bethlehem.

Did you pray at night before going to bed?
Yes, I prayed, and I also did something that I kept up into my teenage years: I'd invent a prayer. I'd ask God for the things everyone asks for, but I'd add other more personal things, as if we were making a deal. But I said the Lord's Prayer as well.

Did you go to mass?
Yes, because my mother always went to church, and she was close to the priest. Also because I'd decided to be an altar boy; that was her idea, she wanted me to be a priest. But my grandmother wasn't keen.

Why not?
When she saw me dressed as an altar boy, she didn't like it. 'Ay, child. What's all this about being an altar boy? D'you think just because you wear that get-up and go to church, that you're with God? Careful with those priests,' she warned. 'Don't believe everything a priest says!' She'd laugh when she heard me reciting in Latin in my room, '*Per saecula saeculorum* . . .' 'So now I've got a little priest at home. Amen,' she teased. She lit candles to the saints so I wouldn't follow that career . . . And when I stopped being an altar boy, she was delighted. She was always joking with me; we were best friends all our lives.

Like accomplices.

Yes, co-conspirators to the last. The day we said goodbye was terrible. I was a captain, it was December 1981, and I came to spend a few days in Barinas, but she was already very ill, very thin, in a bad way. Adán, who lived there – he was a university professor – showed me some X-rays and explained she didn't have long to live. The doctor confirmed it: 'She hasn't got long, her lungs are very damaged, and she's in a lot of pain . . .' She lived in a little room, in my parents' house, I put a mattress on the floor beside her bed and massaged her back. I remember it well. I made her a little nativity scene and spent that Christmas with her. When I left on 26 December I hugged her and she was just a bag of bones, a skeleton, she hardly ate. Then I started crying, and I remember her saying, 'Don't cry, I'm taking so many pills I'm bound to get better.' She knew things were very bad; the pills were only painkillers. But she herself didn't cry, she didn't want to make me sad, she wanted to comfort me . . .

That was my grandmother, like a silent rebel in the world she lived in. And she was wise, with that infinite popular wisdom, because the people are wise. A serene woman. I don't remember ever having seen her angry or wrathful, not once.

Is she buried in Barinas?

Yes, in Barinas.

Was it lung cancer?

No, tuberculosis.

The disease of the poor.

Yes, caused by poverty and hard work; from inhaling a lot of smoke as a child in badly ventilated houses, and exhaustion from working in the fields.

Your mother made you be an altar boy, despite the wishes of your grandmother?

Yes, my mother made me. I began to go to church, I did all the First Communion classes, and then, perhaps for certain verbal skills I had, I was chosen to be an altar boy. Apparently I had the right attitude. I did it for a year, I think. I must have led the 'monastic life' between eight and ten years old.

Did you go to confession and take communion every week?
Altar boys have to go to confession and communion, sweep the church, ring the bells and take the plate round.

Do you remember the priest?
Yes, I think he was South American . . . he might have been from Ecuador. His name was Velázquez. He came to town and installed himself in that large, airy, beautiful church with a thatched roof, on the corner of the Plaza Bolívar. It was where the church is today, but now there's a new one.

Do you remember any conversations with that priest?
Yes, because he initiated me. Don't forget we're in 1964 or '65, I'd just turned ten. I remember the priest talking to me, I haven't forgotten certain things that stuck in my mind because they caught my imagination. I was poor, and all my friends were poor. A few belonged to the rural middle class, perhaps, their fathers owned shops or farms, that kind of thing. But my closest friends were all poor: Laurencio Pérez, for instance, sold *mondongo*, a meat stew, from a delivery bike. We were all penniless country boys. So when the priest talked about the Church's 'preferential option for the poor', I identified with that. And I began to identify with 'Jesus the revolutionary'.

Did the priest talk to you about such things?
Yes, he read to us, he told us Jesus said, 'Come unto me all ye that are heavy laden, and I will give you rest.' I have fond memories of the Church. I took my role of altar boy very seriously. I even remember studying Latin, Father Velázquez taught us a few phrases. What's more, I even remember visiting him after I'd left for secondary school in Barinas. He'd invite all the youngsters studying away from Sabaneta to meetings where he'd get us all talking.

Many years later, I connected the conversations I'd had with Father Velázquez with the theses of Pope John XXIII,[27] that progressive pope, during the Second Vatican Council [1962–1965]; also with those of the Extraordinary Assembly of CELAM [Latin American Episcopal Conference] in Mar del Plata, [Argentina, 1966], and with the conferences of Medellín [Colombia, 1968] and Puebla [Mexico, 1979],[28] and with the Social Doctrine of the Church, a progressive Church that was to spread like wildfire. Presumably our priest, especially if he was Latin American, would have been highly influenced by the ideas of the Episcopal Conference in Mar del Plata, that meeting of Latin American bishops which produced such a progressive document. Those years saw the birth of what came to be known as Liberation Theology.[29] I believe I came under the sway of a progressive priest, a young, good priest, deeply humane and very articulate, who encouraged us to read, and explained the Church's 'preferential option for the poor'. I wonder what happened to him.

It was the era of Camilo Torres, too.

That's right, the Colombian revolutionary priest Camilo Torres [1929–1966] was fighting with the guerrillas of the National Liberation Army (ELN). He had no qualms about taking up arms, because he thought that the Church's commitment, and his as a

---

27   Angelo Giuseppe Roncalli (1881–1963) was elected Pope John XXIII in 1958. He summoned the Second Vatican Council (1962–1965) which transformed the Catholic Church. He was very popular and became known as the 'Good Pope'. He was made a saint by John Paul II in 2000.

28   The 2nd General Conference of Latin American Bishops was held in Medellín, Colombia, in August and September 1968. Its final document called on the Church to transform Latin America according to the Second Vatican Council. The Puebla Conference, in 1979, insisted on the need for a clear preferential option in favour of the poor.

29   Liberation Theology is a theological current that began in Latin America after the Second Vatican Council and the Conferences of Mar del Plata, 1966, and Medellín, 1968. Its best-known representatives were Gustavo Gutiérrez and Leonardo Boff, priests from Peru and Brazil respectively. Liberation Theology tried to answer the question, how to be a Christian in an oppressed continent? One of its foremost exponents, the Spanish Jesuit Ignacio Ellacuría, was murdered by a death squad in San Salvador.

priest, had to be like Christ's: a commitment to the poor, those in greatest need. He started from the Christian premise that poor people deserved preferential care, since Jesus had come to defend the needy.

What else did you learn as an altar boy?
Human values, the human condition. For instance, as an altar boy I had to attend mass with the corpse present; so I was familiar with death, saying a rosary or the Lord's Prayer over a dead body to console widows and sobbing orphans. I also helped the priest baptise babies. So I was in close touch with new life and with death.

Did you attend funerals in the cemetery as well?
Yes, every now and again some service or other was held in the cemetery. So I got used to witnessing the decisive moments of our existence, seeing death close up and the joy of christening a new-born babe. And the thrill of ringing the bells for mass or to launch the feast of our patron saint. What amazing festivals we had! I loved setting off rockets.

Do you remember the religious images in that church?
Of course. A sculpture of Christ, and a cross made of very old wood, brought from Spain many, many years ago. And statues of Our Lady of Perpetual Succour, Our Lady of Mount Carmel, Our Lady of the Rosary, who was the patron saint of Sabaneta, and other figures. Yes, the church had – still has – holy images but it wasn't one of those churches overloaded with saints. It was a humble church, like our town.

Did you talk about religion at school as well?
Well, I must have been really involved in church stuff, because I remember the first visit to Sabaneta of the new bishop of Barinas, Monsignor Rafael González Ramírez. Barinas had been made a bishopric, so that first bishop toured all the parishes in his diocese.[30]

---

30   The diocese of Barinas, part of the Archbishopric of Mérida, was created on 23 July 1965. The first bishop, Rafael Ángel González Ramírez, took over on 29 January 1966.

My school – the Julián Pino – organized an event. I was asked to read a greeting to the new bishop on behalf of the pupils. I did it with a microphone, and the bishop came up to me, put his hand on my head and blessed me, saying, 'Where children speak, peace reigns . . .' I'll never forget it. How could a boy of twelve forget a phrase like that?

Did they entrust you with that role because you'd been an altar boy?
Probably, but mostly because I was a good student. I should mention that by then, my father was teaching at my school; he'd been transferred from his rural school to Sabaneta. He told Adán and me, 'Whenever you get less than twenty out of twenty in an exam, you forfeit your right to the cinema.' So that was motivation enough. Modesty apart, I always got twenty, and in primary school I was exempt from end of year exams. The rule was that pupils who got nineteen or twenty didn't have to take them. I was exempt every year in primary school. I loved studying. And everyone encouraged me, my grandmother, my father. My mum was a schoolteacher too; she'd done her teacher training course and got her diploma. They all inspired me to do better. It may sound boastful, but I guess I was the best pupil the Julián Pino School had in all those years. So, obviously, the teachers would go, 'The bishop's coming, let Huguito Chávez speak.' 'It's National Flag Day, or it's Venezuela National Day . . .'

'. . . let Huguito Chávez speak.'
Yes, and Huguito Chávez ended up speaking a lot.

You weren't shy?
Yes, I was. I was shy, but that's how I overcame my shyness. I'd feel shy with people, but on a sports field, or in a theatre, or on any type of stage, my timidity would disappear. I was shy out of humility, modesty; and I still am, I don't like talking about myself, not even in situations like these, answering your questions. I find it hard to say I was the best student in my school.

Did all those experiences help you in later life?

If we look at my childhood and adolescence – the formative years when my personality was being moulded – we see lots of things that doubtless left their mark and influenced me. I was the child encouraged by his grandmother to appreciate nature, and work in the universe of their backyard; the little street vendor who would sometimes go with Ubaldino Morales in his pick-up to sell bananas in other towns; the boy who would listen to tales of Maisanta, Zamora and Bolívar passing through Sabaneta; the primary-school pupil who loved reading; the altar boy who heard a young priest talk of 'the Church's preferential option for the poor'; the boy who read *Tricolor* and biographies of Venezuelan heroes, who loved history and was fascinated by Marc Bloch's question: 'What is the use of history?'

I approached history down different paths, swept along by the current of that invisible river that flows through plains, woods, towns: the invisible yet immensely powerful current of living history. I dipped my toe in the river of history cautiously, then I plunged into the river, the waters engulfed me and carried me to where I am now.

Did your father, being a teacher, stimulate your interest in history?

Yes, my father encouraged me to study history. He was my class teacher in year five. What a hard taskmaster! Strict and demanding. Boys who didn't do their homework were afraid of him.

That same year I got into the baseball team. And I started speaking at events. I wrote a speech for National Flag Day, which began, 'The flag that Miranda brought and that Bolívar carried to glory . . .' I didn't want to read it, but my father insisted, and listened to me rehearse. Because he was like my grandmother, full of love, patience, kindness – a good man. He always had high expectations, and he passed his standards on to us.

When my father first started teaching in Los Rastrojos, way out in the countryside at San Hipólito, he had only finished year six. But since there was a shortage of teachers, he was given some training and then a job. He kept studying on his own, and doing teacher training courses in Barquisimeto in the holidays of 1957, 1958, 1959, until he graduated. He also went to Caracas to do some extra courses in pedagogy. In fact, he was in Caracas during the earthquake of 29 July 1967. After the evacuations we started weeping for my father, because we heard the whole of Caracas had been flattened. It wasn't until two days later that we got a telegram saying he was all right. But anyway, when he was in Barquisimeto for his exams, he bought these extraordinary books [he shows me].

Dictionnaire encyclopédique Quillet, *it's French. Aristide Quillet was a twentieth-century encyclopaedist.*[31]
These are not the original volumes, unfortunately they got lost. My father's collection had a green cover. This later edition has a red cover. My father had all four volumes in his house. I'd take them to my grandmother's, where I had my desk and my hammock, and immerse myself in the pages of this marvellous encyclopaedia.

So, as well as school, you began learning on your own, you taught yourself.
Yes, this encyclopaedia began to have a huge impact. I'm talking about age ten, eleven, twelve. But then later, when we came to Barinas and I was studying for my secondary-school certificate, *Quillet's* was still my bedside reading. I even brought it to Caracas with me, and consulted it when I was studying maths and chemistry at the Military Academy. And later still, when I was teaching history at that same Academy, I kept on consulting it.

Why did it interest you so much?
The biggest impact on the mind of that eleven or twelve-year-old boy was Volume 1, Chapter 1. It was amazing. I've read it over a

31   Aristide Quillet (1880–1955), self-taught French encyclopaedist, editor and founder of Quillet publishing house. Author of the *Dictionnaire Encyclopédique Quillet*, published in six volumes in Paris in 1934.

hundred times. It was entitled 'How to Succeed in Life'. I took notes in an exercise book. I told myself, 'I'm going to succeed in life. I'm going to succeed.'

At eleven, you set yourself that goal?
Yes. That message reached me at that age, and it spurred me on. What *Tricolor* did for me as a child, this encyclopaedia did for the pre-adolescent beginning to dream of a future life. Maybe I'd climb the Pico Bolívar, the peak I glimpsed in the distance when I was very little . . . maybe I'd reach the summit.

What did 'succeeding in life' mean for you then?
What did I want to do when I grew up? My first real ambition was to be a painter. I felt this when I was a child. I studied painting. I eventually abandoned the idea, but I went on painting.

Do you still paint now?
Yes, I do. In oils. I used watercolour at one stage, but I gave that up. I must show you a picture of mine that survived the hurricane, it's somewhere here. I did one painting when I was in jail.[32] Another one I did during the conflict in the Gulf – the Gulf of Venezuela, I mean – with Colombia. Many of them got lost; some have reappeared. I'm painting a new work at the moment.

Did you admire any particular painter?
To be honest, I didn't gain a very deep knowledge of painting; I only studied for a year, just the basics.

Were there paintings in the church?
No, not in the church. But there were reproductions of paintings in *Tricolor*. And in other books, of course. There were very good reproductions, and even a course on painting, in *Quillet's Encyclopaedia*.

---

32   He is referring to *La Luna de Yare* (Yare Moon), painted in 1993 when he was an inmate of Yare prison after the coup of 4 February 1992.

It's extraordinary that the book fell into your hands at the age when it would be most useful, because if you'd come across it as an adult, it might have been too late. Discovering it aged twelve, when character is being built, most probably shaped your future behaviour.

I love those books. To a certain extent, I'm a child of the written word. The child of *Tricolor* and of *Quillet's*. And many other sources. Knowledge is important, but willpower and motivation matter too. The main thing *Quillet's Encyclopaedia* gave me was motivation.

5

Secondary School in Barinas

The Liceo O'Leary – A country bumpkin
Town and country – Echoes of the guerrillas
Kidnapping of Alfredo Di Stéfano
De Gaulle's visit – Assassination of Martin Luther King
Painting classes – Good student – Love of science
'A Message to García' – Assuming leadership
Baseball fever – Magallanes fan – 'Whiplash' Chávez –
New goal: baseball player – Loss of innocence –
Ruiz Guevara family – Politics – To be a soldier?
Change of direction

When did you go to Barinas to study for your secondary-school certificate?

In 1966, when I was twelve. Raúl Leoni, of Acción Democrática, was president of Venezuela at the time. I went to Barinas as soon as I finished primary school. I lived with my Uncle Marcos in a modest but spacious house which he shared with his wife Josefa, a very kind-hearted, very hard-working Afro-Venezuelan woman with whom he went on to have seven children. At that time they only had one child, their eldest daughter Inés. Adán and I slept in one of their three bedrooms, but at weekends we went home to our grand-mother's in Sabaneta.

Your grandmother had stayed in Sabaneta?

Yes, but not for long. Two years later she came to live in a place my father found for her a couple of blocks from my uncle's. Adán and I went to live with her. Then dad got a job as a teacher in Barinas and brought my mum and their two younger children. My grandmother, Adán and I moved again to a house in their neighbourhood, to be near them.

Had you been to Barinas before?

I'd been once when I was in primary school. My father had an old car and offered to take someone from Sabaneta to a clinic in Barinas. I went with him. It was a private clinic opposite the secondary school. Coming from Sabaneta, Barinas looked like a big city, with things I'd never seen before: tall buildings, wide avenues, huge squares. I was surprised by the height of the pavements. I had to wait outside in the street, and walked up and down. I hadn't been back since then.

What was your impression?

I liked it a lot, of course. Bolívar passed through Barinas in 1813. He raised a small army, crossed the Andes and came down through the state of Portuguesa. In Barinas he found everything he needed for his next campaign: food, water, horses, cloth for uniforms; factories making rifles, bayonets and ammunition; cattle to feed his men; maize and other vital supplies. The city – no more than a quiet rural town, really – had a glorious past, and you could tell.

It was a city with a history.

Yes, it was palpable. At least I felt it straight away, coming from Sabaneta and the countryside. Barinas is a cultured city, home of poets and writers like Alberto Arvelo Torrealba, jurists like Juan Antonio Rodríguez, warrior generals like Pedro Pérez Delgado who was first and foremost a Barinas man, and after Independence, insurgents like the Marquis of Pumar.[1] Like Mérida in the Andes, Barinas also had a long tradition of singers, some nationally and

---

1   See José León Tapia, *Tierra de Marqueses*, ed. José Agustín Catalá, Caracas, 1992.

even internationally renowned, like Carrao de Palmarito.[2] The *carrao* is a bird of the Llanos, with a beautiful warble.

Does Barinas have old colonial buildings?

As I said, it was quite a major city, and you can see that in its architecture, for example in El Marqués palace, which is as big as the Miraflores in Caracas, or the palace of the viceroy of Lima in Peru, or the Moncloa in Madrid.[3] It is something very special. There is also an unusually large old prison. They say there are dungeons and tunnels under the prison and the palace. Legend has it that one tunnel goes from El Marqués to the ranch of La Marqueseña, although no one has ever found it.

Did you live in the Old City?

No, we went to live in a newer, more modern, neighbourhood called Rodríguez Domínguez, it was more or less middle-class.[4] For us this meant climbing the social ladder. From a poor barrio in Sabaneta to a middle-class environment. Tarmacked streets, running water, electricity. I started getting used to it.

Was losing touch with your grandmother a problem for you?

No, because my uncle took Adán and me to Sabaneta in his jeep every Friday, and collected us on Sunday. So we'd left Sabaneta, but we hadn't left. We didn't lose touch with my grandmother that first year. And by the second year, she'd come to live with us.

Your parents came to Barinas too.

Yes, that's right. They were worried about us being in the city. They came to live on a new social housing estate built by the Banco

---

2   Juan de los Santos Contreras, known as the '*Carrao de Palmarito*' (1928–2002), was a famous *joropo* singer from the Llanos.

3   An eighteenth-century colonial palace, residence of José Ignacio del Pumar, first Marquis of Riberas de Masparro y Boconó.

4   José Antonio Rodríguez Domínguez was president of the National Congress which, on 5 July 1811, voted in favour of absolute independence for Venezuela and drafted the Act of Independence.

Obrero as part of a new government project.[5] It was the Venezuela of the 1960s – Saudi Venezuela as it was known – overflowing with oil. And the government started distributing resources to deprived sectors of the population: it was a strategy to prevent revolutionary ideas or left-wing movements from spreading, either by armed struggle or at the ballot box. The Left began to lose its momentum. Those governments were all pretty stable, despite several military uprisings and the actions of the guerrilla movements. On a general political level, the guerrillas did not have the means to destabilize the government beyond carrying out the odd attack, ambush, kidnapping or assassination.

Alfredo Di Stéfano, star of Real Madrid and one of the most famous footballers in the world, was kidnapped in Caracas at that time. Do you remember it?

I was nine when it happened, and I don't know if the news even reached Sabaneta . . . but yes, the event was big news. It happened in 1963 [23 August]. I think Di Stéfano had come with Real Madrid to play a friendly [against São Paulo]. FALN guerrillas kidnapped him at his hotel [Hotel Potomac, no longer in existence, in San Bernardino, Caracas].[6] They used his fame to publicize their demands to public opinion abroad. The FALN originally thought of kidnapping a famous composer, I think it was Igor Stravinsky, passing through Caracas at the time, but he was very old and they were afraid he might die on them. They didn't want to hurt anyone, the aim was to protest against the governments of Rómulo Betancourt and Francisco Franco. They kept Di Stéfano for seventy

---

5   Banco Obrero (Workers' Bank) was an institution created in Venezuela in 1928. Its purpose was to help poor workers acquire houses in the cities. In 1975 it was replaced by the Instituto Nacional de la Vivienda (INAVI), the National Housing Institute..

6   The Fuerzas Armadas de Liberación Nacional (FALN) were founded in 1962 to unite the military forces of the PCV and the MIR. Di Stéfano's kidnapping was the work of the FALN's César Augusto Ríos detachment, led by Luis Correa, alias Comandante Gregorio. The second-in-command was Paúl del Río, the son of Spanish anarchists, who went down in history as 'Máximo Canales'. Gregorio represented the Communists and Canales the MIR.

hours and then released him, safe and sound, in Avenida Bolívar, I think, near the Spanish embassy. There was a lot of press coverage.

He wasn't the first world-famous sports figure to be kidnapped, was he?
No, the Cubans of the 26 July Movement invented that in 1958. They kidnapped the Argentine Formula 1 racing driver Juan Fangio from the Hotel Lincoln in Havana [23 February 1958]. And this twenty-six-hour kidnapping provoked an international media storm, alerting the world to the Cuban insurgents and their leader Fidel Castro. The Venezuelan FALN wanted to emulate that event, and they did.

Nevertheless, according to you, Venezuelan society as a whole never supported the guerrillas.
No. The guerrillas managed to take a city here, or a region there, but they didn't get much support. In Barinas state, as I said, the guerrilla was quickly wiped out. They had more impact when I was in Sabaneta, because it was the country. They were up in the mountains, and I would hear comments in the street; when I got to the city, I didn't hear anything about them.

But the Venezuelan insurgency was taking place in an international context and, although I wasn't aware of it, it was connected with Liberation Theology, with the Vietnam War, with the death of Che, with May '68 in France. This series of circumstances meant many young people – for example my brother Adán – became very active in politics and involved in the issues of that time.

General de Gaulle, president of France, also came to Venezuela then. [7]
Yes, it was when Raúl Leoni was president [1964–1968], at the beginning of his mandate. I don't have any personal memory of that

---

7 Charles de Gaulle (1890–1970), French general who during the Second World War led the resistance against the Nazi occupation of his country. In 1958, he founded the Fifth Republic and was president of France from 1958 to 1969.

visit, of course [21–22 September 1964]. I was ten. But yes, General de Gaulle's visit was important from a political point of view, because a few years earlier he had signed the accords with the Algerian National Liberation Front (FLN) which recognized the independence of Algeria [in 1962] after a lengthy eight-year war. De Gaulle was on a tour of Latin America which was in itself a way to criticize the apparent domination of the United States in this region.[8] He gave a speech in the National Congress in Caracas, in which he denounced 'all the hegemonies' and praised 'the independent nations', in a clear allusion to the need for a 'third way'. Washington was not happy with his trip. By the way, General de Gaulle stayed in the Hotel Ávila and since he was so tall, they had to make a special bed for him.[9]

Let's go back to your adolescence. What were your first impressions of the Liceo O'Leary?[10]
Well, I finished my last year of primary school in June, 1960. I was exempted from taking that end of year exam too, but my father said, 'Look, secondary school is very demanding, so you'd better take this final exam.' So I sat the exam – a roundup of everything we'd done that year – just for fun. I passed it. So let's say I arrived in Barinas with the reputation of being an excellent student.

---

8   That tour lasted over three weeks (21 September–16 October 1964), during which de Gaulle visited ten Latin American countries, in this order: Venezuela, Colombia, Ecuador, Peru, Bolivia, Chile, Argentina, Paraguay, Uruguay, Brazil.

9   Designed by the architect who created the Rockefeller Center and the UN Headquarters in New York, Wallace K. Harrison, the Hotel Ávila is a tropical-colonial-Venezuelan-style hotel in the San Bernardino neighbourhood of Caracas. It was inaugurated by President Isaías Medina Angarita, on 11 August 1942. It became famous in the 1960s for hosting Rockefeller and de Gaulle, as well as Perón and Batista.

10   A *liceo* is the equivalent of the French lycée. Chávez was studying for his *bachillerato* or baccalaureate. Daniel Florence O'Leary (1820–1854) was born in Cork, Ireland, and was an officer in the Britannic Legion which fought with Bolívar for South American independence. He was the Liberator's aide de camp, writing his *Memoirs*, a detailed account of Bolívar's main campaigns.

Did you make friends?
I began to be friends with boys who lived near me. Adán had already been at the school for a year, and in the second year he had a wider range of activities than I did. For me, it was studying, studying and more studying.

Was the school of a good standard?
It was of a very high standard: it was the only public secondary school in Barinas state. It had an excellent tradition, and very fine teachers. I was extremely lucky. That first year I devoted myself entirely to my studies, I didn't even do sports.

Did you already like baseball?
I always liked it. But I wasn't passionate about playing, apart from the odd game in the street. I wasn't committed to a disciplined team that played regularly. No, I was still keen on painting and enrolled in the Cristóbal Rojas Art School, in addition to the art lessons I had at school with a teacher called Ríos, who was excellent.

Those painting classes at the art school, how many times a week were they?
Two or three times a week, in the afternoon.

After the Liceo?
Yes, I studied every morning, from seven to twelve, then a bus came for us, we went home for lunch and came back at two or three. In the afternoon, we'd usually have two hours of class, gym or sport, which I liked, but as I say, I didn't feel the passion for it I acquired later on. At the art school, we had a very pretty teacher. I started painting watercolours, then moved on to oils, and at the end of the year we had an exhibition. I didn't win a prize, I was only a beginner. Some of the boys had been painting for three or four years. I remember the painting which won first prize; it was very good, depicting some doctors performing an operation . . . my contribution was a riverbank scene.

You were a country boy, so how did you get on with your school-mates from the city?

There was the initial shock of being a country bumpkin, a little lost lamb, coming to the city where boys had a different lifestyle . . . actually, the Liceo had very few kids from the countryside. The city boys thought they were superior to us timid country lads, facing a totally new social dynamic. I was lucky, I had my brother Adán already in year two, earning a reputation as a good student, a good all-rounder, so he opened doors for me. Adán was always my advance guard. He had good friends, who became my friends too.

That same year I met Juanita Navas, a black girl from a good family, she was older than me, I liked her, we were together for a while, there was a bit of petting . . . baby love stuff.

Was the school a long way from your house?

Yes, quite a long way. A school bus driven by one Señora Paredes took us there and back. I found being driven to school embarrassing, I never got used it, I don't know why. I thought it was better to walk.

Did you have a place to study at home?

Yes, there was a patio with a lemon tree, a little table and one of those folding chairs. That's where I used to study. Or I'd study in the street, under a street lamp.

Millions of schoolkids – in Africa, say – have no electric light at home, so they have to study outside. You see bunches of kids studying under street lamps at night.

We didn't do it for that reason exactly, sometimes it was just because of the heat.

You took your school work very seriously.

Yes, like I said, that first year my life consisted of studying, studying and more studying. I emphasize this because there have been some distorted versions circulating about that stage of my life, and I don't want to lend myself to that kind of fantasy. I was a simple boy. I wasn't some precocious intellectual prodigy who was reading 'founts of wisdom' like Rousseau, Montesquieu, no. I wasn't a superhero at all.

Studying was your thing.
Yes, I studied hard. As well as my school textbooks, I still had my inseparable companion, *Quillet's Encyclopaedia*. I loved researching, I wanted to get to the bottom of things. I was largely an autodidact.

That first year I happened to have an extraordinary teacher, Carmen Landaeta de Matera, an intelligent woman with a lovely personality, who taught a subject called Leadership. It included activities like group socialization. She became so fond of me that she invited me to her house – she was married and lived near the school – and she put me in a team helping with her Leadership classes. It made a huge impact on me. Every Monday she would read to us from 'A Message to García'.[11] Do you know it? It happened at the end of the Cuban War [1895–1898] between Spain and the US. Someone was given a message to take to General Calixto García, a Cuban revolutionary general. And that someone, without a moment's doubt or a single objection, and after many vicissitudes, delivered the message to García. That's to say, he did his duty.

So in Venezuela, when you say, 'Look, this is a message for García', it means you have to move mountains to deliver that message. Carmen illustrated it by means of group dynamics in her house, outside of school hours. The 'message to García' concept was

---

11   'A Message to García' is an essay by the US writer Elbert Hubbard (1856–1915), published in 1899, which was translated into thirty-seven languages and sold 40 million copies. It recounts the true story of a US army officer, Andrew S. Rowan, to whom President McKinley – preparing the US invasion of Cuba in 1898 – confided the mission of making contact with General Calixto García, leader of the insurgent Cubans during the Ten-Year War (1868–1878) with Spain, who was by then living in clandestinity, and deliver a message to him concerning their joint struggle against the Spaniards. Rowan manages to find García and deliver the message. Hubbard concludes that 'what young people need' is to be 'inculcated with the love of duty' and simply 'do well what has to be done'. A Hollywood film was made in 1936, directed by George Marshall and starring ˈlace Beery.

used a lot in the army as well, and later on in our conspiracy, we used it too. With Carmen, I learned how to become a leader. In Sabaneta, I'd already done things like those Flag Day speeches, but it was a different atmosphere.

You were a teenager by this time.

Yes, as a teenager I was studying, mixing with older, more educated people, secondary-school teachers, professionals, specialists in different subjects, people who were more challenging. I made a commitment to study hard in all my subjects. In English, for example, I was an ace; my teacher for the first three years was Señor Hidalgo. I liked English, I knew all the lessons in the textbook by heart; I remember 'New York, here we are in New York'. I learned it off by heart, so of course I'd get twenty out of twenty, or sometimes eighteen, which was very low for me.

And science subjects.

I always loved science, maths, the laws of physics, Newton's circle, the study of light . . . We made a model of an atom with its different particles: neutron, proton, electron . . . We also began studying the principles of balance, and one day I said to my grandmother, 'Bet you I can balance this lemon on the clothes line!' 'What? Are you crazy?' I took a piece of wire and stuck it through the lemon as if it were the pole a tightrope walker carries on a circus wire, and said, 'Come and see the lemon!' She took a look: 'Ah, but you didn't tell me you were going to put that wire there!' 'I told you I was going to balance a lemon on the wire, didn't I'?

You did experiments.

Yes, I loved experimenting. I also fancied biology, we experimented on ferns, looked for leaves to analyse spores under the microscope. We set up an exhibition about photosynthesis, illustrated it with drawings, and glued stuff onto boards . . . There was usually a group of us, but I'd present the project: finding out how the light of the sun worked, how energy came from the sun, how it was concentrated. We explained the best we could with the limited vocabulary we had then.

At thirteen, I was developing quite a rigorous scientific mind, doing research. One thing secondary school gave me, I think, was a certain study discipline, the search for truth. I had a passion for discovering things. I got excellent marks.

And this gave you kudos at school?

And even outside school. On one occasion, I was walking around the square with Juanita Navas – I told you about her – and as we passed a group of older boys whom I didn't know, I clearly heard one say, 'That kid's a *puñal*, a dagger.' Over here that means I was a bright spark. I was getting a certain status and I began to feel a responsibility to lead.

Didn't the other students think you were a swot and a know-all?

I don't think so, absolutely not. On the contrary, because I wasn't arrogant or aloof, and I always tried to help schoolmates who found things difficult, by giving them examples they could understand. I shared my knowledge. I'd give some of them lessons at home, for free of course. I'd take a blackboard and teach a small group.

If you had to sum up that first year in Barinas, what would you say?

Perhaps the most important thing about that first year in unfamiliar surroundings was that I began to assume the role of leader in my little world. A child becoming a teenager; getting used to a big city; studying loads; getting excellent results, and becoming the leader of a narrow circle of friends. In a nutshell, that was my first year.

And politics?

I started my second year in 1967. Adán and his friends were already in year three, so I began taking an interest in the politics they were into. At the same time, I was still a youngster who liked studying, sports, drama, music, drawing, and so politics wasn't my main concern. When it came to the clashes, demonstrations and protests which were so frequent in those days, I used to participate, but only like everybody else did. I didn't take a lead. For instance, on the square in front of our house lived the Mendoza family and Adán often used to go to their house, he was friends with Iván and Yovani. Their elder brother Baudilio was a member of the youth wing of the recently-formed MIR; Adán and Iván joined it too. My brother tried to get me to join, but I had my limits: I'd listen, learn, take part in a few discussions, read certain materials they printed, but never joined the movement. But Adán was a left-wing activist very early on.

1967 was the year they killed Che . . .
Yes, in Bolivia, on 9 October 1967. And the impact of that terrible news even reached the very provincial city of Barinas.

Did you listen to the radio?
Yes, of course. And that October 1967, as I was beginning my second year, I remember Adán, the Mendoza brothers and my cousin Asdrúbal Chávez, in the square, discussing the death of Che Guevara and the news that was coming out. Because there was a series of news stories lasting days, or weeks. That is, first Che is in Bolivia, they're looking for him; then they kill various guerrillas; then they surround Che, they have him cornered . . . It was a sequence of events that we followed as if it were a film. I remember saying at one point, 'Well, Fidel must be sending some helicopters to rescue him. He can't let them kill him.' I told that to Fidel many years later [in 1994], and he laughed. That operation was impossible. I was just a kid, of course.

For us, that was our first really hard blow. I even drew a picture of Che's face, so we boys could make a stencil and reproduce it.

The following year, 1968, was a very turbulent year globally. It began with the assassination of the black leader Martin Luther King in Memphis, Tennessee, on 4 April. Do you remember hearing that terrible news?
I imagine the press must have mentioned the appalling crime, but I don't remember hearing about it at the time. The media in Barinas probably didn't give it the importance they gave Kennedy's

assassination, for instance. For me it was, at least, equally important. That murder showed the vile face of racism in the US.

Do you think Martin Luther King left his mark on history?

Without a doubt. When I got older, I became very interested in Martin Luther King, one of the main leaders of the Civil Rights Movement in the US. He won the Nobel Peace Prize for defending non-violent resistance to racial segregation, he was a great leader. Not only in the US, but the world over. He preached equality, peace and justice.

He gave that famous and emotional speech, 'I Have a Dream'.

Yes, King led the historic black people's March on Washington [28 August 1963] where, yes, he gave that speech 'I Have a Dream'. And that's where the possibility that he might be killed was mooted. I was in New York once and made several speeches in churches in the Bronx, but I realized very soon that the police were sabotaging the meetings. When I began speaking, the lights would go out. They didn't want me to speak. They might have killed me too if I'd stayed longer, like they killed King and many other US leaders, to stop them bringing about real change in that country.

The Bolivarian Revolution claims Martin Luther King as one of its inspirational figures.

What I say is that King fought for the same dreams of equality, justice and freedom as Simón Bolívar. In his Nobel Prize acceptance speech [10 December 1964], that great visionary spoke of a utopia that is now taking shape in Venezuela. He said, 'I have the audacity to believe that peoples everywhere can have three meals a day for their bodies, education and culture for their minds, and dignity, equality and freedom for their spirits.'

Martin Luther King was a revolutionary who inspired peoples and governments throughout the world, and that includes our Bolivarian Revolution that is attempting to build a country free from discrimination, poverty and war. Here we honour Martin Luther King and have excellent relations with US institutions, like the TransAfrica Forum, which continue his struggle against racism and discrimination, and with leading lights of the Afro-American community like Jesse Jackson, Harry Belafonte, Danny Glover, James Early and others.

That same year, 1968, also saw the May uprising in France; the invasion of Czechoslovakia by Soviet troops; the massacre of students in the Plaza de las Tres Culturas in Mexico . . . Did you hear anything about all those events in Barinas?

I don't have any concrete memory of those three events you mention. I do remember, however, that there was a very close-run electoral campaign for a successor to Raúl Leoni [of AD]. The candidates were Rafael Caldera for Copei, who won by a very small margin, and possibly José Vicente Rangel for the Left.[12] The MIR and the MEP organized various events in Barinas but I don't know which candidate they were supporting, or if they had put forward candidates of their own. But I do remember attending several political events, particularly one at which I heard Alí Primera sing for the first time.[13]

What youngsters of your generation sang most were Beatles' songs, do you remember?

Yes, you heard Beatles' songs here too. Hippies and other young people used to sing them, but we were into different music. The Beatles didn't make much of an impact in our neighbourhood, nor on the working class in general. I had Afro hair, liked baseball and studying, and knew dozens of *rancheras* off by heart.

---

12   The candidate of the Socialist Party of Venezuela was Alejandro Hernández; Luis Beltrán Prieto Figueroa, supported by the left of the AD, was the candidate of the Movimiento Electoral del Pueblo (MEP); and Miguel Ángel Burelli Rivas, supported by the Frente de la Victoria, was the Unión Republicana Democrática (URD) candidate. The Communist Party of Venezuela, under the name of Unidos para Avanzar (United to Advance) participated without presenting a candidate.

13   Famous Venezuelan singer–songwriter (1942–1985), called the People's Singer because his protest songs denounce the suffering of the poor and demand a fairer society.

Is that where this memory of yours comes from? From remembering so many poems and the lyrics of so many songs?
I learned songs as a child. Perhaps it was the result of my wanting to become, as Quillet says, an 'athlete of the spirit', 'an athlete of the mind'. I memorized the poem 'Maisanta', which is very long, by inventing ways of linking one verse to another. Although that was later, of course. In Barinas, I learned *rancheras*. We used to go to a local bar where Antonia Volcán, a pretty Indian woman from Apure, used to sing. The bar was called *Capanaparo*, an Indian name for a river which meant something like 'long snake'.

The most important international political crisis of that time was the Vietnam War. Do you remember hearing anything about that conflict?
To be honest I don't remember any impact the Vietnam War made on our provincial city. I'm sure the news reached us, but it didn't affect me.

No demonstrations against the war?
No, or if there were I didn't take part. I learned about the Vietnam War at the Military Academy.

You still had no interest in party politics?
That's right. As I said, I wasn't in any political movement. I've heard people say I was in one of those 'Che Guevara guerrilla cells'. Not true. Ridiculous. I was barely fourteen. I want to make it quite clear that I wasn't into politics of any kind at secondary school. I obviously leant towards the Left, because I was close to Adán and friends of his like the Mendozas or Fernando Bianco. Adán was much more involved, although I joined in the odd political discussion, like when Che died, for instance, because that had a huge impact. But no, if the truth be told, I led the life of a very normal studious teenager.

When did you start being passionate about baseball?
Well, as I said, I always liked baseball, even in Sabaneta. My father was a real fanatic, he played first base, and I got the interest from

him. But my passion for playing baseball started in 1968, when I really caught the bug.

Next door to us lived – and still does – a journalist called Rafael Guédez Acevedo, an educated man, a good talker, and wise too. He was in AD and wrote for the newspaper *El Espacio*. I practically lived at his house. His wife, Doña Meche, made – still does – exquisite sweets. So, our circle of friends was expanding, we were spreading our wings. I grew away from Sabaneta, we didn't even need to go at weekends. We'd just go once a month to see our parents, but they were looking for a way to move to Barinas too. A year later they came.

That's when you met the Ruiz Guevara family.
Yes, that's when the Ruiz brothers appeared, and they played a lot of baseball, especially Vladimir. He was in year four, two years older than me, so we looked up to him, he had a different circle of friends, but we all played baseball together. We trained by hitting bottle tops . . . we even invented bottle-top tournaments, with a broom handle for a bat.

You start devoting more time to baseball.
Yes, a lot more. Thanks to that group of friends, I began playing in a team, and competing against teams from other areas like La Coromoto or La Aceleración, using a hard ball. The Liceo had a team too, and I started playing in that with kids who were really good at the sport.

Your passion kept growing.
Yes, and I began playing whenever and wherever I could: without neglecting my studies, of course. But now I was spending time on an activity I hadn't done in year one, and this gave me an opening to new friends, new circles and new families. In 1969, when I began year three, I got into the school baseball team.

I also began to make friends in the lower part of Barinas, near the river. I got to know the better players, like Jorge Ramírez, and played at a higher level. By the time I was fifteen, I was playing in the junior major league with some excellent teammates. I remember one black guy, Carlos Daza, very strong, hit the ball really hard. I had to pitch against him once and got nowhere, but later on I figured him out. And another, Lucio Bonilla, a giant of a guy . . . And as I said, Vladimir was another very good player, and he was the one who nicknamed me 'Goofy' because he was called 'Popeye' – *Popeye* Ilyich. His father, José Esteban Ruiz Guevara, was a Communist, he'd set up the first Venezuelan Communist Party cell in Barinas, and had named his son Vladimir Ilyich after Lenin, and his other son Federico after Engels. And a third son he'd named Marleni, after Marx–Lenin.

Vladimir gave me advice, and coached me. And after a couple of months I was taken on by the Transport Union team, the best one. I batted and pitched, and ran really fast. At the same time, I became a huge Magallanes fan. In my neighbourhood, some kids supported Caracas and some Magallanes, the two titans of baseball, irreconcilable rivals.

Historic rivalry.

Yes, the teams were historic opponents: the Caracas 'Leones' and the Magallanes 'Navegantes'. Nowadays [since the 1969–1970 season] Magallanes is based in Valencia, but in those days both teams played in Caracas. Each was a baseball colossus, eternal rivals, and they still are. Our neighbourhood had *caraquistas* versus *magallaneros* and at night we'd turn the radio up full blast to hear which team was winning; we'd shout and whistle along.

When did you first become a fan of Látigo [Whiplash] Chávez?

It was then, when I was a teenager, that I first saw a picture of Isaías *Látigo* Chávez, a brilliant baseball player. I began identifying with him, perhaps because we had a surname in common, and because he too was a left hander. I used to read this sports magazine called *Sport Gráfico* which often published pictures of him, like all the press did. He was a pitcher and played for Magallanes, of course. He was very young, only twenty-one or twenty-two, but already a major league player.

Did he play in the US?

In the US, and in our Venezuelan league.

In both leagues?

Well, now, since baseball got puffed up as a spectacle and a money-spinner, a lot of players aren't allowed to play here even though they're Venezuelan. They give them contracts worth millions in the US and make them sign clauses barring them from playing here. But some refuse, and go back and forth, because here the season lasts three months and is specially timed so it doesn't overlap with the US league; when they finish there, they play here.

Látigo *Chávez played in both.*

Yes, he did, but then a terrible tragedy happened. Chávez was killed in a plane accident. On 16 March 1969, his plane crashed as it was taking off from Maracaibo. I remember the exact minute I heard the news. It was a Sunday, I got up, went to have breakfast, switched on the radio and the news said . . . It was a tremendous shock, I felt as if I'd died. I was about to turn fifteen, and that brutal end to *Látigo* Chávez's life was a real drama, it touched my soul. I was devastated; I stayed home from school that Monday, and on the Tuesday as well.

He was your idol?

Well, in those days I admired him enormously, he was my role model. So, guided perhaps by my favourite book, *Quillet's Encyclopaedia*, and my favourite chapter in it, 'How to Succeed in Life', I promised myself I would follow in the footsteps of *Látigo* Chávez. This vow was a way of refusing to accept his death, of keeping him alive somehow.

You gave yourself another goal in life.

Yes. I stopped wanting to be a painter and put a superhuman effort into improving my sports performance, by running, strengthening my legs, changing my eating habits, studying ball control and all the different types of pitches and grips. I stuck at it by pure willpower, by dint of physical and mental strength. I even got some graphics from the Sports Institute and studied how to spin the ball better.

Were you always a pitcher?

Yes, I dreamed of being a pitcher. A left-handed pitcher. There was a palm tree in the middle of our yard in Barinas. I made it home base and marked it out like a target. I'd pitch stones or small lemons at it, trying to hit the bull's eye as often as I could. Then I'd write down how many times I'd hit the target, and from how far away. So, I'd decided on my new goal, and was heading straight for it.

What team did you play for?

At first with the group of friends I told you about. We organized a team, the Avenida Carabobo team. Although I was one of the youngest, I gradually took on the role of captain. And soon afterwards, we got Mobil to back us.

The US company Mobil Oil?

It wasn't Mobil Oil, just Mobil.[14] A teacher heard the oil company wanted to form a youth baseball team, and asked me to help. So I went to the Mobil office and they gave us t-shirts, jerseys and some mitts. Our first proper team jerseys had the Mobil logo on it, there's a photo of us wearing them. We looked like infiltrators . . .

Imperialist recruits?

Yes, imperialism recruited me via Mobil [laughter]. Just imagine, Hugo Chávez captaining a Mobil team. I remember that the 'o' of Mobil was red, and the symbol was Pegasus, a winged horse. What's more, the Mobil team was league champion two years running, we

---

14   Mobil emerged from the breakup in 1911 of John D. Rockefeller's famous Standard Oil Company. In 1955, it adopted the name Mobil Oil Company but shortened it to plain Mobil in 1963 and launched a world publicity campaign. Giving provincial sports teams (like that of Hugo Chávez) equipment with the Mobil logo in 1966–1971 might have been part of that campaign. Mobil merged with Exxon in 1999 to form what is now ExxonMobil.

hardly lost a match. For example, the players from neighbouring La Coromoto were older and bigger, but they never beat us. We were much more astute, like guerrillas, fewer in number but quicker and more aggressive, whereas those mammoths were slow. We were the youngsters, the new guys on the block, the novices, but we soon got ourselves noticed.

Did you manage the team?

I was the manager. We beat the fiercest of teams, ever the very fiercest of all – the one from the riverbank which had players like Jorge *Pirata* Ramírez, Adolfo *Popo* Espinoso, *Sapo* [Toad] Alemán . . . Can you imagine having a name like that? [Laughter.] 'Toad' Alemán was a sturdy blond kid with a face like a toad. Their team was supposed to be the best, but they couldn't beat us. Our team had some great players too; an outstanding one was a pitcher nicknamed 'Pancake Face'. There were so many funny nicknames. He was a good friend, a with a critical mind.

There was another very aggressive team in Barinas, the one the Reyes brothers, Aníbal and Luis, played in; although the best thing about their family was their gorgeous sister, Virginia Reyes, who I was half in love with, shame she didn't play, but she did come to some of the games . . .[15] Their team was also sponsored by an oil company. It was a good team – they had a player called 'the Bison', a huge aggressive guy – Luis was a very good pitcher, and his elder brother Aníbal batted left-handed. I think this team had a race complex, because there were hardly any whites in it. In Barinas they called them the 'Monkeys', you can guess why.

Was there much racial prejudice against Afro-Venezuelans?

There was prejudice, and there still is. But perhaps less in the Llanos than in the rest of Venezuela. You know that here the Federal War

---

15   Chávez's friend from both school and baseball, army pilot Luis Reyes Reyes, took part in the Bolivarian uprisings of 4 February 1992, and 27 November 1992. After Chávez's electoral victory in 1998, he became governor of Lara state and a government minister. His brother Aníbal Reyes was also in the army with them.

was a class conflict, a war of the rich against the poor. There were huge massacres on both sides, they wiped each other out. It was very savage indeed. The old aristocratic or oligarchic castes were decimated by the war, and the survivors had to mix with non-whites; they got acquainted, and learned to respect one another. There was ethnic and cultural miscegenation. Class didn't disappear, of course, there were still rich and poor, but there was more respect and consideration.

In Sabaneta, for instance, there was this gentleman called Pedro Hurtado, who lived in a big house on the corner of the main square. He was a rich, white guy but he was also a friend of my father, who was black and poor, and welcomed him in his home. We'd drop by there on the way to the cinema, and my father and Pedro Hurtado would talk. So, obviously racism existed, but in a less brutal, violent form than in some other regions.

In the Llanos, black people are treated affectionately. If someone says to a woman, 'Hey, *mi negra*', it's more like an endearment. I remember, for example, my friend *Negro Petróleo*, 'Pitch Black'. We called him *Negro* but he was proud to be black, and nothing was off limits to him because he was black. The Reyes boys were black but they studied in private schools, lived in a big house, their father worked for the oil company, and their home was always full of friends; women, men, white, black, Indian, mestizo . . . shades of all kinds.

Were there places like schools, clubs, bars, hotels, etc., reserved for whites only?

No, there was nothing like that. I never noticed it, anyway, not in Sabaneta nor in Barinas. For instance, I was very poor but I'd go over to the house of Coromoto Linares in the Mobil enclave to give him maths lessons, and his mum and dad, both of them white middle-class, were always sweet to me. I went in and out of the Mobil enclave, which was a very well-protected area, and nobody ever stopped me.

Obviously there were still traces of discrimination here and there, but they were out of place and anachronistic, it wasn't normal behaviour. That's why I say that, although prejudice hadn't completely disappeared, the level of racism seen in other societies, and even in other parts of Venezuela, didn't exist in the Llanos.

When you say your baseball victories brought your team a certain notoriety, does that mean the press talked about you?

No, we didn't get into the newspapers; our fame spread within our own circles, on the grapevine, by word of mouth. People started wondering who this Mobil team were, and where this 'Golden Leftie' Hugo Chávez had sprung from. Perhaps I shouldn't mention it myself, but that's what they called me. I even became known outside our neighbourhood, so that the first prostitute I slept with asked, 'Oh, are you "Golden Leftie"'? My celebrity had spread as far as the brothel.

We were already in the junior league when Radio Continental began to sponsor us; it was a better level. The radio station designated one of their commentators – his name was Alvarado and he was very keen on baseball – as a kind of super-manager. I was still the manager but he helped us a lot, he was more knowledgeable and I learned a lot from him. Not only did he help us with our game, he also helped out financially, because we were all kids from poor families; he got us uniforms, shoes, all our equipment in fact. Alvarado started to publicize our team on his radio show. And he sometimes broadcast live commentary from our games, because we no longer played on the Rodríguez ground.

What day did you play? On Sundays?

On Saturdays and Sundays. In the afternoon, because there weren't any floodlights. We played under lights later on, but by that time we were in the major league.

Did devoting so much time to sport affect your studies?

Well, actually I kept on studying, and giving lessons in the holidays to friends who had to repeat subjects or stay back a year. I didn't charge, of course. That was very important to me, going to the houses of kids my own age, in the evenings or at weekends, out of solidarity, to help them improve. I remember one girl, Inés Rosales, who I liked a lot and we even had a bit of a fling; she was hopeless at maths so I gave her extra lessons. Another of my pupils was Thaís Maldonado, the daughter of Dr Samuel David Maldonado, of the Partido Electoral Popular (PEP), who ran for mayor of Barinas on one occasion.

However, as was to be expected, my grades started to go down as my sporting prowess went up. And here I have to confess the influence of *Quillet's Encyclopaedia* on me as a teenager; it caused a certain conflict of interest.

How come?

Because, like I said, I was a good student, and I enjoyed studying; but when I set myself an objective, as the encyclopaedia encouraged me to, and I began to succeed in that chosen field, then I was forced to neglect my studies. So just let's say, I felt bad when I got a mark that didn't match up to my previous performance.

You spent all your time playing baseball?

Most of it. All of it. I was baseball-mad. You have to remember that I was a lad of sixteen who, through total dedication, had managed to get into the major league in Barinas, play in regional tournaments and represent my state at the national championships.
I was getting into really good physical shape. I was very thin, but I'd started exercising, and doing a lot of running. The result was that my marks suffered. By the time I was in year five my marks were down to fifteen, fourteen, thirteen . . . I even flunked one subject altogether, something I'd never done before. My father asked, 'What happened?' Although of course he knew the answer. Sport.

Did your grandmother approve of you playing so much sport?

Yes, she did. Strangely enough, she who had never liked baseball and had never been to a game, she was happy for me to play.

What profession did she want you to pursue?

She never showed any wish for me to choose any particular career.

But you had decided to be a baseball player?
Absolutely. That became my number one priority and I was doing well. In August 1969, I was selected to play in a national junior baseball championship. The players were supposed be over fifteen and under sixteen, but nearly all the boys had false identity papers. All the teams did that, it was a disgraceful practice. Joel Suárez and I were the only boys from Barinas to have documents in our own names; all the others used false names. They were seventeen, eighteen, even twenty. 'Pitch Black', for instance, he was twenty.

So, you were a boy of fifteen in a group of young adults.
Yes, and it had certain drawbacks and consequences, not only physically but also psychologically. Because that group already behaved like, let's say, mature men, including sexually. And I had to step up to the plate . . . The group used to frequent a brothel, for example.

And you?
Well, I was more or less obliged to go with them, as part of the group, to this Barinas brothel. It was normal in those days, every big town had its red-light district. We'd go there, each guy would choose a girl. It was my first experience with a prostitute, a sex worker.

And you lost your innocence . . .
Yes [laughter], I lost my innocence that first time in 1969. I remember those ladies welcoming us with excitement, because in such a small provincial town, we were – how should I put it? – little local heroes already. For the first time ever, Barinas had reached the final against the Federal District, against Anzoátegui. We came third.

You told me you used to meet up with your school chums in two cafés, do you remember which ones?
Of course. They were more like student bars, now that we were in the last year of secondary school. One was the Noches de Hungría [Hungarian Nights]; we'd meet there to study or play dominoes.

We called it the Faculty, we'd say 'See you at the Faculty.' The other one is called the Rincón Mexicano nowadays, but it used to be the Capanaparo. The baseball crowd would gather there to talk. The most politicized man of our group was Vladimir Ruiz. La Causa R [Radical Cause] was still in its infancy, as was the Movimiento al Socialismo (MAS), and many conversations in those years were peppered with arguments about the unfolding political process. The guerrilla movement was over by then. Fabricio Ojeda, commander in chief of the FLN–FALN, had been assassinated, or rather 'suicided', in the dungeons of the Armed Forces' Intelligence Services (SIFA) in Caracas [21 June 1966]. Raúl Leoni was president. The MAS was growing in middle-class intellectual circles, while the trajectory of the MIR was more tortuous and a little longer.

Vladimir had gone to Barquisimeto to study at the Pedagogic Institute before I'd finished secondary, and he came back in the holidays or at weekends. Barquisimeto had the first La Causa R cell, and he brought news of it. But like all teenagers our main topics of conversation were girls and baseball, and only after that, politics.

So, politics still didn't interest you much?

Not much, really. Although, like I said, I knew Vladimir's father, José Esteban Ruiz Guevara, a historian who had been in the guerrilla movement and then in prison. They'd moved onto our estate, about a hundred yards from our door, in fact. He had a beard, chewed tobacco, studied indigenous communities, edited a magazine and, despite being a man of the Left, worked in the local council. I also spent a lot of time at the house of Eliécer and Jorge Giusti, whose father Carlos was a writer and poet . . .

But did you talk to those fathers?

To be honest, I visited the Ruiz Guevara and Giusti households because I was friends with the boys, of course, but I really enjoyed listening to the old folks; they weren't all that old, I know, forty or fifty at the outside.

I read somewhere that the Ruiz Guevara family was rather important in your political formation, in that their father's library opened a window for you. You discovered political works by authors like Machiavelli and Marx, which subsequently influenced you. Is that true?

Look, let me insist again, it's *not* true that the Ruiz Guevara household was a political school for me at that age. I want to make that absolutely clear. It's not true. There has been speculation that it was some kind of Marxist–Leninist academy, and that I – who was then between fifteen and sixteen – had taken some kind of oath. I never did, that's false, a lie. I did read things, of course; there were magazine articles, conversations with friends. But nothing transcendental. More important than what we read was the direct contact with a person, with circles of people, and with a particular story.

But José Esteban Ruiz Guevara has confirmed the political influence his household had on you . . .[16]

Lots of things have been said. He was old, so he was probably confused. I say this with deep respect, but he was sometimes mistaken. Because I did go back to Barinas in 1975 after graduating from the Military Academy, and naturally I'd changed, I was twenty-one, a second lieutenant and more politically aware. When I returned to the Ruiz Guevara house, our discussions and reading matter were certainly political. But not when I was in secondary school. Not back then.

Some journalists have even claimed that I arrived at the Military Academy with the writings of Che Guevara under my arm. That's absolutely not true. Between 1966 and 1971, I repeat, I was only interested in sports and schoolwork. I had once been approached at school by a boy who was studying in Caracas, and wanted to start a socialist movement at the Liceo. He invited me to a meeting, but I said no. I never participated in any way. For five years, I studied,

---

16   See Cristina Marcano and Alberto Barrera Tyszka, *Hugo Chávez: The Definitive Biography of Venezuela's Controversial President* (2005), trans. Kristina Cordero, Random House, 2007.

played baseball, and had the odd girlfriend – Juanita and Irene were two I remember. I think I was a good boy, with only the normal teenage high jinks.

What did you read?
Well, I've always enjoyed poetry, and I liked talking to poets, I knew Eduardo Alí Rangel, the poet from my town, I often read him . . . I liked regional poetry, and learned several really long poems by heart which I would recite at school and at our get-togethers. And of course, I read my eternal companion, *Quillet's Encyclopaedia*, which provided me with sound advice for everyday life. I'd read any newspapers I could get my hands on, and lots of novels. Some I remember are *Doña Bárbara*, which was obligatory reading, and *Cantaclara*, also by Rómulo Gallegos, and *The Red Lances* by Arturo Uslar Pietri. I also bought *The Green House* by Mario Vargas Llosa, I had to analyse it for a literature class at school, and I got nineteen out of twenty for 'our friend' Vargas Llosa's novel. As well as literature, I was interested in political science and philosophy essays. I was a curious reader.

When did the idea of an army career occur to you?
You could say it was purely by chance. When I started year four, I became friends with an older boy called José Rafael Angarita. He wasn't sporty at all, but he lived on the same estate as me. One day, when we were just finishing year five, it must have been in May or June of 1970 because I was about to turn sixteen, and he was about eighteen, he said, 'Let's enter the Military Academy in Caracas.' Some officer from the Tabacare Fort in Barinas had come to talk about the Military Academy and encouraged us to enrol. And José put his name on a list. I was astonished: 'What a weird idea! What for?'

What did you think of soldiers?
I had a pretty negative idea. I've told you of my reaction when my father was detained in La Marquesena. They represented repression, abuse, arbitrary power. For the circles I moved in, soldiers

were parasites. It was practically a motto on the Left: 'soldier = parasite'.

Although, like any boy, I also liked playing war games. We'd organize Homeric battles in my grandmother's yard, build invincible forts out of tin cans and wooden planks and devise strategies to lay siege to them and conquer them. I relished these battles . . . but one thing was a bit of fun, reality was something quite different.

Did your friend José enlist?

Yes, he had no interest in politics either, and in August 1970 he went off to the Military School. It did make me think.

Was it a School or an Academy?

In those days it was called a School, now it's an Academy.[17] That same year, 1970, under the new 'Andrés Bello Plan', the Military Academy went through a transition and emerged as an Institute of Higher Studies. Until 1970, it accepted boys with three years of secondary education, and they would pass out without a university degree. But after 1970, it only took candidates who had passed their secondary-school certificate, and they left with a degree. Officer training changed completely.

That was when I was at the height of my baseball powers, I was obsessed with the game. I still spent time studying but I wasn't getting good enough marks to please my father, or myself. José Rafael kept trying to persuade me to apply for the Academy, and explained it now had university status. He even gave me a pamphlet. I saw you could play baseball there, and that the coaches were none

---

17 The Military Academy is Venezuela's oldest army officer training institution. It grew out of the institution created by the Caracas Supreme Junta on 3 September 1810. In 1903 President Cipriano Castro created the modern Military Academy, which opened on 5 July 1910. In 1936, General Eleazar López Contreras substituted it for the Military School located in La Planicie until 1949 when President Colonel Carlos Delgado Chalbaud occupied the present site in Avenida de Los Próceres, Fuerte Tiuna, Caracas. In 1971, President Rafael Caldera reorganized it again as the Military Academy, with the introduction of a new curriculum coinciding with the arrival of Hugo Chávez.

other than Héctor Benítez Redondo and José Antonio Casanova, the 'heroes of '41'.[18]

But you couldn't make up your mind?
I was very unsure. In my last year of secondary school, I became very anxious about the career I should choose if I wanted to be a baseball player. Adán had gone off to university in Mérida and was living with some cousins of my father's. It was the nearest university to Barinas. Caracas was the other side of the world. So my first idea was to follow him to Mérida.

Did your brother ask you to join him?
Yes, he encouraged me to, and so did my father. Adán had come over a bit hippy at university, and went around with wide boots and long hair. He had a group of left-wing friends his own age, and they started getting more active in the opposition movements. But I didn't know anything much because the MIR was still clandestine then, and Adán was extremely disciplined. The downside was that they only played football there, and I wanted to carry on with base-ball, and turn professional. So I turned it over and over in my mind: 'Oh god, I don't want to go to Mérida.'

So when it was coming up to February–March 1971, I started to look more favourably at the possibility of applying to the Military School, as a way of getting to Caracas, near the Magallanes team. I planned to get better at baseball and then leave the army and stay in the capital to play professionally. Baseball was my primary objective.

In those days, being 'successful in life' meant being successful at baseball.
That's right. That was my goal, just as painting had been before.

---

18 In 1941, the Venezuelan national baseball team won the World Championships in Havana. The players became popular idols and the sports press called them the 'heroes of '41'.

So, you didn't go to the Military School for hidden political reasons?

No, no, I'll say it again. It was because I was determined to go to Caracas and play baseball. The rest is just made up, pure speculation. At that age, I hadn't even begun to feel history calling me. It is true as you know that at the end of my time in secondary school, I began to hear things, read poems, books, *El Espacio* newspaper, etc. But I'd never thought deeply about the great historical figures, Bolívar, Zamora . . . They had been kicked out of the official version of history, you barely heard their names. Zamora was a bandit, Maisanta was a bandit.

Had you read Bolívar before secondary school?

Very little; like I said, the official history practically ignored him. In the Liceo O'Leary, we studied more world history than we did our own national history. The history textbook for the secondary-school certificate was over one thousand pages long, but the way history was taught was terrible: it consisted of memorizing interminable lists of names and dates . . . However, somewhere deep inside, little seeds of knowledge were germinating, because of the wide range of things I'd read. How often did little Huguito come across Bolívar in the pages of *Tricolor* magazine, for instance? Bolívar was shown delivering the Angostura Manifesto, decorating Páez at Las Queseras del Medio, dying in exile at Santa Marta . . .

The ground was fertile.

Yes, no doubt about that. Ground carefully prepared with fertilizer. And the culmination of those bits and pieces of reading was a mass of questions, which bore fruit later when I reached the epicentre of my education at the Military Academy, with military historians like General Jacinto Pérez Arcay.[19] I became an assiduous visitor to the Academy's huge library, looking for books about Bolívar, reading his proclamations, and getting to know him inside out.

---

19   Author of the *El fuego sagrado. Bolívar hoy*, CLIPER, Caracas, 1980; *La Guerra Federal* (1974), Péndulo histórico bolivariano, Caracas, 1997, 9th edition.

What did your grandmother think of you going to the Military School?

She didn't want me to be a soldier. She was the sort who'd go round whispering to herself, loud enough for you to hear, 'I don't like it at all,' she'd say, as if talking to the birds. She'd surreptitiously put ideas in my head. 'What are you going there for? It's dangerous. You're very meddlesome, too rebellious, you'll get into trouble in no time.' Once when I was a cadet, I found her lighting votive candles on a little altar. She told me, 'I'm begging Santa Rosa and the Virgin of the Rosary to get you out of there.'

She never wanted me to go to the Academy. Naturally, Adán didn't approve either. My parents found out when it was too late. I organized it in secret until it was a fait accompli. A telegram arrived from the Academy giving me a date to go and sit the entrance exams. I was obliged to admit that I had to go to Caracas, that I'd applied to the Military Academy. My father frowned. But my mother agreed. And my younger brothers and sisters also liked the idea.

What qualifications did the Academy require?

I took the first exam in Barinas, at the military barracks.

A pre-selection.

Yes. We were given a very general medical check-up and a 'psycho-technical' interview; there was no physical education or sports exam. The aim was not to eliminate anyone, but to get as many candidates as possible to apply to the Academy. There weren't more than twenty of us, but nearly all went to Caracas.

Had you been to Caracas before?

Never.

Had you already got your secondary-school certificate?

Not yet. I was just finishing the year.

But under the new education guidelines, didn't you have to have the certificate to enter the Academy?

That's right. But unfortunately I had a problem in chemistry. The teacher, Manuel Felipe Díaz, failed me; he awarded me nine out of twenty. But I went to Caracas to take the Academy exams anyway, and I did well. But I couldn't enrol because of that one subject; they didn't accept students who'd failed any subject at all.

So what then?

As well as the academic exams I'd taken, which I passed, there was also a final interview. They sent a telegram asking me to attend, and I took the bus to Caracas again. The interview was conducted by some senior officers, a psychologist and a priest. I remember them asking questions like, 'Do you belong to a political party?' I was very careful and told them that obviously I didn't, which was true. 'But it says here you do,' said one of the jury. 'Yes, but that was a joke, I put the Barinas *Topocheros* Party.' *Topocheros* were the guys who sold *topochos* and plantain. Then they asked me: 'Have you ever had sexual relations with an animal?' Because in the Llanos that was quite common, especially with donkeys. I knew a man nicknamed 'Donkeyman' who had shagged every donkey in the region. I never did anything like that. They asked just to see what reply you gave. The aim was for the potential recruit to show why he wanted to be a soldier.

They were assessing your psychological make-up, your character, were they?

Yes, and I passed that test too, but I still couldn't enrol because of the subject I'd flunked. Then a colonel said to me: 'The only way you can get in provisionally is by excelling at sport. You have to prove yourself.' So that's when I said, 'Well, I play baseball.' 'OK, then show us.' He sent me to the parade ground with other students with subjects flunked who'd said they were good at sport. They split us into groups and took us to the sports ground. There I discovered that José Antonio Casanova, fourth bat for the Venezuelan team which beat Cuba to the world championship in

1941, was the head coach; and the other, shorter, bench coach was the left-hander Héctor Benítez, also a fourth bat. I recognized them from their photos, I admired them, I even used to sell cards with their faces on. And don't forget that major-league baseball, Magallanes, was my primary objective. Joining the army was only secondary.

So, I got ready to demonstrate my pitching skills. But two days earlier, in Barinas, I had pitched for a whole game and my arm was very painful, I was putting ice on it . . .

What was wrong?
Well, by that age, I'd started getting pains in my arms, up here, in the shoulder. It's normal for a pitcher to get elbow pain; anyone who pitches eight or nine innings is bound to get a pain in his elbow.[20] But it's much more serious to get a shoulder pain, because that tends to get worse until you have to have an operation. In Barinas, baseball players didn't get any medical attention.

Did it get better?
No, I had that pain for a long time, until thirty years later Fidel Castro discovered it was my rotator cuff, a group of muscles and tendons covering the shoulder joints. I was pitching in Havana one time and after the game the pain was unbearable; Fidel, who knows everything, felt my shoulder and his diagnosis was, 'You've torn the rotator cuff.' The following day they did an X-ray and it was indeed the rotator cuff.

And that stopped you performing well enough in the sports test?
Exactly, because, as I said, I'd pitched a whole game in Barinas two days earlier and was in quite a lot of pain. So I warmed up, but when they asked me to pitch it was a disaster, I felt my arm seize up with pain and threw the ball way too high. A terrible disappointment . . . They took me off. The guy examining me said, 'You can't

---

20   An inning is each of the segments of a baseball game in which the two teams take consecutive turns at attacking (batting) and defending (pitching and fielding).

play like this; if your arm hurts, you shouldn't pitch.' They refused to let me. I didn't pitch again until I graduated as a second lieutenant. When I went back to Barinas they started giving me injections in my arm. I pitched for another year, but then the pain grew unbearable – the rotator cuff tore completely. I had to give up altogether.

You didn't pass the sports test, then?
Yes I did, because I got lucky. Héctor Benítez was also a left-hander, and he told me to try another position. I decided to bat. I did pretty well. In the end, Benítez told me, 'You can play baseball. We'll put you on the list.'

So it was not far off a miracle you got into the Military Academy.
The tricks life plays! That day, way back in my first life, circumstances could have decided my fate differently, no doubt about it, it was a one-in-a-million chance. There I was, having failed a subject and incapable of pitching properly; just one tiny thing took me on down this road.

We could almost say, one simple strike of a baseball bat changed the course of Venezuelan history.
It was the tiniest stroke of luck. That is, if I hadn't batted decently when my real skill was pitching, I wouldn't have got into the Academy. It also helped that I was left-handed, because Héctor Benítez wrote this down in his notes: 'We're looking for a left-handed hitter. So we're recommending him. Report in eight days.' If by chance I hadn't been left-handed and had missed the three strikes, they wouldn't have enrolled me in the Academy. I wouldn't have been who I am, and we wouldn't be talking about the Bolivarian Revolution.

But you still hadn't passed all your subjects.
Right, and I wanted my school certificate. I worked very hard, took the chemistry exam, and passed with a fourteen. And with that, on Sunday 8 August 1971, I entered the Military Academy.

You went with the idea of becoming a baseball player, but that would soon change.

It certainly did. Because I have to say that I loved the Academy from the very start, and easily adapted to my new life as a cadet. I took my mission as a soldier in the army founded by Simón Bolívar very seriously. I realized I had come to the right place for me: that parade ground, that flag, that uniform, that rifle, those songs . . .

All that transformed you.

That's where the metamorphosis took place. Hugo 'Goofy' Chávez, a simple provincial lad, just turned seventeen, entered the Military Academy with no political motivation. He enlisted to be a pitcher, to train for the baseball wars, yet four years later, in 1975, an extraordinary thing happened: he left as a revolutionary second lieutenant.

You met your destiny there.

It's true. You're born several times, and you live several lives. When I came out of the Military Academy in 1975, I was a changed man, I'd been reborn in a different world, with different perspectives. Many things had happened, of course, personally, politically, nationally and internationally; even merely being in Caracas, mixing with a lot of people. And in any case, the military career is a political career, totally political.

As you say, a metamorphosis.

No doubt about it. When I left the Academy as a young second lieutenant on 8 July 1975, I wasn't yet twenty-one. On 14 July I reported to the commander of the Barinas barracks. I was back in my home town, but I was a different person. In just four years – four years is a very short time – I had acquired a clear political motivation. I was certainly going to talk with old man Ruiz Guevara now. I invited him out, and we went. Vladimir had graduated as a history teacher, and our circle was now having interesting political discussions. I went back to Barinas politicized! And where did I receive my political education? At the Military Academy. Not only in the Academy, of course – but for four years it had been the epicentre of my formation as a young politicized officer. That was absolutely clear.

That's where you came of age politically?
This had obviously been gestating, germinating, incubating, but that's where the explosion happened. An eruption. It's like a volcano. It needs certain geographic conditions, the right temperature, or it will never erupt. So I didn't enter the Academy with a book by Che Guevara under my arm, as some people allege, but I certainly came out with one. What happened during those four years? It would be good to stop here for a while.

PART II

FROM BARRACKS TO BARRACKS

(1971–1982)

VI

Cadet in Caracas

Problems with adapting – Difficulties of being left-handed
Abusive superiors – Discovering Caracas
Chicho Romero – Poor hillsides, rich suburbs
Living in Catia – The Andrés Bello Plan
Progressive officers – Being a soldier
At the tomb of 'Whiplash' Chávez
Singer, painter, master of ceremonies – Felipe Acosta Carlez
Acquiring leadership skills – Courses and readings
A subversive

You started at the Military Academy in August 1971, didn't you?
Yes, on 8 August, it was a Sunday. The boy who entered the Military Academy was an ordinary provincial lad, but one who had just spent five years in a regional capital – in a physically, intellectually, and even spiritually, demanding environment. I was a leader of my student group since I'd got among the best marks, and had even given private lessons to older boys, which was a challenge. They were five years of considerable achievements, but they only got me so far. When I landed in Caracas, I realized this was a defining moment for me. Within a few months, I changed my expectations and circumstances. First, I began to feel like a soldier, then I began

to discover politics and intellectual life, and breathe in a very exciting atmosphere.

How did your military education start?

The selection process in that first year was very strict. About two hundred candidates enrolled on 8 August 1971. However – after being confined to barracks for three months – by the following November, when we received our cadet's insignia, that number had dwindled to half.

Why was that?

Some couldn't stand the pace, physically or academically. Others failed the induction year subjects. First, there was a physical assessment and those who didn't make the grade had to leave. Every day our progress was plotted on an evaluation chart. And each week those with the lowest marks were sent home. We watched them leave. We'd got to know them, so it was sad. Two or three dropped out from my platoon, but we were a good platoon and the third- and fourth-year cadets, called *brigadieres*, helped us.

Did the cadets come from one social class in particular, or did they represent the diversity of Venezuelan society?

They were fairly representative, though the great majority came from the poorer sectors, from the working class and lower middle class. Historically it has always been that way, and it still is. The odd one would come from the upper classes, but they usually didn't fit in; the group would reject them, like a foreign body. The Navy was more aristocratic, but the Army has always recruited from the lower classes, and still does. The Air Force has always taken lower-class recruits, so has the National Guard.[1] The majority of Venezuelan officers in all four sectors come from the lower classes, but especially in the Army.

---

1   The Venezuelan Armed Forces traditionally consist of four parts: Army, Navy, Air Force and National Guard. The militia, a reserve unit complementing the national defence organizations, has recently been added to these four. The National Guard is the body essentially charged with maintaining public order, and also controls customs and excise.

In that sense, Venezuela is quite unusual. The Armed Forces are essentially an institution of the people, very different from the tradition of hereditary 'military castes' existing in other Latin American countries – in Chile, for example – where elite regiments are packed with the offspring of the upper classes. In Venezuela, doubtless because of the Bolivarian tradition, there is no social or racial discrimination preventing youngsters from disadvantaged classes from enrolling in the Military Academy.

That may be why the Venezuelan oligarchy feels a certain animosity towards the military. It is a traditional repugnance: the wealthy classes regard a barracks as home to the hoi polloi. The oligarchy don't address me as 'Mr President'; they say 'Lieutenant Colonel' . . . For them that means I'm a *gorila*, a military brute. They think we're inferior.

Traditionally, senior Venezuelan officers were educated first at the Academy and then abroad.

After the Academy came postgraduate degrees, most of which were obtained here in Venezuela, in our own universities. But a small group of officers, almost always the most privileged, went abroad, especially to the US. From my year, only one – a very intelligent guy, of course – went to West Point. A select few went to Europe; I almost went to Germany on a course when I was a captain.

Were the cadets all Venezuelan, or did they come from other countries as well?

Young men came from other countries. It was a tradition. There were Colombians, Dominicans, Panamanians, Bolivians . . . I remember one Colombian *brigadier* who is now one of his country's senior army officers.[2] One night, he came across me sleeping . . . Lights out was at nine o'clock but students were allowed to go on studying in the classrooms if they wanted to, till midnight at

---

2   In the context of the Bolivarian military schools, the rank of *brigadier* was given to fourth- or fifth-year cadets.

the latest. Despite being tired from the day's lessons, I always stayed until midnight to do an extra three hours.

You did those extra hours voluntarily?

Yes. I'd also write letters home or order my lecture notes. I love studying and learning. I've always been a compulsive student, reader, researcher. One of the things I miss most these days is not having time for it.

You were telling me that a Colombian brigadier found you sleeping...

That's right, his name was González, he was about twenty-five and in charge of the platoon of new recruits.[3] I thought he was going to punish me. He woke me saying, 'Recruit, what are you doing here at this time of night?' It was about three in the morning. Everyone else had left. They were allowed into the dormitories every half-hour. The guards would shout, 'All cadets turning in at eleven, stand in the corridor.' I usually stayed until midnight, the maximum time allowed. On that particular occasion I'd fallen asleep over my books; they'd even turned out the lights. The duty *brigadier* came in, saw a shape in the dark, and turned on the light. He recognized me immediately because I was in his platoon. 'What are you doing here at this time of night?' I didn't know what to say. In the end, he said, 'Congratulations, you fell asleep over your studies. You're a good candidate for cadet, but now get some rest.' I rushed off to bed.

For the first three months, you couldn't leave the Academy, could you?

No, you couldn't. We spent four weeks without going out or receiving visits. After that our families could come and see us at weekends. We still couldn't go out, but they could visit. On Friday nights, they'd show a film, which I loved. And on Saturdays and

---

3 Then a *brigadier*, General Óscar Enrique González Peña would go on to be commander-in-chief of the Colombian Army, 2008–2010.

Sundays, there were visits at pre-arranged times. We'd sit in the recreation room, listen to music, and just chat.

Did your parents come?
They did. My grandmother couldn't come that far; she was waiting for me in Barinas. When my mother saw me, she burst into tears because she thought I was too thin.

Why were you so thin?
I was naturally thin. And also because, although the food was good, the physical effort was considerable. I was like a skeleton. My mother was in tears when she visited, she said she wanted me to come home. There are photos of me looking really, really gaunt.

Did you have any other problems adapting to life in the Academy?
Actually, I did have a problem with one officer who was determined to call me 'Chávez the Cow'.

Why?
To insult me. He'd go, 'You're a cow!' A stupid thing to say. He'd shout, 'Cadet Chávez the Cow!' I didn't reply. One of the arbitrary punishments they went in for was to make you stand to attention on your head, i.e., head on the ground with legs straight up.

Did this kind of abuse happen often?
It wasn't allowed, but it did happen. Another problem I had was that being left-handed, I ate with my left hand. That wasn't tolerated. They wanted to teach us 'good table manners'. The first day in the canteen, I picked up my soup spoon with my left hand. The *brigadier* started shouting, 'Hey, new boy! Eat with your right!' But my right wrist wasn't very strong, so suddenly: 'Recruit, you messed the tablecloth! Wash it, now!' I had to stand up in front of everybody and take the tablecloth outside to wash. I scrubbed it in a pail in the baking sun, although for me this wasn't the torture it was supposed to be, because I grew up washing clothes, getting them down off the line and ironing them.

Being left-handed was also a problem when it came to using a rifle, wasn't it?

Yes. It was a big problem on the firing range. Why, because the rifle's cartridge ejection window was on the side away from the cheek, on the right of the rifle, so that when the cartridge was ejected it didn't hurt the marksman's face. I fired my first shot with my left hand, leaning the rifle butt on my left shoulder with my cheek against the ejection window, I nearly did myself a damage. The officer in charge said, 'Look, leftie, learn to shoot with your right, or it could cost you an eye.' So, I learned right-handed.

Good advice.

In this case, yes. There were no rifles for left-handers.

Was it hard for you to adapt?

It was hard. The first day was frantic, they gave us loads of vaccinations, cut our hair – I used to have an Afro – handed out uniforms, and sent us off on a run. An immediate change.

The next three months were very intense; you were forced to pass rigorous tests, train very hard and simulate guard duties. It was a completely different life. It reminded me of Vargas Llosa's novel, *The Time of the Hero*, set in a military school in Lima.[4] I remember waking up on the first day. Drums were beating at five in the morning, I thought it was an earthquake. 'What on earth's that?' I wondered, and started hurrying, getting dressed on the hoof, because in a couple of minutes we had to be standing to attention on the parade ground. After three months, we were solemnly awarded our insignia, our uniforms, and the rank of cadet, at a ceremony inspired by the ancient investiture of mediaeval knights. We were no longer candidate recruits, we had become cadets. It was a gala ceremony.

---

4   Mario Vargas Llosa, *The Time of the Hero* (1963), Faber and Faber, London, 1998. The original title is *La ciudad y los perros*, The City and the Dogs.

Were your families present?

Yes, my mum and dad came. I remember going out in Caracas that night, we stayed in a hotel in Sabana Grande, and ate in a little restaurant, practically a street stall. We didn't have much money. The following day, on Sunday, we went to the Plaza Miranda and took photos. We walked round the city all day, with me in my impeccable blue uniform, gloves and a cap. That night, I had to go back to the Academy.

What did you feel?

From day one, I realized how seduced I was by the Academy's patriotic symbols. I felt like a fish in water. Even today, when I go back to the Academy, I sense how I entered the womb of a second mother. It was like a mother to me! I'm a child of that Academy, that Alma Mater, that sacred precinct. A child of the Armed Forces! I was born there! You can be born several times. You're born from your mother's belly first, but you're born again when you see the light of ideas and consciousness. The Academy was where everything began. I was hooked on the symbolism. For me, the Academy was a blessing. That's the word, a blessing: because not only was it where I began to feel like a soldier, it was where I became politically motivated. That was a blessing for the Bolivarian process, and let's hope, for our country's sake, that history will absolve us.

What do you mean?

Look at those officers, majors, captains, lieutenants, sergeants, who were merely soldiers. I don't think my influence on them would have been the same. That is, we could not have broken the Pact of Punto Fijo, weak as it seemed in 1990, 1991 and 1992, if it had not been for that military movement that threw in its lot with the people. It was the spark – Lenin called it the '*iskra*', didn't he? – that ignited the prairie.

But independently of everything that happened and the role played by that young Bolivarian movement in 1992 and over the following twenty years, now, today [2009], if I were not a soldier, if I were a civilian president, it would have been difficult for me to have had the same influence over them. That particular context has been very important, and at the same time it has empowered the people at crucial moments, because they know that they have the backing of soldiers who are ready to give their all, in times of crisis like the ones we have been through . . . and those that are still to come.

Let's go back to those first months at the Academy. Did you miss your friends in Barinas?
At first, I did. But it was very much like when I left Sabaneta to study in Barinas, in the sense that when I came to Caracas, I didn't cut myself off from my previous life.

In Barinas, I kept my relationships, contacts and roots from my earlier life in Sabaneta. I don't just mean by going back to see my grandmother, I mean by not losing the spirit, the essence of the place, like a tree doesn't lose its root. The same thing happened when I came to Caracas. During my four years at the Academy, I stayed true to my roots, to Barinas, to my friends – although the sporty ones dispersed to other cities. Every time I went home, I'd go back to my local square as if nothing had changed. I'd take off my cadet's uniform and resume my place, with the same girl, the same friends, the same midnight masses with family at Christmas.[5]

You never stopped going back to Barinas?
Never. Whenever an occasion presented itself, the first thing I'd do was jump on the bus. Once there I'd slip back into the same ball games, the same discussions – now nourished by experience – the same social gatherings in the Noches de Hungría, the Rincón Mexicano, La Facultad. So, there was a continual retracing of steps. I think this made the process easier, it helped me a lot.

---

5   In the Venezuelan Llanos, it is Catholic tradition during Advent, 16–24 December, to go with family and friends to pre-dawn services called 'misa de aguinaldo' or 'de gallo'. Traditional music is played, some pieces based on European carols, both inside churches and with groups playing in the streets, sometimes accompanied by fireworks.

It kept you close to your roots.

And the old fed into the new. It was a sort of dialectical process of encounters and experiences that nurtured my roots during those four years. At the Academy, I wrote letters from the very first day of the first week of the first month. Many have been lost.

You wrote to your grandmother?

To my family, my friends, my grandmother . . . She kept all my letters in a little trunk. Writing every week is good discipline, even though it was imposed on us by the Academy. Perhaps they did it to see what we were writing. But, anyway, it was useful, it kept us in touch with our families and it forced us to write, because some lazy people don't like writing. Plus we received replies. I kept them all. We got photos of our girlfriends, friends, siblings, mothers, and we made albums or stored them in our lockers.

Did you have your own room?

No, there were dormitories for platoons of twenty or thirty cadets, where we each had our own little corner and locker.

You were a boy who'd grown up in the street, with all its freedoms. Didn't you feel constrained by the disciplined life of the Academy?

Well, school and sport had already been an excellent source of discipline for me, but on top of that I resolved voluntarily to change. I accepted the inevitability of change. Of course, I missed the freedom of that kid, in the street, in the wild, playing ball, at home, eating my grandmother's delicious food – and suddenly, there, it was canteen grub. The hardest part was those first three months. After that we were allowed to leave the Academy, and I started discovering Caracas.

Do you remember first arriving at the capital?

Perfectly. I came to Caracas by bus, a little scared. I was on my own. I'll never forget: as we drove down between the mountains, there was a bend in the road, the bus took the curve wide and, suddenly, there before us lay Caracas. The bus arrived at around five in the morning, having left Barinas the previous night. We came into the Nuevo Circo bus terminal, surrounded by indescribable chaos. In those days, Caracas had about 2 million inhabitants; now there are over 4 million, but even then the mountainsides were covered in shanty towns.

Were you surprised by the spectacle of all those shacks?
I didn't imagine Caracas like that, literally enclosed by a gigantic belt of poverty cascading down the hillsides. Later I understood it was the result of what technically is called the 'rural exodus', caused by decades of government policies that neglected the countryside. As oil gradually took over as Venezuela's main source of income, the countryside, which had previously cultivated – and exported – coffee, sugar, cacao and other farm products, was abandoned. The oil model destroyed almost all agricultural production. The rural economy collapsed, and hundreds of thousands of unemployed rural labourers – who had already lost their lands to the big land-owners – were forced to leave the countryside.

And emigrated en masse to Caracas.
Mostly to Caracas, but not only. There were no basic services in the pueblos, no secondary schools or clinics. I myself had to leave my native village to continue studying, although I didn't want to. And my brothers had to go to Mérida to university. If people needed medical attention, they had to go to Barquisimeto or Caracas. Rural society was totally neglected. When young men went off to do their military service in the big cities, and saw all the amenities that existed there, they tended not to go back to the villages where they had neither land nor work. They preferred living in shanty towns on the hillsides to returning to the neglected interior of the country. The result is that 80 per cent of Venezuela's population is concentrated on the narrow coastal stretch in the centre-north which is, to boot, very prone to earthquakes.

And no government ever thought of redressing this balance?
Presidente Jaime Lusinchi [1984–1989] tried something: he established some new towns in the interior. I visited one, Pueblo Bolívar, when I was a captain stationed in Elorza, near the Colombian border. It failed. They transferred rural labourers there more or less by force, without giving them any land, cattle or bank credits. It wasn't long before people started to leave again, to escape.

Have you thought of a solution yourself?
We placed this problem of Venezuela's population imbalance, the unequal relationship between city and countryside, at the heart of our plans from the start. One of the main aims of our revolution was to distribute Venezuelan land in a fairer, more harmonious way. We thought – and we still think – that we had to decentralize, reverse the migratory flow and encourage people to return to the interior and stimulate the rural economy. It's not an easy task. We have introduced an integral development plan for Venezuela. In the last ten years, the revolutionary government has recovered 2,800,000 hectares of uncultivated land and made it productive. We have provided people with land, houses, tools, microcredits, and courses on agronomy and agricultural economics. They also have schools, clinics, sports facilities and cultural activities. The idea is for these population centres to be sustainable, with running water, electricity, phone lines, television, internet, so that people can live a decent life – a better quality of life than many families have in the Caracas shanty towns.

Going back to your first impressions of Caracas, did it have a big impact on you?
Caracas made a huge impression. Firstly, the hustle and bustle . . . I was from a small town, Caracas was a hundred times bigger than Barinas, and that noisy multitude of people from all over, pedestrians running, cars hooting, motorbikes roaring . . . it gave me vertigo. I was scared to go out, even as far as the next corner. I had to get used to it. And I slowly adapted to that social dynamic.

I was astonished at the huge contrast between rich Caracas and poor Caracas. You'd never see such disparities in Barinas, and even less in Sabaneta. I was shocked when I discovered that mass of poverty, compared to the wealth and luxury of East Caracas. I never dreamed such unfathomable poverty could exist in Venezuela, one of the richest countries on the continent. I soon started wondering what kind of democracy this was, to so impoverish the majority and enrich a minority. It seemed to me unjust. And I soon realized that this incredibly unequal distribution of wealth was a powder keg waiting to explode.

Did you know anybody in Caracas?
I didn't have any immediate family, but my father had given me the address of a sort-of relative, *Chicho* Romero, the ex-husband of my mother's sister Joaquina. They had separated and he'd come to the capital. He'd been an army sergeant in the days of Pérez Jiménez. He liked baseball and he was – still is – very llanero, a raconteur and indefatigable talker. He'd been in jail a few years for being a courier for the guerrillas; someone had denounced him, there was no proof but they locked him up anyway.

When I arrived at the terminal that first day, I took a taxi and told the driver to go to Avenida Mohedano – I'll never forget – in La Castellana, an upper-middle-class housing complex, next to Altamira. Dawn was breaking, it was cold, I was wearing a light jacket of my father's. I got out at the address and walked around in the cold until seven o'clock. It was Sunday; the exam at the Academy was on Monday. I rang the bell and a black woman came out. I said, 'I'm looking for Mr *Chicho* Romero.' 'He's not here yet,' she answered, 'and I don't know if he's coming to work today.' 'But he does work here, doesn't he?' 'Yes,' she said, 'he's the family's chauffeur.' A rich family, then. 'Who are you?' she asked. 'A relative.' I still called him 'Uncle'. 'Ah! You're from Barinas?' She invited me in and gave me milky coffee. I waited for a long time. *Chicho* finally appeared, by chance in fact, because he had come to run an errand.

So he didn't know you were coming.
My father had told him, but he wasn't sure what day or what time. He looked after me very well. He drove me to a hotel in the family

car. They had several cars and two drivers. *Chicho* drove the car reserved for errands, shopping, and ferrying the children around. He took me on a tour round Caracas. We passed the Academy. 'Look,' he said, 'that's where you'll be studying.' He was pleased I wanted to be a soldier, because he'd been an NCO. The following day he picked me up at the hotel, took me to the Academy and came back to fetch me in the evening. Although he wasn't involved in politics, *Chicho* was a bit of a rebel. He came to visit me several times during the first three months we weren't allowed to leave the Academy, and he always left me a few coins.

But after three months you had permission to go out, didn't you?
Yes, we cadets got an ordinary pass to go out on Saturday afternoons and Sundays. In the last months of 1971, I'd go to *Chicho's* place. He lived in Colombia Street in Catia, in a very shabby house, more of a shack really: a room with a bed, a toilet, and a small living space.[6] He lived with a woman whose younger sister came to stay every now and again because she lived in La Guaira. I gradually dug myself in, and even had a relationship with the sister, I don't remember her name now . . .

You slept there on Saturday nights?
Well, it wasn't normally allowed. You were supposed to report back at midnight – they called us the 'Cinderellas' – unless you had a special pass. I began earning passes through sport, so I could sleep off base. I'd stay at *Chicho's* house. Sometimes he was working, so he wasn't even there and his lady would take care of me. *Chicho* got me some civilian clothes. I'd take off my uniform and she'd iron it. *Chicho* was always advising me, 'Look after your uniform!' He bought a plastic cover to protect it. 'You have to look impeccable.' And he'd tell his lady, 'Wash and iron his gloves, please.'

---

6   Catia is a huge district made up of several poor neighbourhoods in the east of Caracas.

Could cadets go out in civilian clothes?

No. It was forbidden. Unless you had special permission. If we were spotted in civvies, we were arrested, and if we did it again, we were expelled. It was serious. *Chicho* thought this a bad idea: 'How come they don't let you dress in civvies? That's backward thinking. Put civvies on, lad, no one will see you here.'

You broke the rules.

I liked being in uniform, but I'd change my clothes as soon as I got to *Chicho's*. Near his house, in the old Laguna de Catia area, there was a market, and at weekends people would come from all over. I'd tried Corn Flakes for the first time in the Academy, with milk, plantain and sugar. I liked it. So *Chicho* always bought it for my Sunday breakfast. Despite not being my blood relative, he was very fond of me. He'd say, 'Skinny, you need fattening up a bit.' I was always hungry and tired.

Did you ever go to the wealthy areas of Caracas?

Yes, I did. But not so often. For example, the Massey family from Sabaneta lived there. My father had given me the address of Dr Victor Massey. He worked in parliament, although he wasn't a politician; he was an advisor, or perhaps a lawyer, for the Acción Democrática party. I went to see him, waited for a while, then when he arrived, he invited me into his library. We talked for a time, his son was at the Academy too. He gave me a book – I still have it – an analysis of Bolívar's Angostura Address, published by Congress.

But the area you knew best was Catia?

Yes, Catia, a working-class area. Where *Chicho* lived everybody was poor . . . He was from the countryside, and he was poor too, even though he worked in a rich suburb. He began showing me around his patch. It wasn't prearranged, but this was his world and he was proud of me being a cadet, so he'd take me up the hillsides. 'Put your uniform on,' he say, 'we're going visiting. D'you remember "Birdy", that guy Víctor from Sabaneta?' I didn't remember. 'He works here, and lives in Kennedy.' Kennedy was right at the very top of the hill, in Lomas de Urdaneta, where people were even poorer. I'd go up there in my blue uniform, white gloves and cap, and we'd eat *mondongo* and drink beer. 'Take your jacket off!' ordered *Chicho*. 'You'll spill something down it.'

You could observe the lives of society's most vulnerable people.

Yes, the forgotten people. Although they lived dignified lives. Governments weren't interested in them. Walking over the hillside, I saw all that poverty, the sewers running down dark streets, the mountains of rubbish, the overcrowding, the street children with no shoes, the hunger, the beggars, the marginal, the excluded, the disinherited . . . The staggering inequality between the luxury of La Castellana and the deprivation and squalor of the hillsides began to affect me. I could see for myself what Alí Primera says in one of his political songs: 'The truth of Venezuela / is not at the Country Club / the truth is on the hillsides / with the people and their worries.'

Did you begin to open your eyes?

Faced with such a depressing social panorama, I began to be aware that something serious was going on, that the country wasn't working. In *Les Misérables*, Victor Hugo stated, 'Consciousness is simply the accumulation of science, that is, of knowledge.' The more knowledge you have of any phenomenon, the more conscious you become. That's why the world's tyrants have always wanted to keep their people in ignorance. Keeping them in ignorance is keeping them in unconsciousness. Bolívar said, 'We have been dominated more through ignorance than through force.' Someone who does not know is like someone who does not see. And what I saw on the Caracas hillsides made me indignant and my soul rebelled.

Did you know any other poor areas?

Yes, over the course of that first year, I extended my contacts with the poor of Caracas. As well as Catia, I got to know neighbourhoods inside and outside of Caracas. Another very crowded

neighbourhood was 23 de Enero [23 January].[7] A good friend, a
pitcher in the Rafael Martínez Morales Academy, lived in Tower 49
of the 23 de Enero superblocks, with his parents, sisters and brothers. We became friends, the Caracas hotshot and me the country
bumpkin. So, I got to know that area too. Another friend, José Luis
Vegas Rodríguez, lived in Lomas de Urdaneta in one of those gigantic tower blocks. I gradually got to socializing in the popular barrios,
among parties, friends, girls. And what I saw emphasized the
tremendous contrast between different sectors of the city. Because
poverty is one thing and extreme poverty is another. 'Poverty', said
Victor Hugo, 'is a dark room where you live badly, but beyond that
room lies another where you are in the most complete darkness,
completely black: that is extreme poverty.'

However, even there I found cheerful, welcoming, kind, honest,
hard-working people. I began to get to know them, notice the
conditions they lived in, and wonder, 'Where's the children's
school?' 'Where's the doctor?' Many children didn't go to school,
many sick people received no medical attention, or food. As poverty
grew, so did exasperation and anger, until the social explosion of 27
February 1989. People there often asked me, 'Aren't you afraid to
come here?' A cadet wasn't an everyday sight in the hillside shanty
towns.

Was it dangerous?
There was violence, no doubt about that. There's usually violence
where there is extreme poverty and hopelessness. Criminality
increases when the resort to violence or crime seems the only way to
supply basic needs. I'm not justifying it, I'm just telling it like it is.
And that happened in the opulent Venezuela of the 1970s, in the
midst of euphoria over the explosion of oil prices. How many fathers
had to steal bread to feed their children? How many girls had to sell
their bodies, prostituting themselves to help their families?

---

7   Formerly known as 2 December, after 2 December 1952, when Marcos Pérez
Jiménez took power. It was renamed 23 January to commemorate the date in 1958 when
Pérez Jiménez was overthrown.

But the violence is still continuing on those hillsides; people even say it has increased in the last few years.

Correct, the violence is still going on.[8] We are doing all we can to combat it, using a firm hand and a lot of resources. The insecurity curve is going down. The number of murders in Venezuela, for instance, fell by 4.14 per cent in 2009. In Catia, in the final months of 2009, thanks to the actions of the new Bolivarian National Police, the murder rate went down by 71.43 per cent. Of course, people still do not feel safe, but there are not the same social concerns as there were back then. Nowadays, no one resorts to violence because they're hungry, or can't get medical attention. No one prostitutes herself to feed her family.

Nowadays the causes are different: the main culprit is the drug traffic, and an abundant supply of arms, particularly from a neighbouring country that has been in a state of civil war for decades and in whose interest it could be to destabilize us. Not to mention the settling of accounts between rival gangs of young drug traffickers. I've no doubt that many of those criminal gangs are trained, financed, and supported by the Venezuelan bourgeoisie, and by our international enemies and their lackeys. The majority of victims are aged between sixteen and twenty-two. It wasn't like that when I was a cadet, murder rates were not that high. But there was still terrible violence, and even more so because, don't forget, the worst violence of all is the poverty, the impoverishment, imposed on people. Some were surprised to see me stroll through those shanty towns wearing my uniform.

Didn't any cadets live there?

Yes, like I said, some did live there, but they hardly ever went out in uniform. The Academy still had a rule that cadets didn't wear their uniform in 'dangerous places'. The hillsides were considered 'dangerous'; there had been urban guerrillas in Caracas, tactical combat

---

8 According to a 2009 study by the Mexican NGO Civil Council for Public Safety (CCSP), Caracas was one of the most violent cities in Latin America (96 murders per annum for every 100,000 inhabitants). Source: Radio Netherlands, 7 September 2009.

units. The Academy thought things like going on a bus were too risky for cadets. We had to take taxis.

Who was in charge of the Academy?

The director of the Academy was General Jorge Osorio García. He was from the Andes. He was a good general, very hands-on; he'd appear unannounced on the parade ground, or in the canteen ... My year – the Simón Bolívar – was to all intents and purposes the guinea-pig year for the Andrés Bello Study Plan.[9] We were the first intake of students for this new project which would give the Military Academy university status, or at least make it an Institute which required much higher academic entry standards than those for the previous generations of students. The Academy now had links with other centres of higher education: the Simón Bolívar University, the Central University of Venezuela (UCV), the Santa María University, the Caracas Pedagogic Institute ... This enabled us to establish relationships with other university students in matters of sport, culture, theatre and so on.

Which helped you, I imagine, to get out of that very introspective military environment?

Yes, it was very enriching. It widened our horizons and improved our professional education considerably. The previous Military School had produced students with secondary-school qualifications, whereas in the new Academy, we entered with those qualifications and left with a degree in Military Arts and Sciences. The political context was totally different. These were the 1970s, a very important decade in Venezuela. Rafael Caldera was president, and fought a very hard electoral campaign in the December 1973 elections, which he lost to Carlos Andrés Pérez.

---

9 See Rhony Rafael Pedroza Aguilar and Juan Francisco Escalona Camargo, *Influencia que tuvo la Academia Militar de Venezuela en la formación del Teniente Coronel Rafael Chávez Frías, comandante de la rebelión militar del 4 de febrero de 1992*, especially Chapter III, 'Plan de Estudio Andrés Bello'. Special publication of Venezuela Military Academy, Academic Division, Caracas, March 2008.

What was the long-term aim of these reforms?

This new Venezuelan Integral Educative Military Plan, as I told you, began in 1969–1970 under President Caldera.[10] It was the second big military reform of the twentieth century. The first was implemented by General Cipriano Castro in 1904, and Caldera introduced the second during the first attempts to pacify the guerrillas, but hard-line sectors of the army were opposed to pacification; the same is happening now [2009] in Colombia.

They wanted to wipe out the guerrillas.

Correct. You have to see the reforms in that context. Don't forget – credit where credit is due – Dr Rafael Caldera was an intellectual. He'd had a first-class intellectual training. He was a university professor, had written several books, and was above average intelligence for a traditional politician. He was a cultured man and a great admirer of Andrés Bello, of course.[11] What I'm trying to say is that this reform could not have been achieved without . . .

A political strategy.

Right, because although Caldera belonged to the conservative Christian Democrat political movement, Copei, he was determined to bring the guerrilla war to an end through a peace agreement. That is, he favoured a progressive option, rather than the retrograde solutions of hard-line military officers on the right and extreme right. Caldera took his cue from the progressive officers within the Armed Forces.

In the Academy itself – I can vouch for this because I was there – there was considerable resistance to the changes from more senior

---

10 The Integral Educative Military Plan for Officer Training Schools had different names according to the various institutes. In the Military Academy it was called the Andrés Bello Plan; in the School for Officer Training of the Cooperative Armed Forces (Efocac, National Guard), the Simón Rodríguez Plan; in the Aviation School, the Manuel Ríos Plan; and in the Navy, the José María Vargas Plan.

11 Andrés Bello (1781–1865), eminent Venezuelan humanist, philologist, educator and jurist who spent part of his career in Santiago de Chile. He was the author, among other important works, of *Spanish Language Grammar and Principles of Peoples' Rights.*

officers and some NCOs. But they had to give way to the impetus of a group of progressive officers, headed by the Academy's director, General Osorio. They were progressive in the sense that they allowed us to read a range of texts, and taught us Development Theory, which included views that diverged from traditional right-wing or extreme right-wing theories. It was this context that gave rise to the educative-military reforms of the Andrés Bello Plan. And I'm sure the impulse came from Caldera, who almost certainly chose to name it after Andrés Bello. What was clear was the desire to provide officers with a better level of education, both culturally and academically, and raise the level of the Venezuelan armed forces as a whole.

Were you aware that the officers teaching you were progressives?
Yes, I was educated enough, or rather, politically sensitive enough to see that they were. That first year, I began to notice. Because, apart from our lessons, there were seminars on topics that seemed to me quite daring for an institution like that. Men of considerable intellect, civilian and military, came to speak to us, and they unquestionably opened our minds. There was total freedom of discussion around historical, social and economic themes; there was no dogmatism, or at least everything could be discussed, debated and challenged.

Who organized those seminars?
Some of the officers on the staff, let's see who I remember . . . As well as General Osorio, there was the deputy director, Colonel Rojas Araujo, who had a PhD in history; Commander Betancourt Infante, another excellent history teacher; Lieutenant Pompeyo Torrealba, Captain Ismael Carrasquero Zavala and especially General Jacinto Pérez Arcay, one of those philosophers and teachers you remember all your life, and who lit the Bolivarian flame in me. I've always said he was responsible for my second birth. He had these books and writings that I devoured . . . Books that were ideas, power, fuel for the ideological battle. Because a just idea can win battles. A soldier has to be fired by ideas. Those officers belonged to the tendency within the army that had been responsible for the fall of Pérez Jiménez, and they were unhappy about the current situation in Venezuela.

Was that in 1971?

Yes, my first year. Even though the crisis in the country had not yet reached its peak, there was a diffuse current of discontent. I picked up on it gradually. Anyway, the staff of the Academy included this small group of intelligent, thoughtful officers who were aware of the general social unrest and had a critical theory about what was going on and how it should be resolved. The proof is that they subsequently maintained a very close relationship with us.

Wasn't it odd that the government entrusted such a huge respon-
sibility to those particular officers? Putting them in the Academy
to form the new military cadres?

Because they were the best, the most brilliant. The government took troop commands away from them and assigned what was certainly a very difficult task. But it was a double-edged sword, because while they were undoubtedly brilliant, they were disaffected. There was an underlying discontent which slowly came to the surface in different ways, and was transmitted to the cadets.

Was military service obligatory at the time?

Yes, it was. But the law was never enforced. Despite there being sanctions, the sons of the wealthy were never called up. The poor did military service; sometimes they were practically rounded up like cattle, in police raids on deprived neighbourhoods, hogtied and carted off to the barracks. There was no real willingness to serve. I don't remember a single soldier who had gone voluntarily, it was forced recruitment.

Is it a professional army now?

No, it's not professional. But we've made it compulsory again, truly compulsory for everyone, although for a shorter period.[12]

---

12   In October 2009, the Venezuelan government reformed the Armed Forces Law to include the Military Service Law which determined that all Venezuelans between eighteen and sixty years old must serve a minimum one year's military service.

Did you enjoy the purely military aspects?

I began studying the science of war, military science, and I liked it. I've always had a passion for military history: Alexander the Great, Scipio Africanus, Hannibal, Julius Caesar, Napoleon – one of the greatest captains in history – Bolívar – a magnificent warrior and a strategic genius – Clausewitz, one of the great theoreticians of warfare. And Mao . . .

Did you read Mao Zedong?

Yes, I read him quite a lot. His *Little Red Book* of sayings and speeches was doing the rounds at the time.[13] One of his sayings had a great impact on me: 'Weapons are an important factor in war, but not the decisive one. It is people, not things, that are decisive. The contest of strength is not only determined by military and economic power, but also by human resources and morale. Military and economic power is necessarily wielded by the people.' It was a revelation: the important thing in war, declared Mao, is people and morale, not weapons of war. He also said that the Army must feel it belongs with the people, like a fish in water. And the basis of all victories lies in the union of the Army and the people, a civilian–military alliance.

And did you read Bolívar as well?

Obviously, there was a study group on Bolívar. After all, our class was called Simón Bolívar II. We were given a book called *Seven Essential Documents*, by Simón Bolívar, which we had to study and analyse.[14] I'd ask Pérez Arcay a lot of questions. And from that point

---

13   Mao Zedong (1893–1976) was then the president of China and the Chinese Communist Party. His *Little Red Book* was first published in 1964. Translation of quotes from his Selected Works is by AW.

14   Simón Bolívar, *Siete documentos esenciales*, introduced by José Luis Salcedo-Bastardo, Presidency of the Republic, Caracas, 1973. It includes: Cartagena Manifesto (15 December 1812); Carúpano Manifesto (15 December 1812); Jamaica Letter (6 September 1815); Angostura Address (15 February 1819), Message to the Bolivian Congress (25 May 1826); Message to the Ocaña Convention (29 February 1828); Message to the Colombian Congress (20 January 1830).

my admiration for Simón Bolívar grew and grew. He was a man who was born rich, he belonged to the bourgeoisie of his day, he was a landowner, but along the way he became part of the proletariat, spending his later life among the poor, ending up like Christ, crucified, doing what he thought was right.

That's how I became a little Bolivarian. I read his writings, learned his words by heart: 'Let us behave rightly, and let time work miracles.' Each week we'd sing patriotic songs with the military band, and I always enjoyed singing. I love the Army Hymn, which begins, 'Forward, men of valour / into the wild fray of battle / heads held high for the *Patria* / displaying strength and courage.' It's a beautiful hymn of the people.

Who composed it?

Inocente Carreño, a great contemporary Venezuelan composer.[15] That music, those patriotic anthems . . . the idea of being in the military began to inspire me, and I soon began to feel like a soldier.

But you'd wanted to be a pitcher . . . You said you'd enrolled at the Academy because it would allow you to achieve your aim of becoming a professional baseball player.

That's right, but the Academy changed my life, it had a 'transfigurative' effect. Even though I was, of course, the same person who'd wanted to be a painter and still did, and the same person who wanted to be a baseball player and still did, playing in the Academy team in the university stadium . . . Indeed I felt fulfilled. I'd achieved my dreams, I didn't feel in any way frustrated, but the Academy opened up a new horizon, now I was a cadet, a soldier, I was going to graduate with the first class of soldiers who had a university degree. So, gradually, the idea of being a professional baseball player faded into the background. Three months after enrolling in the Academy, when they presented me with my insignia, I already had a new project, I'd taken my decision: to be a soldier.

---

15 'Venezuelan Armed Forces Hymn' (1962), music by Inocente Carreño, words by Juan Angel Mogollón.

You reneged on your promise to follow in the footsteps of Látigo Chávez . . .

Yes, I no longer longed to be the new *Látigo* and play in the major leagues. Now I wanted to be a soldier. It did cause me some remorse. I had a lump in my throat when I thought about the promise I'd made to *Látigo*. I was abandoning him, and it made me feel bad. Until one day, I left the Academy in my blue uniform and walked alone to the old Southern General Cemetery in Caracas. I'd read somewhere that *Látigo* Chávez was buried there. I found his grave. I prayed and asked him to forgive me. I talked to his gravestone and the spirit that surrounded it. I explained I was no longer going to follow in his footsteps: 'I'm sorry, Isaías, I'm going to be a soldier.' When I left the cemetery, I felt liberated.

You became a soldier, but you hadn't any real military experience.

No, none at all, but I began to enjoy the actual military part. For instance, I liked using a rifle, even though I was left-handed and it was more complicated for me. Some fellow students found it hard, but I didn't, I picked it up fast. You had to learn the parts of the gun, how to dismantle it and put it together with your eyes closed. I got ten out of ten and one of the instructors held me up as an example. I don't remember ever being held up as a bad example, or being punished for doing something wrong, or for being lazy. No, I very quickly fell into step with the beat of the military drum. And I loved the theory of individual combat.

Is there a course for that?

Indeed. The rules of individual combat. I remember perfectly, it was about the best combatant technique. We were told: keep calm, observe from your position, remain silent . . . I really liked it. We'd put on battle dress, the big boots . . . I embraced all that very quickly, I felt like a soldier in a flash.

You'd found your vocation.

I reckon I had. Though I first got myself noticed by singing. I was like a walking jukebox. 'Sing us another, recruit!' the *brigadier* would shout, and I would sing more *rancheras*. I even invented one about a *brigadier* called Rosales Caña. He'd say, 'Recruits, do what I say, not what I do', because while he was very smart, he was physically lazy and the boys had nicknamed him, ironically, 'Lightning'. 'Sing the one about *El Rayo!*' the Colombian *brigadier* would order and, rifle on shoulder, I'd begin to sing it, but changing the words. Marching with us, *brigadier* Rosales Caña, tight-lipped, would whisper, 'Recruit, come and see me as soon as we arrive!' But he didn't do anything, I'd stand to attention for a while, nothing else. He was nice; and deep down, he liked that song.

So, you started to get noticed.

Yes, at least by the new recruits. I swam like a fish in water in that Academy. I don't know why, but it felt like home. I enjoyed myself more than I ever had. We were all young boys, our trainers were only two or three years older than us. And within a few months, we llaneros had formed a group. First with José Angarita whom I told you about, my friend from school in Barinas who had enrolled in the Academy a year before me. There was also this blond lad Felipe Acosta Carlez, from the state of Guárico.[16] He was older than me, almost twenty, and had even done a year at university before choosing the Academy. He was very impulsive, and had a lot of initiative. He soon became a leader. We called him 'Tarzan' because of his strong build. Once I saw him fight ten men, he was hard to beat.

In the dormitory, I ended up in the next bed to him, our wooden cubicles side by side. His first words to me were: 'Hey, kid' – that's what he called me – 'Kid, where are you from?' 'Barinas.' 'Ah, so you're a llanero. Come here, give me your hand.' And he took my hand, but clasped it so hard I thought my bones would break . . . We became great friends.

---

16   Felipe Antonio Acosta Carlez graduated from the Military Academy in July 1975. He was one of the founders of the Movimiento Bolivariano Revolucionario-200 (MBR-200). He swore an oath in the shade of the Samán de Güere tree on 17 November 1982, with Hugo Chávez, Jesús Urdaneta Hernández and Francisco Arias Cárdenas. He died during the Caracazo on 28 February 1989. Hugo Chávez wrote a 'Poem to Felipe Acosta Carlez'.

Did having friends from the Llanos help you fit in better?
Undoubtedly. I first made friends among the llaneros, but then after the first three months, I had friends from all over. As I said, I adapted quickly. I even got used to cleaning the floor, a task imposed on us. Every morning we made our beds and scrubbed the toilet. Lots of cadets complained. I, on the other hand, flew along, used as I was to cleaning our house as a kid, collecting the rubbish, watering the plants. I had no problem with it, but the lads from Caracas, used to cramped apartments, found it tough. Others were just lazy.

There was a good atmosphere.
Yes, excellent. I felt pretty good. What turned out to be really useful was my talent for drawing and painting.

How was that any use in a Military Academy?
Well, don't forget that drawing and painting had been obligatory subjects in the Military Academies for a long time. Art was taught throughout Europe from the eighteenth century, because that was how young officers learned the concept of perspective, something that was essential in modern warfare, especially for the artillery.

In our Academy, there was a weekly competition for the best notice boards, which at that time were like big blackboards in the communal dormitories of each platoon. It was where all the lists, news bulletins, etc., were posted. And our platoon was getting recognition for the best notice board. I wasn't the only one who could draw, but I was good at designing it. For example, if it was 'Academy Week', I'd draw a bust of the cadet, I'd write words round it, and arrange other drawings. And the upshot was that the platoon began to shine . . . and I began to gain the respect of my superiors. In addition, that first year, I also won the prize for the best Christmas card.

You made Christmas cards?
Yes, every platoon had to design at least one, and a jury chose the best. I did a composition reflecting the Academy itself, with the façade and a Christmas tree; it was very nice. Mine was chosen from

among all the platoon, and it went on to win the contest against all
the cadets in the whole battalion. I remember we were called out to
the parade ground, it was December, and the captain called my
name – a captain was already someone important for me – 'Cadet
Chávez!' I ran up, worried, asking myself, 'What can I have done?'
I was received by the captain, the company commander, name of
Zerpa, who said, 'Congratulations, cadet. You won the prize, so our
whole company won.' Our platoon went wild with joy. Captain
Zerpa asked me, 'What would you like as a prize, cadet? A typewriter?' Everyone had to have a typewriter, because there was a
typing course. If I can write on a computer now, it's because I did
that typing course. 'Or would you prefer a weekend pass?' I didn't
hesitate. 'A weekend pass, Captain!' I went to Barinas, they paid the
bus fare. And to cap it all, they sent my card round to all the families as the official cadets' Christmas card that year. Just imagine it!
And underneath was printed: Chávez.

**So, you became even better known in the Academy thanks to your
artistic talents?**
That's right. A combination of all the skills I'd acquired in my former
life: domestic tasks, singing, poetry, painting, baseball . . . when they
were all displayed, they all helped me to make my mark. There were
cultural activities every Thursday afternoon: so-called 'complemen-
tary activities', all voluntary. I signed on for painting, of course, and
I made friends with the art teacher, a civilian, an old guy, quite short,
called Quintanillo Ponce, he's dead now, a very good painter, and a
good poet.[17] We painted pictures and held exhibitions.

**All that artistic activity in the Military Academy? It's hard to
imagine officers receiving that kind of exquisite training.**
You don't know the military very well, then – only through caricatures and distortions. In fact there was a wide range of artistic

---

17 Luis Felipe Quintanilla Ponce (1922–1988), artist, painter, sculptor, musician
and teacher. He painted realistic, especially Andean landscapes, and a variety of other
themes. The theatre in the Military Academy was named after him posthumously.

activity, and I was eager to take advantage of it. After three months, we were dispersed. I was lucky to be assigned to a good platoon, with cadets from different years. We had a very clever *brigadier* called Rojas Díaz, who later became an engineer. We also had Ramón Carrizales, a second-year cadet, and Francisco Arias Cárdenas. And not long after that, I joined a group of cadets in the newsroom.[18]

The newsroom?

Yes, it was a special group who produced the division newsletter, several sheets which we wrote and published ourselves. The newsroom notice board changed weekly. I was the designer. And it meant I could extend my field of activities, I had access to the captain's office. This was not at all usual for a new recruit, but I was allowed. And in December, for instance, the newsroom was responsible for organizing the Nativity scene, and I was a dab hand at that, I did drawings of the Baby Jesus, Three Kings and Star of Bethlehem, and made them in polystyrene.

I was also included in a team of cadets who prepared special cultural and artistic events. We made all sorts of decorative objects. We didn't have a lot of materials or resources, but we improvised and got things done. I applied the thinking of Frederick the Great: 'A man puts his heart into what he does, finds resources where the incompetent give up.'[19] Once we made a gigantic Christmas tree. We put it up outside, in front of the Academy building. We painted the decorations, adorned the tree, and put a big star on top. Then we ran an electric cable and reflectors through it, and at night it shone and glittered in the breeze. In my fourth year, I'd already become official master of ceremonies for the Queen of the Academy beauty pageant.

---

18   Ramón Carrizales (1952–), vice president of Venezuela from January 2008 to January 2010. He was elected governor of the state of Apure for the period 2013–2017.

19   Frederick II the Great (1712–1786), king of Prussia, the epitome of eighteenth-century Enlightened Despotism. Known as the 'Philosopher King', he was also a great military leader and made Prussia into a military power.

There was a Queen of the Academy pageant? Were there women there?

No, but the families came, and they brought their sisters, cousins, friends, etc. There were some very pretty girls. Everybody chose their queens and I ended up being the master of ceremonies for the event. The *brigadiers* and subalterns accompanied the candidates, two or three beautiful girls each. I was just the MC.

Who chose the Queen? The cadets?

No. There was a jury made up of an officer, the general's wife, teachers at the school and some other civilians. Sometimes other beauty queens were invited. I remember that one year we invited a Miss Venezuela, and she was a member of the jury.

And the winner was crowned Miss Military Academy?

No, she was the Queen. Queen of the Military Academy. There was even one girl, Maritza Sayalero, who became a good friend of ours, because after being elected Queen of the Academy, she went on to be Miss Universe, no less. I had the microphone and compered the whole ceremony. I didn't have stage fright or anything; I carried the Academy's big public fiesta off quite naturally. And the general even called me over to congratulate me: 'Congratulations, cadet, for being such a good compere.'

You were practising for Aló Presidente . . .

You could say that . . . [laughter]. That experience of compering and communicating stood me in good stead. It was useful when I took on leadership roles. I became accustomed to handling a microphone, I learned how to talk to large and diverse audiences, without getting stressed or boring them too much. I grew in self-confidence, confidence in my ability to communicate, rouse an audience, transmit ideas and information. The young man who returned to Barinas as a second lieutenant in July 1975 was very different – with the same values, of course – from the one who had left four years earlier. I had matured, I'd undergone an enormous change. I now had a political vision, which had germinated there, in the Military

Academy. My friends were surprised at the change, at my metamorphosis. Although I was still the same person, my development and transformation were spectacular.

Was that also due to the quality of the courses you took?

Partly, no doubt. The level was excellent, especially in the sciences. We were given an introductory science course that enhanced my personal capacity for reflection, abstraction, analysis and synthesis. Apart from chemistry and physics, we studied Introduction to Sociology, Introduction to Law, Constitutional Law, Introduction to Economics, Introduction to Politics, Universal History, History of Political Ideas . . . It was basic knowledge, very elemental, but to me it seemed extraordinary.

And military theory?

Obviously, we had courses on military theory and strategy, and on the history of war. I loved those subjects, I didn't even have to be asked to read Von Clausewitz, not to mention Bolívar. I also discovered the fascinating military memoirs of José Antonio Páez, victor of the battle of Queseras del Medio [1819], and the works of Napoleon and Mao Zedong.[20] All the nuances in these works were revealed to us thanks to the excellence and dedication of the Academy's teachers, who took the new Andrés Bello study project very seriously. We had economists, lawyers and engineers teaching us, as well as military men.

So the quality of the teaching was very high?

Yes. As I said, I was taught by Jacinto Pérez Arcay, author of several books on the Federal War. His *Consequences of the Federal War* had quite a left-wing slant.[21] He explained to us about Ezequiel Zamora and I was completely bowled over. Another left-wing teacher was Colonel Medina Rubio, who taught economic history. One day, he

---

20   José Antonio Páez, *Autobiografía*, Ediciones Antártida, Caracas, 1945.

21   See Jacinto Pérez Arcay, *La Guerra Federal. Consecuencias*, Central Office of Information, Caracas, 1977.

told us quite clearly: 'By the year 2000, there will be democratic socialism in Venezuela.' I made a note of it, and afterwards I introduced myself in the corridor and asked, 'Colonel, what did you mean by that?'

A visionary?

A visionary for sure. He was a man of the Left, who along with Pérez Arcay and other officers formed the progressive wing of the Academy. He subsequently resigned and joined the MAS. Later still, in 1998, he was part of my campaign team when we won the elections. By the way, did I mention that the Academy had an excellent library?

Apart from your textbooks, what did you read?

In the Academy library, I read mostly Bolívar: his texts, his correspondence, analyses of his thought, biographies about him. And also, in 1974 and 1975, when I used to go out at weekends more, I began mixing with university students quite a bit. I'd to go to a bar called El Águila in Los Chaguaramos, there was always some revolutionary discussion going on, and some very pretty waitresses – from Apure, of course. So I had a dual motive, girls and politics. I attended courses at the university as well.

And these students accepted you, a soldier, without reservation?

We did have a few run-ins. When I went to the university, I'd break the Academy rule and go out of uniform, in civvies. And there I'd debate with student groups, basing our opinions on things we'd read, and some of them confronted me: 'You're a soldier, what do you know?' A student once called me a *gusano* [worm]. 'Don't be offensive,' I answered and we almost came to blows. That's what they called soldiers, *gusanos*. I didn't understand why.

We also had discussions at the home of our much loved and sadly missed friend, Doña Carmen Daza from Apure. I'd go round at weekends, I'd get my clothes washed and there was also a little room where I could hang my blue uniform. Her son, Enrique Daza – he's dead now – was left-wing and although he was never in party politics, we'd talk a lot. He gave me the work of that great revolutionary Vladimir Ilyich Lenin, *The State and Revolution*, which provoked a big debate on whether the state had to be eliminated or not. Lenin said, 'The bourgeois state will wither away,' and we'd argue about that. Then I read Lenin's *What Is to Be Done?*, a seminal text that's quickly read. At the same time I read José Martí, and from time to time José Carlos Mariátegui, who wasn't very well known.[22] So, I slowly got myself into circles outside the Academy.

Were politics beginning to interest you?

I grew passionate about political science. In the Academy we used a book by Walter Montenegro, *Introduction to Politico-Economic Doctrines*.[23] And I also started collecting books for myself, on economics, sociology, and politics. I'd go into the centre of Caracas where they sell second-hand books very cheaply. There I bought an old but great book which I still have: *Economía y subversión*, selected essays by John Kenneth Galbraith, which helped me enormously to understand about the economy. In the introduction, Galbraith says the following: 'This essay maintains that the proof of economic success is not the quantity of goods we produce, but what we do to make life tolerable or agreeable.' In my modest opinion, Galbraith is one of the twentieth century's top essayists on economy and society. We cannot say he is a socialist thinker, but he is a progressive, a profound humanist. I subsequently read *The New Industrial State*. What a book! And I recently read his last work, his intellectual legacy, *The Economics of Innocent Fraud*.

---

22   José Julián Martí Pérez (1853–95), Cuban patriot, poet, political thinker and philosopher. Through his journalistic writings he became a figurehead in the fight against Spanish colonialism and also flagged up the threat of US expansionism. He is also an important figure in Latin American literature.

José Carlos Mariátegui (1894–1930), Peruvian writer, philosopher, journalist, considered one of the most influential socialist thinkers in Latin America, author of *Siete ensayos de interpretación de la realidad peruana* (1928)

23   Walter Montenegro, *Introducción a las doctrinas politico-económicas*, Fondo de Cultura Económica, Mexico DF, 1956.

Any other authors you discovered?

On another occasion, I bought a book that struck me as being important – *Evolution, Marxism and Christianity: Studies in the Teilhardian Synthesis*.[24] Fascinating. It demonstrated that Marxism and Christianity could go hand in hand, and I started discussing this with other people.

Had someone told you about Teilhard de Chardin?

No, no one, not at all, but I was intrigued by the title. That is, I'd begun to be politically motivated, not to say *highly* motivated politically. And this came from those conversations at early stages of my life in the Noches de Hungría bar in Barinas, from everything I'd read, and from what I'd seen of the scandalous inequalities in Caracas. I began to get in touch with various young people who were active in politics, and now felt drawn to politics, to the Left, to left-wing ideas. No doubt about it. I had a sense of justice, a sense of the natural balance of society, and I realized that being left-wing means seeking justice, social justice. I'd always been concerned with that, because of my experience as a poor, working child, and because of the social doctrine of the church. A desire for a just world – that was deeply rooted in me.

In what way did the Academy provide new elements to strengthen that conviction?

Well, it didn't, rather the opposite. Because while, on the one hand, there were some progressive teachers, on the other, they tried to eradicate such ideas and brainwash me. The IV Republic said, 'Soldiers should be apolitical!' They even wanted to take away our right to think! I always balked at that. I remember civilian and military instructors being brought in from outside to give some downright political lectures, some of which were supposed to put us on

---

24 Claude Cuénot et al., *Evolution, Marxism and Christianity: Studies in the Teilhardian Synthesis*, Garnstone Press, London, 1967. Essays on the views on the French Jesuit Pierre Teilhard de Chardin (1881–1955), philosopher and palaeontologist who linked science and religion.

our guard against Marxism and left-wing ideas. They talked about the horrors of socialism and the advantages of the capitalist model. According to them, Marxism–Leninism was the ideology of the Devil. But my reaction was to be increasingly drawn to those ideas.

In a spirit of contradiction?

Yes, but also because of my social origins, because I remembered my childhood in Sabaneta . . . The tremendous inequalities existing in Caracas, the emaciated children I'd see in the countryside when we went on manoeuvres, my desire for social justice, for equality, for freedom . . . One day, I realized where I was. I was in the training centre of an army that had confronted a group of idealists in the mountains who were fighting for a just cause: social justice. And I began to feel here inside, in my heart, a big contradiction . . . I resolved the dilemma the day I told myself, 'I'm a subversive.'

7

Young Officer

A cadet's diary – In Che Guevara's skin
Going into politics – Visit to Peru
Velasco Alvarado – Omar Torrijos – Juan José Torres
The army and the people – Theory of leadership
José Vicente Rangel – Farewell to the Academy
Back to Barinas – Baptism in a whorehouse
On the Colombian border – Ilich Ramírez, 'Carlos'
Head of Recruitment – Columnist in *El Espacio*
Political discussions in the Noches de Hungría
Role of individuals in history
Rehearsal for the Plan Bolívar 2000 – Nancy

Do you remember your final years at the Military Academy?
Very well. Because from the second year, in 1972, I began jotting
down everything I did, with occasional comments . . . Every year
I'd buy my little diary, and fill it in every day. I never missed a day.
I kept up the habit when I was a second lieutenant, a lieutenant and
a captain. In the first year, however, when I was new, I didn't have
time. Sadly some of my notes have disappeared. They'll reappear
one day.

Were they lost or confiscated?

The night of our uprising [4 February 1992], the intelligence services ransacked my house. They took everything, including my uniforms. I even had piles of old sports magazines. I'd been buying the two main ones, *Sport Gráfico* and *Venezuela Gráfico*, since I was a cadet. I was mad about sport, especially baseball. Now I've switched allegiance to football and volleyball. There were also two very good political magazines, each with its own perspective. One was *Zeta*, which is still going; it used to be a serious magazine but now it's just a rag. The editor then was Rafael Poleo, the same Poleo who now lives in Miami.[1] The other side of the coin, *Resumen*, was edited by Jorge Olavarría, a man of the bourgeoisie but also a very serious intellectual, who at one stage held some interesting views.[2] He was close to Alfredo Maneiro, the founder and leader of La Causa R. I knew Olavarría well.[3] He visited me in prison after 4 February [1992], and after I was released [26 March 1994] I went to his home several times. He was a friend.

Many friends from those days are now in the opposition, because they were always bourgeois politicians. Olavarría was a very intelligent man, and in the early 1980s, Alfredo Maneiro made a tactical alliance with him, even putting him up as presidential candidate for La Causa R in 1982. During the campaign, however, Maneiro died prematurely.

Let's go back to what you were saying about keeping a diary when you were in the Academy . . .

Yes. The pages of my diary I've preserved – thanks to my friend Herma Marksman who typed them out, although the originals still exist – begin in September 1974, when I was in my fourth year at

---

1   Rafael Poleo (1937–), journalist, editor and owner of the newspaper *El Nuevo País* and the magazine *Zeta*. In 2008 he went to live in Florida.

2   Jorge Olavarría (1933–2005), politician, lawyer, journalist and historian who supported Hugo Chávez in his first electoral campaign of 1998, but defected to the opposition from 1999, although he criticized the petrol coup of 2002–2003 and the biased attitude of the media.

3   Alfredo Maneiro (1937–1982), politician, communist guerrilla in the 1960s. He taught at the Communications School of the Central University of Venezuela, and founded the workers' party La Causa Radical.

the Academy and had just become a subaltern.[4] Herma's a history professor and a good researcher; she's disciplined, and very methodical with documents. And this is the result. All nicely classified by date and subject.

It begins like this: 'Fort Guaicaipuro, Wednesday 11 September 1974'. Exactly a year after Pinochet's coup against Salvador Allende in Chile. I wrote, 'After a twelve-kilometre march, we pitched camp in a wooded area. I put up my tent with Ordóñez Montero' – a *compañero* who was nicknamed 'Repellent' because he was so haughty. 'I've been made commander of the first platoon. In the afternoon, Ordóñez and I gave instructions to purify the water and check the electric generators; it all went quite well, and I made some arrows and signs to facilitate vehicle circulation.' The officers would use me to make signs, traffic signals, etc., because, as I said, I was good at painting and I liked our camp looking neat. 'Tonight I'm on third watch. I've decided to write a diary about this camp with this year's new recruits. It's raining lightly. Am very tired. Everybody is asleep. Silence in the camp.'

Friday 13 September, there's one detail I want to flag up: 'Lieutenant Serrano Zapata assigned me to give the new recruits the preliminary theoretical training. Afterwards, I set up a role-play, with myself in the role of Comandante Ernesto Che Guevara.'

In other words you had to play the baddy . . .

Yes, I was the baddy, the 'insurgent' . . . It says a lot about how they saw me at that stage in the Academy. At the same time this diary, written when I was twenty years old, already showed social concerns, we could almost say, pre-revolutionary concerns. We even built a fake guerrilla camp where we sang protest songs. I wrote: 'I had a whale of a time, I'm hoarse from belting out, now writing on a

---

4   Herma Marksman (1949–), Venezuelan historian, met Hugo Chávez in 1984, and had an affair with him until 1993. She was in the Movimiento Bolivariano Revolucionario (MBR-200) and took part in the conspiracy and uprising of 4 February 1992. She published her version of their relationship, claiming 'Chávez used me', in a book of interviews with the journalist Agustín Blanco Muñoz, *Habla Herma Marksman. Chávez me utilizó*, Fundación Cátedra 'Pío Tamayo', Caracas, 2004.

plank, with a torch. In the distance I hear toads croaking from a nearby lake, in unison with the crickets, and again I'm thinking back to far-off days of childhood, back in my village . . .'

You were twenty . . .
I'd just turned twenty. And thereby hangs another story. Saturday 14 September: 'We left at six p.m. straight for our night training ground where we waited for our dinner, which came late; all the rookies were rather nervous.'

How long had these new recruits been in the Academy?
Less than a month. The training's tough, you have to shoot and be shot at, all that.

Did some quit the course?
Many dropped out. They couldn't take it. But the Academy expelled other cadets for ideological reasons.

For ideological reasons?
That's right. They chucked them out if they suspected they were left-wing and wanted to infiltrate the Armed Forces, or only wanted to do the training so they could go off and join the guerrillas.

Were there cases like that?
I remember them expelling the son of José Vicente Rangel, because he was the 'son of a communist'.[5] It was in 1973. There were elections that year, and José Vicente was the presidential candidate for the MAS. His son Pepito enrolled in the Academy that same year. I was a *brigadier* by then, and he was in the platoon of new recruits under my command. That's how I met his father, because he and his wife Anita [Ávalos], the great Chilean sculptress, came to visit at weekends. I began chatting to

---

5   José Vicente Rangel (1929–), Venezuelan journalist and politician. He was a presidential candidate in 1973 and 1978 for the MAS party and in 1983 for the PCV. In 1998 he supported Hugo Chávez, who appointed him from 1999 to 2007 as minister of foreign affairs, minister of defence and vice president successively.

José Vicente quite a bit about politics, the situation in Venezuela, the Left in general, the electoral campaign . . . So much so that one of the officers summoned me, and criticized me for talking at length to a 'communist'. Not long afterwards I found out Military Intelligence had stepped in and decided to expel Pepito Rangel from the Academy on a false pretext. I informed José Vicente discreetly. There was nothing that could be done.

What did you think about that?
The day Pepito said goodbye to me, I wrote in my diary, 'Pepito Rangel left today. He showed promise.' That is, I saw him as some-one who could have joined our radical group within the Academy. A young man of promise . . .

Do you remember any other cases of 'ideological exclusion'?
No, all the other recruits were expelled because they couldn't cope with the physical training aspect. As well as the lifestyle being differ-ent, the work was difficult and the training very hard.

You say you'd already read Che's Bolivian diary.
Yes, of course. By then, I'd also read the diaries in which Che tells the story of the Cuban guerrillas' exploits against Batista.[6] They circulated here in a compilation entitled *The Olive Green Book*.[7] It was the one I had. It was only recently that Che's widow Aleida March sent me a copy of the first edition of *Pasajes*, edited in Cuba at the beginning of the 1960s.

It was called The Olive Green Book?
I lost my copy. My brother Adán had given it to me. I used to read a lot. I was finishing that particular stage of my military training, but at the same time I was giving myself a sort of advance training in politics, studying Bolívar and reading a lot of Ezequiel Zamora. When I was at

---

6   Ernesto Guevara, *Pasajes de la Guerra Revolucionaria*, Ediciones ERA, Mexico DF, 1969. Extracts in English in *Secret Papers of a Revolutionary: The Diaries of Che Guevara*, American Reprint Co, Mattituck, 1975.

7   Ernesto Guevara, *El libro verde olivo. Antologías temáticas*, Editorial Diógenes, Mexico DF, 1970.

secondary school in Barinas, I'd gone with some other boys to Santa Inés, the site of Zamora's great battle [10 December 1859]. So, I'd been imbibing military knowledge, imbibing the theory and practice of chieftains . . . because we were also taught the theory of leadership.

Leadership lessons?
Yes – until the module changed its name and became 'Command and Guidance'. The Academy was seriously committed to the preparation of leaders, in both scientific and humanist terms. For me it was a training ground for leadership. It was there I learned that a true leader needs to be in touch with his people, and only then can he be considered an authentic statesman. The course at the Academy complemented my own experience as a leader very well – remember I'd managed a boys' baseball team, etc.

The Vietnam War was going on then. In the Academy, did you ever discuss why the US couldn't win that war despite its superior military strength?
We read this book about fighting guerrillas . . .

A counterinsurgency manual?
That's right. And you could see the intention was to manipulate the minds of our young cadets, because it was produced by the Empire, and a group of Venezuelan officers who had been trained in the US.

At the School of the Americas?[8]
A lot of officers went for training there. So, I mean, it was

---

8   The United States School of the Americas (Escuela de las Américas), located in the US-controlled Panama Canal Zone, cooperated for decades with a range of Latin American governments, some of them dictatorships. Its training courses included counter-insurgency strategies, commando operations, and interrogation techniques. In 1977, the US agreed to the Panamanian request to relocate the School on US territory, at Fort Benning, Georgia. The School was officially closed in 2000 during Bill Clinton's presidency. However, the Western Hemispheric Institute for Security Cooperation, inaugurated in 2001, appears to be the heir to the School of the Americas, although more respectful of democracy. In 2004, Venezuela stopped sending cadets to this US Institute.

impossible for them to tell us what was really happening in Vietnam. There was hardly any discussion of that conflict in the Academy, but I'd go out at weekends . . .

And you got information yourself.

By now I was socializing in another area of Caracas, Prado de María, at the house of a relative of mine called Raúl. He was in Acción Democrática, and there were always some quite high-up Adecos there. There was a lot of discussion, especially in 1973–1974 during the Carlos Andrés Pérez election campaign. But the most radical gatherings were at the El Águila bar in Los Chaguaramos. I hung out with other people outside Caracas too, in Barinas, or with my brother Adán's friends . . .

When you went home on holiday . . .

Yes, when I had a long weekend, I'd hop on the direct bus to Barinas. What did I get up to? All sorts of movements were growing there: La Causa R, MAS, or Movimiento Ruptura, which was the political face of Douglas Bravo's guerrilla organization. Debate flourished in those groups, and many documents and pamphlets were circulating. La Causa R's magazine had very interesting articles, especially about Carlos Andrés Pérez's 'Great Venezuela' project, the Fifth National Plan [1976–1980], the national debt, corruption, oil politics, international affairs.

It was at one of these meetings – when I was still in my first year at the Academy – as I was going through various newspapers, that I read about Fidel Castro's visit to Salvador Allende in Chile and to Velasco Alvarado in Peru.[9] When I saw the photo of Fidel with the Peruvian leader for the first time, it dawned on me that at the helm

---

9   Fidel Castro's visit to Salvador Allende's Popular Unity government in Chile lasted from 10 November to 4 December 1971; General Juan Velasco Alvarado (1910–1977) was president of Peru from 1968 to 1975. At the head of the Revolutionary Government of the Armed Forces he nationalized key sectors of the economy – oil, fishing, mines, telecommunications, energy – and introduced important agrarian reforms. He was removed on 29 August 1975 by a group of army officers, and replaced by General Francisco Morales Bermúdez.

of a great brother Latin American country was a progressive, nation-alist general who was introducing important reforms.[10] My interest was aroused.

And you went to Peru, didn't you?

Yes, a few years later, in 1974. A dozen cadets from the Academy were picked to go to Peru for the 150th anniversary of the Battle of Ayacucho [9 December 1824]. I was one of them. Before leaving, I read up on what was happening in Peru. And I learned about Velasco Alvarado's 'Inca Plan'.[11] Then, in Lima and Huamanga, I got to know Peruvian cadets, and cadets from Panama, Colombia, Ecuador, Bolivia, Chile . . .

What did you talk about?

Mainly about the role of the armed forces in Latin American poli-tics.[12] I talked quite a bit to a Chilean cadet called Juan Heiss, and asked him why Pinochet's military coup had happened the previous year. He didn't want to answer, he seemed reticent, and I felt he was uncomfortable. The Panamanians, on the other hand, expressed their fervent anti-Americanism with no inhibitions at all.

I got the chance to shake hands with General Velasco Alvarado when he made a brief speech and gave each of us a signed copy of two books: *The Manifesto of the Peruvian Revolutionary Government of the Armed Forces* and *The Peruvian National Revolution*, the latter bound in blue.[13] I witnessed the close relationship between Velasco and both the Peruvian people and the Armed Forces. I read the

---

10   On his way home from Chile on 4 December 1971, Fidel Castro stopped in Lima and had a three-hour meeting with General Velasco Alvarado.

11   General Velasco Alvarado's Inca Plan was unveiled in Lima on 28 July 1974, on the 150th anniversary of Peruvian Independence.

12   In Hugo Chávez's account of his visit to Peru entitled 'A Flag in Ayacucho' (*Una bandera en Ayacucho*) he says that he and his colleagues, Dumas Ramírez Marquínez and Carlos Escalona, 'gave our opinions on the role the Armed Forces play in society and particularly the unconditional support the Armed Forces in Venezuela have given the democratic process over the last sixteen years'. See Hugo Chávez, *Un brazalete tricolor*, Vadell Hermanos Editores, Valencia-Caracas, 1992.

13   In fact, the Constitution of the Bolivarian Republic of Venezuela, of 1999, bound in blue, looks very like Velasco Alvarado's 'little blue book'.

books and learned some of the speeches almost off by heart. I kept them until they disappeared when my house was ransacked after our 1992 uprising. The only survivor from that trip is *Peru, Military Socialism?* by Juan Aguilar Despich, which I've kept ever since.[14]

What did that meeting with General Velasco Alvarado mean to you?

First, I believe he was a great soldier, a great patriot and a revolutionary. His government showed that the Armed Forces can help a country develop and bring about social change. In a gesture of cultural justice and recognition of the ancestral Inca culture, he gave the Quechua language equal status [with Spanish] as a national language. In several aspects, his thinking reflected what I felt – and still feel. It helped me realize the need for a close relationship between the people and the military. As Mao said, a soldier should be like a fish in water when he is among the people.

And his economic policy?

Velasco Alvarado's Peruvian Revolution was a socialist project. I'm sure of that. He introduced the most far-reaching agrarian reform of the twentieth century in Latin America, and nationalized the strategic sectors of the economy: oil, gas, mining. He encouraged worker participation in the management of nationalized industries. He aimed to raise the living standards of the poor through state-sponsored public works, while at the same time leaving an important space for the market economy, the private sector and small and medium-sized companies.

For example, Velasco once wrote [he reads], 'When we talk about the oligarchy, we are emphatically not referring to industrialists, or to entrepreneurs who contribute to producing our country's wealth, and who understand the need for capital to fulfil its social responsibility in Peru. The small and medium-sized industrialists, and the major modern entrepreneurs, are not the oligarchy we are fighting. Oligarchs are the wealthy financiers and financial institutions who use their economic power to buy a political power that goes on to serve their own economic interests. Oligarchs are those who

---

14   Juan Aguilar Despich, *Perú, ¿socialismo militar?* Editorial Fuentes, Caracas, 1972.

monopolize wealth and form financial cartels for their own benefit, to crush the small and medium-sized industrialists.'[15]

I would say the same applies here, today, in Venezuela. Although, in retrospect, I'd make one criticism.

Of those economic decisions?
No, this is a political point. Velasco's government was made up exclusively of military men, there were no civilian ministers. I think that was a mistake. I've thought about it a lot and I've come to the conclusion that the best road is a civilian–military alliance. An alliance that had been proposed here in Venezuela by Fabricio Ojeda, the intellectual, guerrilla and martyr who I've already mentioned. In his 1966 book, *La guerra del pueblo* (The People's War), Ojeda stated, 'The anti-feudal and anti-imperialist basis of our revolutionary process suggests a model of alliances which are more important than the background, political credo, philosophical leanings, religious convictions, economic or professional standing, or party affiliations of the Venezuelans. The strength and power of the common enemy demands a united struggle to overcome it . . . The forces with the greatest propensity to fight for national liberation' – and I agree with Ojeda's idea here – 'are the workers, peasants, petty bourgeoisie, students, employees, intellectuals, professionals, the majority of officers, NCOs and soldiers of the Armed Forces (air, sea and land), national industrialists, agricultural producers, non-importing businessmen' – I'd say certain importers as well, because we also import – 'non-independent producers and small-scale artisans.' In Fabricio Ojeda's view, which I share, all these sectors of society – civilian and military – have the vocation to form a true national revolutionary alliance.

In those days you were also interested in the policies of General Omar Torrijos in Panama, weren't you?
That's right. I also started getting news about Panama in those years, via four Panamanian cadets who were studying with me in the

---

15 Juan Velasco Alvarado: *La Revolución Peruana*, Editorial Universitaria, Buenos Aires, 1973.

Academy and told me about the transformational changes General Torrijos had been introducing since 1968. One of those cadets, Antonio Gómez Ortega, once brought me copies of the Panamanian National Guard magazine, and I read several speeches by Torrijos, the 'general of national dignity'. I remember his favourite saying: 'I don't want to go down in history, I want to go into the Canal Zone.' There were several photos of him surrounded by *campesinos*, and I could see how popular a progressive officer, leading a government of the people, might be. So different from Pinochet and the reactionary Chilean generals whom I loathed.

I went on to read a lot more about Torrijos, notably the biography-reportage *Getting to Know the General*, by the English novelist Grahame Greene; and another extraordinary book, *Mi General Torrijos*, by one of his closest collaborators, José Jesús Martínez.[16] I still remember the Panamanian general's definition of what real leadership by the armed forces should be: 'Military rank is awarded by decree,' said Torrijos. 'Authority, on the other hand, is achieved by exemplary actions. Rank is when a soldier orders: "Go!" Authority is when he says: "Follow me!"' That distinction remained engraved on my mind forever.

Did you also study the experience of General Juan José Torres in Bolivia?

Absolutely. Although Torres was in the early 1970s, before Torrijos. His mandate was very short [7 October 1970–21 August 1971], less than a year. Yet I read a lot about that experience of military socialism. Torres was a mixed-race soldier, from humble beginnings, who became a left-wing officer. He had been a very popular minister of labour, then chief of staff of the Bolivian Armed Forces when

---

16 Graham Greene (1904–1991), *Getting to Know the General*, Bodley Head, London, 1984; José Jesús Martínez (1929–1991), philosopher, professor, poet and playwright, was born in Nicaragua but took Panamanian nationality. He joined the Panamanian National Guard and as a sergeant became bodyguard and confidant to General Omar Torrijos. Author of, among other books, *Mi General Torrijos*, Editorial Contrapunto, Buenos Aires, 1987, which won the Casa de las Américas prize, Havana, 1987.

Bolivian Rangers, with the help of the CIA, killed Che Guevara in La Higuera in October 1967. Just think of the historical paradoxes. With a group of intellectuals and progressive officers, the good revolutionary and socialist General Juan José Torres created a programme called the Armed Forces Revolutionary Mandate, and defined a Socio-Economic Strategy for National Development. This gave them a left-wing theoretical framework with which to govern. The people knew the progressive nature of General Torres's plans, and came out to support the powerful Bolivian Trades Union Federation when it moved to prevent a reactionary coup [led by General Rogelio Miranda]. That popular uprising brought Torres to power. His left-wing military government relied on what he called the 'four pillars of the revolution': workers' unions, peasant organizations, student movements and progressive officers.

I imagine you were pretty interested in that.
Yes, enormously, because it proved the need for a civilian–military alliance. What's more, Torres had a very interesting thesis: the concept of the 'internal frontier'. He said we naturally have to protect our external frontiers, but that the 'internal frontier' – social equality, economic justice, development – needed even greater protection. We can protect external frontiers all we like, but if we neglect our 'internal frontier', poverty and injustice will increase, and society will explode. As happened in Venezuela in February 1989, with the Caracazo.

In the short time his mandate lasted, General Torres nationalized part of the mining sector, developed education, increased wages, and created the State Bank. He was eventually toppled [21 August 1971] by a group of right-wing officers under General Hugo Banzer, on orders from Washington. Torres went into exile, but was still very popular in Bolivia. So much so that he was kidnapped in Buenos Aires [2 June 1976] and murdered – part of the sinister strategy of Operation Condor.[17]

---

17   Operation Condor is the name given to the project carried out by the military dictatorships of the Southern Cone of Latin America – Argentina, Bolivia, Brazil, Chile, Paraguay and Uruguay – through the 1970s and 1980s to jointly coordinate their repressive mechanisms with the help of the United States.

So, in the midst of the whirlwind of ideas and debates at home,
you were interested in what was happening then in Latin America.
They were unforgettable years, of reading, discussion . . . And Latin
America was a continual subject of debate . . . Although I have to
admit that, in 1974 – my military studies finished and just turned
twenty – I also tried to have a good time, like all youngsters my age.

What did you do for fun?
Well, for instance, on Saturday nights, lots of cadets took off their
uniforms and invaded the Caracas discos, sometimes the Cueva del
Oso (Bear Cave). Those were the days of the unforgettable music of
the Bee Gees, the Rolling Stones, the Beatles . . .

They'd just opened the Poliedro, a huge new entertainment
complex in the south of Caracas. I remember seeing the American
boxers George Foreman and Ken Norton training in the Academy
gymnasium, and hearing they were going head-to-head in an
historic fight in the Poliedro.[18] Foreman won that night, but a few
months later he would be fighting in Africa, in Kinshasa, capital of
Zaire, against the great Muhammad Ali, who knocked him out in
the immortal Rumble in the Jungle, organized by the famous
boxing promoter Don King. Muhammad Ali, the former Cassius
Clay, was our idol.

It was also the time of the 'disaster movies' that filled cinemas
with thrills and dread: *Earthquake, Airport '74, The Towering Inferno,*
The Poseidon Adventure . . . and scary horror films: *Jaws, The Exorcist,*
The Prophesy.

But politics interested me the most. Don't forget that a lot of
very important global events happened in 1974. In April, in
Portugal, the Carnation Revolution brought a fresh wind to Europe:
young army officers and the Portuguese people overthrew a dictatorship, started a revolution and brought about the decolonization
of Portugal's African colonies – Angola, Guinea-Bissau and
Mozambique. In July, we saw the fall of the Greek Colonels' fascist

---

18   The world heavyweight championship was held on 26 March 1974 in Caracas.
George Foreman won in the second round with a technical knockout.

regime. And in August, US President Richard Nixon resigned over the Watergate affair. The Vietnam War was still going on but the Paris Agreement had already been signed [27 January 1973] which finally brought the conflict to an end. In 1973, we'd already had the first Oil Crisis with its spectacular increase in the price of oil, which naturally had big repercussions in Venezuela. And prior to that, in 1972, the massacre at the Munich Olympics had been another event with global repercussions.[19] We're talking about prodigious times.

The end of Francoism.

To all intents and purposes, the end of Francoism. Franco died in November 1975 – I'd already left the Academy – and not long afterward [in October 1976] King Juan Carlos and Queen Sofía came on a visit to Venezuela.[20] I think it's fair to say that the big powers have always treated Venezuela carefully because of its oil wealth. Our presidents have always been rather spoiled in the US and Europe, especially by right-wing governments. We were a neo-colonial country treated with kid gloves.

Nevertheless, it was only natural that we were mainly interested in national politics; it's what motivated us the most . . . I thought of these discussions as a kind of training, a preliminary period, prior to my real political training.

In 1975, you graduated.

Yes, I was twenty-one. It was 5 July 1975, the anniversary of Venezuelan Independence. President Carlos Andrés Pérez presented me with the Academy's graduation sword. I graduated as a second lieutenant, with a degree in Military Arts and Science – speciality in engineering, ground forces.

---

19   In the 1972 summer Olympics in Munich, Israeli athletes were taken hostage and assassinated by the Palestinian commando 'Black September'.

20   Francisco Franco (1892–1975), Spanish general, instigator of the uprising in 1936 against the Second Republic, which resulted in the Spanish Civil War (1936–1939). Helped by Fascist Italy and Nazi Germany, Franco won the war and installed a cruel dictatorship (1939–1975).

What did leaving the Military Academy feel like?

I'd just spent perhaps the most decisive four years of my life there. I became a Bolivarian, discovered the political thinking of our 'three roots': Simón Bolívar, Simón Rodríguez and Ezequiel Zamora. I left with leadership experience and incipiently revolutionary ideas. People sometimes say I went into the Academy with a Che book under my arm. It's not true. I didn't have any books, let alone one of Che's. What I do know is that, when I came out of the Academy, I had a Che book under my arm. I had my road map engraved on my mind, I knew where I was headed.

You're stationed in Barinas, and another stage of your life begins.

Yes, I spent my first two years as a second lieutenant in Barinas; at the Tabacare Fort, in the Manuel Cedeño battalion.[21] Of the new second lieutenants from my year, I was the only one sent there. A new stage of my professional life was beginning, but also of my political life.

What were your first months at the barracks like?

Getting on with the other officers was not easy at first. I clashed with them, not so much about ideological or political stuff, just everyday barracks life. We still had a lot of those horrible Prussian habits that had permeated our army for so long – and that of many other countries too.[22] These Prussian influences were entrenched in

---

21   Manuel Cedeño (1874–1821), Venezuelan army general who distinguished himself in the War of Independence. He died at the battle of Carabobo on 24 June 1821. His remains lie in the National Pantheon in Caracas.

22   After the Franco–Prussian War (1870–1871), defeated France ceased to be considered an important military power, a role subsequently assumed by the victorious Prussians. The tight tactics and the uniform of Count Helmuth von Moltke became the new role model. The first Prussian military mission to Latin America went to Chile in 1885. Its reorganization of the Chilean Army was such a resounding success that several other countries in the region, including Venezuela, decided to follow their example. President Juan Vicente Gómez inaugurated the new Military School in La Planicie in 1910, and authorized a military training mission to professionalize the Venezuelan Army. The head of the mission, the Chilean colonel Samuel McGill, played a significant role in reorganizing the Army and training the future officer corps. Prussian-trained himself, McGill imposed on the Venezuelans the traditional Prussian hallmark of plumed helmet and goose-step, and many other Prussian influences.

the late nineteenth century when Juan Vicente Gómez, a well-known Germanophile, modernized the Venezuelan Army along Prussian lines. And our rules were still very Prussian. For example, officers weren't allowed to eat at the same table as their men. It was an authoritarian fascist-military model, based on abuse of the human being; the exact opposite of the Bolivarian tradition of the People's Army, the union of the people and the army.

What's more, I was the only second lieutenant in the barracks with a university degree; none of the other officers were graduates. So there was a generational battle.

Do you remember any other friction?

Yes, the other shock was the so-called baptism. I was taken to a brothel where a group of officers ordered whisky, rum and women. I ended up with a woman as well, of course, and drunk. They 'baptized' me . . . which consisted of 'bathing' me with a bottle of rum, with the 'baby' paying. It was all pretty pathetic. Vulgar macho customs; pitiful.

They initiated you.

Yes, someone sometime invented that. I imagine it happened in other places too. But I was shocked, because I had a different perception of morality. For me, the Army was something different. Pérez Arcay used to say, 'Don't ever stop being a cadet in the ethical sense.' Because many cadets ditch the code of honour when they leave the Academy. General Osorio, the Academy director, said the same. So, very early on I got into arguments for the most stupid things. In that phase – 1975, '76, '77 – I was all over the place emotionally, very uncertain about things, in some existential dilemma. Should I carry on with a military career, or should I get out while the going was good? I once said to Ruiz Guevara, 'Maybe I'll drop out, ask for a discharge.'

What advice did he give you?

He said I mustn't leave, that it was more useful and more important for me to stay on. He said, 'Look, Hugo, to the Left you're worth more than twenty unions.' I spoke to my dad, and he also said, 'How can you think of leaving?' Adán the same, 'You can't leave. You're one of "ours" inside the Army.' But I said, 'OK, but what's the plan? You don't have a plan, so what am I here for?'

Did you feel depressed?
Very. Barracks life began to bore me. It was very routine. And often absurd. For instance, they wouldn't let me play baseball in a non-army team. I never understood that. I kept disobeying the order and getting arrested. Until one day I said to the commander, 'I was arrested for playing baseball, but what about officers who spend the whole night at La Guyanesa's brothel, that's allowed. I don't understand.' The commander finally gave me permission.

But, was there anti-guerrilla activity?
Very little. Except that one day, it was 1 December, I arrived at the battalion and the major said, 'Lieutenant, get ready. You're leaving for El Cutufí tomorrow. Pick twenty soldiers.' El Cutufí is on the border with Colombia. The border conflict with Colombia was just beginning, there were some Colombian armed groups, but there was never any fighting. They'd kidnap someone, but it wasn't a big deal. It wasn't my turn to do that patrol, I'd already done it. But the next day, there I was, heading for the border in an M-35 truck.

You'd already been there?
Yes, and they were sending me again, but I was glad, it got me out of the routine. I gathered my platoon: 'Let's go!' We reached the Cutufí jungle, and installed ourselves in a village called El Nula. The following day there was an attack on the village store and some people were killed. They blamed the guerrillas. We went downriver for about a week on the Sarare, patrolling almost down to Guasdualito. We saw many undocumented Colombians and a lot of illegal logging. The situation was becoming critical. I got malaria, and came back on 30 December seriously ill.

Just about then, on 21 December 1975, to be exact, a spectacu-
larly dramatic event happened, which would have ramifications
for the entire world, and especially Venezuela: the taking hostage
of the OPEC ministers in Vienna by a pro-Palestinian commando
led by the Venezuelan Ilich Ramírez Sánchez, alias 'Carlos' [the
Jackal].[23] Do you remember it?

Yes, very well. The news shocked the whole of Venezuela. Because
our energy minister, Valentín Hernández Acosta, was a hostage in
Vienna and it soon became clear that, as you said, 'Carlos' was
directing the action.[24] What's more, if I'm not mistaken, it went on
for quite a few days, from Vienna the commando took the hostages
to Algeria, I think, and then to Tripoli, then back to Algeria where
the ministers were released. The entire media were talking about it
here. Audiences were enthralled.

Years later, in March 1999, when you had just become president,
you sent 'Carlos' a personal letter. He was in a Paris prison at the
time, yet you addressed him as 'distinguished compatriot'. It
surprised people a lot, because 'Carlos' had been convicted of
particularly serious acts of terrorism.[25]

Yes, there was a poisonous campaign against me because of that
letter. But, look, I've already explained what happened . . . I wrote
in reply to a letter of his. I won't comment on the acts he may have
committed, which may well have been odious, terrible . . .
Everybody knows I'm against violence and terrorism. What I do say

---

23   Organization of Petroleum Exporting Countries (OPEC), founded in Baghdad,
Iraq, in 1960 on the initiative of the Venezuelan Juan Pablo Pérez Acosta.

24   Valentín Hernández Acosta (1925–1989). In 1974, he was appointed minister of
mines and hydrocarburants by Carlos Andrés Pérez and oversaw the nationalization of the
Venezuelan oil industry. During his kidnapping in Vienna, the hostages chose him to
negotiate with the kidnappers, since both he and 'Carlos' were Venezuelans.

25   On 15 August 1994, 'Carlos' was captured in Khartoum, Sudan, and handed
over to the French police. He was taken back to France, imprisoned in Poissy, Clairvaux
and finally in the Paris prison of La Santé. In 1997, 'Carlos' was sentenced to life for the
murder of two French policemen and an Arab civilian back in 1995. In a subsequent trial
in 2011, he was accused of killing eleven people and injuring 150, in 1982 and 1983, on
French territory. On 15 December 2011 he was given a fresh life sentence.

is that, as president of Venezuela, it's my duty to take an interest in the situation of Venezuelans imprisoned in other parts of the world. Out of patriotic solidarity. Whatever the crime they may have committed or are accused of. Every country does the same. Consuls visit prisoners, they assist them, without expressing an opinion on the trial or the sentence. Why shouldn't we do the same for 'Carlos'? He's a human being sentenced to life imprisonment. I know what being in prison is like.

But in 2009 you called him a 'revolutionary fighter'.
And that's true. Or isn't it? He took on the Palestinian cause, a just cause. He even became a Palestinian, he risked his life for Palestine. He fought with the PLO but he was not a leader. He was not responsible. Yet there he is, paying for it, in prison for life. The French police kidnapped him in Sudan, they put him in a sack and took him to Paris. That's how they arrested him. That's not justice. I repeat, to me 'Carlos' is a fighter. He followed his orders.

Let's go back to Barinas. When you returned, as a second lieutenant, did you meet up with your old friends?
Yes, I went back to my old circle of friends, but now as a soldier. I remember one Sunday, I took them shooting . . . I was on duty at the firing range at Fort Tabacare, and I invited those left-wing friends – my brother Adán, Vladimir Ruiz, and other friends from Mérida, some hairy hippies – to take some potshots . . .

Were you authorized?
No, absolutely not. I invited them and we fired off a few rounds. Nobody found out. The captain was a friend. That was when I began to forge a closer intellectual relationship with José Ruiz Guevara, the father of the Ruiz brothers; he became an influential teacher for me, a reference in terms of morality, politics and ideology. We talked about everything, Bolívar, Ezequiel Zamora, Simón Rodríguez, the history of Venezuela . . . I'd spend whole afternoons reading in his modest library. It was there I read Jean-Jacques Rousseau's *Social Contract*, a seminal text. Georgi Plekhanov's *Role*

of the Individual in History was a present from Ruiz Guevara.[26] That
text was a compass, a guide to the awareness of individual freedom,
a maxim for life.

You also met your first wife around then, didn't you?
That's true, something very positive happened in 1976, I met Nancy
Colmenares and fell in love with her; she was eighteen.

How did you meet her?
Our commander in Barinas liked going out in his white uniform
and full regalia, and his wife loved the social whirl. And every year
in Barinas they used to have a Miss Barinas pageant. So with the
experience I'd acquired at the Academy, I became the master of
ceremonies for the pageant. That's where I met Nancy. One of the
contestants was a girl called Pilar, and she and her sister Moraima
were Nancy's close friends. I fancied Nancy straight off, she was the
prettiest. Pilar was pretty too, but she already had a boyfriend, a
lieutenant. Nancy and I started courting. I fell for Nancy so hard
that I didn't have eyes for any other woman. But my mother
objected, and it turned into a battle. She didn't like Nancy. I quarrelled with my mother, I stood fast and my free choice in love
prevailed, of course.

And politics?
Well, by this time, I was in La Causa R. My friend Vladimir was a
Causa R leader and we'd often see each other at political meetings
in the Noches de Hungría. I'd also visit Adán in Mérida, which was
three hours' drive away. We'd go over to the University of Los Andes
and join the political discussions; I loved La Hechicera, a debating
place in the Science Faculty. Most of the students didn't know I was

---

26   Georgi Plekhanov (1856–1918), *On the Role of the Individual in History* (1898),
in *Selected Works of G. V. Plekhanov*, vol. 2, Lawrence & Wishart, London, 1961. Plekhanov
was a Russian revolutionary and Marxist theoretician. In this work he demonstrates how
Marx gave philosophy and history a rigorous scientific order, thereby making the proletariat a theoretical instrument of huge transformational potential. For Lenin, 'what
Plekhanov has written about philosophy is the best in global Marxist literature'.

a soldier. As I said, between 1975 and 1977, I even thought of dropping out of the army to continue with my studies.

You were entering a period of uncertainty and drift . . .
Yes, uncertainty, and doubt. I felt as if my heart would burst from the contradictions, until . . . And this, I believe, is very important. Ruiz Guevara was researching into Pedro Pérez Delgado.

Maisanta?
Yes, my mother's grandfather. We've already talked a lot about him. But what I mean to say is that Ruiz Guevara was from Puerto Nutrias, further down the Apure river, so he too was interested in that story. I told him the subject was taboo in our house when I was a child, my family called him a murderer. So he told me about class struggle in the early twentieth century. He said, 'History is the story of class struggle.' I started to read Marx and Engels, the *Communist Manifesto*. Ruiz Guevara never wrote his book about Maisanta, but he passed on a lot of information to José León Tapia, who was a doctor rather than a professional historian. I knew him in those days.

The first edition of Tapia's book about Maisanta came out in August 1974, when I was still in the Academy. I bought it when I went back to Barinas as a second lieutenant. Tapia was an empirical researcher, he investigated stories, followed trails; what they call living history. I followed his example.

Let's go back to your first experience of barracks life in Barinas; you said you were bored.
Yes. I was so bored, I asked the commander for permission to write a column in the local newspaper, *El Espacio*. Because, among other reasons, the editor was a neighbour of mine, Dr. Guédez Acevedo and his wife Rafaela, I got on really well with them. I've already mentioned them. He encouraged me to write. Strange as it may seem, the commander gave me permission. He asked me what name I would give the column. And between us, we chose 'The Cedeño Patriotic Cultural Project'. It was a weekly chronicle of

events at the barracks. It came out on Thursdays, and began to attract readers.

Did it just talk about the barracks?

The barracks, and history. For example, who was Manuel Cedeño? A great soldier who died at the battle of Carabobo. When Bolívar was told, 'General Cedeño is dead,' he exclaimed, 'The bravest of Colombia's braves has died.' The column also gave news of the soldiers, sports, the firing range, cultural activities . . .

What else did you do to escape from barracks routine?

I went out recruiting candidates for the Military Academy.

Recruiting candidates?

Yes, let me tell you. Just after I graduated, a lieutenant friend of mine, a very smart guy called Pedro Salazar Monsalve, was appointed head of Academy admissions in Caracas. His job was to find applicants for the Academy. And he, in turn, appointed me . . .

As local recruiter.

Exactly. He suggested me to the director of the Academy and submitted the proposition to the Army's director of personnel, whose office was in the same complex. And out came the official decision to appoint me. Every garrison had a 'Head of Recruitment'.

Salazar Monsalve knew my skills as an orator. He said, 'Get cracking, here are your admission prospectuses.' And I took my responsibility seriously, as ever. My advantage was that I knew Barinas inside out. I went to the workshop of a baseball buddy, a mechanic known as *Tripa*, and said, 'There's an old bus with a broken engine at the barracks. It needs repairing.' The battalion didn't have the funds to do it. And *Tripa* fixed the engine for nothing.

The administrator in charge of sports for Barinas was old Agustín Tovar – they recently named the local football stadium after him. I knew him well. I put it to him: 'The battalion has 300 soldiers who want to play sports.' 'OK, we'll integrate the battalion with the city, so they can all play.' I added, 'I've got a bus, but it needs some tyres.' He got me five tyres, one as a spare, and the bus looked good as new. Luckily there was a group of soldiers who were good ball players, and we made a good team.

But the stadium at Fort Tabacare was useless. I went back to Agustín Tovar and got some funds to refurbish it. I took some soldiers out to a beautiful prairie, to dig up squares of turf. We went looking for red sand in riverbeds and laid it round the diamond. Technicians from the National Institute of Sport helped me to do the measuring, make the dugout and the backstop. It all cost very little, about two thousand bolívars. They paid for everything. The stadium looked brilliant! The commander couldn't get over it.

I'm not surprised: the bus, the stadium, the team . . .
But what's more, with that bus, I began a recruitment drive in the secondary schools all over the state of Barinas, including the O'Leary where I had studied myself. I remember arriving there to give a talk and seeing my very beautiful ex-girlfriend, Irene Rosales. She was still doing year five because she'd got married, then divorced, and had gone back to school. I saw her, called her over and invited her for a coffee.

But I thought you were in love with Nancy, with eyes for no other woman!
I hadn't even met Nancy then! Then Nancy appeared and that was that [laughter].

Oh! Sorry. So, you threw yourself into a serious campaign to recruit candidates for the Military Academy.
Yes, very systematic. I visited all the secondary schools in the state. Private schools as well. I took slides with me, the boys asked questions, and filled in the forms. It was actually a motivational campaign. I did it on the radio too: Radio Barinas and Radio Continental. I had access to all those stations, I knew nearly all the presenters. So, guess how many boys we sent to the Academy that year? More than fifty.

A success.

Undoubtedly. My idea was to establish, through my personal contacts, a more fruitful relationship between the barracks and the town, to illustrate how important the civilian–military union could be. For instance, I organized an agricultural programme at the barracks with the help of my brother Narciso, an agricultural expert at Inagro, the National Farming and Livestock Institute. I asked him to teach the soldiers for free. The commander was soon impressed to see them sowing tomatoes, maize, passion fruit and papaya on some waste ground behind the barracks. Nacho brought a tractor and started clearing and raking. One day, I told the commander, 'We'd like you to present diplomas to the soldiers.' He gave out diplomas signed by the director of Inagro. In these ways I took maximum advantage of my contacts to integrate the barracks with the town.

You foresaw what after your election in 1999 would be the Plan Bolívar.

Yes, it was a mini Plan Bolívar 2000 . . .[27] In embryo, because my idea of the relationship that should exist between soldiers and the people was very different to the one that prevailed in our army back then. I was inspired by the great tradition of Bolívar and Zamora, and also by what had been achieved by Velasco Alvarado in Peru and Omar Torrijos in Panama: cooperation between soldiers and the people, united in the cause of development. But you're right, to a certain extent I was actually putting into practice something that after we took power in 1999 we called the Plan Bolívar: social missions run by the army in poor neighbourhoods, so people would have an image of soldiers that was not about repression, coups, authoritarianism. It would show that soldiers could also make war on poverty, disease and hunger.

---

27   A civilian–military plan, launched in February 1999, by President Chávez's first government, put the resources of the Armed Forces at the service of the civilian popula-tion as a way of meeting their social needs.

The other officers must have envied you, didn't they?

No, they were excellent *compañeros*. Some even helped out. Another thing we did, this time to benefit the soldiers, was a literacy campaign. My father was director of the 24 June school group, and my mother gave adult education evening classes. With their assistance, we started a literacy programme designed for soldiers.

Were many of the soldiers illiterate?

Too many. It was a serious problem. Most of the soldiers were country boys, so they were illiterate or had reached first or second grade at best. Graduating from secondary school was the bee's knees. We had to teach them to type. I also gave history lectures at the Liceo O'Leary. The teachers knew me. My father invited me to talk to his pupils about Bolívar and Venezuelan history, which I was very proud to do.

How long did you stay at Barinas barracks?

From September 1975 to May 1977. Then guerrilla activity flared up again in Oriente, and the Army decided to send us to Cumaná. This affected me deeply.

Why?

Because Nancy, the love of my life, was in Barinas. I came back a month later, on furlough, Nancy and I were desperate. I decided to talk to her mother and ask permission to take her with me.

Nancy? To Cumaná?

Yes. I'm very fond of that old lady, Rosa Luciani de Colmenares, her mother, but my request triggered an explosion in that humble home . . .

Why?

I was breaking all the rules. I was even a rebel in that sense . . . I had the cheek to ask for Nancy. Not to marry her, but to take her away with me. Her mother burst out crying. Nancy wanted to go with me. Her brother Carlitos got angry. Harsh words were exchanged.

The eldest brother, Rafael, was sent for. He agreed: 'Hugo is relia-ble, he'll take care of her.' I guaranteed that Nancy would continue her studies. They also consulted her sister, Miriam, God rest her soul. 'They love each other,' she said. They called her father, Don Darío Colmenares, whom I barely knew. He's dead now. He worked in the Institute of Public Health's anti-malaria campaign. To cut a long story short, I took Nancy, my woman, with me.

But you weren't married. Did your parents agree?
Well, I already told you my mother didn't like her. But I dug my heels in and she had to understand that when love comes calling . . . My father agreed, and even let me take his car. I left him my Volkswagen, a lovely red Beetle that Commander Estrella had sold me. It had wheels with magnesium rims. As Cumaná was a long way away, we decided to swap cars. My father who seldom travelled kept the Volkswagen, and I took his Dodge Dart which lasted a good many years. Nancy and I were very much in love. And off to Cumaná we went, to start another stage of my life.

8

In Cumaná

Counterinsurgency operations
Campaign diary – Joining the guerrillas?
The importance of communications – Leaving the Army?
Quoting Che Guevara – Cowardly ambush
A guerrilla army disconnected from the people
The Venezuelan People's Liberation Army
A secret intelligence operation
Thinking about the civilian–military union
Reading Lenin – Jesús Urdaneta – Violence and ethics
Military executioners – Corrupt generals

How big a city was Cumaná?

Cumaná lies in eastern Venezuela, on the Caribbean coast facing the Araya peninsula. It must have been home to about 40,000 to 50,000 souls in those days and, as one of the oldest cities on the continent, it was still very traditional. The birthplace of Marshal Sucre, it has always been guerrilla territory par excellence. Defeated in central Venezuela and in the west – and with the Spaniards occupying Cartagena de Indias and dominating the whole Caribbean-Pacific arc as far as Panama – Bolívar returned from exile in Haiti and came to Cumaná via Isla Margarita. The Spaniards never controlled Cumaná, it was always insurgent territory. Between

1960 and 1970 the Antonio José de Sucre guerrilla front was active in that area, and our battalion was in hot pursuit of what was left of them.[1]

Did you know anyone in Cumaná?
Hardly anyone; but I began to make friends. I bumped into *Negro* Reyes, a friend from Barinas, now a technical sergeant, and second lieutenant Brito Valerio, another good pal. One night we saw the stadium lights were on, and went in. Argenis Bastidas was pitching. He was a lad of my own age from Barinas who'd been to the World Series. I waited till the game was over, then went up to say hello. He invited us back to his house, introduced us to his wife and we drank a few beers . . . Through him I began to meet more people, especially in sports. He got me a trial at the University of Oriente (UDO) in May and June 1977, and I began to play baseball, and make friends.

You didn't have any political contacts.
That's right. I was away from my political circles. But talking to Argenis – who worked in the municipal council and, being only interested in sport, was in no way a man of the Left – I learned there were some left-wing people in the University team.

And did you detect any left-wing officers in the Cumaná barracks?
No. I was in a counter-insurgency unit. Our unit and the Left were like oil and water. And anyway, I was a new boy. I talked to Lieutenant Brito Valerio about a few things, but never about [political] commitment. Don't forget I was still in my period . . .

Of uncertainty?
Yes, uncertainty, oscillation; an existential dilemma.

---

1   The Antonio José de Sucre guerrilla front, armed wing of the Bandera Roja (Red Flag) organization, operated in the mountains of Anzoátegui and Monagas. Among its commanders were Carlos Betancourt, Américo Silva, Tito González Heredia, Gabriel Puerta Aponte, Miguel Salas Suárez and Pedro Véliz.

Were you still thinking of quitting the Army?
I questioned everything, and felt more and more inclined towards the Left, increasingly attracted by the revolutionary movement. I read books . . . In fact, near a former anti-guerrilla army post, I came across an old black Mercedes which had belonged to some guerrilla couriers. It was all beat up and riddled with bullet-holes, forgotten for years and covered in earth in the middle of the undergrowth, but in the boot was a veritable treasure trove of disintegrating Marxist books. I took them, patched them up, and read them.

Do you remember any titles?
Yes, I still have some. For example, there was *Imperialism, the Highest Stage of Capitalism*, Lenin's classic work, but that interested me less than *Economic Structure of Colonial Venezuela*, by Professor Federico Brito Figueroa.[2]

Did reading these books make you feel any less confused?
No. In Cumaná I still thought about leaving the Army. I remember when I was sent to Cutufí on the Colombian border, I'd jotted down a few observations, like, 'This area is ideal for guerrilla operations' – thinking like a guerrilla, not like a counter-insurgency soldier. 'If you had to open a guerrilla front, this area is ideal because of its rivers, forests, jungle . . .' And yet the guerrillas had already been defeated, politically, socially and militarily, and I thought I must be crazy. In the east of the country, however, there were still guerrilla hubs and the front was still operational, and I had access to military intelligence about it; I began juggling with the idea again. I told myself, 'Well, I actually could join the guerrillas.'

---

2 Federico Brito Figueroa (1921–2000), Venezuelan historian and anthropologist, Marxist, author of among other books, *La estructura económica de Venezuela colonial*, UCV-Ediciones de la Biblioteca, Caracas, 1978; and *Tiempo de Ezequiel Zamora*, UCV/ECUC, Caracas, 1981. He was the coordinator of the Constitutional Front for Culture, which in 1997 designed Hugo Chávez's cultural programme when he was presidential candidate.

Were you really tempted to join the other side?

Yes, absolutely, to be a guerrilla. The most powerful impediment was Nancy, I was responsible for her. It would have been madness.

You didn't want to abandon her.

No. That was probably the decisive factor. Love. And then they decided to send me out on field operations for a few months – September, October and November of 1977 – and Nancy stayed in Cumaná.

A few months?

Yes, or rather, out for forty days, back for three or four days, then out again.

What did those operations consist of?

There was a new outbreak of guerrilla activity. These were the last remnants of the Bandera Roja [Red Flag] guerrilla army, which had turned down the amnesty offered by ex-President Rafael Caldera [1969–74]. The new president, Carlos Andrés Pérez, had been Rómulo Betancourt's interior minister; he was a hardliner with an intransigent stance, like 'shoot first, ask questions later'. There was a lot of repression, disappearances, torture, and other aspects of the 'dirty war'. The sinister Henry López Cisco was chief of operations of the Intelligence and Prevention Services (DISIP) in those days.[3] And the Cubans were in there too . . .

With the guerrillas?

No! Cuban terrorists, anti-Castroists like Orlando Bosch and Luis

---

3   Henry López Cisco, chief of operations of the DISIP, the secret police. He was accused of the massacre of Yumare on 8 May 1986 during Jaime Lusinchi's presidency, when nine students were killed in Yaracuy state. He was also accused of taking part in the massacre of Cantaura, in October 1984 in Anzoátegui state, when twenty-three insurgents were assassinated.

DISIP: intelligence and counter-intelligence service inside and outside Venezuela between 1969 and 2009. It was dissolved on 4 December 2009 by President Chávez and replaced by the Bolivarian Intelligence Service (SEBIN).

Posada Carriles, CIA operatives working in the DISIP.[4] Posada Carriles was head of the DISIP's operational commandos, no less. And there were Israeli military advisers, too. I saw them. Bosch, Posada Carriles and their commandos went out on sorties using weapons of war, day and night; they kidnapped, tortured, raped, murdered, set fire to crops and terrorized the peasants. There wasn't anything they didn't do! And as part of this effort to annihilate the last remnants of the guerrillas and wipe them off the map, in September 1977 my battalion was sent to join in the dirty war against them.

And where were these counterinsurgency operations?

Our field operations HQ was at the Hato Las Flores, a ranch about twenty kilometres to the south of Barcelona, capital of the state of Anzoátegui. I remember it well, because when I was going through some old documents, I found this other diary that my friend [Herma Marksman] had kept and transcribed. Its title is 'Guerrilla Operation, October–November 1977'.

A campaign diary, like Che's?

Well, you can't compare it. But I'd kept a journal ever since I was at the Academy. My original diary was handwritten; my friend must still have it. I'll read an extract if I may, it's not very long:

'Friday 21 October 1977. We've set up camp, communications, canteen, showers, latrines, first aid. Each work team needs a leader, and leaders are in short supply, the corporals are NCOs and, with a few rare exceptions, don't know how to give orders. We're not working well together; we lack coordination, information, experience and work ethic. Food is crucial, we need to establish a minimum ration for each individual and make sure everyone receives the same. A good leader needs to keep an eye on the tiniest details, have his finger on every pulse. That night, being present at an

---

4   Orlando Bosch (1926–2011) and Luis Posada Carriles (1928–), notorious Cuban counter-revolutionaries trained by the CIA, accused by the Cuban and Venezuelan governments of having committed numerous attempts to topple the Cuban government. They are famously accused of being the intellectual authors of the sabotage of a Cubana plane which blew up on 14 October 1976, killing seventy-three people.

interrogation session, listening to a boy who'd been fighting with
the guerrillas, was a new experience for me. He said his name was
José Domingo Centeno, and his nom de guerre was 'Rafael', he had
been at the attack on Urica, a nearby town. At times he appeared
sincere, but I'm sure he was trying to confuse the military intelligence officer, Commander Carlos Barreto. They took him away to
wait for his comrades. I wonder how my *negra* is? With every day
that passes I'm more convinced that I love her, *mi negra*.'

Nancy?
Yes. Nancy Colmenares . . . The diary continues, 'Anyway, life goes
on . . . new experiences . . . waiting, waiting . . . Is this what I
should be doing?' The following day was Saturday, and I wrote,
'This is my first guerrilla operation, so I've decided to refresh the
theoretical knowledge I acquired as a Military Arts and Sciences
graduate about this particular kind of warfare, advocated by Mao
Zedong and Ernesto Che Guevara. This war started in Venezuela
many years ago, and a large number of diverse individuals have filed
past in its ranks – the majority Army officers and soldiers, the
minority guerrillas, although in different conditions and circumstances – and here I am playing an insignificant role, in a way, when
it could be a bigger and more productive one.'

**Did you think it might be 'bigger and more productive' among
the guerrillas?**
I already told you, I was once more thinking of joining them at that
time. I couldn't write it, of course. It was just a crazy thought.

But did you have any contacts with the guerrillas?
Well, I was in touch with people who had links to the guerrillas, but
that was in the cities: students, a professor at the Universidad de
Oriente and so on.

Naturally you didn't mention that in your diary.
No, absolutely not. But I wrote every day, often about the guerrillas, here for instance:

'A group of twenty armed men took the town of Oricual at 23.00 hours on 23 October 1977, called a meeting and were there for two hours.' 'Oricual' was Orijuán, in Anzoátegui. 'You find them where you least expect them. They bite and flee. We got a message at three in the morning. We mobilized immediately, combat rations, trucks, radio, pursuit, aggression . . . Result: negative. They disappeared into thin air. Those selective military actions by the guerrillas are not intended to win an olive-green victory, but to generate a gradual process of counter-revolutionary attrition, erosion of confidence and loss of credibility. In the afternoon, Captain Manzanares and his company arrived at our command post.'

Was there any fighting?

On Monday 24 October, there was fighting but no casualties, they all managed to escape. As communications officer at the command post, I had two radios and received all the messages. So I knew everything, because I had to encrypt and decipher them. I wrote in my diary, 'They all managed to escape. They sneaked past Captain Pérez González. Since the guerrillas have the support of the *campesino* masses, they'll be difficult to defeat.'

I kept on writing, only now a bit more explicitly, 'Tuesday 25. We're going to San Mateo tomorrow, further south. Last night I took Manzanares to his departure point for El Turimiquire, up in the mountains, it was pouring with rain. Yesterday's fighting was near here, at the Hato La Centella. Our tactics are poor, at least I think so. The incursion patrol arrived today, the SWAT, with Parra Pereira; but Piñero, the logistics man, didn't come.[5] I sent a letter to *mi negra* via him. It's a good thing to start operations near a well-chosen road, and use four-wheel drives. One, two Vietnams in Latin America . . . He failed too.'

---

5 In the US, SWAT (Special Weapons and Tactics) is a special police unit used for very dangerous operations. In Venezuela, tactical groups with a similar function are the Brigadas de Acción Especiales (BAE) belonging to the Cuerpos de Investigación Científicas, Penales y Criminalísticas (CICPC), formerly the Policía Técnica Judicial (PTJ) created in 1958 and disbanded in 2001.

An allusion to Che Guevara?

Yes – I'm setting out my stall now, aren't I. Deep inside I've defined my position, and what's more I'm daring to write down these things. I hid my notebook in my campaign equipment, among some other books. And I wrote this: 'One, two Vietnams in Latin America. He failed too. Death is welcome. Villa, Che, new battle cries, new hands. Like that man who had an epiphany on the Chimborazo, he too must have felt he was ploughing the sea.'[6]

I'm effectively talking about Bolívar and Che. And listen to this next bit: 'It doesn't matter, it could happen here. All those who failed, let them come back.'

Meaning Ezequiel Zamora, Maisanta, Pancho Villa, Zapata, Sandino, Che Guevara . . .

All of them. Now, look what comes next. I wrote every day and, at a certain point, things started hotting up. We moved to a pretty little town, San Mateo. Further on I write about logistical support, but first I say, listen, 'A battalion of 324 soldiers is a lot of men, but they are not very effective. They lack morale, they lack conscious-ness. The soldiers neither feel nor understand what they are fighting for, because their interests, as a social class, do not coincide with the aims of this war. The guerrillas, on the other hand, generally possess the necessary qualities to withstand the sacrifices, privations and solitude.'

Very lucid. How old were you?

I'd just turned twenty-three.

You had to choose between three options: stay in the army, join the guerrillas, or devote yourself to Nancy.

Well, my love for Nancy was very strong. See what I wrote: '*Mi negra* is so far away . . . If only I could be with her, feel her warmth,

---

6 Mount Chimborazo, a volcano on the equator in Ecuador; its peak is the farthest point away from the centre of the earth. Bolívar wrote a poetic text about it, 'Mi delirio sobre el Chimborazo'.

be happy with her, I truly love her, it's hard to live without her.' I loved Nancy to pieces. And here: 'Perhaps one day I can bring you with me, *negra*, and you can learn with me, be victorious with me or die with me.' Because I'd ask myself, how can I leave her? I'll take her along.

Where? To join the guerrillas?
I was terribly tempted. In my diary, I suggested some operational solutions:

'The guerrillas are still there. They're seasoned veterans. Gabriel Puerta, Andrés Cova, Carlos Betancourt, old man Ruperto, they know the terrain backwards, they have support, but they also have one great disadvantage: they're divided. Unite, unite or anarchy will devour you. My people are still the same. In the same situation. My passive people. Who will light the flame? We can make a huge blaze.'

That alludes to a revolutionary song you used to hear a lot in those days. It talks about lighting a flame to make a blaze, but the wood is wet, the conditions are not right, conditions are not right, conditions are not right . . . 'Damn it,' I wrote, 'when will they ever be right? Why not create them? Soldiers raising their swords to defend social justice, that's where hope lies, perhaps.'

You already had that idea.
Yes, and by then I was expressing it clearly. But I also wrote, 'This war will go on for years and "it gives us the opportunity to be revolutionaries, the highest form of the human species".'[7]

Quoting Che Guevara's phrase.
A famous phrase. And I went on, 'I have to do it, although it cost me my life. It doesn't matter, it's what I feel I was born for. How long can I go on like this? I feel impotent, unproductive, I must prepare myself to act.'

---

7 Ernesto 'Che' Guevara, *The Bolivian Diary*, Harper Perennial, London, 2009, p. 208 (entry of 8 August 1967).

But you didn't join the guerrillas.

That was my dilemma. But then something happened that knocked the idea of the guerrillas on the head once and for all: an ambush where seven soldiers were killed, for no good reason. I saw those boys, one practically died in my arms. They were peasant soldiers and they killed them just for the heck of it, with no military objective.

The guerrillas killed them?

Yes, but a lot of mistakes were also made. I knew that because, as the communications officer, I listened to all the messages. They arrived in code and I'd decipher them.

They fell into an ambush.

That ambush shook me to the core. So much so that during those operations, I formed the first cell of my Liberation Army, the Ejército de Liberación del Pueblo Venezolano (ELPV) – the forerunner of the Ejército Bolivariano Revolucionario (EBR–200) – with a group of soldiers from my communications platoon. The cell was made up of: Sergeant Mario Núñez Hidalgo; First Corporal Agustín Moros; Corporal José Rodríguez Toro; Private Esteban Silva. Men accompanying their leader.

You had a special relationship with your men.

I always have had. On several occasions a captain at the Cumaná barracks ticked me off for listening to music by Alí Primera in the patio or the mess, whenever I was on guard duty. I'd bought one of those huge 1970s ghetto blasters at the Army store and used to play protest songs. What's more, I'd tell my soldiers about Bolívar, morning, noon and night. So, I won over the soldiers in my patrol with ideas.

That's why you founded the ELPV with four of them.

Yes, like I said, I was running around with a hurricane inside me, I was desperate, I had to do something. To give you an idea of my state of mind, look what I was writing in my diary on 25 October

1977: 'Vietnam, one, two Vietnams in Latin America. Bolívar, Che Guevara, come back! Return! This may be the place to do it.'

And later on, I wrote, 'This war will go on for years, I have to do it, though it may cost me my life, it doesn't matter, it's what I was born for. How long can I go on like this? I feel impotent, unproductive, I must prepare myself to act.'

And this is how I decided to act. The night of 28 October on Mount Zamuro, I suggested to four soldiers – Núñez Hidalgo, Moros, Toro and Silva – that we form a Bolivarian cell. I made the group swear an oath, and we formed the first ELPV cell. During full-scale anti-guerrilla operations.

What was your plan?

The first thing we did was bury some grenades, in case something happened, and we had to take to the hills. Although we didn't have a clear strategy or objectives. I was a rebel without a cause. Looking back, I see it as more of a Quixotic gesture of protest against the overall situation, the country's predicament . . .

Why didn't you take to the hills?

Because fortunately we were let down by a contact, a lecturer at Cumaná University, who didn't show up. If contact had been made, I'd have become a guerrilla. That would have been lunacy, because in Venezuela then the conditions weren't right for a guerrilla war. And a few weeks later, I was transferred to Maracay . . .

Was that after the ambush?

Yes, I remember clearly it was after the ambush because, as I said, that ambush shocked me to the core. I asked myself, what kind of guerrillas would kill simple soldiers for no reason?

Poor peasants, humble people.

Yes, and they weren't even killed in combat. The soldiers were in a truck, some of them were asleep. And they were massacred. I was sympathetic to the guerrillas, but when I saw those bodies . . . My command post was in San Mateo, Anzoátegui, but every now and again they'd send me to fetch combat rations and munitions in the town of Barcelona, almost an hour away, where there was a big military logistics post. The day of the ambush, I happened to be in Barcelona when I saw some helicopters land on the parade ground of the Pedro María Freitas barracks.[8] Out of one of them jumped Commander De la Costa de Parra, of the Pedro Zaraza Battalion, whom I knew from meetings. He saw me and shouted, 'Over here! Help us take out the wounded.' We ran over to the helicopters, to help with the wounded, and we saw such corpses . . . I'll never forget it. I helped one soldier out, we looked at each other, I picked him up in my arms, he was bleeding . . . He said, 'Don't let me die.' I tried to reassure him, 'You're not going to die, boy.' I carried him as fast as I could, but I lost him. I asked about him later, and was told that a bullet had gone right through him; he'd bled to death.

This shook you.
Very much. When everyone had gone, I got in my truck with a few of my soldiers, and we drove off at top speed towards our command post. I went into my communications tent and began to exchange messages. Later, in the silence of the night I got to thinking, and asked myself, 'What kind of guerrillas are those?'

Did you have any information about who they were?
We knew they belonged to Bandera Roja's Américo Silva Front, but not much more.[9] That was the information we had from military intelligence.

Were you directly involved in field operations?
No, like I said, I was a communications officer. Although one day I did ask the commander if I could take part in an operation. And, perhaps to get me off his back, he sent me on a covert intelligence

---

8   Pedro María Freitas (1790–1817), hero of the War of Independence, shot by the Spaniards aged twenty-seven.

9   Américo Silva (1933–1972), Marxist leader, one of the founders in 1960 of the MIR and subsequently, in 1970, of Bandera Roja. Died in combat against the National Guard.

mission with Lieutenant Parra Pereira who led a group of elite commandos called SWAT. We arrived in San Mateo where the grandfather of a woman guerrilla leader was dying, and army intelligence wanted to know whether or not she was coming to see him, so they could capture her. The commando group was in a Ministry of Public Works truck, pretending to be workmen, except we were all armed. There was another truck on the outskirts of the village supposedly mending some electricity cables. Lieutenant Parra and I were in the front seat watching the house where the old man lay ill. I was secretly praying his granddaughter wouldn't come, but I had to carry out my mission. I wrote about it in my diary:

'Last night, Saturday 29 October 1977, went on a mission with Parra Pereira. The grandfather of guerrilla leader Ciriaca Carvajal is seriously ill in San Mateo, and the commander thinks Ciriaca might come. Lieutenants Arleo and Urbina staked out the house. I was with a SWAT group in civilian clothes. There were ten of us in an old truck belonging to the Ministry of Public Works, and we had to "crash" it, then stagger off on foot into the drunken, noisy streets of San Mateo on a Saturday night. We bought a bottle of rum and behaved in true party style, Parra Pereira strumming on a cuatro and me singing. We looked just like any other town drunks. We sat down at a corner and began singing "*No basta rezar*" [Praying's not enough, one of Alí Primera's revolutionary songs].'

There were lots of people in the street and on the corner, because on Saturday nights in those pueblos of the interior, everyone, families, mothers, grandmothers, children, sit out on the doorstep, while the youngsters promenade around, or ride bicycles. We started singing the song, which goes like this [he sings]:

'No, noooo, praying's not enough / For peace much more is needed / When the people rise up and make things change / You will say along with me it's not enough to pray / No, noooo, praying's not enough / They pray in good faith and from the heart / But a pilot also prays when he boards his plane / To drop bombs on children in Vietnam / No, noooo, praying's not enough.' [A cock is heard crowing.]

The cock has started singing with you!
Well I never! He was listening. We're on the same wavelength. [The cock crows again.] This cock's a baritone. Do you know his name?

Llanero?
No. He's called Fidel [laughter].

Ah, I see you're a pair of conspirators!
We're old mates, mountain mates. He was quiet the whole after-noon, did you notice? And suddenly he starts singing, and what's more, in tune with me. What's up, little rooster? [The cock crows again] There's no stopping him now! [Laughter.] Anyway, as I was saying, when the village folk heard us singing, they came up and clapped, a lady came out and offered us coffee. People in the East are very hospitable, and very rebellious as well. They're guerrillas at heart. That's why the guerrillas lasted a bit longer there.

Didn't you get to know some of those guerrillas later on?
Yes. Well, I met Gabriel Puerta Aponte in prison.

And Carlos Betancourt?
Carlos was another one. But they split. There were only about forty of them left, and of them, about twenty, led by Puerta Aponte, founded the Bandera Roja group, while the others were in 'Bandera Roja Marxista–Leninista' [laughter].

Going back to the intelligence operation, what happened when you finished singing?
We were amazed, people got so excited they offered us cigarettes and other stuff. We had to sing the song again, and then they asked for more, and I sang my head off, like this cockerel [laughter].We were only a block from Ciriaca's house, because our job was to watch it. In this way I was able get to know the villagers, sincere, plain folk, fertile terrain for planting the seed of disinterested friendships. Next morning I woke up in the truck: Ciriaca hadn't come, I was glad to note. Thank goodness she didn't.

So there were women guerrillas too?

Yes, there always have been fighting women in Venezuela, and else-where too. This one, Ciriaca, *La Negra* Ciriaca, was famous. They say she was beautiful, brave and also very clever. Apparently she had managed to infiltrate her band of women into military units, to get information. When she was detected she had to head for the hills, but until then she was in charge of a group of urban women, in cities and towns. After that she became ill.

Did you write about this in your diary?

Of course. And also about the need to have the support of the people. For example, 'It's vital to discard sentimentality, or at least its outward manifestations, if you want to survive this war. It's also vital to get the support of the people, but to do that you need to motivate them, and keep them motivated, by making them under-stand that their interests and the objectives of the struggle are the same. You need to introduce programmes that get a positive reac-tion from the people, by making them more attractive than the existing ones. The question to ask is, what are the interests of the Venezuelan people? Land? Weapons? Religion? Equality? Land is no longer, these days, the primordial interest of the *campesino*. Why not? Simply because, according to the latest survey, the *campesino* is no longer in the *campo*.'

Which survey?

The one showing that 70 per cent of people who did live in the countryside were old. They were tied to the countryside by their great love for the land, and their wish to die under the same sky that saw them born. The rest had all left for the cities to make their fortunes.

And the guerrillas moved among them like fish in water?

Well no, not really. On the contrary. I realized that the guerrillas were totally disconnected from the social reality. And I came to the conclusion that the old guerrilla army no longer made any sense, yet nor did creating a new one.

So you abandoned the idea of creating one.
Yes. That conclusion, and my love for Nancy, stopped me. Then came the ambush and the deaths ... Those guerrillas, killing humble soldiers. What cause could justify a crime like that? From then on, I closed my mind to that crazy notion I'd had in Cutufí, Cumaná, and during the anti-guerrilla operations, of leaving the Army. My doubts faded, I decided to go on with my military career, and I began a revolutionary process inside myself, with the idea of a civilian–military alliance already in my head.

Who did the campesinos tend to vote for?
Well, it was interesting to see that the *campesinos* – poor, easily manipulated people – mainly voted for the Adecos. The Acción Democrática party would give them a couple of concrete blocks, a sheet of corrugated iron, a bag of food, a couple of cents. Populism. But maybe the fault didn't lie with the people, the manipulated victims. It was clear to me that Venezuelans were a good, noble, but manipulated people. That's why I wrote in my diary, with a certain pessimism, 'This is what's left of your people, Guaicaipuro, and yours, José Leonardo [Chirino], and yours, Miranda, and yours, Bolívar, this is what's left of your people, Zamora, *Negro* Pérez, Arévalo Cedeño ... Come on, it's time to act, not sleep.'

You were actually writing a diary of political thought.
Yes, a political diary. I enjoy writing, and I was telling the story of those operations, in which I was the officer in charge.

Your journal is also a commentary on the situation in Venezuela: the cause of the guerrilla armies; the reasons for the insurgency; the relationship between the guerrillas and the people; and the Army itself. You're very critical of the way the Army carried out its military operations.
They weren't on the ball. Troop movements were noisy and exaggerated. The officers weren't up to scratch. I didn't idealize the guerrillas, though. I was critical of them too. I criticized both armies.

That's when I began to see there were other paths. Like the one which reflects what Bolívar said about soldiers raising their swords . . . and that's what we did over the next twenty years, working within the Army, creating Bolivarian cells, of which there were eventually quite a few. Nevertheless, the 'detonating spark', as I describe it in this diary, was 4 February 1992. A 'detonating action' envisaged by a young second lieutenant in 1977. You can see it was a long time coming.

What books were you reading at the time?
I was reading Lenin's *What Is to Be Done?* and, of course, Che's *Bolivian Diary*.

Did you tell friends among the other officers that you had created the ELPV?
We had taken an oath of secrecy, but I took the risk of confiding in a young officer called Jesús Urdaneta Hernández, a llanero two years my senior but in the same year, who had also been critical and had become a friend.[10] I told him I'd formed that group. I trusted him. I confessed that I was disappointed with military life and was thinking of leaving the Army.

What did Urdaneta say?
He showed interest. He said we had to talk some more. That I shouldn't leave the Armed Forces. I said in that case we should start thinking about creating a movement inside the Army itself. We both agreed that joining the guerrillas wasn't our thing, that it didn't suit us. We spent a whole night talking politics, having a very animated discussion. And the seed was sown for what, fifteen years later, would become the uprising of 4 February 1992.

---

10   Jesús Urdaneta Hernández (1952–), founding member on 17 December 1982 of the Ejército Bolivariano Revolucionario-200, with Hugo Chávez, Raúl Isaías Baduel and Felipe Antonio Acosta Carlez. He took part in the uprising of 4 February 1992 and in the 1998 election campaign which led to Chávez's victory. He was head of the DISIP, but has now retired from politics.

I want to put two questions to you. How do you explain the fact that the guerrillas were still operating in that area, when they had disappeared from the rest of Venezuela? And how did the guerrillas survive if, as you said, they were disconnected from the people?

They were small groups on their last legs. That was the last ambush of that particular period of the Venezuelan guerrillas. I may have held in my arms the last soldier the guerrillas killed. It was like a tree dying a natural death, but still standing.

Would you describe those guerrillas as 'focalists'?[11]

Well, many such experiments, all over Latin America, were described as *foquistas*. Because they were implanted, artificially, by an armed group in a rural area – preferably mountainous and remote – from where they carried out military operations, mainly ambushes and attacks on small military outposts, in the hope that in the process they would galvanize the peasant population into supporting them. This was successful in the Cuban Revolution. But it did not work anywhere else.

The great error of 'focalism', in my view, resides in the lack of serious preparatory work done by the revolutionary organization among the masses in the theatre of operations. This was fatal, for example, in the case of Che Guevara in Bolivia. He was attacked before he had time to gain the support of the peasant masses.

What happened to the Venezuelan guerrillas?

They all took advantage of peace agreements a few years later. One of them, Gabriel Puerta Aponte, is now on the extreme right along with his group: Bandera Roja, which in the early days was the most hard-line of all the Marxist–Leninist groups, and left the MIR because it considered it to be 'revisionist'. In fact, Bandera had always been infiltrated to the core. Puerta Aponte was one of the

---

11   From the *foco* theory of revolution, theorized by Che Guevara and Régis Debray. The central idea is that small paramilitary revolutionaries can provide a focus for discontent, and by doing so inspire insurrection in the general population.

most renowned leaders of the guerrilla front in the East, but he ended up supporting the coup against us on 11 April 2002. He's still the leader of Bandera Roja, although it has hardly any members. I wonder whether he was always an infiltrator? Or merely a traitor?

Nowadays he and his tiny group are on the far right; they support AD candidates, and receive money from the US embassy. Those last remnants of the guerrilla armies were artificial groups, riddled with gangrene. You asked me how they managed to survive. The information we had was that they lived off cattle rustling, and collecting ransoms for the people they kidnapped.

Would you say they'd turned into outlaws?
Yes, the pejorative word used then was 'bandits', and I really think they'd become more like bandits than guerrillas.

Many guerrilla armies had heroic reputations, yet as Che Guevara says in his diaries, they sometimes killed soldiers who were just poor country boys. For example, in Che's Bolivian Diary, we can see that the Bolivian soldiers are mainly poor and indigenous, but the guerrillas shoot at them and sometimes kill them. Aren't guerrillas armies always like that?
Yes, it would seem a contradiction, but Gramsci explains it as bourgeois civil society taking the reins of the state and what he calls 'political society'. This means the Armed Forces are subordinate to a bourgeois state. But the upper classes don't serve in the army, except as officers. So the foot soldiers are always made up of the common people. In Latin America, this is a given. Bolivian soldiers are indigenous Bolivians, the poorest of the poor. The same goes for Venezuela. The dominant class controls military power, and uses the Armed Forces to preserve its class interests.

Against the interests of the popular classes.
That's right. The upper classes use the poor to put the brakes on those same poor. Since 1999, we in Venezuela have turned that

process on its head. There are now no soldiers defending the interests of the rich. That's why I say ours is a revolutionary army. And it grows more revolutionary by the day. That still makes some people uneasy, but they either accept it or they leave. Of course, no process is irreversible. We can't say the Bolivarian Revolution is irreversible. But for the time being, we're here to keep pushing and seeing it isn't reversed.

Of those soldiers facing the Venezuelan guerrillas on the day of the ambush, not a single one was from the wealthy classes, defending their class interests. Thanks to brainwashing with counter-insurgency manuals, they indoctrinated the mostly middle- or lower-middle-class officers and, especially, the troops. They used the poor to fight the poor. That's why Bolívar said, 'Cursed is the soldier who turns his weapon on his people.' However, none of this justifies the way those guerrillas – some of whom ended up on the far right – slaughtered those soldiers.

So you think that the guerrillas' behaviour should meet certain ethical standards.

Exactly. Otherwise, what's the difference between one side and the other? A revolutionary's concept of violence should have an ethical dimension. Not only respecting the innocent, that's obvious, but also displaying an exemplary morality, irreproachable conduct towards prisoners, never using torture . . . because the Army did resort to torture, disappearances and extra-judicial killings.

Did you witness that in the Armed Forces?

There were excesses on all sides, as there are unfortunately in all wars. But a real soldier should try to do his duty within an ethical framework. That is what the Geneva Convention is for, to guarantee respect for human rights. And, for his part, a revolutionary should be incapable of torturing anyone, even less of killing or giving orders to kill defenceless people.

To answer your question, I remember once, when I was in San Mateo, a military intelligence patrol brought some captured men to our camp, some very scrawny *campesinos*. They accused them of being guerrillas and locked them in a hut. During the night, I began hearing noises, shouts, screams. I went out and saw the men being tortured. A colonel, an old man, was hitting them with a baseball bat wrapped in a cloth. I was outraged, and wrenched the bat from his hands. The *campesinos* were spared further torture that night, at least. But when I asked after the prisoners the following day, I was told they had been taken away. A few days later, we heard they'd 'committed suicide'.

I didn't know that the crimes typical of the Latin American military dictatorships of the period had also been committed in Venezuela. Was it the norm?

You could not protest peacefully here. The regime used openly repressive measures like shooting, beating, tear-gassing protesters, and also covert measures, like clandestinely 'disappearing' and killing opposition leaders. For example, a student leader from the 23 de Enero neighbourhood was killed while he was playing basketball. They said he'd been mugged. *Campesino* leaders were disappeared, political leaders were thrown into the sea from helicopters.

But Venezuela was a democracy . . .

Yes, formally it was. But in those years, the atrocities committed by the repressive forces of the state were similar to those committed by the dictatorships. There was a lot of corruption in the Army. A few years earlier, in 1965, Alberto Lovera, leader of the Venezuelan Communist Party, had been disappeared and his body subsequently found on a beach at Puerto la Cruz.[12] The following year, in 1966, Fabricio Ojeda was arrested by the Armed Forces' Intelligence Services (SIFA), taken to a cell in the Palacio Blanco, opposite the Miraflores Palace, and 'suicided'. And in 1976, Jorge Rodríguez, secretary

---

12   Alberto Lovera, left-wing professor and political leader, secretary general of the Venezuelan Communist Party. Detained on 17 October 1965 by the DIGEPOL, the intelligence services of Raúl Leoni's AD government, he was taken to their headquarters in Los Chaguaramos suburb of Caracas, tortured and murdered. His disfigured body turned up in a fisherman's net ten days later.

general of the Socialist League, was found beaten to death. He was the father of the Jorge Rodríguez who became mayor of Caracas.[13]

Was there corruption in the Army?

In those days, 99 per cent of the generals were corrupt. And almost all of them – with honourable exceptions – were drunkards. The majority of defence ministers were appointed by their cronies in the two main parties, Acción Democrática and Copei. The same thing applied to commanders of the Army, Navy, Air Force and National Guard. The party leadership would subsequently come crawling for their reward: 'Hey, I scratched your back giving you the Army Command, it's time you scratched mine.' Many were compromised even before they were appointed. Some were even card-carrying members of the ruling party. The Casa Militar was at the service of the mistresses of the president of the day, or of any bourgeois grandee.[14] And the presidential residence on La Orchila island, what was that? A brothel. And the Miraflores Palace? Just a place to do business. It was so flagrant that three defence ministers in a row had to flee the country, I remember, because warrants were out for their arrest.

Were they civilian or military?

Military, of course, and they'd been Army chiefs of staff. There was the famous Margold case, for instance, with its consignment of Yugoslav munitions . . .[15]

---

13   Jorge Rodríguez (1965–), psychiatrist and politician, has been president of the National Election Board (2005–2006), vice president of Venezuela (2007–2008), mayor of Libertador Municipality in Caracas (2009–2015) and coordinator of the Partido Socialista Unido de Venezuela (PSUV).

14   In several Latin American countries, the Casa Militar is the administrative body, made up of officers from the different armed forces, which supports the commander in chief of the Armed Forces in his dealings with the Presidency. Another of its functions is the protection and security of the president and senior government ministers.

15   The Margold case was a fraudulent munitions supplies contract entered into by the Venezuelan Armed Forces with the Margold Corporation, which received full payment for a shipment of 105 mm artillery shells which were never delivered. The contract was signed with an army supplier, Gardenia Martínez, who was a protegée of officers linked to President Carlos Andrés Pérez.

They got rich off Army supplies?
Yes, by stealing military supplies or doing business with the
political class. They'd taken over the Armed Forces Social
Prevention Institute (IPSFA), and used its funds for whatever
they fancied. The endemic corruption in politics also penetrated
deep into the Armed Forces. Many officers stole part of the
supplies budget meant for the soldiers, and diverted it for their
personal use.

There were so many different ways of stealing. Some superior
officers even got rich by stealing the soldiers' food. I saw it in
several of the barracks I was in. I denounced them, because that
immorality clashed with the Bolivarian principles and values
instilled in me at the Academy. I was revolted by so much cyni-
cism and hypocrisy. All that corruption was the result of a
general crisis in politics and a widespread moral decay. Moral
above all.

*So the political parties bought the compliance of the Armed
Forces by allowing some officers to line their pockets.*
That's right. Rómulo Betancourt, in the 1960s, was responsible for
the moral decline in the Armed Forces.

That corruption began with Rómulo Betancourt?
Betancourt coined a phrase: 'You have to keep the military happy
with the three C's: *caña* (alcohol), *cobre* (money) and *culo* (sex).'
They turned the barracks into taverns. The best officers I knew
when I was a cadet, or subsequently in the garrisons, never became
generals.

Because those posts were already taken?
No, it wasn't that. The rank of general was reserved for the Adecos
and the Copei cronies. You had to run the gauntlet of Congress and
kowtow to the politicians. It was an abomination. You'd hear senior
officers say, 'You need to learn dominoes, you won't get promoted
playing softball.' A captain advised me, 'Learn to tinkle your whisky
glass.' Social skills were the most important asset, hobnobbing,

networking, schmoozing, sweet-talking. You had to rub shoulders with important people, and then toady up to them. And most of all, you had to have the 'gift': 'Where shall I send the gift?' The situation was summed up in a horrible phrase, accepted by everyone, even those who protested in silence: 'The military career stops at lieutenant colonel.'

From there on rank was a purely political matter?
Yes, political. That's all over now. Last night, for instance, I was up late reviewing the list of promotions. I have them all here, colonel, navy captain, general, admiral, vice admiral, brigade general, division general, even most senior generals . . . political party doesn't come into to it, and nobody would dream of putting in a good word for someone.

But what happens if this officer isn't a socialist, or that officer isn't a revolutionary?
No difference. It's all decided on merit, qualifications, performance in current posts. And, of course, diligence and professionalism.

That's rather hard to believe . . .
Well, I'm telling you. We are not the caricatures our adversaries have made us out to be. That adherence to party politics is long gone. For example, when I was a captain, it was Sodom and Gomorra. There was a group of generals we called the 'Blanca Ibáñezes'. Blanca Ibáñez was the mistress of President Jaime Lusinchi [1984–1989], and she decided who got promoted.

Was she the lady who once dressed up as a general?
Yes, that's the one. She once wore a uniform, not a general's, though; I think she only dressed as a private. I was away on the Colombian border at the time, I didn't see the pictures, but I heard the gossip. That woman had a lot of power. I met her when I came here to the Palace during Lusinchi's last year as president. She was a very hard, arrogant woman, people were afraid of her. I saw her in the corridors, and at various ceremonies in 1988. She and

Lusinchi left in 1989 when Carlos Andrés Pérez came to power for the second time.

But we've got well ahead of ourselves. I suggest we go back to Cumaná, to the end of the 1970s when I left my posting there and went to Maracay.

9

In Maracay

Living in a shack – Bravos de Apure Battalion
Fidel's speech – Wedding to Nancy – Douglas Bravo
The PRV-*Ruptura* Movement – Hugo Trejo – William Izarra
Tank man – Alfredo Maneiro – Fragmentation of the Left
Fidel Castro and Cristina Maica
Protest songs in barracks
Training recruits – Political reading
Christ, revolutionary radical

When did you go to Maracay?
At the end of 1977. One day I was on guard duty in the Cumaná barracks when a lieutenant came up to me. It was José María Morales Franco, known to all at the Academy as 'Willy Mora'. We'd been chatting for a while, when he said, 'You were in communications like me, weren't you? How long have you been in Cumaná?' Two and a half years, I told him. 'And how do you feel? Would you like to leave?' 'I wouldn't mind,' I told him, 'but I have to wait until July to see if I get promoted to lieutenant.'

He himself was dying to get out of Maracay, where he was clocking up a lot of sanctions in the Bravos de Apure Battalion, so he suggested, 'Why don't we do a straight swap? You to Maracay and me to Cumaná?' 'That would be tricky, between a lieutenant and a second lieutenant,' I said, 'and I don't have an uncle who's a general who can fix it.' So he said, 'If you agree, I'll ask my uncle to get us a straight swap.' His uncle really was a general!

Did you know him well?
Very well. Willy Mora is a real character. Not long ago, I mentioned him on *Aló Presidente* and three days later the head of the Presidential Guard called up: 'Willy Mora has just checked into the Military Social Club. He says he's not paying, that you sent for him, and he's not leaving until he sees you.' That's him all over.

Quite cheeky.
When we were cadets, he once sang during the inauguration of some Inter-Institute Sports, and landed up in the glasshouse. He began singing a Sandro number called 'Rosa, Rosa' which went, 'Ay, Rosa, Rosa, magnificent rose / like a white goddess / such a beautiful blossom / your love condemns me / to suffer sweet pain . . . Ay, Rosa, Rosa, give me your lips / this furious passion / that my love provokes / causes such tears / because I love you, and you alone.'[1] And he dedicated the song – with those words! – to the general's wife, who was very beautiful. Willy was wearing the blue cape of student music groups and when he finished, he flung the cape at the lady's feet, like a bullfighter. The general, one of those stern men from the Andes who never crack a smile, was furious. 'Lock him up!' he shouted, there and then!

On another occasion, when we were cadets in Caracas, we took some girls to La Cueva de Oro disco. We weren't in uniform and didn't have permission. Trying not to be noticed, we sat with the girls in a dark corner. Suddenly, there was guy in a *liqui-liqui* on stage, singing. It was Willy Mora! He finished his song, and shouted down the microphone, 'I dedicate my second song to *brigadier* Chávez Frías, *brigadier* Pérez Isa . . .' He named us all, one by one!

---

1 Sandro (1945–2010), real name Roberto Sánchez, was an Argentine pop singer of romantic ballads, famous all over Latin America.

Did you finally manage to get transferred to Maracay?
Yes. At the beginning of December 1977, I got an unexpected radiogram: 'Second lieutenant Hugo Chávez, present yourself to the Bravos de Apure armoured battalion, Maracay. Post of communications officer.' A few days later I was in Maracay, being received by Lieutenant Camejo: 'You've no idea what you've got yourself into.' For me, this was a second education.

Did Nancy go with you?
Sure, I brought Nancy. We came to live in the big, beautiful city of Maracay, in the shanty town of Francisco de Miranda, with *Chicho* Romero, that same relative who had helped me in Caracas. It was only a cardboard and corrugated-iron shack, but I was relieved because Nancy would be living in a family. *Chicho* drove a public minibus in Río Blanco. That December, Nancy became pregnant, although we didn't find out till January. The beautiful result was my daughter Rosa Virginia.

Another stage of your life began.
Yes, you could say that. Another stage of my life took off.

What happened to the ELPV?
When I came to Maracay, as the 'commander' of that 'Liberation Army', I was still thinking about leaving the Armed Forces. And the other members, all enlisted men, had already been discharged. Only Silva and I were left. The other three, Moros, Toro and Núñez, were sergeants; Silva was a corporal. Anyway, that 'army' was put on ice. But let me tell you a story.

Thirty years later, I mentioned it in *Aló Presidente*, and said, 'That army only lasted a month, because I went to Maracay and the soldiers all left.' A few days later, I went to the Llanos to inaugurate a natural gas well. There was big crowd there. I got out of the helicopter, greeted the people, and a National Guard officer came up to me and said, 'Comandante, a sergeant in my squad wants to talk to you.' I thought it was a soldier with personal problems, so I said, 'Let me finish my schedule, I'll see him at the end. What's his problem?' He replied, 'Nothing, he just wants to talk to you. He's right here'.

A short, fat, white-haired sergeant came forward: 'Comandante, Sergeant Toro. At your service.' I stared at him. 'Are you . . .?' 'Yes,' he said, 'from the ELPV.' He was almost in tears. And he added, 'Over there, that tall white-haired man is Núñez.' I turned round and saw Núñez in civvies. I called to him, and we embraced in silence, overcome with emotion. Núñez said, 'I've got 3,000 reservists here in Portuguesa state. The ELPV has grown.' And Moros was in San Felipe, apparently. A few days later, they all came to see me in the Miraflores Palace. Silva came too, from Barinas, where he had a plot of land. He was very thin: 'I've been going hungry,' he said. We gave him a little tractor. They told me, 'We always kept track of whatever you were doing, and we wanted to join the 4 February rebellion. We called ourselves "the reserve".' So, that 'Army' was never disbanded after all. The following Sunday on *Aló Presidente*, I set the record straight: 'I'd like to inform the country that the Ejército de Liberación del Pueblo Venezolano never died.'

Did you come across any friends in Maracay?

After a while *Negro* Piña, my old friend from Sabaneta, appeared on the horizon. One Friday afternoon, I was in uniform, shopping in the Capcimide Commercial Centre, when I suddenly heard, 'Huguito!' Only in my village do they call me Huguito; my father is Hugo, and I'm Huguito. It was *Negro* Piña, the nephew of my godfather Eligio Piña, the one who told me about Bolívar.

Was he your age?

No, he was a bit older. He was a radio commentator, with a deep growl of a voice. He was going bowling with some friends and invited me. I put my shopping – milk, tomatoes, kilo of meat – in the boot of the car and stayed out bowling. Poor Nancy! I got home at five in the morning. There were no mobile phones back then. The heat had ruined the food. Nancy was furious.

And were you reunited with any friends from the Academy?
Yes, there was a group of former cadets: Antonio Hernández Borgo, González Guzmán and Pedro Ruiz Rondón. Pedro and I had an ideological affinity: as cadets in 1973, we had listened together to the speech Fidel Castro made when he came back from India, after the coup in Chile topped Salvador Allende's Popular Unity government. Fidel was in India when Allende fell. He'd been to Guyana, Trinidad and Tobago, and to the Fourth Summit of Non-aligned Countries in Algiers, before going on to India.

And Vietnam.
Yes, India and Vietnam. Between Algeria and India, he had stopped off in Iraq. Fidel told me himself that on 11 September he was dining, or having a meeting, with Indira Gandhi when he was told the news of Allende's death. He then went on to Vietnam, and on his return to Havana, he delivered a major speech. Ruiz Rondón and I listened to it live.

Is it the speech in which he gives the details of the coup, and how Salvador Allende died fighting?
Yes, he gave all the details. It's the one where he says, 'If every worker and every peasant had had a gun in his hand, there would not have been a Fascist coup!' Ruíz Rondón and I took that to heart. It confirmed in my mind the necessity of a revolutionary civilian–military alliance. After that, whenever we'd meet, I'd say, 'If every worker . . .' and he'd reply, 'and every peasant . . .' He did a good job on the day of the coup against us [11 April 2002]. He was in Maracaibo and took control of the base at Fuerte Mara. We subsequently made him commander of the armoured brigade in Valencia, he was a colonel. He died suddenly, of cancer.

The military regime in Maracay was very harsh, wasn't it?
It was a forge, for tempering character. I felt braced by the change at once. From a battalion in Cumaná where discipline was relaxed, and where rules and regulations weren't strictly applied, I went to a

school of first-rate captains like Alvarado Pinto, Jon Díaz, Pedro Salazar Monsalve, Yanoguiski Hernández, etc. Second Commander Salazar was very good, and the commander was Luis Pulido.

I was on guard duty on New Year's Eve. *Chicho* went to Barinas for the holidays, and Nancy and I had the shack to ourselves. I remember the neighbours asking me, 'Lieutenant, don't you mind living in that shack, among us poor people?' The commander found out . . .

That you were living there?
Yes, that we lived in this slum and that I had a woman. He called me in, and we talked. He turned up at the house one day.

Nancy was pregnant?
Yes, but it didn't show. Commander Pulido wanted to see how Lieutenant Chávez lived. That was very much his style; he used to visit his officers at home. We sat down, offered him coffee, and he went away impressed. The following day he called me in again: 'Are you thinking of marrying your girlfriend?' 'Yes, Commander.' 'Fine, apply for the permit.'

What permit?
The authorization an officer has to get from the Army to allow him to get married. You have to present a report and dig out I don't know how many documents. But eventually, in July 1978, the permit arrived. We got married in August that year, and Rosa Virginia was born shortly afterwards. She's the eldest. Later on, Nancy and I had two other children: María Gabriela and Hugo Rafael. The best man at my wedding was Captain Alvarado, my company commander.

Did you fit into this new environment without any problems?
Yes. I felt great there, right from the start. From the commander down, everyone gave Rosa Virginia the nickname *Maisantica*. I had begun to research Maisanta. I wasn't as yet obsessive about his story, but I'd found evidence that he was an officer in Cipriano Castro's

Army and had joined the guerrillas against Juan Vicente Gómez. I'd read José León Tapia's book, and had talked about him with José Esteban Ruiz Guevara.

Did your existential confusion disappear?

Not at all. I went to Barinas in December 1977, I remember how the dilemma was still hanging over me. I told Adán, 'I'm still thinking about leaving.' Adán nearly lost his temper: 'How long are you going to keep on about that?' 'I want to study,' I told him. I'd asked permission to study in the Armed Forces' Polytechnic (IUPFA), I'd even bought some books on physics, and sat an exam. I liked engineering; I wanted to be an electronics engineer. 'You're crazy,' said Major Alfonso. I filled in the forms, but never got accepted in the IUPFA. So I kept insisting to Adán that I wanted to study and asked him to help me get a place at the University. He was now a lecturer in the University of the Andes in Mérida, and a married man.

What did he teach?

Maths and physics. He'd always been a good student, dedicated, serious and modest. So he repeated what he'd said before, 'How can you think of quitting? We in left-wing politics have got our hopes pinned on you. Look what's happening in this country.' 'That's exactly why I want out'. His expression turned serious. 'You can't leave the Army, Hugo.' And he revealed – for the first time – that he was in a movement called the Partido de la Revolución Democrática–Ruptura, which was the legal political wing of the PRV–FALN, the guerrilla organization founded in 1966 by Douglas Bravo and Fabricio Ojeda, after they broke away from the Communist Party.

The PRV had a big intellectual influence on left-wing circles in Venezuela at that time, didn't it?

Yes, for the political, economic and social ideas they put forward about social exclusion, negritude, oil, the need for an alliance between Latin America and the Muslim-Arab world. And also because its supporters included intellectuals of the stature of the writer and artist Carlos Contramaestre, the novelist Salvador Garmendia, Dr Bernard Mommer, the architect Fruto Vivas, the lawyer Alí Rodríguez Araque . . .[2] My brother Adán had been a member of the MIR, but was persuaded to switch to the PRV by one of his professors, Juan Salazar, a physicist friend of Douglas Bravo.

Was Douglas Bravo no longer a guerrilla?

No. In 1962, in line with the Communist Party strategy of the time, Douglas had founded the José Leonardo Chirino Front in the Falcón hills. Under his command were Alí Rodríguez and Teodoro Petkoff. At the time we're talking about, though, the Front had dissolved and Douglas went on to found the PRV–FALN. Neither he nor Alí Rodríguez accepted the amnesty offered to the guerrillas, and were still in clandestinity. They had spent a long time planning to infiltrate the Armed Forces with a view to creating a civilian–military alliance. This was one of the missions of the PRV; it was always a very serious group, despite many of their leaders being underground in the cities.

What did you think of Douglas and the PRV's plans?

To infiltrate the Army?

Yes.

It didn't seem very realistic. There was a very strong anti-Marxist culture at the heart of the Army, and any attempt of this kind would give the Army – even the progressives – the feeling that they were being manipulated. Like Douglas, I was all for a civilian–military alliance, but I thought the seed of the movement should be sown and developed in the heart of the Army itself, from inside.

---

2   Dr Bernard Mommer, with mathematics and social science degrees from the University of Tübingen, is considered a global expert in hydrocarbons. Author among other works of *Global Oil and the Nation State*, Oxford University Press, 2002.

Did you know of any movement of this kind within the Armed Forces at that time?

No, I didn't. I sensed that younger officers were very unhappy with the scandalous level of corruption among the top brass. They were also concerned about the way the country was being governed. But, as a young officer, I was quite isolated and didn't have many contacts with officers in other garrisons, so I didn't know what might be being hatched in this or that barracks.

Why was there so much discontent? The country was developing, living standards were rising, the middle class was growing...

That was on the surface. The reality of Venezuela was still widespread poverty, and huge corruption in the governing classes. Democracy was just a façade, behind which politicians and businessmen had established a Mafia-like pact to achieve unimaginable levels of mutual enrichment. Remember that oil prices had shot up exorbitantly because of the Arab–Israeli war in 1973. I think our crude, that was at $1.76 a barrel in 1970, tripled to $3.56 in 1973, and then, in 1974 when Carlos Andrés Pérez came to power, it went through the roof to $10.31 a barrel! The country's income multiplied tenfold. What's more, in 1976 Carlos Andrés nationalized the oil companies. An excellent decision, and a very positive one in terms of sovereignty, but which aggravated social problems because the state's new and copious resources were not used to reduce inequalities. On the contrary, the differences between rich and poor were accentuated, and the feeling of injustice was compounded ...

Uslar Pietri wrote that 'between 1973 and 1984, Venezuela earned over $200 billion from oil exploitation alone, the equivalent of twenty Marshall Plans'.

And one Marshall Plan was enough to rebuild the whole of a Europe destroyed by the Second World War.[3] So just imagine. Here, it sent

---

3 The European Recovery Programme (ERP), also called the Marshall Plan after the US secretary of state at the time, George Marshall, was launched by President Harry

corruption sky-high. Anyone who had the tiniest bit of power began stealing shamelessly. Resources which could have been used for social development programmes, to improve the lives of the forgotten masses of Venezuelans, were squandered. This created a feeling of deep unease among many intellectuals and political activists. And within the Armed Forces, especially among young officers.

That's why various military conspiracies emerged, wasn't it?
Yes, although I didn't know of them at the time. I've already mentioned the revolts in 1962, in Carúpano and Puerto Cabello, organized by army officers with the support of left-wing activists – from the Communist Party and the MIR – and where the civilian–military insurgents were massacred. At the end of the 1950s, even before the triumph of the Cuban Revolution, the Venezuelan Communist Party (PCV), to which Douglas Bravo then belonged, had defined a strategy for working with the Armed Forces. It aimed to incorporate army officers into the revolutionary project. In a few years, dozens of officers from poor backgrounds were won over by the PCV. Many of them took part in the *Carupanazo* and *Porteñazo*. When these uprisings failed, many of the surviving officers headed for the hills to join the FALN guerrillas, and several of them commanded guerrilla fronts of various kinds.

What was happening within the Army meanwhile?
Well, after those two uprisings, there was a ferocious purge in the Armed Forces. It was during the presidencies of Rómulo Betancourt and Raúl Leoni, close allies of the US and enforcers of their anti-Communist and anti-Castrist policies. Their intelligence services mercilessly pursued any left-wing sympathizers within the Armed Forces. Nevertheless, it didn't eradicate the influence of one extraordinary man, someone I have already mentioned: Colonel Hugo Trejo.

Truman (1945–1952) to reconstruct the sixteen countries in Western Europe after the Second World War. The amount of aid is estimated at $13 billion.

The leader of the military uprising of 1 January 1958.

That's right; he prepared the popular uprising that caused the fall of the dictator Pérez Jiménez. Trejo's motto was 'Democratize the Armed Forces and integrate them with the people of Venezuela'. He gained a great deal of prestige, so the new government transferred him from the Army to an embassy abroad. But his influence within the military remained, and even increased among certain dissenting sectors. He wrote a book called *The Revolution Is Not Over*, which became essential barracks reading.[4] It coined the term *Trejismo*, a movement which advocated uniting the military and the people. When Trejo returned to Venezuela at the end of the 1960s, he re-established contact with many of the officers who had voiced criticisms and who later joined our Revolutionary Bolivarian Movement.

You said you knew him well.

Yes, but not then, much later on when, after the Caracazo, he decided to return to the political struggle and created an organization, the Movimiento Nacionalista Venezolano Integral (MNVI) [Venezuelan Nationalist Integral Movement]. I got to know him even better after our rebellion of 4 February 1992, and our detention in Yare prison. He supported us, defended us and backed our political approach. I knew him as a white-haired old man; I learned a lot from talking to him, he told me about Bolívar and how Acción Democrática had betrayed democracy. He was a great leader; he sowed the seeds of rebellion.

Among the young officers you knew, were any involved in conspiracies?

Yes. Although I wasn't aware of it at the time, in 1978–1979 a well-respected Air Force officer, Colonel William Izarra, had formed the

---

4 Hugo Trejo, *La Revolución no ha terminado*, Vadell Hnos. Editores, Valencia-Caracas 1977.

Revolución-83 (R-83) group of young officers.[5] Subsequently, in 1980, Izarra created another important clandestine organization called Alianza Revolucionaria de Militares Activos (ARMA) [Revolutionary Alliance of Active-Service Soldiers], which was made up of about a hundred Air Force officers with an excellent ideological training. That group did not prosper, because Izarra was betrayed and expelled from the Air Force. However, it sowed revolutionary seeds too.

William Izarra made international contacts.
Yes, many. At the beginning of the 1980s, Izarra and others of his group travelled abroad, without official permission, to countries which had undergone what in those days were considered progressive political experiments, in which the military had played a part.

He was in touch with Saddam Hussein and Muammar Gaddafi, I believe?
Well, I don't know if he met them personally, but yes, he did travel secretly to Baghdad and had links to the Ba'ath Party in Iraq. He also went to Libya, whose leader was then, and had been since the revolution of July 1969, Colonel Muammar Gaddafi. Izarra also went to Cuba. He was interested in all those political experiments, and they were subsequently useful to us.

He was in contact with Douglas Bravo too, wasn't he?
Yes, they'd met through Izarra's brother, Richard, a very polemical journalist who edited the left-wing magazine *Reventón* [Explosion].

---

5   William Izarra (1947–), Air Force colonel, completed his training in the US. In one of his first missions, when he was nineteen, he had to wipe out a column of guerrillas who had come from Cuba. Two guerrillas were taken prisoner and interrogated. One of them was Lieutenant Antonio Briones Montoto, who told Izarra that he had not been forced to fight in Venezuela but had come out of international solidarity. Izarra began to question what he had learned at the Military Academy. He contacted Douglas Bravo's group and began to collaborate with them while in the Air Force. He later joined Hugo Chávez. He is the father of the journalist Andrés Izarra (born 1969), several times minister of communications and former president of the TV channel Telesur.

Colonel Izarra and Douglas Bravo had secret meetings. Douglas had left the Communist Party by then because of theoretical differences over Soviet orthodoxy. He harked back to our own national history to reconfigure ideas inspired by Bolívar, Rodríguez, Zamora and other Venezuelan thinkers. This 'repatriation' of revolutionary theories appealed to military officers, many of whom felt Bolivarian, and helped disseminate throughout the barracks the idea of an uprising led by a civilian–military alliance. Douglas's project was to persuade officers from the various forces to join the revolutionary movement.

Didn't your brother Adán try to recruit you?
He tried, naturally. I'd already told him, 'OK, to convince me not to leave the Army, tell me what your plan is.' He replied, 'Hugo, I don't have the authority to tell you anything, it's a matter of discipline; but I've told our leaders about you and what you believe in.' Then he said, 'Do you want to meet Douglas Bravo?' Of course I did!

Douglas Bravo was something of a legend, wasn't he?
Yes, Douglas was a legend.[6] That same month, January 1978, or maybe it was February, Adán came to Maracay and we met up with his maths professor friend, Nelson Sánchez alias 'Harold'. He was to be my contact and would introduce me to Douglas. We met in the Parque Aragua.

In secret.
That's right, I wasn't in uniform. From then on, I would be leading a double life: my army life and my other, clandestine life. A few days later I was in Caracas. I'd started off in my Volkswagen, changed cars somewhere, and was taken to a house in south Caracas. That's where I met Douglas Bravo.

Was that your first meeting with Douglas?
The first. It was then that I accepted that I had a role to play.

---

6   See Douglas Bravo, *Douglas Bravo Speaks: Interview with Venezuelan Guerrilla Leader*, Pathfinder Press, Atlanta, 1970.

A mission.

A mission within Douglas's organization, PRV-Ruptura. I asked him the same question I'd asked Adán, 'What's the plan?' Douglas replied, 'The plan is to construct a civilian–military–religious insurrection'. I liked the idea, because it was what I'd been thinking for quite some time. I decided to go down that road with them. So I started reading documents, texts and manifestos written by Douglas, and going to meetings in Maracay, Valencia and Caracas.

Always clandestinely?

Of course. This new activity dispelled all thoughts I'd had of leaving the Army. I took on a role for the long haul in the PRV-Ruptura movement, with a view to a general civilian–military insurrection. It was what I had always believed in. I began reading a very interesting collection of essays edited by the Mexican sociologist Claude Heller, entitled *The Army as an Agent of Social Change*, in which he stated, 'In circumstances in which military officers consider the civilian leadership to be corrupt, incompetent or in some way incapable of carrying out the basic tasks of government, their motivation to take over those functions themselves increases proportionately.'[7]

As you can imagine, that sentence struck a chord in me given the rampant corruption in Venezuela under Presidents Carlos Andrés Pérez, Luis Herrera Campíns and Jaime Lusinchi.[8] I thought of the contrast between them and Velasco Alvarado in Peru, Torrijos in Panama, and Torres in Bolivia. All this helped entrench even more the values I'd learned as a soldier. I wasn't a bad soldier, but I told myself that I had to be the very best, and surround myself with soldiers of the same mindset. At the time I was alone.

---

7 Claude Heller, *El Ejército como agente de cambio social*, Fondo de Cultura Económica, Col. Tierra firme, Mexico DF, 1979. The book brings together the papers on military intervention presented during the XXX International Congress of Human Sciences in Asia and North Africa, held in Mexico City, 1976.

8 Luis Herrera Campíns (1925–2007), lawyer and leader of the Copei party, elected on 13 December 1978, president of Venezuela 1979–1984, succeeding Carlos Andrés Pérez (AD) and preceding Jaime Lusinchi (AD).

You needed to build a network.

Right, and to build a network, to attract other soldiers to my cause,
I needed be one of the best officers and study a lot more. So I began
preparing myself, reading up . . .

Can you remember any of the books you read?

I bought books about socialism. I also read the polemical works of
the day, like Antonio Stempel's *Venezuela: An Ailing Democracy*, or
Américo Martín's *The Big Fish*, which described how the new
corrupt oligarchies operated in the shadow of power.[9] Martín
affirms, for example, 'With oil, a new asset appeared in Venezuela
and a new object of plunder for those in positions of power. . . .
Any professional nowadays negotiates his cut at dead of night,
assesses offers in the silence of an office where noises disappear into
deep-pile carpets, and becomes a partner in a company on condition of anonymity.'

The dirty deals, made with government complicity, meant the
rich got even richer and amassed colossal fortunes, while the poor
received mere crumbs from the oil money table.

Do you remember any other books?

Yes, for instance, *When the Man Sure Isn't Walking*, by Sanín. The title
was a pun on the Carlos Andrés Pérez campaign jingle, 'That Man
Sure Is Walking'.[10] Another best-seller by Sanín was called *Saudi
Venezuela*. And I also remember reading *After the Tunnel* by Diego
Salazar, an account of how twenty-three guerrillas escaped from the
San Carlos barracks.[11] The break-out proved there were political
prisoners in Venezuela, contrary to the claims of the Pérez

---

9   Antonio Stempel, *Venezuela, una democracia enferma. Apuntes para el estudio del
desarrollo político venezolano*, Editorial Ateneo de Caracas, Caracas, 1981; Américo
Martín, *Los peces gordos*, Vadell Hnos. Editores, Valencia, 1977.

10   'Sanín' was the pseudonym of Alfredo Tarre Murzi. The campaign jingle was '*Ese
hombre sí camina*', hence the book's title *Cuando el hombre no camina*, Vadell Hnos.
Editores, Valencia-Caracas, 1976.

11   Diego Salazar: *Después del túnel*, Editorial Ruptura, Caracas, 1975. The San
Carlos barracks is now a historical monument.

government. Another book I bought in August 1987 was *The Power Within You*.[12] I found it incredibly interesting, I read and reread it. It's a self-help book. I studied it very seriously. It was a period of enlightenment for me, you know? I'd say it was one of the best times of my life.

Because your destiny became clear . . .
Yes, I had chosen my path. I was taking on a revolutionary commitment. What's more, my wife was pregnant, Rosa was born, I became a lieutenant in a real battalion, which I was proud to belong to. The Bravos de Apure had French AMX-30 tanks in those days.

You decided to become a better soldier.
Yes, I wanted to be an expert in my speciality. Though I had problems to begin with.

What sort of problems?
The first conflict arose when I was put in command of an armoured battalion communications squad. The battalion commander, Luis Pulido, a harsh but humane man, called me in and said: 'Your fellow soldiers hold you in high regard, so I'm going to put you in command of a tank squad, because I'm short of officers . . .' I didn't know the first thing about tanks.

How did you get on with the tank squad?
I didn't get just one; they gave me two squads, six enormous tanks. Each tank had a maintenance manual the size of a telephone directory. If a part got damaged, we had to send to France for a new one. I was pretty out of my depth. The captain calmed me down. 'Trust your sergeants.' So I started studying tanks. I immersed myself in the subject, day and night, with my sergeants and my men.

---

12   Claude M. Bristol and Harold Sherman, *TNT: The Power Within You*, Prentice Hall, New York, 1954.

It can't have been easy.

No, it wasn't, so I decided to change my speciality from communications to armoured vehicles. I applied for reclassification, and
enrolled in a basic tank course. I spent my whole time studying,
and came out top of the class. It's not that I'm a great brain, but
when I decide to do something, I put my heart and soul into it.
The sergeants had all attended courses in France, at the workshops
of SOFMA, the French armaments company that manufactured
the tanks. They had studied the operating manual.

So when I was on night duty, I'd get a blackboard and ask the
men questions like, 'How does the engine cooling system work?
How do you fire straight? How do you fire in a curve? How do you
calculate distance?' All sorts of details. I went into it in depth. Every
evening I'd study the concept of 'armoured warfare', analysing wars
in the Middle East, the Arab–Israeli war . . . In the end, I won the
prize for best tank instructor.

You liked armoured vehicles.

Yes. I was finally on my chosen path, and was forging my character
in the forge of the Maracay battalion. I was promoted to
lieutenant.

In July 1978, Luis Pulido was promoted to colonel, and moved
on. He handed over the battalion to the new commander, Hugo
García Hernández, a severe disciplinarian.

By this time, Carlos Andrés Pérez was no longer president.

Right, his first mandate was over. The elections of December 1978
were won by Luis Herrera Campíns. Carlos Andrés had talked
about our 'Great Venezuela', but had presided over the greatest
wave of corruption in living memory. Luis Herrera confirmed, 'I've
been handed a mortgaged Venezuela.' That phrase passed into
history. Meanwhile, I continued my meetings with Douglas Bravo.

In the PRV-Ruptura movement?

Yes, and shortly afterwards, I was elected to the central committee
of PRV-Ruptura. Douglas broke the news: 'Look, "José Antonio"'

– that was my *nom de guerre* – 'I proposed, and it was unanimously accepted, that you form part of the central committee of PRV-Ruptura, although for obvious reasons you won't be attending committee meetings.'

But you were also sympathetic to La Causa R, weren't you?
Yes, my spectrum of political activity widened in 1978. I met Alfredo Maneiro, general secretary of La Causa R, while the electoral campaign was in full swing.

How did that come about?
Nancy and I had left the shack we were living in and set ourselves up in a little apartment a friend had managed to get for us. Maneiro came to that apartment. Our contact was my friend from Barinas, Federico Ruiz, Vladimir's brother. We met up in the Plaza Bolívar in Maracay, my car led the way, Maneiro followed in a jeep with another Causa R leader called Pablo Medina and Federico.[13] Maneiro drove very gingerly along the side of the road. We reached my house, which was on an upper floor, and spent all day talking.

What did Maneiro say to you?
He said something like, that with me 'they'd found the fourth leg of the table'.

What did that mean?
That they already had the first three legs: the working class, especially in Ciudad Guayana; the middle class; the intellectuals; and now, with me representing the Armed Forces, they had the fourth leg.[14] They did important work among the masses, and that interested me for the civilian–military alliance that I was seriously

---

13 Pablo Medina was one of the founders and secretary general of La Causa Radical. He was a deputy in 1993 and one of the founders of Patria para Todos (PPT, *Patria* for All) when La Causa R split. He is now in the Frente Social Civico-Militar (Civilian–Military Social Front), which opposes Hugo Chávez.

14 From its beginnings in 1971, La Causa R managed to create a workers' bastion and electoral base in Sidor, the steel industry complex near Ciudad Guayana in Bolívar state.

thinking of. To get an idea of the tasks involved in that kind of political work, I joined – clandestinely – a group of La Causa R militants who'd go into the poor areas of Caracas, like Catia for example, to distribute leaflets and put up posters.

What else did Maneiro say?

That a revolutionary needed two main qualities: profound ideological conviction, and absolute efficiency in carrying out his mission. Not the easiest qualities to find in a political activist, actually. How many times have I been reminded of Maneiro's words! Since I've been president, I've seen again and again how certain comrades, given basic tasks to do, prove incapable of carrying them out – whether out of stupidity, ineptitude or laziness. Or else they forget this government is a revolutionary government that serves the people, and behave like little bureaucratized satraps, when they're not downright corrupt.

Good observation from Maneiro, then.

Yes, very good. He had a great strategic sense. He talked about the need to create a vanguard because, without it, the popular movement would fail no matter how much impetus it had. He had done a theoretical study of it in his book *Negative Notes*.[15] I'll always remember him saying, 'Listen, Chávez, don't you forget, we're in this for the long haul . . .' He knew I was meeting Douglas Bravo and other people from Ruptura. I even began to suggest uniting the movements, but it was never possible. The years passed, 4 February [1992] arrived, but the Left was never united. In the end the military movement did it pretty much alone, after trying out many ways of building a mass movement, a political movement, that would include the working class, the students, the peasants and the urban masses. It was impossible! Couldn't be done.

Perhaps Maneiro saw I was impetuous, because he advised me, 'Don't make any short-term commitment to any movement, it will fail. This is for the long haul, a decade or more; always remember that.'

---

15   See Alfredo Maneiro, *Notas negativas*, Editorial Venezuela 83, Caracas, 1971.

Did you try to get Maneiro and Douglas Bravo together?
Yes; I used to meet each one separately, it was absurd. And I started
asking them why they didn't try to join forces. But there was no way;
each rejected the idea of meeting the other. Like the soldiers grouped
around Hugo Trejo, they didn't want to meet us Bolivarian officers
either. Not even meet. Each organization sniped about the others.
Everything was division, dispersal . . . A disaster. Time went by and
when the Caracazo happened [27 February 1989], the left-wing opposition was still fragmented, disjointed, divided into a thousand pieces,
a tower of Babel. Even when the rebellion of 4 February [1992] took
place, we revolutionary soldiers had to act on our own because the left-
wing political organizations couldn't agree on whether to join the
Bolivarian Revolution or not. They were all obsessed by the same thing:
hegemonizing the revolutionary movement, yet this priority objective
led them to fight among themselves. A tragedy. Bolívar was right when
he demanded 'unity, unity, or anarchy will devour us', and when he
declared, 'Unity is all we need to complete the work of our regenera-
tion.' The Left's fragmentation, discord, lack of historical vision and
inability to achieve long-term unity are among the main reasons for the
frequent victories of the Right in Latin America.

***What doctrinal differences were there between the PRV-Ruptura
and La Causa R?***
I'd say that Maneiro and La Causa R aspired, in the long term, to
organize a massive general strike which would lead to a working-class
uprising, supported by some sectors of the Armed Forces, and bring
a revolutionary workers' government to power.[16] Douglas Bravo and
Ruptura, for their part, proposed a civilian–military revolutionary
uprising to topple the existing corrupt order and replace it with a
Bolivarian, patriotic, revolutionary government. Both options
seemed legitimate and interesting to me. And there was a possibility,
I'm convinced of it, of making a synthesis of the two positions.

But the divisions and rivalries were so strong that I began to

---

16   See Alfredo Maneiro, *Ideas políticas para el debate actual*, texts selected by Marta
Harnecker, Editorial El perro y la rana, Caracas, 2007.

wonder, rather anxiously, if one day they would quarrel with me too. And I'd be in danger if someone informed about me being a soldier. In any case, those fratricidal struggles made me think, however confusedly, that ultimately the movement should emerge from inside the Armed Forces themselves. And that *that* movement itself, in essence Bolivarian, had the capacity to unify the civilian–military alliance we needed, and to guide it.

Meanwhile, then, you kept building your own network inside the army.

Yes. And not only the army; I began to make friends through sport, culture, at the University, and to organize artistic events on our parade ground. Maluenga, the NCO who conducted the military band, was from Barinas. He was a real musician, he played the harp and also had his own band; he earned his living playing here and there. One day I asked him, 'Maluenga, why don't we put on shows here in the battalion?' On Fridays, they showed films, so the idea would be to put on groups for half an hour or so. That's what we did. One night we brought Cristina Maica, she'd have been about fifteen at the time.

Who is she?

A great singer. I remember Maluenga telling me, 'Don't forget the name. Cristina Maica. That kid's going to be a great singer.' He wasn't wrong. She's one of the best. Fidel took a shine to her. When he came [in October 2000], we had lunch in the Ministry of Foreign Affairs, we invited Cristina and she sang, walking from table to table. She performed a song that was very popular at the time, 'The Neighbour', about a jealous woman singing to her rival: 'He's mine, he's mine / don't mess with what's mine / if you play that kind of game / you have to be a real woman.' Fidel couldn't take his eyes off her. When the song ended, Fidel hugged her and said to me, 'Mine, mine . . . don't mess with what's mine.' He was warning me to stay away. Cristina was very impressed by Fidel.

On another occasion, we brought Reyna Lucero to the barracks. She hadn't even made her first record then, she wasn't famous. She was a friend of Maluenga's.

Were you still expanding your circle of friends?
Yes, my social circle in Maracay was widening. I was on top form. Just think, the PRV-Ruptura and Douglas Bravo on one side, La Causa R and Alfredo Maneiro on the other. And in the midst of all this spiritual, personal, moral and political growth, I found myself painting and writing. That was the time I wrote short stories. I even sent one off to a short-story competition in *El Nacional*, a very prestigious competition held every year. It's lost some of its prestige lately. Within the Armed Forces there was a history competition, and I did some research on Maisanta for it. He reappeared in my life more clearly.

In what sense?
In the sense that the life and example of that old guerrilla, my great-grandfather, would have more influence on my personal trajectory than other political contacts. For example, I was still meeting with Douglas and Maneiro, two living, even legendary men, and yet the principal influence on that young man of twenty-four, alongside Bolívar and his thinking, was a dead man: Pedro Pérez Delgado, Maisanta. I was in search of historical roots. Not only mine, from mine I jumped to the collective, the Army's, and beyond that, Venezuela's.

Were you still playing baseball?
Yes, I found sport in Maracay too. Through *Chicho* Romero, I started to play baseball. But the battalion was my main day-to-day responsibility.

And your main concern?
Absolutely. I received the Best Instructor award in the tank unit. I've always loved pedagogy. When the new recruits arrived, I'd take them to some small training fields at the end of the barracks where there wasn't much room to fire. The recruits had to run through barbed-wire fences while blank cartridges were shot at them. But if blanks are shot at close range, they burn. So, what did I do? I got a load of small limes and dunked them in

whitewash, so they were coated white. Then I positioned the shooters along the route. Any recruit who arrived stained with white paint was 'dead' and had to run through the wires again. The recruits fairly flew along . . .

Did that work with tanks?

No, that was individual instruction, training in tanks came next. We'd sow a minefield with whitewashed mines, and any tank that touched them . . . The sergeants would use visual aids, drawings and wooden shapes to simulate tank parts, to better explain tank structure. We were very creative. Fridays were maintenance days. The recruits had to clean and grease the tanks. We were under the tanks, covered in grease, from five in the morning. The commander would come and inspect – 'Open the battery!' to see if it had water in it. 'Check the oil!' He'd test the recruits with questions. Sometimes he'd punish some squad or other, and on several occasions I had to spend my Saturday repeating the maintenance class. Or he'd congratulate them: 'Special pass for this squad!' After inspection, the officers would play petanque or dominoes with the commander in the officers' club.

Were the soldiers in your tank unit volunteers?

No. In those days we still had military service, and the recruits were distributed according to which sectors of the Armed Forces needed what. I often went to fetch recruits, interviewed them and chose the ones I wanted. Each officer tried to bag the best ones. Some youngsters had psychological problems, but the majority were fine boys. Many applied because they were unemployed and didn't have anywhere to study, or were excluded from schools, work schemes, etc. It was a way of finding something to do, if only for a short time.

Did you come across any other progressive officers?

I remember there being a lawyer, Dr López, who came to the battalion on Friday afternoons. He was an intellectual, and had been an activist in the Movimiento Electoral del Pueblo (MEP). He helped us organize consumer cooperatives. Each officer would put in some money, then we'd go to a wholesale market and buy stuff for everybody. On another occasion, López, Lieutenant Alastre and myself discussed how to find collective solutions to the problem of officer housing. López was undoubtedly left-wing. And one day, the intelligence services stopped him coming to the battalion, because of some remark he made. That was strange, because López never said anything explicitly political.

Was there an intelligence service?

Of course. My colleague Salazar, the one who got me recruiting candidates, was our intelligence officer. He was nicknamed *Pedro el malo*, 'Bad Pedro'. He kept his eye on me because he could see that I read a lot. A guy came round the barracks selling books and I bought some. At once Salazar called me in: 'I heard you bought some books.' I asked, 'How do you know? Are you watching me?' 'No, but remember I'm an intelligence office and I know a lot of things.' 'OK, but what's that got to do with my reading?' I stood up to him. But afterwards, I wondered, 'Was that an intelligence operation?'

What? The books?

Yup! To find out what individual soldiers read. It's true I bought some books on the twentieth century's big political movements. Four of them. I have them to this day. *Communism: From Marx to Mao*; *Fascism: From Hitler to Mussolini*; *Capitalism: From Manchester to Wall Street*; *Socialism: From Class Struggle to Welfare State*.[17] The authors were different, but the most interesting was Irving Fetscher, author of the volumes on Communism and Socialism.[18] Have you heard of him?

---

17   A political encyclopaedia in four volumes edited by Plaza & Janés, Barcelona, 1975.

18   Irving Fetscher (1922–), professor of political science and social philosophy at Frankfurt University from 1963 to 1988. Expert on Jean-Jacques Rousseau, Hegel and Marx, and author of a dozen books translated into several languages.

No.

He's a very interesting German political scientist. The four tomes form a political encyclopaedia. I read it thoroughly, and I started thinking about primitive socialism, the first Christians, and Christ's socialist message. The Church domesticated Jesus, they made him out to be a fool ... When Christ was, in truth, a radical revolutionary.

10

Conspiring and Recruiting

Gently flowing water – *The Power Within You*
Sandinista victory in Nicaragua – Marx and Bolívar
'About-Turn' – First micro-cell – Winning over cadets
Crisis theory – Trip to Dominican Republic
Back at the Academy – Tools for thinking
First appearance on television – The Popy Show
Advice from Hugo Trejo – General Olavarría
Seedbed of revolution – The death of Mamá Rosa
A poem and an oath

My impression is that at the end of the 1970s and beginning of the 1980s, you experienced a kind of blossoming in personal, intellectual and professional terms. Your character grew more assured, you were more confident in yourself, your abilities, your potential. You seemed ripe for action.
During those years – 1978, '79, '80 – I felt a whole set of spiritual, ideological, political triggers ready to go off, yet at the same time these were also years of study and reflection. I started seriously to prepare political briefings and reports on military matters for my meetings with Douglas Bravo and the PRV-Ruptura central committee. It was now called the Civilian Military Movement, although not yet the MBR-200. I also remember reading a lot of

Alfredo Maneiro's work, he was much more intellectual than Douglas, although I respected Douglas intellectually as well. Maneiro's work [he shows the book] was bedside reading for me in those days, it contains Maneiro's ideas, speeches, his 'negative notes', as he called them. He died of a sudden heart attack before he was fifty.

This [he holds up a pamphlet] is one of Maneiro's speeches in 1971. La Causa R used to bring out a cultural magazine called *La Casa del Agua Mansa* [The House of Gently Flowing Water], a line from Bertolt Brecht, something like, 'Over time, gently flowing water triumphs over hard rock.' The water does not pierce the rock by force, it wears it away. It was part of our philosophy; not to become a waterfall, yet. Waterfalls would come, whirlwinds would come, but for the time being we were gently flowing water.

I also spent time researching Maisanta, reading the history of twentieth-century Venezuela, and trying to better understand its political processes. At school we'd only been taught the half of it, the 'heroic' history, and only the nineteenth century, as if the twentieth century didn't exist.

They only taught 'heroic' history, no social history.
None at all. Only the heroic history of battles, wars, events without any social or economic context.

I also read a book at that time which had a huge impact on me. I mentioned it before: *The Power Within You*. In Maracay, in August 1978, I read in it something Victor Hugo said that stayed engraved on my mind for ever: 'There is nothing as powerful as an idea whose time has come.' That book helped me mature, in the same way *Quillet's Encyclopaedia* had done. I had become a father, a lieutenant with responsibilities, etc. . . .

July 1979 saw the Sandinista victory in Nicaragua. Do you remember what was said about it in the political circles you moved in?
For us, the Sandinista victory was a very positive step forward. We had been following that epic tale with the utmost interest. The

battle for Managua . . . I was meeting Douglas at the time. We'd talked about it a lot. And then Colonel Hugo Trejo appeared, and we met his group of nationalist officers. William Izarra also appeared; he was still serving in the Air Force then. And we began having contact with his group ARMA, I've mentioned them before. That group subsequently 'went with the wind': some of them joined us, others dropped away.

I also found time to devote to painting, I painted a few canvases. So as you can see, it was a time of splendid fulfilment.

From the emotional, intellectual, professional and political points of view . . .

Yes, in all aspects of my life. This portrait of José Antonio Páez [he shows it] won a prize in Valencia, in an exhibition of officers' paintings. And this canvas, *Shadow of War in the Gulf*, is of the parade ground in Maracay, which is identical today, as if time had not passed. It was the view from my room. I opened the window and could see the troops' dormitory block, a soldiers' washroom, a weapons storeroom and the parade ground; and on the other side, a row of buildings.

I painted that canvas in very particular circumstances. It was 1980, war was about to break out with Colombia and we were being sent to the frontier via the Gulf of Maracaibo. I was leaving at daybreak, with a now fully trained tank squad. I got up really early, opened the window, it was cold, and I suddenly saw the sky lit up, a fiery red, and cried out, 'My God, the war!'

But it was only a sumptuous dawn . . . I suddenly sensed the brute horror of what war could be like. And I told myself, 'If I come back alive, I'm going to paint.' And when I came back, I painted that scene. The following year, when I went back to the Military Academy as a captain, I took it with me. My painting teacher, Quintanilla, liked it. He said, 'Will you let me touch it up?' I've never told anyone this before. 'Your painting is beautiful, Chávez, but let me add a couple of touches.' And he put this shading here, some shadows that are trees, and that gave the painting a whole other dimension. A real eye-opener.

Did you learn any lessons from the Sandinista victory?
The Sandinista Revolution of July 1979 was a major boost for us. I remember being in a meeting of the PRV-Ruptura, chaired by Douglas, where we analysed the whole experience and particularly the importance of the people and the Armed Forces acting in unison. The Sandinistas showed – as the Cubans had previously – that a guerrilla force was capable of defeating a regular army. Why? Because that army did not have the support of the people. It was used by a tyrant to oppress the people, and that debilitates an army. We also spent a lot of time analysing Mao's fish in water theory.

Did Douglas find justification for the guerrilla strategy in the Sandinista victory? Did you consider reviving the guerrilla war?
No. Renouncing the armed struggle was irreversible.

So the Sandinista victory didn't make anyone want to take up arms again?
No, absolutely not, because the guerrillas had been beaten here. Besides, Venezuela wasn't Nicaragua, our Armed Forces weren't like Somoza's army. Conditions weren't ripe. What's more, I don't think conditions had ever been ripe for launching a strong guerrilla movement. Che Guevara had weighed up whether to come to Venezuela before going to Bolivia, and for various reasons he opted to go to the Bolivian Andes. Objective conditions never really existed here.

Not even in the 1960s, when the Cubans were fighting alongside the Venezuelan guerrillas?
Those Cubans suffered a surprise attack from the Venezuelan army the moment they landed, and some lost their lives. Comandante Arnaldo Ochoa and his men had to retreat by way of Falcón and, not long after that, they went back to Cuba. And look at the unhappy fate of several of the guerrilla leaders: Gabriel Puerta Aponte, one of the greatest, and Teodoro Petkoff? Where do they stand today? Systematically opposed to the revolution, in the reactionary camp. The only one of those leaders who is respected, because he rose to the occasion, is Douglas Bravo. And others like

Alí Rodríguez, whose actions have always been consistent with their ideas. Unfortunately, not enough grass-roots work was done. In addition, Nicaragua was, and still is, a heroic people of *campesinos* – and great poets – whereas here, as I said before, the *campesinos* all moved to the cities in the 1960s; the countryside was to all intents and purposes abandoned.

I suppose you can't compare Somoza's dictatorial political system with Venezuela's 'imperfect democracy', either.
They were very different systems, although there was torture and repression here too. But the situation did not compare. Venezuela may have been plundered and fleeced, but the government had enough resources to distribute *something* to its citizens, enough at least to maintain a minimum of stability. That's doubtless why the guerrilla leadership, engaged in a process of intense revision, was never able to create a powerful guerrilla movement. This was true of both Douglas and Maneiro – and Maneiro's rethink was possibly more thorough than Douglas's, because Douglas never got further than organizing small groups.

Alfredo Maneiro concentrated his efforts on the working class in the region of Guayana, and the Matanceros worker contingent who controlled the trade union in SIDOR, Venezuela's biggest steel complex. I also remember discussing Catia, the revolutionary movements in Caracas, and the poor neighbourhoods of all the major urban concentrations. La Causa R also did good work with intellectuals. I've already mentioned the cultural magazine *The House of Gently Flowing Water*. I remember writing it a letter, which I immediately regretted because I wrote it in longhand, totally careless. I realized, 'My God! I've violated security codes!' Maneiro told me later that he burned it after reading it.

What did the letter say?
It was a complaint, or suggestion, whatever you want to call it, because in one edition there was a chapter called 'The Ghosts of the House of Gently Flowing Water', and when I started reading, I saw that the 'ghosts' were Marx, Lenin, Che, etc., but there was no

mention of Bolívar, Simón Rodríguez, Zamora . . . I wrote asking them to include our own 'ghosts'. I've always thought it a mistake to peg everything on the thinking of great international figures, forgetting our roots, our Bolivarian tradition.

Many Marxists are unfamiliar with the wealth of authentic revolutionary thinking that has come out of Latin America.
I think that has been a huge mistake. Fidel has often criticized the lack of knowledge about that immensely important revolutionary, José Martí. And Mariátegui, despite dying very young, tried to elaborate a theory of an original Marxism rooted in Latin American reality.[1]

You have made the Latin American sources an original characteristic of your own thinking.
I've tried to. I'll tell you an anecdote that a lawyer told to me, in prison. It's an experience he had when he was a young law student and left-wing activist. His organization used to send him to liaise with the guerrillas in Guárico at weekends . . .

Only at weekends?
Yes, lots of students would do that. They'd join the Communist Party and the party would send them on missions to urban or rural guerrillas for a few days during the holidays, or at weekends. They'd go to the guerrillas in the Llanos: there was no social base there, so they'd make do with those students from the cities.

What did the lawyer tell you?
He said that one winter he and about fifteen armed guerrillas arrived on horseback in Corozopando, a village in Guárico state, near the Apure River, in the middle of the savannah. While taking the

---

1 José Carlos Mariátegui (1894–1930), Peruvian writer, philosopher, journalist and political activist. Although he died at only thirty-five, his thought and work has had a major influence on left-wing intellectuals in Latin America. His most important book is *Siete ensayos de interpretación de la realidad peruana* (1928).

village, they detained two policemen and confiscated their old Mauser rifles. They gathered about 200 inhabitants together, and wham! Straight into the political harangue. Informing the masses, you know. Since he was a student and could write nicely, the guerrilla leaders gave him the job of spraying graffiti and slogans on the walls of ruined houses. He went round spraying but when he got back to the plaza, there was no one there! The guerrillas had vanished. And they'd taken his horse.

He legged it out fast but spent several days lost in the savannah. When he finally caught up with the guerrillas, they asked, 'Where were you, comrade? You put the patrol in danger!' He protested, 'I was obeying orders.' He was tried. They sat him down in front of the two top commanders. Since he was a law student, he put up a good case, insisting, 'I was carrying out my mission, painting slogans.' 'What were you painting?' they asked. He replied, '¡Viva Lenin!' So one commander asked him: 'Who's Lenin?' And the other one interrupted: 'Lenin is our leader in Caracas, so let's pardon him' [laughter]. They hadn't the slightest notion of revolutionary history. This lawyer may have been exaggerating a bit, but it shows what it was like here. There was never any proper ideological work.

You were still in Maracay?

Yes, I spent three years in the Bravos de Apure Battalion, and pretty well kept up all those political, intellectual and cultural activities. I started writing, too . . . Some of my writing turned up in an old briefcase not long ago. Among the short stories was '*El brazalete tricolor*' ['The Tricolor Armband'] which I wrote in Maracay, and others like '*Vuelvan Caras*' ['About-Turn'] which talks about soldiers' lives in Maisanta's days, in the early twentieth century.[2]

---

2   *Vuelvan Caras* is also one of the Bolivarian Missions – a series of anti-poverty and social welfare programs – concerned specifically with land rights and endogenous and sustainable social development.

Did you invent the expression Vuelvan Caras?

No, it comes from the War of Independence, when José Antonio Páez faced Spanish General Pablo Morillo at the battle of Las Queseras del Medio, in 1819. Páez simulated a withdrawal of his cavalry. When Morillo's cavalry chased after them, he ordered, '*Vuelvan caras!*' In a skilful manoeuvre with horses and lances, the pursued whipped round to face their pursuers who, dispersed and unprepared, were routed. Watching from the far bank of the Arauca, Bolívar drafted a dispatch praising the 'valiant soldiers of the Apure Army'. He decorated the men with the Liberator's Cross. There were 150 of them. They rode back across the river with their lances ready, and surprised the enemy camped in a thicket on the opposite bank. That's where the expression '*Vuelvan Caras*' comes from.

Let's go back to the main story. In this period, when I decided to play a greater part in the revolutionary process, I needed to develop a lot of skills. I was learning the whole time. I began looking for like-minded officers, because I wasn't going to make a revolution on my own. First to appear was Lieutenant Alastre, who later took part in the rebellion of 4 February 1992. He had just returned from a course in France; he was a tank specialist.

How did you make contact?

We were on guard duty one night, and he caught me reading a political book . . . I can't remember which one. We were pals already, because he also played baseball. When he saw what I was reading, he said, 'Did you know that my dad, Pedro Alastre senior, was a guerrilla?' I said, 'How come?' And he said, 'Yes, my dad was in the Communist Party. When my mum was pregnant with me, they were both arrested. He was tortured, and afterwards he took off for the hills.'

So, I began to get closer to him politically. Another day, I asked, 'What about your dad? Have you seen him again?' 'No, he's ill in Puerto Cabello. My parents separated. They're from Humocaro.' Humocaro Alto, in the mountains of Lara state, was a guerrilla town. That's also where Argimiro Gabaldón was from.

Who?

Argimiro Gabaldón, son of General José Rafael Gabaldón [1882–1975], leader of an uprising, the *gabaldonera* [April–May 1929], in the time of the dictator Juan Vicente Gómez. He became a guerrilla in the early 1960s. He died in the mountains. It was an accident: one day in December 1964, the guerrillas were cleaning their rifles when one went off by mistake and killed Argimiro.

Did you and Alastre form the first nucleus?

We were the first 'micro-cell', that's what we called it. Shortly afterwards, Lieutenant Carlos Díaz Reyes joined the battalion. He was in the 4 February 1992 rebellion too. I heard by chance that his father, too, was also an old communist, from Los Teques. I started up a conversation: 'So, when's your dad coming to visit?' One day his old man came to the barracks. With that there were three of us: Díaz Reyes, Alastre and me.

I also remember one weekend being with several comrades from the central committee, one of which was 'Harold' (real name Nelson Sánchez, my original liaison with Douglas), and I said, 'D'you want to see the tanks?' And we went into the battalion on the pretext of going to the softball pitch. I wanted to show them that we already had a cell. Alastre came and talked to them. I said, 'The day the rebellion starts, we'll take all these tanks out.' They were impressed.

Did that cell grow?

Yes. The barracks had a firing range, and units from other garrisons would come and practice. Whenever a battalion of paratroopers came, for instance, I'd ask if they wanted a coffee, or any help, etc. I'd form relationships, establish contacts, make friends.

The Flying School was also in Maracay, and my old friend Luis Reyes was a flying instructor. I used to visit him. On one occasion, I invited him to a meeting with Douglas. By then we had taken the decision to form a revolutionary organization within the armed forces. Luis took on the task of forming cadres in the Air Force, as I was doing in the Army. We were indefatigable. I'm talking about the period before 1980, especially 1978, 1979 . . . We worked hard, winning over officers and cadets alike. For almost twenty years . . .

The situation favoured you, didn't it?
Indeed, conditions in Venezuela were deteriorating. The economy was a disaster, corruption was out of control. Carlos Andrés Pérez finished his mandate at the beginning of 1979, leaving Venezuela in debt, bankrupt. His successor, Copei's Luis Herrera Campíns, declared an economic 'freeze'. Then came 'Black Friday' [18 February 1983], when the bolívar was abruptly devalued; the economic history of Venezuela changed overnight. The crisis may have erupted that day, but like a volcano it had been rumbling for a very long time. The country was mired in poverty, unemployment, underemployment, corruption . . . It was what I once called the 'theory of crises', the accumulation of crises, one after another.

Did you feel a sense of urgency, did you want to take action?
Yes, but we also remembered Maneiro's advice, that you have to let things mature, that the time for our idea will come. Meanwhile, we made progress, but slowly, like gently flowing water, calm but unremitting. And against that backdrop, things were happening in my personal life. One propitious day in 1980, my second daughter María was born, a sister for Rosa. I was still in the battalion.

Still in Maracay.
In Maracay. That's when I went to the Dominican Republic, to Santo Domingo, that beautiful Caribbean city. I went to play baseball and softball in an international competition. The president in those days was Antonio Guzmán Fernández, who later committed suicide while in office [3 July 1982]. He was from the Partido Revolucionario Dominicano (PRD), Juan Bosch's old party, although he had left it in 1973 to found a more left-wing party, the Partido de la Liberación Dominicana (PLD).[3]

---

3   Juan Bosch (1909–2001), founder of the Dominican Revolutionary Party (PRD). Exiled during the dictatorship of Rafael Trujillo (1939–1961), he was elected president in

In Santo Domingo I discovered the great Dominican poet, Pedro Mir [1913–2000], who wrote the poem 'If Someone Wants to Know of My *Patria*'. I learned it and have often quoted it. It's very long, but some of the lines are worth remembering: 'If someone wants to know of my *Patria* / Don't search for it, or ask after it / No, don't search for it. You must fight for it . . .'

Despite your political activity, you didn't give up baseball.
No, on the contrary, I consolidated my place in the Army's baseball and softball teams in national and international competitions. I played in the Inter-Forces Games in Maracay, and we won the championship in Barquisimeto.

When did you go back to the Academy as an instructor?
In 1981. One day in March, the new commander, Humberto Prieto, summoned me and said, 'Chávez, did you request a transfer?' 'No,' I said. Transfers usually take place in August. But he said, 'Well, anyway, I'm happy for you, because you're going to Caracas, to the Military Academy.'

How did you take the news?
On the one hand, I was glad to be going back to the Academy, which had a very particular significance for me. But I was sorry to leave because, quite honestly, I'd been happy in that battalion. You can sometimes get fed up of being in the same place, but not me, the Bravos de Apure was special for me. Even today when I see them march past, my heart misses a beat. Its anthem is a hymn to the *Patria*, a perfect anthem. Leaving Maracay also meant leaving behind our growing organization.

In what sense?
We'd already put feelers out in the paratroopers. I'd begun talking to Jesús Urdaneta and Felipe Acosta Carlez who were there. We'd

1962, introduced a series of progressive social reforms, and was toppled by a military coup on 25 September 1963. In 1973 he founded the Dominican Liberation Party (PLD)

had meetings. No commitment had been made but there was an identity, a shared sense of indignation. To be honest, they weren't very clear-sighted politically. They just rejected the establishment and clashed with the older generations of officers. So it wasn't so much because of the state of the country, despite the fact that there were protests everywhere. I tried to orientate them politically, man to man, one to one, at their homes. At weekends we'd go to the beach with our wives, most were married with small children. So we'd talk, have a few beers, walk along the beach, go jogging, discuss stuff.

How was your return to the Academy?
Well, that same month of March 1981, from one day to the next, I presented myself at the Military Academy. They were playing the Inter-Institute Games, I remember, and my return to the Academy suited them down to the ground. I've said it before, sometimes everything seems to conspire to help me, as if there was a hidden plan or plot. I arrived at the Academy at the top of my game, I'd been a lieutenant for two years, I had another year and a half before I made it to captain, but I was already 'matured'. At the Bravos de Apure, Commander Luis Pulido used to say 'I want swashbuckling officers', and I tried to become a 'swashbuckling officer'. In my political life, I'd taken important steps to forge my destiny. In my personal life, I was married, with two daughters. I had the wind in my sails. With it blowing in my favour, I landed back in that cere-monial parade ground – the *patio de honor* – with its code of honour and idealistic cadets. I could see it clearly: here was the 'eagle's nest'. It was obvious to me from then on that the Academy had to be the nest . . . how do you say it?

The cradle of the revolution.
The cradle of the revolution, the eagle's nest. There, our movement fell on fertile ground. On arrival, I was given command of a platoon of cadets until July 1981. I had to make a big effort to reach the standard of fitness, because in the tank battalion we didn't do much sport. Here you had to go jogging every morning. And even as

platoon officer, you were just another cadet, you had to do everything they did, physically at least. I had to push myself hard at first.

Did you start doing political work?

Yes, very soon. Acosta Carlez was already there, he'd arrived before me. And there were other good friends, like Brito Valerio, from Cumaná, and Luis Edelmiro. The commander of the cadet corps was Colonel Troconis Peraza, from the Andes. From the political point of view, I could soon see the potential there. And ignoring the officers, I started relating to some of the cadets, making friends, trying to be a good superior to the juniors. I told myself, these boys have good qualities, they're not only army recruits.

They were future officers . . .

They would be officers; they were set to be in the armed forces for thirty-something years.

That's to say, fate put at your disposal, laid out on a silver platter, the men you needed for your project.

Exactly. It's as if it was all planned. I began to 'work' the cadets. I began a campaign of recruiting them for the revolution.

Were you sure you wanted to make a revolution?

Well, I was sure that we had to bring about radical change, to found Venezuela anew. But we still didn't have a structure, a movement. There was still nothing organic. We were looking for cadres. We didn't have to look for long, candidates began to appear. One of the first cadets I talked to was – he's currently a serving general – Euclides Campos Aponte. He joined us. I also signed up Blanco La Cruz, who was a subaltern. Another early convert was Frank Morales, who was also in the 4 February 1992 rebellion. He was from Guárico. We made a commitment to keep in touch while we assessed the situation. Those first lads I recruited were mainly llaneros, because I'd begun running cultural activities and I formed a llanero music group, with a harp, a cuatro, and maracas. I also started a painting workshop, and joined the baseball team. Dynamic as ever, in other words. I was on fire.

Did you start organizing beauty pageants again?
Yes [laughter]. I went back to being master of ceremonies. I remember our Queen at the time was Astrid Carolina Herrera, who went on to be Miss World in London, in 1984. We put on an amazing pageant for her in the parade ground. The comperes were myself and Gilberto Correa. Can you imagine! Gilberto Correa, one of the best comperes on TV.

The army discovered her first?
Yes, before anybody. She was Queen of Cadets in 1982, I think, then won the Miss Venezuela contest, and finally was Miss World.

Did you make contact with your old friends in Caracas?
I did. I returned to my old haunts: Los Chaguaramos, El Águila, etc. I went back to Prado de María, even stayed in that same house sometimes. Some of my mates were still students, others had graduated, and several were professionals. Other places were found for my clandestine meetings with Douglas Bravo and the team from La Causa R, especially Pablo Medina. I didn't see Alfredo Maneiro, for security reasons. He had named Pablo Medina as my contact.

When were you promoted to captain?
In July 1982. I came fifth in my class. I was improving: I'd come fortieth out of eighty when I was promoted to lieutenant. The Academy got a new director, upper-class: General José Antonio Olavarría.

What were your exact duties at the Academy?
I was an instructor. I gave classes in tactics, history, war games, leadership . . . I loved teaching. Sometimes I couldn't sleep, I was so engrossed in preparing my classes. It was a way of getting close to the cadets. I was still quite young, twenty-eight years old.

What teaching experience did you have?

Don't forget my parents were schoolteachers. And I'd volunteered in the literacy campaign. And when I was at the Liceo O'Leary in Barinas, I gave extra tutoring to some of my classmates. But at the Academy, I also took a teacher training course. Some lieutenants from the Academy were sent to do a course in 'intelligence development'. I know, it sounds like a joke. Every day we went to the Parque Central, where the course was being run by Corina Parisca de Machado, wife of one of the Machado-Zuloagas, and Thaís Aguerrevere, of the Aguerrevere y Zuloaga clan. Both are families of the Venezuelan haute bourgeoisie. Olavarría sent us to do the course so we would be able pass on the method within the Academy. There were both civilians and military personnel attending. Olavarría was very keen on it, and attended every now and again. He was a friend of Corina, Thaís, and even Machado, the minister.

Did you know Olavarría well?

No, I had no dealings with him whatsoever. He was the director of the Academy, and I was a simple lieutenant. At the end of the course, when they were handing out the diplomas, Corina said, 'Hugo, I want you to come on TV with me, Napoleón Bravo is waiting for us.' I'd never been on TV. Venevision's Canal 4 had this lunchtime programme called 'Hello, Venezuela', super-famous. Have you heard of Napoleón Bravo?

No, a TV celebrity, I suppose.

Arch-iconic. Super-famous. He's in Miami now. He was one of the leaders of the 'media coup' inside the political coup against us on 11 April 2002. He read out on TV the decree proclaiming the post-coup president: 'Today Venezuela is a different place . . .' He was very young in those days.

It was a problem for me. I told Corina, 'I can't, I'm a serving army officer, I have to follow the rules.' There were more senior officers on the course, Lieutenant Roberto Fajardo, for example. 'No, it has to be you,' said Corina. She chose four or five students

who had finished the Intelligence Development course to appear
on TV. As if to say, 'Look, these soldiers were dead stupid, and now
they aren't quite so bad . . .'

What did you do?

I said, 'Corina, first let's ask Fajardo, he's the most senior . . .' She
called him immediately, 'Roberto, Thaís and I have decided to take
Chávez.' 'Fine by me', said Fajardo. So I asked Thaís to phone
General Olavarría: 'He's a friend of yours. I can't go on TV just like
that. I'll be arrested.' She called him straight away. 'José Antonio,
we're going on TV, they're waiting for us, and I want to take Chávez.'
'Put him on,' said Olavarría. She passed me the phone. 'Chávez,
you can go, but don't talk politics. Be careful! I'll be watching.' And
we left for the TV station.

Your first time on TV?

Yes. It was a live interview.

Were you in uniform?

Of course. My lieutenant's uniform. Then up came Napoleón and
asked me, 'Lieutenant, do you believe in the development of intelligence?' I've no idea what the hell I replied [laughter]. But he
pushed on: 'Don't you think it might be dangerous to develop
intelligence in the army?' 'Why dangerous?' I asked. 'Well, because
subalterns might disrespect their officers.' So then I gave a Major
League answer: 'No, on the contrary, developing the ability to
think helps to strengthen discipline. We are a new breed of soldiers
for a new era, a different time: the time for the development of
ideas.'

General Olavarría must have loved that!

You bet he loved it! Olavarría was watching the programme with
several officers and apparently they all clapped. When I got back,
they were waiting for me: 'Congratulations, Lieutenant! Have a
seat! These new lieutenants are quite something, look how well they
speak on TV.'

You earned yourself a reputation.
I certainly did. 'Chávez live on television!' The other lieutenants were impressed, they'd all seen the programme. And Olavarría put a recording on the Academy's closed-circuit TV, so everyone could see it in the classrooms, even in the dining room. I was getting embarrassed . . .

So you became even more well known in the Academy.
And not only in the Academy. Because not long afterwards, Popy arrived. Know who Popy was?

No idea.
The clown Popy, in real life the actor and singer Diony López, had a very popular children's programme – *El Show de Popy* – on Radio Caracas Television.[4] He was always accompanied by some cute girls, the 'Popyanas'. General Olavarría liked the programme very much. He called me one day and said, 'Look, lieutenant, Popy wants to do a show about the Academy, with the Popyanas, of course.' He asked me to coordinate it with Popy. I came up with the idea of filming the cadets doing a march-past, so the world could see them. Popy asked the general. He accepted: 'Whatever Chávez says . . .'

Did you do it?
We filmed the whole battalion marching past, we recorded in the dining room, and the parade ground.

You became a popular figure.
You've no idea! We lived in an apartment block in Baruta with my little girls. And there were lots of children living there. When I got home one day, they all began shouting, 'It's Popy's friend!' What a party we had!

---

4   Dionisio López Ramos (1946–2010), singer, comic and children's TV presenter. Since 1971, famous as Popy the clown.

So you extended your radius of action . . .

It's just an anecdote. But it showed me the importance of mass communications. As well, it may help give you an idea of the whole host of things accumulating inside me, all the different experiences I was having . . .

Did you have political contacts outside the Academy?

The ones I've already mentioned: Douglas Bravo's people and the activist groups around Alfredo Maneiro. And the new and important relationship I had with Colonel Hugo Trejo was consolidated. He lived in Caracas, but he also had a beach house in Macuto, not far from the capital. I'd often go there with my wife and daughters to swim and stay the night. I discussed lots of things with Trejo. He'd get out his files and papers. Once I even managed to bring him and Douglas Bravo together, and I wrote a 'poem of unity' for the occasion: 'Commandante Trejo, Comandante Bravo / Together we'll make the Revolution, ¡carajo!' But they didn't hit it off. Trejo helped me a great deal in coordinating what we could call the 'technical details' of the conspiracy.

What technical details?

For example, he advised me, 'Hugo, when you talk to the officers, be very careful in those meetings with the ones who drink alcohol. It loosens their tongue . . .' And he went on, 'And be equally careful with those who don't drink. They might be writing everything down!'

So you couldn't trust anyone?

Exactly. He said, 'Be careful with telephones.' And he warned, 'You have to prepare yourself mentally for the worst, for being in prison, interrogated and tortured. Train yourself. It could happen to you.' I did what the old man said. He prepared me. He sometimes put me to the test: 'If they ask you such and such, what will you say? If they ask the other, what will you answer?' He prepared me very thoroughly. He had a lot of experience. I'll never forget him. I've been interrogated several times, and that preparation served me well.

And finally, was that course of 'intelligence development' useful?
Well, I started to apply Edward de Bono's methods in my Military
History classes. I set the cadets to evaluating and analysing the situation in Nicaragua with those tools. It was 1982, the height of the
Sandinista government.

Wasn't that a politically 'dangerous' topic?
Yes, but I was taking a calculated risk. Olavarría was a man with
intellectual leanings, with a certain culture. He inspected the classrooms, and saw the kind of thing I was doing. I'd have the cadets'
desks in circles, with different groups reading newspapers, or cutting
out articles. One day, Olavarría visited the class unannounced:
'Carry on, Chávez. Pretend I'm not here. Carry on.' I was actually
quoting Mao Zedong at the time: 'The people is to the army as water
is to the fish'. And I quoted Bolívar. The cadets were all fired up by
the method and the work, and reached the conclusion that, in this
kind of conflict, it was crucial for the armed forces to have popular
support. I told myself, 'This general is going to kick me out!'

What did Olavarría do?
When the class finished, he beckoned me into the corridor. 'Chávez,
I congratulate you. You're the only one applying the methods. I've
spent a week observing and haven't seen anyone else doing it.' He
added, 'Next Friday, at the instructors' meeting, I want you to do a
presentation of the Thinking Tools method.'

I prepared my presentation. Friday came. Olavarría opened the
meeting: 'Please proceed, Lieutenant.' Using a projector and slides, I
explained how the class had been taught, stressing the tools I'd employed,
and the conclusions the cadets had reached. When I'd finished, a colonel who was a guest instructor from the intelligence services got to his
feet. Olavarría invited him to speak, and the colonel asserted loud and
clear that I was 'encouraging the cadets to be subversive'.

No less?
No less. Just like that. Murmurs ran round the classroom. I said to
myself, 'Holy shit!'

You'd been unmasked...

Yes, I was only just beginning and they'd already found me out [laughter] . . . I put my hand up straight away, but Olavarría intervened: 'You don't have to answer, I will.' And he embarked on my defence. He swept aside the colonel's criticism, and left him looking two inches tall: 'That's precisely why we're not progressing, why the Army is stagnating. These young officers of the Andrés Bello Plan are the new generations . . .'

An interesting man, General Olavarría.

I have a lot of respect for him. When I became president, I appointed him head of the Negotiating Commission with Colombia. He was an expert in border issues. He is a patriot, and born with a silver spoon in his mouth. When I came out of prison he invited me to his house for lunch – he lived in Lagunita Country Club, one of the most exclusive areas of Caracas – and gave me, in good faith, some advice, to get me to moderate my behaviour. We even went out for a walk: 'I want people to see you with me, so they stop thinking you're a demon.' An intelligent man.

Did you talk to the colonel who made the accusation?

Yes, when we went out to the parade ground, the colonel called to me, 'Lieutenant, you know I'm right.' I said, 'The one who's right is the general. I'm obeying orders. I followed a course on developing intelligence, and I applied it.' The colonel worked in the military police. He was one of those old-style officers, with bad manners. I never saw him again. I don't think he came back to the Academy, I don't know if Olavarría sacked him. Just anecdotes, again.

But significant.

I had a big thick black exercise book where I wrote up my notes about my classes, cadet by cadet. There I also noted, in my own code, whether or not a particular cadet could be part of our movement. I was hardly ever wrong. I detected Ronald Blanco La Cruz, for example, and Oswaldo Aquino Lamón. The Academy became a seedbed, a cradle of revolution.

It was around then that your grandmother died, wasn't it?
Yes, my grandmother Rosa Inés died in January 1982. It was a hard blow for me, very hard.

Were you still in touch, did you write to her like you did when you were a cadet?
That and more. I used to go and see her in Barinas. I'd been there in December 1981. She seemed so ill that I left Nancy and the girls with my in-laws and went to sleep in her room. I put a mattress on the floor beside her and spent Christmas with her. I made her a Nativity scene, she always liked that. I gave her back massages, her back hurt, her lungs had given out.

Did you talk to her doctors?
Yes, and one doctor warned me, 'She hasn't long to live.' But on 26 December I had to get back to the Academy, I was still a lieutenant, after all. Our goodbye was very painful, our last embrace. I started crying. Something told me I would not see her again. I left in tears. Nancy and the girls stayed. In Caracas, I had to do two weekend guard duties. I phoned constantly to ask how she was. My brother Adán was with her. She was as sick as ever, and in great pain. I had guard duty on 31 December. I talked to Adán but not to her, because she couldn't get up.

I was due to hand over on 1 January at nine in the morning. Just before that, Colonel Tovar Jiménez came to inspect us. He was a good man, known as 'The Horse' because he ran like the devil. He was also in a nationalist movement, along the lines of Hugo Trejo's, who was a friend of his. I told him, 'Colonel, my grandma who brought me up is very ill.' And I explained the situation. I was director of Culture and Sport at the time, so he said, 'We have no competitions at the moment, so as soon as the officers and cadets who are on leave for 5 and 6 January come back, you can take a few days off to see your grandmother.'

But you still had five or six days to wait . . .
I was desperate. I decided to visit Colonel Trejo, because the rebellion he led in 1958 took place on 1 January and I went to wish him Happy New Year at his beach house. I remember him saying, 'You'll

be promoted to captain this year! So, be prepared . . .' I headed back that same afternoon, but I had an old car with an engine that burned the oil and gave off lots of smoke. It struggled up the hills and kept stopping. I went to Villa de Cura to see Ana [Maisanta's daughter], arriving late at night. I called Barinas. 'How's the old lady?' 'Still very bad.'

I stayed the night at Ana's, but had to be back in Caracas for work on the 3rd. I looked pretty rough, unshaven, my hair too long, so I went to find a barber in the Plaza Bolívar. When I came back, Ana was crying, 'Your brother called. She just passed away.'

My car just about made it back to the Academy, but it wasn't fit for a trip to Barinas. I called Adán: 'I don't know how I'm going to get home, because the buses are all full on 2 January. I'll go to the terminal anyway.' I found a seat on one bound for Trujillo, passing through Guanare. My brother picked me up at the Guanare check-point and we drove to Barinas.

We buried my grandma on 3 January 1982. I changed into my olive green fatigues, and helped carry her coffin to the church; we had the service and then buried her. Straight afterwards I wrote the poem I told you about, a few definitive lines like an oath or a promise, a sort of 'Motherland or Death', and it ended,

'And then the happy smile on your absent face / will illuminate this scorched plain, / and men on horseback will suddenly appear. / The federal army, with Zamora at its head / and red-haired Páez with his thousand brave hearts, / and Maisanta's guerrillas and followers aplenty.'

And now comes the vow about 'Patria o Muerte':

'Or perhaps never, my dearest, will such happiness come / to this place. And then, only then, at the end of my life / I will come to find you, my sweet Mama Rosa / I will come to your grave and water your flowers / with my sweat and blood, and find comfort in your maternal love / and tell you all my misfortunes in this world of mortals. / Then you will open your arms and give me a hug / like when I was a child, and you will rock me with your soft lullaby / and take me through other places and raise a victory cry / that will never die.'

So you see, it was a hymn to her and to rebellion.

A very painful moment, I imagine.

One of the hardest moments of my life. But, as poets and entertainers say, 'the show must go on . . .' The next day I returned to Caracas with Nancy and the girls.

Your grandmother would be proud of you now, wouldn't she?

I think so. Although at the beginning she used to say, 'Get out of that place, being a soldier isn't for you.'

Did she ever change her mind?

Yes, she stopped saying that. She was glad in the end. When I went back to Barinas after graduation, she exclaimed, '*Ay*, how nice you look in that uniform!'

PART III

THE ROAD TO POWER

(1982–1998)

11

Rebellion in the Making

Paratrooper captain – Speech of 17 December 1982
'Bolívar still has work to do in America'
The Oath of Samán de Güere – 'Black Friday'
Creation of the Revolutionary Bolivarian Army (EBR)
Head of the Military Academy's cultural department
Visit of Pope John Paul II – Death of General Omar Torrijos
Bolivarianism, a Latin American revolutionary path
Growth of the EBR
Against the idea that 'the Party rules by the gun'
The tree with three roots
The Bolivarian Revolutionary Movement-200

You were promoted to captain in July 1982 and left the Military Academy again, didn't you?
Yes, I was promoted on 5 July and in August I was sent back to Maracay. To the parachute regiment this time. I was there until December 1982 as commander of the Antonio Nicolás Briceño Battalion; the battalion with which, ten years later, I would lead the uprising.

I arrived at the end of August, and presented myself to Colonel Manrique Maneiro, nicknamed 'The Tiger' because he had stripy eyes. He was a veteran paratrooper. He said, 'I know who you are,

Chávez. Your friends here, Urdaneta and Acosta Carlez, think a lot of you.' And he added, 'I want you to be part of my staff. I've only got two colonels – nobody wants to be a paratrooper.'

You weren't a paratrooper.

No. Well, I'd done a basic parachute course when I was a subaltern, but I hadn't jumped out of a plane since then. I'd gone into communications and armoured vehicles. Urdaneta and Acosta Carlez, meanwhile, were paratrooper officers. Although they'd been on other courses, they'd always gone back to the parachute regiments. Officers who weren't professional paratroopers were usually terrified of accidents, getting injured, dying. Not me. I told the colonel that whenever they did parachute training, I wanted to jump. I was ready for anything. *El Tigre* Manrique told me he didn't have a G1 or G2 on his staff.

What's that?

The G1 officer is in charge of personnel, while the G2 directs military intelligence operations and electronic warfare. So I was made the G2, responsible for intelligence. But I told the colonel, 'I have to leave in December, to go on an advanced course. I can only stay for three months.' 'No problem, Chávez, devote that time to me. Help me organize my staff.' 'Yes, Colonel.' So I spent three months there. It was a very special time. And as I said, I was there with Urdaneta and Acosta Carlez.

Is that the same Acosta Carlez you mentioned before?

No, that was his brother, Felipe Antonio Carlez, who was killed during the Caracazo [27 February 1989]. Old friends were meeting up again and groups were re-forming. Luis Reyes Reyes was in the Air Force, Pedro Emilio Alastre was in tanks. I went to visit them, helping set up groups. Meanwhile, relations between myself and Douglas Bravo were still tense.

Did you like parachuting?

I started getting used to it again. I even did a very risky jump, in Caicara del Orinoco. The colonel warned me, 'This jump is very dangerous, I'm not doing it, Chávez. My staff are all landing in a Hercules. Come with us.' I replied, 'No, Colonel, I'm a captain, what would my men say?' We went up in a small plane, a Cessna 208, and I jumped. It was horrible. Contrary to all security norms, there was a twenty-something knots per hour wind.[1]

The exercise wasn't suspended?
No. We had to jump. A group of senior officers from some country or other, I can't remember which, had come to see us demonstrate a jump over the Orinoco river and the airport of Caicara and Cabruta, two towns on opposite sides of the river. It was a joint operation with the Jungle Infantry Division which was coming overland. A big manoeuvre. Our mission was to parachute in and take the airport.

Was anybody injured?
Yes, quite a few, and several broken bones. I came down on the asphalt with a terrible bang, I saw stars as I got to my feet. When there's a high wind, the parachutes don't collapse when they hit the ground; the wind catches them and drags the paratrooper along. One soldier fell face downwards; the parachute dragged him across the tarmac, ripping half his face off. If we hadn't got to him, the parachute would have killed him. Worse still, one lieutenant fell into a bush and disturbed a nest of African killer bees. He almost died.

From the stings?
Yes, the bees got everywhere. A helicopter evacuated him. It was a miracle he survived. And the cloud of killer bees still hung around, buzzing. Urdaneta and I went round collecting the wounded. The observers were standing on a podium in the shade, drinking cold water, calmly watching the spectacle. Suddenly, Urdaneta said to me, 'Look, *compadre*, the killers are heading straight for the podium' [laughter]. It was so comical. The guests all fled, hats and drinks left scattered behind them. We were in heaven.

---

1 Corresponds to a Force 6 gale, or 40 to 50 kilometers per hour.

Some time later, I was summoned by Colonel Manrique. 'Chávez, tomorrow is 17 December [anniversary of Bolívar's death in 1830], I want the whole regiment gathered together and you'll say a few words.' It was perhaps the most significant event in the three months I spent in the parachute regiment. Like I said, I'd already been talking to individual colleagues: Urdaneta, Acosta, an Air Force doctor who was with Douglas, Carlos Zambrano, etc. But nothing concrete had been decided.

So, on that 17 December, at 12.30, two battalions were lined up in the parade ground, the commando unit and the communications unit: the communications unit was commanded by Raúl Isaías Baduel, then a lieutenant; Jesús Urdaneta was a captain in the Chirino Battalion, and Felipe Acosta Carlez was a captain in the Briceño Battalion. After a minute's silence, a major acting as MC announced, 'We shall now hear from Captain Hugo Chávez Frías.' I went up to the microphone and the major asked, 'Chávez, where's your speech? Haven't you written one?' 'No, Major, I'm going to talk without notes.' I don't write speeches [laughter].

It wasn't your style.
No! But speaking off the cuff was not allowed. 'How dare you?' whispered the major, 'regulations say you have to write the speech.' I whispered back, 'The colonel only asked me late last night.' 'Well, you had all night to write it!' 'I didn't write anything. And I'm not going to read anything.' He was furious: 'You've got some cheek! We'll discuss it later. Here's the microphone.' Everybody was waiting.

The speech was impromptu.
Live! To hundreds of soldiers lined up in front of me. And it occurred to me to start with the words of José Martí: 'There is Bolívar in the heavens of America, vigilant and frowning, still seated on the rock of creation, with the Inca at his side and a pile of flags at his feet; there he is, still wearing his campaign boots, because what he left undone, still has to be done today; because Bolívar still

has work to do in America!'[2] I knew the piece in its entirety. And whatever barracks I was posted to, the first thing I always did was to paint Bolívar's face; the soldiers helped me.

So that's how I began. My speech wasn't recorded because they didn't record things in those days, but I remember the general idea. Martí ends by saying, 'Because Bolívar still has work to do in America', and my response was, 'Why wouldn't Bolívar still have work to do in America, when we have a continent mired in poverty?' I was careful, however, not to refer to internal politics, or to the Venezuelan government.

You kept to generalities.
Yes, dwelling on Latin American unity. We're talking about late 1982; I'd been analysing documents in regular meetings with Douglas Bravo and his comrades for four years by then. And don't forget I'd been studying Bolívar since I was a cadet. I had my own intellectual artillery, and my own personal take on things.

How long did you speak for?
About half an hour. It wasn't *Aló Presidente*, you know ... [Laughter.] It was one in the afternoon. When I finished, the atmosphere was electric with tension. Colonel Manrique called us and we jogged over to him. The major was standing beside him; he was furious and said in a loud voice, 'Chávez, you sounded like a politician.' The major's name was Flores Guilland, nicknamed 'The Cat'; he wasn't a bad guy, nor a bad officer, just right-wing. In those days, calling someone a politician was an insult, as if you'd said 'grafter', 'liar' or 'demagogue'. Anyway, there we were: Urdaneta, Acosta, commanders, captains, lieutenants, over thirty officers in a semi-circle round the colonel. Everybody heard what he said. I was going to reply but Acosta Carlez, who was very quick-witted, thundered back, 'Major,

---

2 Speech given at a soirée of the Hispanic–American Literary Society on 28 October 1893, and published in *Patria*, New York, on 4 November 1893.

what do you mean, "a politician"? The fact is, we captains are graduates of the Simón Bolívar year, we're Bolivarian captains, and when we speak like Chávez just spoke, you all pee your pants . . .' I would never have dared.

Pretty strong!
Wasn't it. There was still bad blood between the new graduate cadets and the older officers. I mentioned it before. And it was still going on.

Because they were suspicious.
Suspicion, inferiority complex . . . They tried to humiliate us, and we'd defend ourselves against that constant aggression. Sometimes we'd exaggerate and go over the top. So, when Acosta Carlez said that to 'The Cat' and all hell was about to break loose, the colonel yelled, 'Silence!' And, with a little white lie, he took responsibility for what I'd said, 'Gentlemen, Captain Chávez cleared what he was going to say with me last night in my office. I authorized it. It was an interesting speech. I hope everybody will reflect on Bolívar and this patriotic act. You may disperse.'

A gesture of solidarity.
Later, he sent for me, and we went for a walk. He kept saying, 'You realize what you're carrying inside you? Be careful, be very careful!'

You said that was on 17 December 1982. Isn't that the same day you swore your Oath of Samán de Güere?
Yes, that same day. Because following that incident, Felipe Acosta Carlez was fired up like a raging bull, so he said, 'Hey, compadre, let's go for a run, we need to calm down and talk.' We asked Urdaneta and Baduel to come too. Baduel was still only a lieutenant, but a close friend. We appreciated his intellect and his human qualities. The four of us first jogged over to La Placera, where there were a few chicken and pig farms. Then, on our way back, we did a two-kilometre detour to the monument to Bolívar at Samán de

Güere, where, underneath the giant tree, we swore the oath. It was dark by the time we got back to the regiment.[3]

Was the oath planned, or did it just happen on the spur of the moment?

We reached the famous *samán* tree and stopped. It was then I suggested the oath, we made it up it on the spot.

Were you thinking of Bolívar's Oath on the Monte Sacro in Rome?

Yes, adapting it, of course.[4] On that anniversary of Bolívar's death, we uttered the following words:

'I swear by the God of my fathers, I swear by my homeland, I swear by my honour, that my soul will not be at peace nor my arm at rest until the chains with which the powerful oppress my people have been broken. Free elections, free lands and free men, horror to the oligarchy'.

A reference to Bolívar and also to Ezequiel Zamora.

Yes, because as I said, although officially governments went on a lot about Bolívar, the icon of Venezuelan political identity, they did

---

3   The *samán* is a native tree of the South American tropical rain forest, also known as the rain tree. It is massive, sometimes growing to sixty metres, with a span of eighty metres across. Bolívar camped under this very same tree during his military campaign in the region, and a simple monument was subsequently erected on the historic spot. Bolívar is supposed to have said on 3 August 1813, 'Perhaps the soul of this tree and the spirits of our indigenous peoples will give us the courage to reach the glory our *patria* deserves.' Venezuelan oral tradition has it, as do the written records of scientists like Alexander von Humboldt and Agustín Codazzi, that the Samán de Güere was sacred to the Arawaks and other Carib tribes. Women would come to give birth in its shade, and tribal leaders met there to seal alliances.

4   On 15 August 1805, twenty-two-year old Símon Bolívar, the future Liberator, climbed up the historic Roman hill of the Monte Sacro and swore to free Venezuela: 'I swear before you, I swear by the God of my forefathers, I swear by my ancestors, I swear by my honour, and I swear by the Patria, that my arm will not rest, nor my soul repose, until we have broken the chains that oppress us by the will of the Spanish power.' He was accompanied by his teacher Simón Rodríguez and by Fernando Toro.

not follow the Liberator's core message: referring to him was just a formality. In those days in Venezuela, they distorted and falsified Bolívar, just as people did with Christ. Not to mention Ezequiel Zamora, who had been practically obliterated from official history altogether. So we decided to rescue them. Bolívar began to assume his rightful place at the head of a movement which was Bolivarian, and also revolutionary.

Could you say it was the founding action of the Bolivarian Revolution?

Symbolically, no doubt about it. That was the movement's formal point of departure. After swearing that oath, we set to work very seriously. We decided on strict criteria for recruiting other officers; we would only accept candidates by consensus. None of us could do it on our own. It was an indispensable precaution. So, in that December of 1982, the Ejército Bolivariano Revolucionario [Revolutionary Bolivarian Army] was born. The initials EBR also stood for **E**zequiel Zamora, Simón **B**olívar, and Simón **R**odríguez. The name was later changed to the Movimiento Bolivariano Revolucionario (MBR-200).

Why the 200?

Well, at first the intelligence services said we called ourselves the EBR-200 because there were 200 of us. That made us laugh, I remember us saying, 'Wish we *were* 200 . . .' There were only a handful of us. In reality, it was because we were entering the year of the two hundredth anniversary of Bolívar's birth [24 July 1783]. That's why we annexed the 200 to the initials EBR.

How did you start organizing?

The movement's initial structure was by rank: captains, the most senior, then lieutenants, second lieutenants and cadets – because we started organizing at the Military Academy as well. As I explained, we'd already been working on individuals. Shortly afterwards, we called a meeting. In addition to the four of us, there was Ronald Blanco La Cruz, paratrooper second lieutenant; Pedro Alastre

López, armoured division lieutenant; and Luis Reyes Reyes, of the Air Force. We were now a group of seven officers. So we decided to call ourselves the EBR High Command. That's how 1982 ended. And at the beginning of 1983, I found myself doing an advanced course at the Armoured Vehicles School in Caracas.

That year also saw elections to find a successor to President Luis Herrera Campíns, right?
Yes, Jaime Lusinchi of Acción Democrática won the elections at the end of that year. But, more importantly, that was the year of 'Black Friday' [18 February 1983]: economic collapse, massive capital flight, and an external debt crisis – partly caused by the previous government of Carlos Andrés Pérez – which led to a violent devaluation of the Venezuelan currency. The bolívar went from 4.30 to the dollar to 15. It was traumatic in the extreme.

Were you in Caracas when that happened?
Yes, I was doing a residential course at Fuerte Tiuna. I spent six or seven months and took advantage of it to proselytize. I succeeded in getting some of the officers on the course to join the movement.

Was it all clandestine? Did no one discover those connections?
Absolutely no one. And, with the odd exception, it invariably stayed that way until 4 February 1992. And even those exceptions didn't endanger the movement.

When the armoured vehicles course finished, did you stay in Caracas?
I finished the course in July 1983, having managed to recruit several fellow captains: Pedro Ruiz Rondón, Willy Fernández, Pérez Isa, José Angarita. I'd come top of the class, so they offered me the job of instructor. I maintained close ties with the Academy, where I was still teaching cadets. The two buildings were fifty metres apart on opposite sides of the road.

So you were an instructor in the Armoured Vehicles School, and still teaching at the Military Academy?

No, I stayed on as an instructor at that school from July 1983, until the start of 1984, when from one day to the next I was unexpectedly moved, as had happened on previous occasions. I received an order: 'Present yourself at the Academy.' So I did.

Like a kind of promotion.

That's right. I was going back to the Academy again. That meant, as you can appreciate, wider scope for action. Being a captain in an isolated frontier unit is not the same as being a captain at the very heart of the system. Besides, and I say this in all modesty, I was gaining more kudos by the day, I'd come out top of the class . . . The job was to teach at the Army's Senior Officers School. They'd asked the Armoured Vehicles School for an instructor, and the logical thing would have been for Colonel Ojeda to send a colonel to teach lieutenant colonels. But Ojeda decided, 'Send Chávez!' So I picked up my maps and off I went. Next thing I knew, I was giving classes to senior officers.

What did you teach?

Tactics and strategy. It was a preparatory class, prior to the course for the Army Staff College.

And at the Academy?

They made me head of the Cultural Activities Office, or the Culture Department, I don't remember the exact name. I'd already been head of the Sports Department. The director of the Academy at the time was General Peñaloza Zambrano. To all intents and purposes there was no cultural programme, so I enthusiastically began drawing up a study plan and fixing aims and objectives in music, theatre, etc.

How long were you in that job?

Six months. I organized art exhibitions, choir exchanges, student music groups, beauty pageants, etc. We even brought the famous singer–songwriter Simón Díaz to the Academy for Mothers' Day.[5] I stayed in the post until July 1984, when I received one of the greatest honours of my life – because I'd barely been a captain for two years – which was to be suddenly put in command of the military course. Something normally taught by a very senior captain. That academic year, 1984–1985, was extraordinary.

Were you still into sport?
Of course. I was still playing baseball with the cadets, in the team.

In the Academy team?
I couldn't compete in the inter-military institutes' championships but, as a graduate, I could take part in the inter-university competitions. Because in the University of Caracas league, they took up to five graduates. So we played some really good teams: Central University, the Santa María University, the Pedagogic University. I carried that team, that's where its nickname, the 'Famous', came from.

The 'Famous'?
Yes. I invented that name because we had a weak team, not many good pitchers, and not a single good catcher. We had no good artillery, so to speak. We hardly ever won. So, to get them fired up, I started invoking Maisanta, 'Maisanta, help me!' and the cadets followed suit. One day, in the parade ground, I was commanding the battalion as duty officer, and my team was playing that afternoon. And since I had to send them to lunch before the rest of the unit, I said, 'Those in the "famous" baseball team, over here.' I meant it ironically, the team was famous for being useless. From then on it was called 'the Famous'.

---

5   Simón Díaz (1928–2014), famous singer and composer of popular Venezuelan music. Considered the father of *tonada* music, typical of the Llanos. Among his many awards was the Latin Grammy 2008.

Pope John Paul II came on a visit to Caracas, do you remember it?
Very well. It was at the end of January 1985. He stayed three days. He arrived on a stifling hot afternoon. President Jaime Lusinchi met him at the airport, and a cadet unit from the Academy provided the guard of honour. I also remember the Pope making hostile statements against the Theology of Liberation, which he called 'a grave deviation', and stigmatized the movement's leaders: Gustavo Gutiérrez, Leonardo Boff, Jon Sobrino, Ernesto Cardenal, and Ignacio Ellacuría who was assassinated in El Salvador in 1989. John Paul's visit was politically exploited. Conservative business-men tried to capitalize on the people's enthusiasm, and allied themselves to retrograde elements within the clergy. But the more technocratic and 'modern' people within the Opus Dei resisted them. On the other hand, the Pope ended his visit with a speech in the working-class city of Ciudad Guayana in which he called for 'an end to social injustice', something we fervently agreed with.

John Paul II came back to Venezuela in February 1996, when Rafael Caldera was in power. I remember him again denouncing, in a speech he gave in the Teresa Carreño theatre in Caracas, 'the dramatic increase in poverty which often amounts to outright destitution'.

Did you ever meet him?
I had an audience with him during my early years as president. He received me at the Vatican on 1 October 1999. He had made his famous visit to Cuba the previous January. I invited him to visit Venezuela again, but as you know he died in 2005.

Going back to the early 1980s, General Omar Torrijos died in 1981. Do you remember that moment?
Perfectly. Torrijos died on 31 July 1981. I was playing baseball in the Dominican Republic; it was my second tournament there. After one game, I remember going with a group of officers to a swimming pool, at a military club. That's where I heard the news of the plane

crash. It was a huge blow for me. He was a revolutionary officer who got the Panama Canal back for his people. Many historians claim it was sabotage by the CIA. We thought about him a lot, him and his example.

Was Torrijos an example for you personally?
At one stage, yes, absolutely. As I've said, his example stimulated us to put a lot of effort into political education. Because – and I want to make this clear – I always stressed the importance of ideology: in the meetings with Douglas Bravo and the PRB; with Alfredo Maneiro and his people; with Hugo Trejo and his group . . . I always emphasized the ideological basis of Bolivarianism.

The officers who joined your movement favoured, I imagine, an autochthonous, Venezuelan, Bolivarian, road to revolution, and were opposed to any Marxist-type experiment, weren't they?
Absolutely. I began to see very early on, as early as 1978, that I could talk to some fellow soldiers about politics in the sense of dissatisfaction with the current state of affairs in Venezuela; but whenever I did, extremely cautiously, mention Douglas Bravo or Alfredo Maneiro, they'd reject it out of hand. Marxism was seen as something very hostile, negative. My colleagues were not ready to go that far.

Did they know you knew Bravo and Maneiro?
Oh, no. I had to be very careful. I gradually realized that some of them were prepared to go down that route; Reyes Reyes, for instance, even came to several meetings with Douglas Bravo. But he too soon distanced himself from the group. Captain Dumas Ramírez also met Douglas once, after which he told me, 'These are men from the past . . .' I began to realize that even the officers closest to me felt uncomfortable with it. I could see going down that route would lead nowhere. Marxism was the opposite of everything the Armed Forces stood for: it was impossible to combine Marx and Lenin with the idiosyncratic Prussianism of our military education. Besides which, most Marxist political circles in Caracas accepted

the theory of the 'armed wing'. I disagreed with that thesis, and argued for a combined civilian–military movement.

They thought the Armed Forces should be just an instrument.

Yes, the 'armed wing' of the civilian rebellion. Only the wing; they were the brain. It was based on the old Maoist idea that 'the Party commands the gun', that the Armed Forces should be under the direct control of the Party.[6] I didn't agree. I said this on several occasions, and sensed that Alfredo Maneiro was losing interest. I stayed in touch with Pablo Medina. But when Maneiro died, Jorge Olavarría [1933–2005] became the leading light in La Causa R, and I never really thought of him as a man of the Left.

So I began to distance myself, met these groups less and less frequently, and intensified my work within the Army.

The idea of your military friends was, I suppose, that the Armed Forces should lead the movement.

They balked at the idea of meekly taking orders from a political party. That idea was quite simply unacceptable. They were afraid they would be used, like 'useful fools'. Nevertheless, I thought we had to move towards a synthesis of the two positions and build, I repeat, a civilian–military movement. But for the time being, I devoted myself to consolidating our movement inside the Armed Forces. I proposed we study everything we could about Bolívar and immerse ourselves in his thinking.

On the basis of his own writings, or critical studies?

Both. Rereading and studying his writings was an indispensable return to the source, the original spring, the foundation. But we also needed analysis by historians and academics. For instance, we read several essential books: *Introducción a Simón Bolívar*, by Miguel

---

6   'Our principle is that the Party commands the gun, the gun must never be allowed to command the Party.' Mao Zedong, *Problems and Strategy of War*. See Peter D. Feaver, 'The Civil-Military Problematique: Huntington, Janowitz and the Question of Civilian Control', *Armed Forces & Society*, 1996.

Acosta Saignes; *Bolívar*, by Indalecio Liévano Aguirre; *Bolívar de carne y hueso*, by Francisco Herrera Luque; *Bolívar: Pensamiento Precursor de Antiimperialismo*, by Francisco Pividal; and *El Culto a Bolívar*, by Germán Carrera Damas, among many others.[7] He appeared to us in all his clarity, the statesman, the visionary of Latin American integration. We studied his decrees on the distribution of uncultivated land. We tried to define a Bolivarian ideology because, for us, in our situation, it provided the perfect theoretical tool: no soldier could reject it, it had historical weight and contained all the revolutionary elements we needed to mobilize discontented officers.

Were you interested in Miranda, the 'Precursor'?
Yes, we also studied Francisco de Miranda, his *Colombeia*, his vision of Europe, his geopolitical prognosis.[8] Sucre as well. We deepened our knowledge of Venezuela, of indigenous resistance and the figure of Guaicaipuro. We also researched the thinking of Bolívar's teacher Simón Rodríguez, his social vision, his ideas about ethics, education and economics. And the thinking of Ezequiel Zamora. We decided to assemble the essential ideas from each of them, to build up a body of original doctrine, of political thought that was revolutionary yet at the same time profoundly Venezuelan. It began to take shape bit by bit. In this way, we created the 'tree with three roots' as a fundamental ideological concept, one of the mainstays of our political project.

---

7   Miguel Acosta Saignes, *Introducción a Simón Bolívar*, Siglo XXI, Mexico DF, 1983. Indalecio Liévano Aguirre, *Bolívar*, Ediciones Cultura Hispánica, Madrid, 1983. Francisco Herrera Luque, *Bolívar de carne y hueso* [Bolívar of Flesh and Blood], Ateneo de Caracas, Caracas, 1983. Francisco Pividal, *Bolívar: Pensamiento Precursor del Antiimperialismo*, Ateneo de Caracas, Caracas, 1983. Francisco Pividal, *Bolívar: Pensamiento Precursor del Antiimperialismo*, Ateneo de Caracas, Caracas, 1983. Germán Carrera Damas, *El Culto a Bolívar*, Universidad Central de Venezuela, Caracas, 1969. Reprinted by Editorial Alfa, Caracas, 2003.

8   Francisco de Miranda and Josefina R. de Alonso, *Colombeia*, Ediciones de la Presidencia de la República, Caracas, 1978. See also *Francisco de Miranda, Palabras Esenciales*, Ministerio de Comunicación e Información, Caracas, 2006.

Was it your idea?

Yes, in all honesty I have to admit it was mine. I proposed the concept and even drew the tree . . . I also designed the first logo for the EBR-200: I envisaged an arm, a fist and a sabre with its sheath in the form of an E, a B, an R, and a 200. Later, it seemed too militaristic for my liking and we discarded it; besides, tactically we couldn't use it. But I got that far, imagining how to give graphic form to the ideology. 1983–1985 were years of expansion for our movement. Numbers grew, especially in the Academy where we incorporated Ronald Blanco La Cruz, Diosdado Cabello, Jesse Chacón, Edgar Hernández Behrens, Moreno Acosta, Florencio Porras, Moro González who died, and Llanos Morales who was unfortunately killed in a light aircraft. By then, we were about eight or ten officers with some twenty or thirty cadets, each of which would eventually bring a colleague or friend.

Had Francisco Arias Cárdenas joined by then?

No, Arias joined in 1985. He was just back from doing a postgraduate degree in Colombia and, like I said, he was in the ARMA movement. Not directly with William Izarra, the founder, but with the then Colonel Ramón Santeliz. They were more like discussion groups, they didn't have many cadres. For us, on the other hand, and this is important, the Academy was like a seedbed. We achieved everything I envisaged when I arrived: 'If it can't be done here, it can't be done anywhere; conditions here are perfect.'

Yet it was still clandestine?

Yes, even though we sometimes did provocative things. For instance, when we were out jogging with the colonel, I'd sing Zamora's anthem, 'The lowering sky announces a storm! / Tremble, oligarchs, long live freedom!' And over a hundred cadets would repeat the chorus. On the centenary of Zamora's death, 10 January 1985, we spent the whole night sticking huge polystyrene letters to the top of the building where the military course was held: 'General Zamora, a hundred years after your death, your song is still with us.' It was an open conspiracy.

And nobody said anything about it?

Yes, the colonel sent for me: 'What's the meaning of this?' 'Colonel, it's the anniversary of Ezequiel Zamora's murder'. He replied, 'I'm not sure what you mean by it, but get rid of it; I don't want to see it there tomorrow.' We had to take it down. But we went on filling the whole Academy with symbols. It was also the year of the black flags. José Antonio Páez put a skull on his, but even more important than the skull.

Was his motto, 'Freedom or Death!'

That's right. 'Freedom or Death!' Those flags were everywhere. Symbols, anthems . . . Those were years of expansion, until July 1985. The cadets – we called them the Centaurs – graduated. The movement kept growing. We had even organized the movement's first National Congress, with some twenty delegates representing different regions. I got that idea of a congress from seeing how the Venezuelan Communist Party organized things, I plagiarized their methods. We divided the country into regions and gave them indigenous names. So, the Guaicaipuro Revolutionary Area Command (CAR) was the central states of Miranda, Vargas and Caracas; the Variná CAR was Barinas and Apure; the Mara CAR was Zulia, the Timotucuicas CAR was the Andes, etc. Then we introduced the Simón Bolívar National Project, defined lines of strategic planning, did in-depth studies of the economy, agrarian problems, education, urbanization, health, international relations . . .

How many congresses did you organize?

Five, I think. We held them at weekends. The last one was in Maracay in 1989, after the Caracazo; we didn't hold another one for security reasons.

Did you invite leaders from other parties?

Not to the congresses, but they came to our other meetings. People like Pablo Medina and Andrés Velásquez from La Causa R, some people from the PRV linked to Douglas Bravo, and other independent intellectuals.[9] The idea of forging links with civilians on the Left was to reaffirm our intention of moving forward to civilian–military unity.

Did you produce theoretical documents?

Yes, we wrote papers. We prepared agendas for our meetings, and made photocopies. We wrote several theses on Bolívar and asked members to produce discussion papers on specific subjects, for example, 'You two, please prepare a discussion paper on Zamora for the next meeting.' We also decided, at our congress in San Cristóbal in 1986, to bring out a magazine called *Alianza Patriótica*. But as with *El Agua Mansa* magazine ['Gently Flowing Water', see Chapter 9], its articles were all about world revolutionary leaders – Marx, Lenin, Mao, Che, etc. – and none about Venezuelans, not even Bolívar! I think I burned the two hundred copies I was sent. I was furious. We didn't bring out a second issue.

And all without being rumbled by military intelligence?

Well, at one point we realized we were under surveillance. The intelligence services did actually start coming after us, and we had to destroy some of our documents: papers, reports, etc.

Did you impose a code of confidentiality?

Yes, it was very strict. We even went as far as admonishing officers. In coded language, of course, but we had a functioning command group which recognized merit and meted out sanctions. For example, an officer who missed a meeting without good reason would be sent a brief caution.

Discipline was imposed.

Yes. And we also tried to foresee the evolution of the political situation in Venezuela. And look what a coincidence this was: I

---

9   Andrés Velásquez, former trade union leader, was presidential candidate for La Causa R in 1983, 1988 and 1993. He is currently [2009] a member of the National Assembly for a party opposed to President Chávez.

remember the opinion polls we did among members of our movement foresaw a rebellion taking place around 1990, 1991 and 1992, that is, ten years from then. So, that's what they had in mind.

They anticipated what would happen ten years later.
That's right. Our people thought in terms of a decade. It arose out of our debates and discussions. No one thought in the short term. The consensus was that we'd have to put in a lot of effort, and wait for the right conditions. Not only that. Some of us said in various meetings, 'Let's hope the Venezuelan political class pulls the country out of the mire, then we wouldn't have to intervene.' We didn't want to create a movement just for the sake of it. Do you see?

You saw yourselves as a resource, an alternative. You were only going to act if the situation in the country got worse.
Of course. If the government, through a political accord, changed tack and dragged the country back from the abyss, we wouldn't have to intervene. But Venezuela was still engulfed in poverty, misery, corruption, and the surrender of the country's resources.

Were you concerned with economic issues?
Enormously. We studied economic matters very closely. Many members of our movement went on to university, to further their studies and acquire more tools for political, social and economic analysis. We all read a lot. Samuel Moncada, a history professor at the Military Academy, published his book *The Serpent's Eggs* around then, and was forced to resign: they fired him from the Academy because he told the inside story of the Fedecámaras [Venezuelan Chamber of Commerce] case.[10] I was duty officer when that book was published.

All in all, from 1980 to 1985 we were maturing and gaining even more experience than we had expected. I was surprised myself. As a result, in 1986 we organized another national congress, to further

---

10   Samuel Moncada, *Los huevos de la serpiente. Fedecámaras por dentro*, Editorial Alianza Gráfica, Caracas, 1985.

consolidate our ideas. We were some fifteen officers, some from very far away, all well prepared for that meeting. But we were growing so large that, in 1986, we decided to stop. Continuing to expand was just too risky.

Statistically, the danger of informers increases in proportion to the number of members.

It's mathematical. That's why we decided to stop expanding, and didn't accept new members for a prudent period. We wanted to consolidate what we had achieved, man by man, structure by structure. So we re-analysed everything: the cells, the Revolutionary Area Commands, the ideology, the civilian–military alliance, the revolutionary aspect. Because some *compañeros* had joined without having a very clear sense of our identity, of who we were. We even had to explain that this wasn't a right-wing movement. That issue showed up again later, especially in prison [1992–1994]. Some didn't stick with it long, they lacked a solid political consciousness. Others came out of prison and joined the other side.

And eventually, some even went over to the opposition, like Jesús Urdaneta and Raúl Isaías Baduel.

Jesús Urdaneta never had much of a grasp of ideology; that says it all. He was ideologically weak, and the enemy rapidly spotted it. The same happened with Baduel. To be fair, Baduel was never wholly committed to our movement. He came to some meetings, but then, when 4 February 1992 happened, he didn't take part, he decided to become a reservist. He was already showing signs of weakness. But anyway, when we get to that point, we'll talk about those people if you like.

Going back to 1986, what I want to stress is the very rapid expansion our organization went through. That's when we decided to change the EBR-200 [Revolutionary Bolivarian Army] into the MBR-200 [Revolutionary Bolivarian Movement]. We changed the E for Ejército [Army] into the M for Movement, because we said, 'We have a big group of officers in the Air Force, so how can we call ourselves an Army?' There were Navy officers too, not very many, but some. And civilian movements were also beginning to join. That's why we decided to change the name. From then on we were the MBR-200, and under that name we carried out the rebellion of 4 February 1992. But before we get on to that, we have to talk about the Caracazo.

12

The Caracazo

Three years in Elorza – Back to Caracas
Studying political science
Return of Carlos Andrés Pérez – The 'Great U-Turn'
27 February 1989 – Causes of the Caracazo
Impact on the Armed Forces – Death of Felipe Acosta Carlez
Under suspicion – In the Senior Defence School
War of nerves at Los Pinos – General Peñaloza
Manoeuvring – In Provisioning! – The 'invisible conspiracy'
Commanding the parachute regiment in Maracay

In 1985, they took your post in the Military Academy in Caracas away from you, and transferred you to Elorza, a town in the state of Apure, in the far west of Venezuela near the border with Colombia. Why did they send you so far away?
Perhaps they thought they were sending me into exile [laughter]. The reason was very simple; it was becoming increasingly difficult to keep our organization secret, and its activities eventually reached the ears of the Directorate of Military Intelligence (DIM). They almost certainly heard from our sworn enemy, General Julio Peñaloza, the army chief of staff, about the radical lectures we were giving at the Academy. Yet they weren't Marxist speeches; they were about Bolívar, Miranda, and the heroes of Venezuelan history, so it

was difficult to sack us or discipline us. What's more, the officers involved were considered the most brilliant of the current crop. The armed forces couldn't afford to lose a whole generation. So the DIM didn't arrest us, or accuse us of being subversives, they just made sure we weren't given command of troops in the centre of the country. They dispersed us to the four corners of Venezuela in the hope that we'd lose touch with one another.

Were you surprised to be sent so far away?

Not really. I didn't even see Elorza as a punishment. On the contrary. I was recommended for that post by Ramón Carrizales, a great cavalry officer and a friend. I was given very important military responsibilities in a strategic location: the border with Colombia. I remember that when I received the order to transfer to Elorza, I packed my things, left the Academy, got into my old blue jalopy, started the engine, and shouted, 'Mission accomplished!' The seed had been sown, nobody was going to stop the birth of the revolution. The Movimiento Bolivariano Revolucionario-200 was the expression of the purest dreams of the 1970–1980 decade of heroic young soldiers.

What lessons did you learn from your time in Apure?

I spent almost three years in that beautiful state. First in Elorza, as commander of the town's garrison and the Francisco Farfán Motorized Cavalry Squadron.[1] My post was what they called a Remote Basic Unit. That is, I had no senior officer within a five-hundred-kilometre radius. I felt like a fish in water in Capanaparo, Sabanas del Viento, Barranco Yopal, Caño Caribe, Cubarro, Cinaruco . . . all in the central Llanos where I was born. It was like coming back to my nest, my cradle, my origins. The time I spent there was one of the happiest periods of my life, I felt fulfilled militarily, socially and politically. Elorza became a kind of sociological laboratory, where I put into practice our theories of creating a

---

1 Francisco Farfán (?–1841), colonel in the Venezuelan Army during the Independence War. He fought under the command of José Antonio Páez, in the battles of Las Queseras del Medio (1819) and Carabobo (1821).

relationship between the armed forces and the people. Something I'd never done before.

So, you used Elorza to test your theories about governing society?

Yes, because I had to solve concrete problems, not virtual or theoretical ones. I had more time to reflect, to read and study. It was like a mini human laboratory where I was faced with very specific economic and social challenges. Normally, of course, it would not have been up to me or my garrison to solve these problems. So, at the beginning, if I had any ideas about ways of helping, I would seek the permission of my superiors, who were some distance away. The answer always came back, 'No, Captain, that's not your job. Your job is to guarantee the security of the border.'

But I'd say to myself, 'Good grief, doesn't the fact that the indigenous people round here are dying of hunger bear some relation to security? Or that the river fishermen are exploited by the boat owners? Or that local people are living in extreme poverty?' Of course it was relevant to security. That's what, in the early 1970s, General Juan José Torres and Bolivia's socialist soldiers called the 'interior frontier'. And part of my mission to safeguard Venezuelan territory – in the most intelligent way I could think of – was to look after that 'interior frontier'. So I decided to stop consulting my superiors, or asking their permission, and I devoted myself to resolving concrete problems in that region.

Such as what?

The problem of the *latifundio* and exploitation, for example. And in Elorza I came up against the 'Indian problem'. I've mentioned that already. The indigenous people of this region, the Cuivas and the Yaruros, lived the same tragic lives as indigenous peoples all over Venezuela. You had to see it to believe it. There I was tested as a leader, no longer of cadets and soldiers, but among a ragbag of different groups: students, Indians, sportspeople, etc. A genuine people, in other words. A microcosm of society – like society as a whole, but in miniature.

What was Elorza like in those days?

A typical abandoned Venezuelan town. A dusty main street, a small hotel, a few Syrian-owned shops, several Colombian-owned restaurants, and on the outskirts, the wretched shacks where the Cuivas and the Yaruros lived. And a military base some ten kilometres away. Images of poverty characteristic of those godforsaken pueblos of the Venezuelan plains, straight out of *Doña Bárbara*, or Otero Silva's *Casas Muertas* [Dead Houses].[2] And the same political set-up, but writ small, so it was easier to understand the manoeuvrings of the Pact of Punto Fijo. Corruption at every level, and a neglected underclass with no government, no social programmes of any kind. Schools without water, blackboards, desks, toilets or food. A hospital with no doctors or medicines. Nothing. Even ice had to be brought from San Cristóbal. An abandoned town, with no drinking water, appalling roads, impossible to drive on in winter. All this in such a rich country . . .

So what did you do?

I was the military commander, but I had to become a social leader. I got the soldiers out of their barracks-life routine, and into the life of that community, by providing support for social and economic development. We went out into the savannah and onto the rivers to gather the poor and organize them. The folkloric fiestas of 19 March, Saint John's Day, are very important there now – all the best singers and musicians come to town. But not in those days. We used the local interest in the fiestas to organize the people, rouse them out of their lethargy. We asked for volunteers to contribute time or money to help organize and finance local pageants. We got hold of some old, thin cows and fattened them up to sell. The money went into the coffers of the Festival Committee. We'd erect stalls on street corners to sell food at weekends, and liquor as well.

---

2 Miguel Otero Silva (1908–1985), great progressive intellectual and one of the best Venezuelan writers of the second half of the twentieth century. Founder of *El Nacional* newspaper (1942) and author of *Casas muertas* (1955); *Oficina Nº 1* (1960); *La muerte de Honorio* (1968) and *Cuando quiero llorar no lloro* (1975).

We brought musicians like Luis Lozada *El Cubiro* – God rest his soul – to sing *joropos* and liven things up. Money left over from that also went into the coffers. The town began to spring to life, people started to cooperate, to collaborate. I also worked a lot with the Cuivas and Yaruros, going deep into the Cajón de Arauca, following the banks of the Cubarro stream.

With your soldiers?
Yes. I commanded a patrol of bearded soldiers who looked more like guerrillas. I myself started to resemble the ragged character Lorenzo Barquero in *Doña Bárbara* . . . With the help of a great ethnologist, Arelis Sumavila, I got to know the Indians, to appreciate and respect their customs and culture. I spent weeks in the savannah with them, living the way they did. At the same time, I was able to keep researching Maisanta, whose memory was still fresh in the minds of many old people in the region. It was very important for me to dig more deeply into my family roots. And into the history, geography and culture of the Llanos.

So it was a fruitful 'exile' for you?
Yes, very fertile. I came out of that laboratory stronger mentally. It made a big impression on me, and reinforced my sense of the need for cooperation between the military and civil society. Those experiences were what I needed to form a more complete, integrated vision of the real Venezuela. Although the DIM were on my back even there.

They didn't lose track of you?
As a precaution, we'd decided to suspend looking for new officers to join the movement. But one of our lieutenants [Ramón Valera Querales] asked me to let him finish the work he was doing with one particular second lieutenant. I gave him permission. Then this second lieutenant, nervous and scared, went and told his commander everything. He mentioned me by name. I didn't know it at the time, but one day I started noticing agents following me everywhere.

Did you have any compromising documents or papers?
That was the trouble. I kept very important documents, books, notebooks in my bedroom. As it happened, when I heard about the informant I was away having an eye operation in Fuerte Tiuna, Caracas. Luckily I was able to alert some friends to 'clean' my room, and burn all those incriminating documents. Just in time, because the next day DIM and DISIP agents landed in Elorza in a light aircraft. They searched my room but didn't find anything. But when I got back to Elorza, they stripped me of my command. I was left with no troops, no budget, nothing. The DISIP kept watching me, however, and in one of their reports they even linked me to the Colombian guerrillas, and said I was preparing an indigenous revolt! [Laughter.]

Were you still in touch with the other MBR-200 cadres?
It was more difficult, of course, because of the distances involved and the surveillance we were under. But these obstacles didn't stop us organizing, in May 1986, our third National MBR-200 Congress in San Cristóbal, capital of the state of Táchira. I went there under the pretext of some armoured vehicle manoeuvre. During that congress, we discussed the main planks of what action to take, mainly those proposed by Arias Cárdenas and myself.

Apparently there was tension between you and Arias Cárdenas.
Arias had joined our Movement a few months before that congress, at the end of 1985. He was an exceedingly intelligent man, with experience of conspiracies within the Army. But, initially, there were things we disagreed about – like working methods, the ideological line to take, the strategy of uniting soldiers and civilians. These differences came to a head during the congress and we had a heated discussion about whether or not to incorporate popular organizations into our movement. But it didn't stop us moving forward. We finally defined the Movement's philosophical principles, based on the ideas of Bolívar, Miranda, Simón Rodríguez, and the social vision of Ezequiel Zamora: the four figures who nourished our political philosophy and our plan of action.

After this congress in 1986, we really did have an organization capable of preparing the civilian–military insurrection. And that was indispensable, because in the following months I was to feel the full pressure of the army intelligence services. What's more, Generals Ítalo del Valle Alliegro, Manuel Heinz Azpurua, and especially Carlos Julio Peñaloza Zambrana, were out to get me.

Despite that, you were transferred back to Caracas, weren't you?
Yes, but later. In 1986, I was promoted to major. One day, when I was just back from visiting a Yaruro area and my soldiers were so bedraggled, long-haired, and bearded that they really looked like veteran guerrillas, a general called Arnoldo Rodríguez Ochoa came on a visit of inspection. He was astonished by our appearance. Still, he and I talked at length, and eventually he asked me to be his second-in-command in San Juan de los Morros [capital of the state of Guárico], gateway to the Central Llanos. I accepted. And a mere three months later, he was appointed to run the National Security Council. He took me with him to Caracas to head up his staff. So, by way of a series of coincidences, from one day to the next, I was back in the capital.

What date was that?
Mid 1988, in the final days of Jaime Lusinchi's presidency. In a trice, I had gone from the banks of the Arauca to the shores of the Guaire, I hadn't even finished picking off the ticks. Once again, it was as if someone had conspired in my favour, like a cosmic conspiracy, with fate moving the pieces at the right time and place. There I was again in Caracas. My offices were in the Palacio Blanco [across the street from the Miraflores Palace], in the Seconasede [Secretariat of the National Council for Security and Defence, or Homeland Security]. It was an important position. Several generals opposed my appointment.

Did you revive the MBR-200?
I was under strict surveillance, but I did my best to get things going again and reactivate groups from within the Palacio Blanco and the

Miraflores Palace. It was not easy. The Movement's activity was at a low ebb. Everything, or almost everything, had been deactivated. I felt really deflated. I began to think about leaving . . .

About leaving the Army, again?

Yes. I'd been away from the capital for three years, and back in Caracas I was being watched very closely. I was under a lot of pressure, and forced to lower my level of activity. Several officers had deserted the Movement, others had left the Army, and some had even gone abroad . . . So, I took the decision to go to university and study political science; I was also considering leaving the Army altogether, to join the political struggle as a civilian.

You started at university, then.

Yes. I took advantage of being at the Seconasede to enrol, in July 1990, at the Simón Bolívar University to do a Masters in political science. I used my recent promotion to lieutenant colonel to ask permission, and General Rodríguez authorized it. The course was at the Valle de Sartenejas campus in Baruta [a smart neighbourhood in the east of Caracas].

With one exception, none of my lecturers was left-wing, so I argued with them and learned quite a bit from some of them. One day, one of these conservatives asked me, 'What's in your head, Major?' 'Ideas, Professor, ideas,' I replied, to the lecturer's alarm. 'Those ideas of yours are rather worrying, seeing you're in uniform . . .'

My main aim was to work hard and learn as much as possible about politics, economics and society. I remember my mentor, General Pérez Arcay, repeating, 'Study! Study!' He was always saying, 'You have to learn a lot. One day you'll be head of state, and you have to be a good head of state'. Personally, I had no wish to be head of state, what I wanted was to see change.

Did you specialize in any subject in particular?

Well, on the postgraduate course I signed up for I had to prepare a thesis. One of the subjects I took was National Projects, Planning and Development, and I wrote a paper on Carlos Andrés Pérez's VIII Plan, known as the *Gran Viraje* [Great U-Turn].[3] This U-turn was the one imposed on Venezuela by hegemonic global capitalism and the International Monetary Fund through a harsh programme of structural adjustment, which ultimately caused the mass protests and popular uprising known as the Caracazo.

What was the topic of your thesis?
Transitional government. I'd already done several papers on it for my Master's.

Did you study political transitions here in Venezuela, or did you look at transition abroad? In Spain, for instance?
I looked at several places. One of my papers was on the political transition in Spain, from Francoism to democracy, and one of the books I cited most was by a French professor, Maurice Duverger. It was entitled *Political Institutions and Constitutional Law*.[4] I was fascinated by Duverger's thesis, and took it as my main point of reference. A left-wing professor in the university at the time recommended it. In my day, there were good lecturers, a handful of left-wingers. The subjects I chose and the papers I wrote during my Master's were orientated towards the political movement we were preparing. In the country in general, there was a lot of political activity going on. This was 1988–1989.

What other papers did you write at the University?
Well, I also wrote on economic matters. I remember doing research on the Sidor steel plant in Ciudad Guayana, and the Matanceros, a political movement that had emerged in the heat of the Venezuelan state steel industry. I had strong links to the leaders of that movement, militants of Maneiro's La Causa R. They passed me documents that proved very useful in my research on Sidor. I offered a

---

3 *El Gran Viraje. Lineamientos generales del VIII Plan de la Nación (1990–1995)*, Oficina Central de Coordinación y Planificación (CORDIPLAN), Caracas, 1990.
4 Maurice Duverger, *Institutions politiques et droit constitutionnel*, PUF, Paris, 1970.

critique of neoliberal policies, since there was already talk of privati-
zations. I researched the new political actor born in the heat of the
workers' struggles, the Matanceros and their history, and what
made my work of particular interest was that I more or less took on
the voice of the Matanceros themselves.

At the University, didn't the students shun you for being a soldier?
Absolutely not. There were other soldiers there. Some were right-
wing, others left-wing. I remember one National Guard colonel . . .
I was very careful not to show my political colours. But I got along
fine with the students. I was good friends with most of them: some
very pretty girls, even a priest, and a businessman . . . I made friends
with the lecturers . . . Recently I met a woman who said, 'Hugo,
don't you remember me? I was the secretary in the Rector's office.'
Because I knew everyone in the administration too. That's the way
I am. I like being friends with everybody; I make friends no matter
what colour or class they are. I got along just as well in the salons of
the bourgeoisie, chatting to the elite, as I did among the Indians of
the Capanaparo. Military life is good for that. One day you're with
your soldiers, most of whom are illiterate *campesinos*, and the next
you're at a party in the Miraflores Palace.

How long were you at the University?
A year and a half. I tried to get my thesis finished, but when it
became clear the army high command wanted to scupper my career,
I had to devote myself full-time to the Bolivarian Movement. So I
opted to deal with that problem first, and leave my thesis for later.

Were those university studies useful to you, though?
Very. I learned an enormous amount. And they helped me at a later
date to research the evolution of the Venezuelan flag. I became an
expert. At the Seconasede, I even produced a leaflet on the history
of our national flags, starting with Miranda's in 1810. We held a
ceremony inaugurating a Flag Room. That was several months after
the Caracazo. Carlos Andrés Pérez came and the general in charge
said, 'You're the expert, Chávez, explain it to the president.' We

walked along, with me telling him the history of each flag. When we got to the Angostura standard with the eight stars, I said, 'Mr President, this is the flag you decreed should have an eighth star, but it couldn't be done during your first mandate . . .' And Carlos Andrés replied, 'Ah! Quite right, Major, you're reminding me of something very important, the eighth star . . .' I was making a coded reference to the Bolivarian star.[5]

Did you have any other contact with President Pérez in those days?
Carlos Andrés knew me. He saw me in the corridors of the Miraflores Palace several times. One evening he found me working on a computer in the security office. He came in and said, 'What are you doing here at this time, Major Chávez?' 'Some work for the University,' I said. 'I don't have a computer and Major Frank González lets me use this one.' He was the chief of security. 'What are you studying?' 'Political science, Mr President!' 'Aha, you're interested in politics?' he enquired, suspiciously.

You MBR-200 officers were waiting for the state to be in terminal crisis before you took action.
Yes. But we saw no sign of a serious crisis. The system was in permanent crisis, in fact, but proving to be highly flexible and resilient. It was, as the saying goes, in rude ill-health. At the end of Lusinchi's presidency, the election campaign began; Carlos Andrés Pérez threw himself into battle with the slogan '_Ese hombre sí camina_' [That man sure is walking].

And he won.
Yes. The day Carlos Andrés won [4 December 1988], I was on high alert in the Miraflores Palace. When I finished, I remember going

---

5   On 20 November 1817, Simón Bolívar decreed that 'another star will be added to the seven stars of the Venezuelan national flag as an emblem of the province of Guayana, so that from henceforth there will be eight stars'. This was in force from 1817 to its derogation on 4 October 1821. On 9 March 2006, the inclusion of the eighth star was approved by the National Assembly, in compliance with the Liberator's decree.

out for a walk. I could see a crowd around the Palace gates where a group of Carlos Andrés supporters, most of them drunk, had crashed their vehicle into railings while trying to get into the Palace. Soldiers arrived, and a lieutenant punched one of the drunks. I intervened and the rowdies were arrested and taken away. I then got my car and drove around the city. There was jubilation everywhere, people drinking, celebrating . . . The people didn't realize Carlos Andrés would not solve anything.

I went to bed feeling disheartened. I thought to myself, 'Ten years ago, Carlos Andrés left the presidency with accusations of corruption hanging over him and, now he's back, re-elected president with a very high percentage of the vote. Media manipulation has even robbed the people of their memory, it's lobotomized them. And the left-wing parties are still divided, ineffective, inefficient. What hope is there for this country?' Going to bed totally depressed, I wanted to leave the Army, finish my university studies, and see what could be done on the streets, as an activist.

But not long afterwards, that same people rose up in the Caracazo.
Yes. The Pérez government took power and almost immediately came *El Sacudón* [the Big Shake-Up]. What a surprise! And that hurricane – sad, of course, for the deaths and grief involved – unleashed the internal forces we had been cultivating.

Why did the Caracazo happen?
Well, I've already told you how far political, economic and social conditions had deteriorated. The country was going nowhere, like a rudderless ship. The political system was in a state of putrefaction. The discourse of the political class was completely discredited, its leadership and demagogic populism exhausted. And in the 1980s, things got even worse.

In what way?
First, at the end of Luis Herrera Campíns' Copei presidency, came Black Friday [18 February 1983], the brutal currency devaluation and the severe financial and economic crisis. People were shocked

and scared. The growth rate plummeted, while the national debt skyrocketed despite big earnings from oil exports. Venezuela had to declare itself bankrupt and submit to the dictates of the IMF. It was already a dependent country, with limited sovereignty, but all the more so from then on.

Did the situation change under President Jaime Lusinchi, between 1984 and 1989?

No, the economic crisis got worse during Lusinchi's AD presidency. The bolívar was devalued on several occasions. The government's inability to mitigate the effects of the crisis on ordinary people unleashed a wave of social discontent. What's more, public opinion was critical of the adverse influence of Blanca Ibáñez, Lusinchi's secretary and lover. As on the eve of the French Revolution with the 'Austrian' Marie Antoinette, popular discontent focused on Blanca Ibáñez. The people hated her. They said the president was not at the helm in the Miraflores Palace, that the real power was held by Blanquita, the daughter of Colombian immigrants.

This destroyed the legitimacy of the Pact of Punto Fijo. The people were beginning to understand just how widespread clientelism, nepotism and general corruption were. There was an increase in social ills across the spectrum: hunger, prostitution, begging, crime . . . All the signs of a deep crisis in society. Strikes and demonstrations became frequent. The government responded with repression: violence against students, the 'disappearance' of political leaders, assassinations of labour leaders and attacks on *campesinos*. In Mérida there was a real popular uprising, known as the *Meridazo*, which took the government a week to put down.

There was also the 'night of the tanks'. Do you remember that?

Perfectly. That peculiar event – which, by the way, was never explained – happened during Carlos Andrés Pérez's election campaign, while President Lusinchi was out of the country. Tanks suddenly appeared in front of the Miraflores Palace, and also surrounded the Ministry of the Interior on Carmelitas Corner, office of the caretaker president in Lusinchi's absence. It was all very strange, and set alarm bells ringing. There was nothing casual about it. An extreme right-wing military movement was at that time being directed from the US embassy in Caracas. It consisted of mainly high-ranking officers who were plotting a pre-emptive coup, to prevent the Left from taking power first.

Tumultuous times.
Yes, turbulent, chaotic and violent. It's also when the Las Coloradas canyon massacre occurred, in El Amparo [Apure state], where DISIP special forces murdered fourteen fishermen. Lusinchi ended up tremendously unpopular. Subsequently, in 1991, he and Blanca were tried and found guilty of corruption.

Nevertheless, in December 1988, voters chose a candidate from the same Acción Democrática party to replace outgoing President Lusinchi: Carlos Andrés Pérez. How do you explain that?
It seems pretty inexplicable. Something to do with personal charisma, perhaps; his strong leadership, especially on an international level. And also because certain positive moves during his first mandate [1974–1979] might have left good memories among the lower classes. Don't forget, the vast income Venezuela had reaped from the two oil shocks had turned the country into 'Saudi Venezuela', a culture of extravagance fuelled by the large amounts of money in circulation and a false illusion of opulence.[6] It deepened the inequalities: on the one hand we had indolent millionaires enriched through corruption, and on the other, a mass of poor people going hungry, eating dog food. Carlos Andrés nationalized the steel and oil industries. He created the huge oil company Petróleos de Venezuela (PDVSA), passed a law against unfair dismissal and introduced the minimum wage. He was a traditional populist caudillo, but claimed to be a 'socialist' – and indeed in

---

6 The first oil crisis (or shock) was in October 1973, during the Arab–Israeli war. The Arab members of OPEC, meeting in Kuwait, decided to reduce the sale of hydrocarbons to 'countries supporting Israel'. In a few weeks, the price of oil went from $3 a barrel to $18. The second oil shock came in 1979, with the victory of Ayatollah Khomeini's Islamic Revolution in Iran.

1975 he was elected vice president of the Socialist International. All this helped create the myth that he was a 'progressive', a 'friend of the people'.

But after he was re-elected, his discourse changed.

Totally. He made the 'great U-turn' almost overnight. He came to office on 4 February 1989, and on 16 February, to the surprise of his own followers, he declared he was going to apply a neoliberal, IMF-dictated 'shock therapy' to the country at once, and without anaesthetic. Supported by his development minister, Moisés Naím, and his planning minister, Miguel Rodríguez Fandeo, and advised by Jeffrey Sachs – then a huge fanatic of ultra-liberalism – Carlos Andrés announced the ominous measures of the 'neoliberal package': trade liberalization, abolition of exchange controls, massive privatization of state enterprises, drastic cuts in social programmes, increases in the price of essential products and services.[7]

Of all these decisions, two put people's backs up the most, both related to the price hike of oil-based products: an unbelievable 100 per cent on the price of petrol, and 30 per cent on public transport fares. The poorer classes, who three months earlier had voted for Carlos Andrés, viewed this savage 'structural adjustment plan' as a stab in the back.

When did the protests begin?

As soon as the government applied the measures. That is, about ten days later. On Sunday 26 February, the Ministry of Energy and Mines announced that the rise in the price of petrol and of public transport would come into force the very next day, the 27th. At the end of the month, when workers don't have a cent! It was the last straw.

On the Monday, at six in the morning, in Guarenas, a satellite town thirty miles outside Caracas, the first workers boarding the

---

7   Moisés Naím (1952–), Venezuelan economist and journalist. He writes on international affairs for *El País* (Madrid) and was editor of *Foreign Policy* magazine (Washington). Jeffrey Sachs (1954–), US economist, promulgator of neoliberal 'shock therapies' in Bolivia (1985), Venezuela (1989), Poland (1989) and Russia (1991).

buses to the capital refused to pay the new fare. They confronted the bus drivers. That's where it all started. The people said, 'Enough!' It was a popular explosion, the start of the clamour of 'No to the IMF!' The inhabitants of the area around the bus station, Menca de Leoni [now renamed 27 February], goaded by exasperation, joined the commuters' revolt. The people's fury was unleashed. They burned buses. The few policemen present were overwhelmed. The riots spread like wildfire through the hillside shanty towns and the lower-class neighbourhoods like El Valle, Catia, Antímano, Coche . . . Many shops and businesses were looted by hungry crowds.

By the afternoon, the riots had spread to the centre of Caracas and to several cities across the country. It wasn't just a Caracazo, it was a *Venezolanazo*. True, its epicentre was Caracas, but it spread to Barquisimeto, Cagua, Ciudad Guayana, La Guaira, Maracay, Valencia, Los Andes . . . The government panicked, imposed a curfew, and activated the Ávila Plan. This placed the capital under martial law and allowed the army to use heavy weapons against civilian protesters. The social protest was put down with the utmost brutality; massacres were committed in the poor areas, a repeat of Rómulo Betancourt's mantra: 'Shoot first, ask questions later!'

Where were you when the Caracazo broke out?

I spent the night at the Seconasede, in the Palacio Blanco, and the following morning I woke up with a temperature and aching limbs. My kids had German measles and I must have caught it. The doctor confirmed I had a contagious viral infection and said I couldn't stay in the Palace. He sent me home. I had no troops to command, and didn't know about the uprising. I passed by the university first but, seeing classes had been suspended, I went home. I was living with Nancy and my three children in San Joaquín [Carabobo state, some one hundred kilometres from Caracas]. We'd just bought a modest house there. One of my neighbours, and a *compañero* in the MBR-200, Major Wilmar Castro Soteldo, told me what was happening: 'What do we do?' he asked. But it had caught us on the hop, uncoordinated. There was nothing we could do.

Hadn't you foreseen it from way back?

Of course we had, but then we had no plan. It was exasperating. The moment and opportunity we'd waited for so eagerly had finally arrived, and we were incapable of acting. I remember phoning Arias Cárdenas and saying, 'The people have pre-empted us. They came out first.' The people had caught us scattered and unprepared; we didn't even have a system for communicating between members of the MBR-200. A few of us took individual steps to try and halt the massacre. Several officers who received orders to open fire on the people did not do so; instead they ordered their troops not to fire. But they were a minority . . .

How many victims were there?

It was never known. A lot of blood was shed that day. The official figure was about three hundred dead, but there were probably several thousand, buried in communal graves. And not by an invading army – by our own police and military forces. I saw children shot to pieces by our own soldiers. They even killed patients in a mental hospital. The government brought soldiers from the interior like an invading army, as if they were the Armed Forces of the IMF. Many officers who took part in the repression felt remorse and shame afterwards. They got a lot of stick. Weeks later at an officers' meeting, I reminded them of Bolívar's famous phrase: 'Cursed be the soldier who turns his weapon on his people'. I couldn't help myself, I shouted at them, 'Bolívar's curse has fallen on us. We are cursed!'

Did it have a big impact on the Armed Forces?

It was very painful for us. It marked our generation; it left indelible traces. In fact, it was inside the Forces that this 'shake-up' had the greatest long-term impact. Months later, I remember an officer coming up to me as I was going into the Palacio Blanco one night: 'Major, apparently you're in a movement, I want to join.' For security reasons, I denied it. But I asked him why he wanted to join, and this is what he said:

'On 27 February 1989, I was on guard duty around the Miraflores Palace and caught some youngsters breaking into a bakery. There were a dozen of them, mostly teenagers. I arrested them. I let them eat the bread they'd stolen because they said they were hungry. I gave them water. We spent several hours talking. They told me about the terrible conditions in the shanty towns; poverty, unemployment, hunger. They begged me to let them go, but I couldn't. I had to wait for orders. The DISIP arrived to question them. I handed them over. They shoved them in a pick-up and drove off. A few hours later, going down a nearby street, I found them all: machine-gunned down, executed . . .'

That officer was devastated. He wrote a report. His superiors ordered him to keep quiet, it wasn't his problem, they were just delinquents, and democracy had to be saved. That officer belonged to the presidential guard, a totally trustworthy cog in the state apparatus but, from that day on, he was closer to us than to the government. The regime used the Caracazo to terrorize the poor and teach them a lesson. So they wouldn't rise up again. On that day, the biggest massacre of twentieth-century century Venezuela was committed. On that day, the mask of Venezuelan 'democracy' fell and revealed the oppressor's most hateful face. Because in the early days of March, after the rebellion had been put down, the government pursued the systematic and criminal use of state terrorism. We must recognize the fact. It was a dictatorship disguised as a democracy. That's why I so often say we must not forget.

Were any of your military friends among the victims?

Yes, unfortunately, we lost *compañeros*. I received news on 1 March: 'They've killed Felipe Acosta Carlez!' He was one of the founders of the Bolivarian Movement, a loyal comrade and a great friend. It's unclear how he died, but I'm convinced the army high command and the DISIP, knowing he was one of the leaders of our Movement, used the general chaos to set a trap for him.[8] Perhaps, if I hadn't been ill that week, the intelligence services might have killed me too.

---

8 The strong evidence that makes Chávez believe Acosta Carlez was killed by the Army is found in Agustín Blanco Muñoz, *Habla el Comandante*, Fundación Cátedra Pío Tamayo, Universidad Central de Venezuela, Caracas, 1998, p. 124. [The facts referring to Acosta Carlez are mistakenly attributed to Acosta Chirinos in this book.]

That's when you dedicated a poem to him?

Yes, I wrote a poem to him right there and then, on 1 March.[9] Mourning that tragedy, my heart spilled over onto the page. Although I dedicated the poem to Felipe, I was really thinking of all the victims. But at the same time, the pain acted like a detonator. The popular explosion of the Caracazo broke the cement that was walling up Venezuela in a collective tomb. Because, in the international context, that popular uprising was admirable.

In what sense?

The Caracazo was, in my opinion, the major political event of twentieth-century Venezuela. And it marked the rebirth of the Bolivarian Revolution. After all, the same year the Berlin Wall fell – 1989 – Caracas rose up against the IMF. While international intellectuals went on about 'the end of history', while here in Venezuela the political, financial and economic community lay prostrate at the feet of the IMF and the Washington Consensus, a whole city, a whole country, rebelled. With that uprising of the poor, with that insurrection of the secular victims of inequality and exclusion, with that heroic blood of the people, a new chapter in Venezuelan history was beginning. In less than ten years, our Bolivarian government would come and propose alternative formulas. Venezuela rose up against neoliberalism. And we in the Army understood there was no going back.

On the personal level, I told myself, 'I'm not leaving the Army now. Even if only five of us storm the Miraflores Palace one night, we will not leave without having our say.' The others felt the same. Our Movement was relaunched, it grew, consolidated, went onto the attack . . . We started meeting again. Although, from then on, the government increased its pressure on us, because we were becoming an open and defiant threat.

---

9   Hugo Chávez, 'Mataron a Felipe Acosta Carlez'. English translation in Bart Jones, *Hugo*, Bodley Head, London, 2008, p. 157.

How did they put pressure on you?

They began a 'dirty war' against us inside the barracks, in an attempt to discredit us in the eyes of young soldiers. They began calling us pejoratively the *Comacates* [commanders, majors, captains, lieutenants]. They said we were a sect. At the end of 1989, on 6 December to be precise, just as elections for governors and mayors were about to be held for the first time, they even accused me of plotting to assassinate the president and senior army officers.[10] This was a trumped-up charge to alarm the president and get rid of me and other officers from the Miraflores Palace. We were arrested. As all of us held the rank of major, it was known as the 'Night of the Majors'.

And did they manage to get rid of you?

Yes, by the end of 1989, they'd got me out of the Palace on that charge.

And where did they transfer you to?

I was sent to Maturín [capital of Monagas state, over five hundred kilometres east of Caracas] where I was made officer in charge of civilian affairs for the Chasseurs brigade. Initially I wasn't allowed to leave the city without a special permit. But I managed to get back to Caracas shortly afterwards, to do the two-year Command and General Staff Course [obligatory for assuming command of a battalion] at the National Defence College in Los Pinos, Fuerte Tiuna. I began the course in October 1989, and finished it in 1991. With great difficulty, because the gloves were off, it was war . . .

War?

Well, a rebellion by us students against the army chief of staff, General Carlos Julio Peñaloza Zambrano, who had given orders for

---

10 The effects of the Caracazo were felt in the 6 December elections. Despite the bi-partisan AD and Copei pact holding strong, there were some surprising victories in the states of Aragua and Bolívar, where Carlos Tablante of the MAS and Andrés Velásquez of La Causa R won. The abstention rate was 54.9 per cent.

me and my group to be prevented from graduating. We were seen
as conspirators. They'd never been able to prove it, though they'd
arrested me several times, but it still hadn't stopped me being
promoted to lieutenant colonel. So they thought, 'Since we couldn't
stop him being promoted, the only way to stop Chávez and his
group is to make sure they flunk the general staff course.'

Who was behind all this?
I expect the decision came from the army high command. The
plan was executed by Military Intelligence and a group of senior
officers teaching on the course. Their mission was to see that I
failed by any means possible – disciplinary, academic, even physical. The one who hated me the most was Peñaloza . . . But they
couldn't stop me being promoted. I'd been top of my year when I
was made a major, and objectively, in terms of qualifications I
should have been first in line to be made a lieutenant colonel. And
there wasn't any evidence or witnesses against me. On the contrary.
So the only thing they could do was to change the order of profi-
ciency, and make sure I wasn't No. 1. They made me No. 12. But
at least I was promoted.

That's when Peñaloza decided I must be prevented from graduating. A real war broke out. Even a gringo got involved. Because some
of the officers were foreign. One US officer on the course got so fed
up with the atmosphere that he complained to his embassy and
asked to be sent home. He couldn't stand the tension.

It was psychological warfare, a war of nerves.
Yes, they were waging an internal war against me. Not only was I
arrested several times, they even tried to eliminate me. One night
we went to a party. A Guatemalan officer had had too much to
drink and I had to drive him from Fuerte Tiuna to his hotel in my
car. When we arrived, he confessed, 'Commander, I'll never betray
you, but they're paying me in dollars to spy on you and record your
conversations. They're after your head, you know. They're stalking
you and want you dead. Watch your step. I'm taking the dollars,
but I'll never betray you. You're a patriot.'

What were the courses like?

Some instructors were excellent, but those didn't last long. General José Luis Prieto was sacked for making 'comments'. He was subsequently minister of defence in one of my governments [July 2002–January 2004]. Academically it was a disaster. I enrolled expecting to further my previous studies: learning advanced strategies and the science of modern conflicts, by analysing what was currently going on in the world.

For example, I began the course in October 1989, and barely two months into it [20 December 1989], the US bombed Panama and ousted President Manuel Noriega. That sister republic, of Amphictyonic Congress fame, so beloved of Bolívar . . .[11] I happened to ask, 'Are we going to talk about the invasion of Panama?' Nothing, no comment. And then, in the second year, came the first US attack on Iraq [16 January 1991], the so-called Operation Desert Storm. Not a word was said about that, either. Nothing about anything. Ludicrous.

Were you aiming to get promoted again by doing this course?

No, I'd already been promoted to lieutenant colonel in July 1990, as was my due. I was top in my year. But if I finished the general staff course, it would be very hard for them to stop me being given a battalion to command.

So your objective was to have troops under you?

That's right. That's what was at stake: I wanted the chance to command troops. Besides, if I didn't pass, it would pretty much be an end to my career. Any officer who didn't pass the general staff course would have a blot on his CV.

---

11   The Amphictyonic Congress of Panama (named after the Amphictyonic League in Greece) was called by Simón Bolívar on 7 December 1824, to bring together in an alliance or confederation all the new states which had been created out of the Spanish viceroyalties in America. The Congress was held in Panama City from 22 June to 15 July 1826. Present were representatives from Gran Colombia (present-day Colombia, Ecuador, Panama and Venezuela), Peru, Bolivia, Mexico, and the United Provinces of Central America (Guatemala, El Salvador, Honduras, Nicaragua and Costa Rica).

How did your fellow officers put up with that abuse?
Badly. The majority were firm friends and showed solidarity with
one another. But the less able academically, the weakest students,
began to lose their nerve and snapped. About a dozen officers were
thrown off the course. The storm began turning into a high-
intensity cyclone. We were treated abominably. They secreted tape
recorders under our desks. They made us jog through the streets like
cadets. It was like a boot camp.

**Didn't the college try to negotiate with you, to calm thing things
down?**
Well, something of the sort did happen. One day, we were in the
classroom when a sergeant popped his head in and signalled to me
discreetly. I asked permission to go to the toilet. The sergeant said
he'd been sent by the inspector-general of the armed forces, No. 2
at the Ministry of Defence, and Peñaloza's superior. He gave me a
piece of paper: the inspector-general wanted to see me at the ministry. 'Nobody must know you're going there,' added the sergeant.

I went back to class and told the instructor I didn't feel well: 'Can
I go to the clinic for a few minutes?' The clinic was next door. I
went out of the building and into the car the sergeant had kept
hidden. We went round in a few circles to shake off any surveillance. When we reached the ministry, I was taken up a back lift
directly into the inspector-general's office. He was there, waiting for
me . . . along with the director of the general staff college. I thought
it was a trap, and they were going to arrest me. I remember leaving
a note for a comrade: 'If I don't come back, it's because I've been
arrested.' No one knew where I was.

I was wrong. The inspector-general said, 'We're concerned about
what is happening. I'm asking you, in front of my friend, director
of the college, to be disciplined, study hard and pass your remaining exams. I guarantee you will not be expelled.' I replied, 'General,
you know what's going on, I won't go into details, but I request they
leave my fellow officers in peace and treat us with respect.' They
told me not to worry. That meeting helped lower the tension a bit.
The war did not stop, but open hostility diminished.

So things calmed down.

A bit, but only for a while. General Peñaloza was still determined I shouldn't pass. On that course, you couldn't fail three subjects. If you failed two, they gave you the chance to retake them. But if you failed a third subject, you couldn't try again. They threw you out.

Did you fail any?

I managed to retake two, but when I saw there was no way I could avoid being failed in the third subject, I went to the Palacio Blanco to talk to General Arnoldo Rodríguez: 'They're going to kick me off the course, on Peñaloza's orders, it's completely arbitrary.' I told him what was happening: 'You know I'm not a man to fail exams, they've already failed me in two subjects, the third is coming up; they've arrested me twice, they're harassing me, they're even paying foreign officers to spy on me . . .' I knew General Rodríguez was at odds with Peñaloza Zambrana and Ochoa Antich, it was an old quarrel. General Rodríguez asked me, 'Do you have some civilian clothes?' 'No, but I can get some'. 'Well, come here in civvies at noon, we're going to have lunch with a friend'.

I came back and we went for lunch. We arrived at a restaurant in an East Caracas neighbourhood, and there sitting at a table was General Herminio Fuenmayor, a *compadre* of Carlos Andrés Pérez and head of military intelligence. All three of us were in civvies, because they too were conspiring against Peñaloza.

You took advantage of the rivalry between them.

That's right. I used the internal rifts between the generals to my benefit. But I was on a knife edge. We sat down, had a drink, and General Rodríguez said, 'Chávez, I called Herminio, as head of the DIM, so you could tell him what you told me.' I began, 'General, if someone doesn't put a stop to this, there will be serious problems in the Army. We are being abused, not only me, but my fellow officers on the course. About ten or a dozen have already been unfairly dismissed. We're being put under unbearable pressure, treated like new recruits, etc.' Fuenmayor asked me several questions, then said, 'But, Chávez, you're said to be part of a movement that wants to topple the government . . .' 'You know that's not true,' I replied. 'The truth is that there's a rivalry between certain generals which is causing divisions in the lower ranks, among commanders, captains, and so on. Tensions like that in the army are very dangerous because the social situation in the country after the Caracazo is highly precarious, it won't be long before . . . It could explode, you both know that.' Fuenmayor listened to me thoughtfully but didn't say anything, except, 'Alright, take care and don't go getting into any trouble.' We finished lunch and left.

Did that meeting change anything?

There were immediate consequences. The next morning, when classes started at seven, Peñaloza stormed in like a wild animal, shouting, 'There are some grasses here!' That morning he'd received a telegram from Military Intelligence warning him of the dangers of splits in the Army, and ordering him to take action to reduce the tension. That is, repeating almost exactly what I'd told General Fuenmayor. Peñaloza was beside himself, and I was quietly laughing: 'If only he knew it was me who had grassed him up!' He suspected everyone except me. He suspected some of the DIM informers on the course, but no one dreamed it was me who'd let the cat out of the bag. Only a few *compañeros* knew, Urdaneta and the others.

Was the tension reduced?

Yes, there was less harassment. And a few days later, a huge scandal broke out. Perhaps as a reprisal against the intervention of the DIM, or at any rate something to do with the feuds inside the army high command and its confrontation with the government, Peñaloza clashed with Carlos Andrés Pérez. Congress accused Peñaloza of being involved in a fraudulent arms deal.[12] The president ordered

---

12 'Venezuela has accused the Spanish arms company Santa Bárbara of failing to deliver a cargo of weapons, valued at US$4.5 million. The agreement between the Venezuelan Army and Santa Bárbara was brokered by an intermediary, the Margold Corporation, represented by the Cuban Gardenia Martínez.' *El País*, Madrid, 4 June 1991.

him not to come to the Congress building. But Peñaloza arrived anyway, carrying files he proceeded to distribute to various deputies, denouncing alleged corrupt dealings committed by a Cuban lady called Gardenia Martínez, of the Margold Corporation, a friend of the president's lover, Cecilia Matos. In his statement to Congress, Peñaloza accused the Margold Corporation of having swindled the Venezuelan state out of 5 million dollars, for armaments which were paid for but not delivered. It turned out the Margold Corporation's main shareholder was none other than Orlando García, lifelong friend of President Pérez, chief of presidential security . . . and lover of Gardenia Martínez.

What an atmosphere!

An air of decadence and *fin de régime* . . . It led one Adeco leader [Gonzalo Barrios] to declare, 'Venezuela is a country in which there is no reason not to steal,' and on another occasion, 'The Constitution is like Sofia Loren, you can violate her a thousand times.'[13] Primitive machismo, shameless corruption, public immorality, delinquency, decomposition – all this in a country still traumatized by the Caracazo and exhausted by social protests. What happened then was that Orlando García was dismissed, obviously; so was the DIM's General Herminio Fuenmayor, for various statements he made and also for being implicated in the drugs traffic; and, last but not least, so was Peñaloza.[14] It was an historic day. When I saw the news on television, I exclaimed, 'Fuck! Peñaloza's gone before me!'

---

13   Gonzalo Barrios (1902–1993), founder member and one of the main leaders of Acción Democrática.

14   'President Pérez removed the head of military intelligence (DIM), General Herminio Fuenmayor, for the grave error of making unauthorized political statements, after a luxury car he owned was impounded from an alleged drug trafficker. The DIM director's BMW was found in the possession of Edwin Rincón Rodríguez, the prime suspect regarding a recently confiscated 621-kg consignment of cocaine in Peracal, on the border between the [Venezuelan] state of Táchira and [the Colombian city of] Cúcuta.' *El Tiempo*, Bogotá, 14 June 1991.

You saw it as a personal victory.

For sure, to a certain extent it stemmed from my manoeuvre with General Rodríguez and that conspiratorial lunch. However, the day after Peñaloza was dismissed, there was the public award ceremony, and that's where they made a mistake. Under those circumstances, if you dismiss a top-ranking Army officer, you don't hold a public ceremony. If I'm punishing him, why would I then give him a platform, and let him make a speech? We were at the ceremony and I deliberately sat in the front row, near the lectern where he was going to speak. Peñaloza began his speech with ' "Tiger" Clemenceau said that "war is too serious a matter to be left to the military", and I say, "politics is too serious a matter to be left to the politicians."' It was a direct attack on President Pérez. Several television channels were broadcasting the speech live.

When Peñaloza finished, I went up to him. He saw me and took a step backwards, thinking perhaps I was going to assault him. I congratulated him, 'General, what a fine speech! Well said.' He stared at me, he couldn't tell if I was poking fun at him or not. He finally said, 'Chávez, you heard what I said, didn't you?' 'Yes, General.' A very clever man, Peñaloza, with some advanced ideas. He liked progressive thinking, but on a different level, of course.

Did you eventually get your diploma from the General Staff College?

Yes, I passed the course, the whole thing ended in our favour. We won that war, and it wasn't me but Peñaloza who left the Army. That's life. As if the invisible hand was still guiding my destiny, don't you think? Everything conspired to resolve the conflict in my favour. Pérez Arcay quotes a certain phrase a lot, I don't know who said it: 'When you really want something, the whole universe conspires to help you obtain it.' And, a couple of weeks later, after going through that sort of labyrinth, I was given command of the parachute battalion in Maracay.

So quickly?

Well, not that quickly, as it happened, but the 'invisible conspiracy' continued. I finished the General Staff College course and was sent

– wait for it – to the Armed Forces Provisioning Service. Incredible! A slap in the face for me.

Why?

Because I had already had an armoured vehicles command, and I'd just finished the course with excellent marks: I should have got a tank battalion.

And they didn't give it to you.

No! They rotated officers who were already commanding other battalions, and I and my comrades were left out. I was sent, on 17 July 1991, to the Army Provisioning Service, a place for officers with careers in logistics. It was a blow. Military Intelligence clearly did not want me in command of troops. They were trying to isolate me at all costs.[15] So anyway, I presented myself in Catia, where the Provisioning Service was. I had nothing to do, they had absolutely no need of me. I just walked up and down the corridors, thinking. Then three weeks later, on 13 August 1991, on the orders of General Fernando Ochoa Antich, the new army chief of staff, I was appointed commander of the Colonel Antonio Nicolás Briceño Parachute Battalion, at the Páez barracks in Maracay.

What happened during those three weeks?

The 'invisible conspiracy' . . . Like I said, I presented myself to Army Provisioning determined to do my time in the wilderness again. 'Better days will come,' I told myself. Besides, by then the MBR-200 had been deployed; it didn't depend on my having a command, even though, of course, I remained the head of the Movement. We had a lot of captains commanding tank companies, infantry, cadets; and several commanders – Francisco Arias Cárdenas, Jesús Urdaneta, Joel Acosta Chirinos, Jesús Ortiz Contreras – had been given battalions.

---

15 This is confirmed by General Herminio Fuenmayor, head of the DIM from February 1989 to June 1991: 'Chávez represented no danger because he had been removed from the chain of command, as had other commanders. They had been sent to the military provisioning department, they were not given [troop] commands.' *La Razón*, Caracas, 29 November 2009.

So how come you got the Maracay parachute battalion?
Because sometimes fate drops a gift in your hands. Several things
happened. Since there was not much to do in Army Provisioning, I
spent my time at the Academy attending ceremonies for my fellow
officers' new assignments. I'd just listen and converse. I always felt
my batteries recharge when I went to the Academy. Outside I was
being watched and harassed, but inside the Academy I was in my
world, I had friends all around me. One afternoon I was attending
the ceremony of my friend Jesús Ortiz Contreras, who was being
given command of the Colonel Genaro Vásquez Chasseurs battalion, and I spoke to him about my problem.

That they hadn't given you a troop command.
That's right. A few days later, while I was visiting him in Chaguaramal,
Miranda state, he said, '*Compadre*, army high command is on the
phone for you!' What had actually happened was that, a couple of
nights earlier at a party in the Academy, Jesús had been talking to
the new minister of defence, General Ochoa Antich. Ochoa had
asked, 'What's Chávez up to?' Jesús told him I'd been given a post
in Army Provisioning. Ochoa didn't know this, and he said, 'Tell
Chávez I want to talk to him'.

   Jesús told me, but I said, 'I don't want to talk to Ochoa, tell him
I'm fine where I am.' But while I was in Chaguaramal, this phone call
came from a colonel in army high command: 'Commander, the
minister of defence wants to see you.' 'Alright,' I said, 'when?'
'Monday.' I went. Ochoa called me in. We knew each other from the
Academy. He said, 'Chávez, we know your career path. The Army
Provisioning job must be a mistake, because you're an officer who is
good with troops. You just need to modify your behaviour, fit in a bit
better.' They knew, of course, that a large group of officers was discontented, and my leadership of that group made them uneasy.

They were trying to enlist your help to calm things down.
Exactly. That's why Ochoa's attitude was so conciliatory: 'Chávez,
help me patch up these internal squabbles.' I said, 'General, they're
the ones picking on me, I get along with everyone.' And then, right

there in front of me, he used the internal phone to call General Pedro Rangel Rojas, chief of the general staff, and said, 'Rangel, I've got Chávez here, I'm sending him to your office. Give him a command, you'll know where.' I went to see him.

Was General Rangel a friend or enemy?

He was a declared adversary. I knew him well when I was head of culture at the Academy, and he was the corps commander. He called me *paisano*, because he was from Guasdualito.[16] So I went in, and he said, 'Look here, *paisano*, help me out, let's restore some peace to the army, let's calm things down.' 'Very well, General,' I said, 'I'll do what I can, and as far as I can, but I'm a simple lieutenant colonel, you're the general.' Then he asked me, 'Where would you like to go as commander?' I replied, 'Wherever you send me.' 'I want you to go . . . back to your wife and children. Where are they?' 'In San Joaquín, Carabobo.' 'Well, go home, rest for a few days, and wait for our call.' I went home. But first I went to the Officers' Department to see my friend Frank González – the one who'd been chief of security in Miraflores, and had lent me his computer – and said, 'Here's my phone number, when you know where I'm being sent, call me.'

Three days later, in August 1991, Frank called me and announced, 'Commander, I'm not going to explain much, but there's a parachute regiment vacant, and pretty well nobody wants to go. Would you be up for it?' I didn't need to think twice: 'Put me on the short-list.' He rang me back that afternoon: 'You've been put in command of the Colonel Antonio Nicolás Briceño Parachute Battalion, at the Páez barracks in Maracay. Present yourself tomorrow.' So I turned up the next day and took command of the battalion in a handover ceremony.

So you finally achieved your objective.

When I took command of that battalion of 'red berets', with the banner of that elite troop in my hand, the words that sprang to my

---

16   Translator's Note: Someone who is from the same region, 'countryman'.

mind were: 'They're fucked!' I thought it, but didn't say it aloud. I had over five hundred well-trained men, in a strategic place like Maracay, near Caracas. In addition, I had a group of MBR-200 officers already in positions of command; our Movement, mature, and poised to rise up ... and an entire people clamouring for rebellion.

The Rebellion of 4 February 1992

Commander of the Parachute Battalion in Maracay
Frente Patriótico – Assassination attempt – The rebellion
Arresting President Pérez – Plans A, B and C
Jesús Ramón Carmona – History and destiny – Chávez myth
Role of the individual in history
Simón Bolívar national project
Bolivarianism and socialism
Why the rebellion failed – Surrender – 'For now'
Hope is born – Rebellion in Caracas vs coup in Moscow
Popular support – '*Golpista*'?

After the Caracazo, the Bolivarian Movement was revitalized.
Yes. The socio-political context changed, became more polarised.
The number of social protests increased, and so did the repression.
In 1991 alone, twenty-five students were murdered by the regime.
The economic and moral fabric of society was fraying. All this
contributed to the objective conditions which favoured an action
such as ours. You could hear the hurricane approaching. Nothing
could stop it. I've already explained why.

The Caracazo certainly jolted us out of our lethargy, and revitalized our Movement. The many years of work finally began to bear
fruit. How much time had passed? Two decades in the making. Since

1972. Two decades! First, the genesis, the embryo; then the long, slow gestation; then the consciousness-raising, proselytizing, recruitment; followed by the painful birth of February 1989, when blood flowed in the streets of Caracas; and finally that 4 February 1992, which divided Venezuelan history into two parts, and the *Patria* emerged. The fact is, the country was going under. And young military officers could not stand by and watch the ship go down.

What was your main motivation? Taking power?
There was no personal ambition on anybody's part. None of us wanted power for power's sake. The main motivation was the poverty in the barrios, the slums, the countryside. We saw ourselves as soldiers of a people, not guard dogs of the oligarchy and their gringo masters.

From the international historical perspective, the 4 February rebellion looked as if it was going against the grain of the times.
Yes, that's true, against the dominant ideology of that era. Neoliberalism was taking root all over the place: Margaret Thatcher's conservative revolution in the UK, and Ronald Reagan's in the US. The great leap backwards! In contrast, our Movement, an example of historical awareness, joined the Venezuelan people in shouting, 'No!' to the IMF and 'No!' to neoliberalism.

When you arrived in Maracay to command the parachute battalion, was everything ready for the next step, for taking action?
By the time I was posted to Maracay in 1991, other officers who'd been in my year at the Academy were already in control of barracks in Maracaibo and other cities. They had troops, tanks and heavy weapons under their command. We had active support from the very best young officers; a necessary prerequisite for action.

But you didn't know the parachute battalion very well. How could you trust it?
Well, it didn't happen overnight . . . It took months of hard work. I'd go with the battalion out on manoeuvres; we'd do parachute jumps together. I always went first. I made myself available, I talked

to the officers, and they got to know me. Several joined our Movement: Jesús Suárez Chourio, Celso Canelones Guevara, Jorge Durán Centeno; and sergeants like Julio Marciales Casanova. I soon had the battalion eating out of my hand. Ready for anything. In every one of my speeches to the soldiers, I repeated my message quite openly, reminding them of the battalion's own motto: 'If the *Patria* is in danger, our flags will fly and we will soar like eagles.' Venezuela was in danger, we had to act now!

Didn't your senior officers notice?
They never said anything. I'd sometimes wonder, 'Are my superiors deaf? Don't they understand what I'm saying?' Some didn't understand because they were always drunk . . .

Only a couple of weeks after your arrival in Maracay, there was a military coup in Haiti against President Jean-Bertrand Aristide. It was condemned worldwide. Did that make you reflect on how a military uprising against Carlos Andrés Pérez would be received?
The coup in Haiti happened on 30 September 1991, exactly one month after I took charge in Maracay. Aristide was a very popular and progressive leader, who had been elected with a large majority the previous year [16 December 1990]. We all supported him. He was the first democratically elected president in Haitian history. I actually met him personally in 2008 in Pretoria, on a visit I made to South Africa, where he had been living in exile ever since George W. Bush's administration ousted him again in 2004 [29 February]. In 1991, General Raoul Cédras, head of the Haitian Army, replaced Aristide with a military junta that went on to kill thousands of people. It was an extreme-right-wing military junta, typical of a *'gorila'* coup. The exact opposite of ourselves.

At the time, several democratic states thought of intervening militarily to reinstate President Aristide. Wasn't Venezuela among them?
Yes. Carlos Andrés and the Canadian prime minister [Brian Mulroney] tried to push forward a project – called the Caribbean

Plan – to intervene militarily under the auspices of the Organization of American States (OAS). But Washington and George Bush Sr. nipped it in the bud. I was on manoeuvres in El Pao at the time, retraining in parachuting; it was years since I'd done any. While I was there, I received the order: 'Urgently needed in Maracay'. They got all the commanders together and explained the Caribbean Plan to us.

What mission were you given?
My mission was to parachute my battalion into Port au Prince, capital of Haiti, take the airport and hold it until the allied forces' airborne troops landed. Our Movement had previously agreed that the order to leave for Haiti would be the moment to launch our own uprising. But the plan was aborted and we had to wait for another opportunity. We continued our preparations.

What political support could you count on, outside the Armed Forces?
We were still working with people from La Causa R, like Pablo Medina, Alí Rodríguez, Ebert José *El Cojo* Lira, Julio Marcelino *El Cabito* Chirinos, Lucas Matheus, Andrés Velásquez, and from the Movimiento Electoral del Pueblo (MEP) [People's Electoral Movement], men like Eustoquio Contreras. We also had the support of almost all the activists of the short-lived Frente Patriótico [Patriotic Front], a party formed in 1989, after the Caracazo, around Luis Miquilena, a man of great stature with long experience as a left-wing militant.[1]

---

1 Luis Miquilena (1919–), leader of the bus drivers' union in Caracas in the 1940s. He was a militant of the Communist Party (PVC), allied to the government of Isaías Medina Angarita (1914–1945) and firm opponent of President Rómulo Betancourt and the dictator Marcos Pérez Jiménez. He broke with the PCV and, together with the brothers Eduardo and Gustavo Machado, founded, in 1946, an anti-Stalinist organization – the Unitarian Venezuelan Communist Party. With Professor Salvador de la Plaza, known as the 'red monk', Miquilena helped revive the tradition of socialist nationalism which had a great influence in sectors of the Venezuelan Left from 1940 onwards. He retired from public life in the 1960s, but came back thirty years later when he met Hugo Chávez and his political project. Miquilena held important posts in public administration, was president of the Constituent Assembly in 1999 and minister of the interior (1999–2002). But serious disagreements led President Chávez to break with him politically. Since then, Miquilena has been active in the opposition to the Bolivarian Revolution.

Others leaders of the Frente Patriótico were Douglas Bravo; philosophy professor Pedro Duno; former Marxist air force officer William Izarra; writer Juan Liscano, the Frente's president; former guerrilla commander Lino Martínez; and the lawyer Manuel Quijada, who had taken part in the military uprisings of 1962 and was the Frente's coordinator. At that critical time for Venezuela, they aimed to create a civilian–military movement in the tradition of Venezuelan dissidence from Ezequiel Zamora onwards. That is, a political instrument for a broad church of civilian forces to join with the military in a change of direction.

Were you in contact with that Frente?
Yes, of course. Discreet contacts, obviously, because we were being watched very closely, especially me. But we had meetings and some joint activities. The Frente published some manifestos entitled 'Three Decades of Frustration', calling for a National Constituent Assembly to create a new Constitution. This was our primary demand, too. But the Frente didn't even last a year. The people involved were from very different, sometimes opposing, tendencies. They had come together in the heady atmosphere following the Caracazo, but when the emotion of the moment passed, they returned to their own corners. Eternal demons of the Venezuelan Left . . . We kept in touch with some of the individuals: Douglas, Izarra, Miquilena, Duno, etc. And we took a permanent distance from others who claimed to be on the far Left, like Gabriel Puerta Aponte of the Bandera Roja [Red Flag] group, who turned out to be very dangerous.

Why did you choose 4 February?
We didn't choose it, events dictated it. My army contact within the presidential palace, Lieutenant Pérez Ravelo, was to let us know when the president was coming back.

The president was abroad, wasn't he?
Yes, he was returning from the World Economic Forum in Davos, Switzerland, via New York. Our Movement had gone on the alert

the moment he left Caracas for Davos. We had meetings with our Air Force people, Luis Reyes Reyes, Francisco Visconti, etc. At midnight on Sunday, 2 February, Pérez Ravelo called me. He said in code, 'My uncle is arriving on . . . at . . .' When we learned the president's plane would be landing in the early hours of 4 February, we decided to activate the operation. The action would take place before dawn that day.

What did the action consist of?

While officers of the MBR-200 – Arias Cárdenas, Urdaneta, Blanco de la Cruz – were taking control of strategic points in several cities, my Maracay garrison drove tanks and armoured vehicles to Caracas, a distance of about eighty kilometres.

In Caracas itself, several units had been given precise objectives: that led by Joel Acosta Chirinos would take the small military airport of La Carlota, in the city centre; others would take Fuerte Tiuna and the Ministry of Defence, and arrest the Army High Command; others would occupy the Miraflores Palace and La Casona [the president's official residence]; others would take over the main television channels. As for me, I took my men to the Military History Museum, which is on a hill looking over the centre of Caracas, where we were met by gunfire . . .

But didn't you take them by surprise?

No, because we'd been betrayed. They knew about the uprising, but they didn't know which troops had rebelled. I managed to talk to the officer on duty at the museum and convince him that we were reinforcements, come to help them protect the site. We occupied it without firing a shot, and no blood was spilt. I'm no fan of the trigger-happy approach. My mission was to direct and coordinate operations nationally from this command post. Arias Cárdenas would be joining me as soon as his plane arrived from Maracaibo. But I could see straight away that the museum didn't have the equipment I needed to be able to communicate with the other leaders of the uprising or with the public.

What was the main objective, to arrest the president?

Well, the main political aim was to topple the government and take power. But the most effective way of achieving that was, in our opinion, to arrest the president when he arrived at Maiquetía airport; and also to detain the Army High Command. The aim was political, not military, and its realization involved the capture of the president so he could stand trial, not his physical elimination. I want to stress this point.

We intended to present the detained president to the country on television, and order the commanders of the garrisons who had not joined the rebellion to obey the new authorities. Meanwhile, in several cities, our comrades in the MBR-200 would have already taken power locally and be controlling the situation. However, the plan didn't work.

Why not?

As I said, our project was betrayed by an officer [Captain René Gimón Álvarez] who went over to the enemy, though he didn't know where or how the coup would take place. Nevertheless, reinforcements were summoned. At Maiquetía airport, for instance, all sorts of precautionary measures were taken: the minister of defence, General Ochoa Antich, brought National Guard and Navy troops to the airport to personally welcome Carlos Andrés home; there was nothing we could do. The president was well protected. Our people couldn't act. But the operation didn't end there – we switched to Plan B.

What did that consist of?

Ambushing the presidential convoy in the tunnel of the Maiquetía–Caracas motorway, after we closed the motorway by burning a car. But that didn't work out either. The forces deployed to protect the president were too numerous. We had to resort to Plan C.

You had a Plan C?

Yes. It consisted of arresting the president at either La Casona or the Miraflores Palace. Carlos Andrés headed straight to his residence, but there again we were outnumbered and our attack went on for too long. Carlos Andrés was alerted, and turned back. He went to the Miraflores Palace and got inside a few minutes before our tanks appeared. So, for one brief moment, he was at our mercy. In other words, our plan had worked. Because, I repeat, the aim was to capture him, take him to the command post at the Military History Museum, and present him to the country saying, 'The president is under arrest!' It was a good plan. Although chances of success were low, and we knew it.

It failed because you didn't capture Carlos Andrés.

Exactly. He managed to escape the trap. A year later, I was watching television in Yare prison and saw Admiral Carratú Molina, head of the military HQ inside the palace, describe how when our tanks came to the Miraflores and the shooting started, he was able to get the president out of the palace through the Plaza Bicentenario. Luckily for him, our tank which should have been there . . . wasn't there! The order had been to encircle the whole palace. But thanks to the admiral, Carlos Andrés managed to give us the slip and make a getaway in some nondescript car. Carratú described how, when they were driving up the Cota Mil highway, a furious President Pérez kept repeating, 'This is Carmona's fault. Phone Carmona!' [Laughter.]

Who's Carmona?

Jesús Ramón Carmona was one of his former ministers. In photos of Fidel's visit to Caracas in January 1959, when he spoke in the Aula Magna of the Central University, you can see him being welcomed by a young man. That's Jesús Ramón Carmona. Back then he was the president of the Central University Student Union. The years passed and Carmona became a minister in Carlos Andrés's government.

Did you know him?

Yes, I first met him one winter in Apure. I was patrolling a river with some of my men, when I was informed that a motorboat had run out of petrol. I sent someone to rescue it. Sooner afterwards, a man in a cowboy hat stepped onto the jetty: it was Jesús Ramón Carmona. We greeted each other. I'd been in Elorza for over two years by then, and everyone had heard of me. He was very chatty and introduced himself: 'I'm a lawyer, with a practice in Caracas.' I was impressed by his loquacity and quick mind. He was from Apure, and had a ranch in the region. He gave me his card, which I kept. Not long afterwards, when I was made president of the Festival Committee in Elorza, I started looking for support.

And you remembered Carmona.

That's right. One of the people I called was Dr Carmona. Once I went to Caracas and met up with him. He was working in the Ministry of Transport and Communications, his nephew was a deputy minister in Lusinchi's government. Thanks to him, I got jerseys and balls for the Elorza baseball team, and bulldozers to mend the roads. He came to our fiestas, and once he brought a minister, Juan Pedro del Moral. To cut a long story short, Carmona and I became great friends.

Friends for life . . .

No, because after I left Elorza, we didn't keep in touch. Then, in December 1988, after Carlos Andrés won the elections, I was attending the official results ceremony at the National Electoral Board headquarters, as assistant to General Arnoldo Rodríguez, a member of the Army High Command. Through all the hubbub of journalists and cameras, I heard, 'Chávez!' It was Carmona. 'What are you doing here?' he asked. 'I'm the General's assistant, and you?' 'I'm a friend of Carlos Andrés.' Just like that!

He introduced me to some friends of his, a gang of Adecos: Henry Ramos Allup, Antonio Ledezma, Alberto Federico Ravell . . . all Carlos Andrés riff-raff. They were his campaign team; Carmona, a very astute man, was the coordinator. 'Where are you based?' he asked. 'In the Palacio Blanco.' '*¡Hombre!* Opposite Miraflores. OK, that's a good place, I'll be around.' And pointing to the General, he enquired, 'Is your boss one of us?' General

Rodríguez was more of a Copei man, but what could I say? 'Of
course he is!' [Laughter.]

That reassured him, I suppose.
Yes, and it allowed me to weave a web of deceit that was very useful
leading up to 4 February. Because Carmona had the president's ear.
Anyway, he gave me his phone number and added, 'You and your
general are invited for drinks afterwards, just a few of us, in
here . . .'

In those days, the president of the electoral council was a man
called Carlos Delgado Chapellín who could never be far from a
glass of whisky. So, any ceremony was an excuse for a drink. After
the election results were announced, General Rodríguez said, 'Let's
go.' But I said, 'No, General, we've been invited for drinks with the
president.' 'Are you pulling my leg, Chávez? They see you as a revolutionary.' 'Well, it just goes to show.' [Laughter.] He knew something was afoot, but he protected me. 'Don't get in too deep,' he'd
say, 'they're after you; don't talk so much, you're always
chattering.'

So that's how you got to know Carlos Andrés?
We went into a little room, no more than thirty of us: Carlos
Andrés, his campaign team, the president of the electoral board,
and a few celebrities. The only army officers were the general and
myself. We tiptoed in. I looked around for Carmona; he was talking
heatedly. He was an extrovert, always very effusive. He saw me and
called us over. Next thing I knew, 'Carlos Andrés, I want you to
meet a friend of mine, Major Chávez. And General Arnoldo
Rodríguez. Let's drink a toast.' We stayed until the president-elect
left at three in the morning. The general said, 'Chávez, I didn't
know you were friendly with those people. You surprise me.'
[Laughter.]

You were infiltrating . . .
I was getting closer to the centre of power. Two months later [2
February 1989], Carlos Andrés took office, at sixty-six years old.

Fidel Castro came to the inaugural ceremony. I saw him close up; the first time I'd seen him in person. When the president announced the members of his government, Carmona was made ombudsman. Then a few months later he became a minister, heading up the president's office in Miraflores. So I got to spend a lot of time in that office, having coffee, phoning, doing university business. As I told you, Carlos Andrés sometimes came in when I was there. That's why, when the episode with the flags happened, I took the liberty of telling him about the Bolivarian standard with its eighth star. There's even a video of me explaining things to the president. He got used to seeing me; I had a pass for the Miraflores, so I had no problem getting in. Thanks to Carmona, I became a regular visitor to the president's office. And when I was arrested [6 December 1989], accused of preparing a coup and wanting to assassinate the president, the only person who stood up for me was Jesús Ramón Cardona.

That accusation got you taken out of Miraflores and sent to Maturín, didn't it?
Yes, they sent me to Maturín. But I'd barely been there a week when Carmona phoned, asking me to come back to Caracas because . . . they had given me a decoration and wanted to organize a presentation ceremony. Talk about a surprise! I went, and Carlos Andrés Pérez himself presented me with the Seconasede Medal. The Seconasede was within the remit of the head of the president's office. And that was Jesús Ramón Carmona. That's why, on 4 February 1992, President Pérez . . .

Accused Carmona.
Right. He didn't know for a fact I was involved, but the old fox sensed something was going on there . . . He understood, in retrospect, that the intelligence service reports of a potential coup instigated by me were actually correct. In December 1989, Carmona must have convinced them they were unfounded. So, my 'friendship' with Carmona fitted my purposes like a glove . . . Again, that invisible conspiracy in my favour.

As if history, once again, was helping you along the road to power.
My stint in the palace was like a practise obstacle course, tough but
short. But I'd already done twenty years of obstacle courses . . .

Didn't you ever feel discouraged?
Never. A voice inside me always kept alive the hope that I could
change things and build a Venezuela with more justice. Let me tell
you a story. During my years in the wilderness, in Elorza, I came to
Caracas one time and went to visit the Military Academy. In a
corridor, I ran into Argenis Paredes, who had taught our Philosophy
of War course. He told me something that struck me very much:
'You must know there's a myth surrounding you here in the
Academy. You're a myth. Nourish it, Chávez, nourish it.' I was
astonished. That advice did not fall on deaf ears.

'Nourish it.'
The more they attacked and persecuted me, the more they contributed to feeding the myth. Everything derived from that. Like a
huge conspiracy, as I say. We're back with Marc Bloch . . . Mind
you, you can be helped by history as far as history itself allows. The
conditions history imposes are like a game of chance. I always felt it
was highly probable things would work out for me. Because the
right conditions are indispensable. If I'd have been born in 1930,
and enrolled in the Military School as it was then, I would never
have become Colonel Chávez. What could I have done in the
Venezuela of the 1950s? Not much . . .

If you'd been born in the same place, in the same social condi-
tions, but in another historical context, you don't think your
destiny would have been the same?
I'm absolutely certain it would not. But it's good to pose the question, at least from the theoretical point of view, and try to find an
answer. I've never felt that my progress through life was predestined . . . I already told you that I never felt predestined to make
a revolution. I've always been aware of the precariousness of
things.

Sometimes, when objective conditions for a great social movement exist, you need the catalyst of a special individual in order to also create the subjective conditions, and bring about the explosion. It's the role of the leader to unite, although it doesn't seem very Marxist to say so, but without the will and charisma of a leader, divisions persist and nothing changes. What would have become of the powerful social movements of recent years in Latin America without a generation of exceptional leaders: Lula in Brazil, Rafael Correa in Ecuador, Evo Morales in Bolivia? In Cuba, in the 1950s, that historic leader was Fidel Castro. In Venezuela, in the 1990s, in very different conditions, wouldn't you say you took on that mantle?

After the Caracazo, everyone knew something was going to happen. They could see it coming. The country was effectively in a situation we could call pre-revolutionary. It is also possible that, if it hadn't been for our rebellion of 4 February, Venezuela might have had a civil war. I don't know if I played a particular role at that particular time, but it is true that a series of factors placed me in a decisive position. Fidel is always saying, 'Look after yourself, Chávez! If something happens to you, this is all going to the dogs.' I think he's exaggerating.

Going back to 4 February. How did you actually mobilize your paratroopers? Did you tell them they were going to be involved in a coup?

They suspected we were preparing an action. But we couldn't shout about it, or give precise details. We were under heavy surveillance, remember. My men more or less got the idea; we'd done a lot of political work, their consciousness had been raised, and they'd bought into the Bolivarian project. We'd explained the ideology of Bolívar, Zamora, Robinson, the 'tree with three roots'. I was always repeating the slogan, 'If the *Patria* is in danger . . .' And they'd chorus, 'We'll soar like eagles!' When the moment came, they fell over each other to join the action.

Were they volunteers?

They were all volunteers. Here's another story. When we were planning the rebellion, among the thousand things we had to think of was the possibility of a rear-guard attack on us, by tanks from Valencia. We decided on a plan to block the two possible approach roads those hostile tanks could take: through the tunnel from La Cabrera, or down the old road through Güigüe. The evening before D-Day [Monday, 3 February], I asked Jesús Urdaneta, also a parachute brigade commander, to stay in Maracay and protect our backs. Urdaneta called me: 'You're giving me an order, *compadre*, but I don't have any anti-tank weapons. Give me some, and soldiers to operate them.' So I told Sergeant Marciales, an MBR-200 member and anti-tank weapons instructor, 'Take a squadron of anti-tank weapons to Commander Urdaneta's position immediately, with operators and plenty of ammunition.' We, the elite paratrooper battalion, had numerous AT4s, portable high-precision anti-tank rocket launchers.[2] It was about five in the afternoon. I reviewed my troops, checking every detail because with only a few hours to go, maximum tension, we had to make sure there were no mistakes, nobody entering the barracks, nobody leaving the barracks, and no betrayals.

Were any of the soldiers in your barracks against the rebellion?
Yes, there were some who didn't know what we were planning, and even some opposed to our action. So we took various precautions, first internally . . . We knew which officers to detain, and what to do with the other battalion that was not committed.

Was there any violence?
No, fortunately no bloodshed. We were very careful. Besides, I was checking everything, buses to take us to Caracas, weaponry . . . A full revision. Suddenly I noticed Sergeant Marciales was still there. I called him over, irritably, 'Why are you still here? It's urgent. Urdaneta's waiting for you!' He replied, 'Permission to speak, Commander.' 'OK, tell me.' 'Commander, you know I've spent my whole life as a professional soldier in this battalion.' He was on the

---

2   Anti-tank rocket launchers, 84 mm calibre, easily operated by individual soldiers, and only used once, manufactured by the Swedish company Bofors.

verge of tears. 'Commander, I beg you. If I die, I want to die with my battalion.' He didn't want to do rear-guard duty. I embraced him: 'Stay with me then, my boy.' And he ran off to join his troops.

And Urdaneta?

I phoned him: '*Compadre*, I'm sending you the weapons and men with Sergeant John Muñoz. He's an administrator and doesn't know anything about the Movement, be careful . . .' Urdaneta arrested him [laughter].

So your men preferred joining the active rebellion to staying in less risky positions, did they?

Everyone wanted to take part. Although most of them didn't yet know the dangers they would be exposed to. Officially we were going on parachute manoeuvres to El Pao, actually planned for the following day, anyway. That was another 'providential coincidence', because troop movements that day wouldn't seem strange. See how it all fitted together, in the end.

When did you decide to tell your men that the real objective was overthrowing the government, and taking power?

When I considered everything was ready, I told the battalion to fall in. And then I thought, 'I can't take these boys without telling them. I'll put it to the test. If my leadership is just hot air, the soldiers will arrest me on the spot.' I told my officers to be on the alert, 'because I'm going to tell the troops what we're going to do. I trust these kids.' I stood in the middle of the parade group, facing the lines of men, and cried, 'The *Patria* is in danger. What shall we do?' With one voice, they shouted, 'We'll soar like eagles!' Then I explained, 'That's the situation this country is in.' I gave a political speech, and then announced, 'A military uprising is underway. We're going to overthrow the government.'

How did they react?

With a roar of support that echoed far and wide. It still gives me the shivers. Deep down, they knew . . . From my speeches, my conversations with them. They all came aboard. Even those in the glasshouse wanted to join in. They started banging their cell doors: 'Let us out, Commander!' [Laughter.] I had them released and given rifles. Even the dog who was our mascot signed up.

Did you tell them it was a risky operation?

I told them, obviously. It wasn't a training session, or manoeuvres, we had live ammunition; they ran the risk of being killed. As, in fact, turned out to be the case. It was a daring operation, reckless even, because we were in a minority compared to the Armed Forces as a whole. Not a single general was with us. Our highest rank was lieutenant colonel. There were no officers from the Navy, nor the National Guard.

How do you explain that?

The Armed Forces were divided into different branches, so they were tightly compartmentalized. This stemmed from the *Carupanazo* and *Porteñazo* uprisings of 1962. Rómulo Betancourt changed the structure of the military by doing away with the Basic Training School, where cadets from the four branches of the Armed Forces had lived together and got to know one another. We didn't know the officers of our year in the Navy or the National Guard. We never had any real contact. With the Air Force it was different, because the parachute brigade acted as a link between the Army and the Air Force.

Had you prepared any political documents to disseminate, were the operation to be successful?

I wanted to talk about that. Look, this is my Commander's brief-case [showing it to me]. I had it in my vehicle the day of the rebellion. It's pretty beat-up: the DIM confiscated it and only gave it back two years ago. It's like opening a Pandora's box. Look what's in here: my house keys, car keys, notebooks, armband, photos, my last cheque book from the Banco Industrial. I had twenty-five thousand bolívars in my account. It's what I left Nancy on the eve of the uprising. It was Monday . . . When I was already kitted out in my battledress, I suddenly thought, 'My God! What if something happens to me?' I went to the bank and withdrew everything I had, for Nancy and the children . . . it's hard to leave your wife, your children, your home. But as Bolívar said, 'He who abandons everything to serve his country, loses nothing and gains whatever he devotes himself to.'

What did you want to show me in the briefcase?

Oh yes, I wanted to show you this: an abstract of the 'tree with three roots' that we drafted just before the rebellion. It's called the 'Simón Bolívar National Project. Government of National Salvation. General Procedure for Construction'. Lieutenant Lugo Salas wrote it on his computer.

Can you summarize its main points?

We began with a quote from Thomas Jefferson: 'The tree of liberty must be nourished from time to time by the blood of patriots and tyrants. It is its natural manure.'[3] And then an explanation: 'Why are we, here and now, announcing and fomenting profound changes at the beginning of the last decade of this lost century?' We went on to refer to the 'EBR System' of Ezequiel [Zamora], [Simón] Bolívar and [Simón] Rodríguez, the three roots.

Did you refer to socialism at all?

No. It was too soon. Nowhere did we refer specifically to socialism. Although there were elements of it. For example, we said, 'The objectives of the Bolívar Project lie in the most urgent human, individual and collective needs; not only material needs but also political and cultural needs.'

This is very 'Varsavskyan', that is, based on the theories of Oscar Varsavsky [1920–1976], an Argentine academic who maintained, in his influential book *National Projects*, that a socialist model

---

3   Thomas Jefferson (1743–1826), third president of the United States (1801–1809). He founded the Republican Party in 1792 with James Madison. Main author of the US Declaration of Independence. The quote is from a letter to William Stephens Smith on 13 November 1787, and refers to the Shays Rebellion in Massachusetts after the American Revolution.

must be based on the real needs of the population.[4] 'Satisfaction
of such needs is the ultimate objective. All other objectives, and
temporary and sequential goals, are subordinate. In the Simón
Bolívar National Project, we distinguish the following needs and
objectives. . . .

'Social objectives: to guarantee the highest level of individual and
social freedoms; fair distribution of income; appropriate and timely
administration of justice; maximum security for the individual, the
nuclear family and society as a whole.

'Cultural objectives: education and training, sport and recreation
for the masses; national identity; opportunity for creativity, and
artistic and scientific invention; a harmonious living and working
environment.

'Political objectives: national sovereignty; a worthy place in the
international community; gradual participation in the decision-
making that affects the social group; political freedom; authentic
democracy.'

We drafted this abstract in the days prior to our action, and
distributed it to all the Movement's leaders.

**What were the first measures you would have taken had your
uprising been successful?**
If the rebellion had succeeded, we had prepared decrees to be put
into immediate effect in order to run the country. We'd worked on
them with revolutionary intellectuals like Kléber Ramírez, Pablo
Medina and others. We wanted to create a General National
Council, comprising army officers and civilians, which would
appoint the new president and introduce a Constituent Assembly
capable of founding a new Venezuela and a new democracy.

You were already thinking of a Constituent Assembly?
Yes, because remember, that's what they were talking about in
Colombia after 1990. It gave rise to a wide-ranging debate which we

---

4   Oscar Varsavsky, *Proyectos Nacionales, Planteos y Estudios de Viabilidad*, Ediciones
Periferia, Buenos Aires, 1971.

followed with great interest. The M-19 guerrillas were negotiating with President Virgilio Barco to end the guerrilla war, and one condition for giving up their weapons was the election of a Constituent Assembly.[5] The Constitution in force at the time was not very democratic: among other things, it did not allow more than two political parties [Conservative and Liberal].

The idea took root among the Colombian people, and the student movement held gigantic national demonstrations to demand it. They proposed the idea of the 'seventh ballot box' or 'seventh voting slip', I don't remember which, so that in the general elections of [13 March] 1990, the public could choose if they wanted a Constituent Assembly or not.

Like Manuel Zelaya did in Honduras.

Yes, the same, the only difference being that Manuel Zelaya was toppled by a coup in 2009 for merely suggesting it.

While in Colombia the idea was adopted, wasn't it?

Yes, it was. And it triggered energetic discussion around the new Constitution. One former leader of the M-19 guerrillas, Antonio Navarro Wolff, was joint president of the Assembly that drafted the new Magna Carta [promulgated on 4 July 1991]. The Venezuelan Armed Forces were in touch with organizations on the Colombian Left, and we followed the process, discussions, proposals and changes, very closely. Following a serious analysis, we included the idea of a Constituent Assembly in our strategy for government, in the event that the rebellion were to succeed. But, as we know, it failed.

What was it that didn't work?

First and most important, we didn't manage to arrest Carlos Andrés Peréz. And everything else hinged on that. Second, the Ministry of Defence and the High Command knew – because one of our number betrayed us – that an uprising was imminent, and so they had taken

---

5 The M-19 Movement was one of the three main guerrilla groups in Colombia, together with the FARC (Colombian Revolutionary Armed Forces) and the ELN (Army of National Liberation). The M-19 was founded in 1970 and dissolved itself in 1990.

extreme precautions. Third, there were constant failures of communication between us: I was supposed to coordinate the uprising, but I didn't have the technical equipment for contacting the others; and in the cities of the interior, some of our officers were either indecisive or could not take control of their barracks. Fourth, under those circumstances, our Air Force officers thought it too dangerous to send their planes up. Fifth, the civilian groups whose job it was to help us take Caracas, and control the radio and television stations, did not show up.

Instead, at four in the morning President Pérez spoke to the nation on TV. That was the defining moment, wasn't it?
Beyond all shadow of a doubt. Those images of Carlos Andrés Pérez, broadcast every five minutes, caused the officers who weren't sure whether or not to join the rebellion to either freeze or decide to side with the government.

When did you realize that everything was lost?
At that moment, pretty much. Although in some places, battles were still going on.

But you took the decision to surrender?
Yes. Too many things had gone wrong . . . In the Military Museum, where I was, the communications equipment never arrived. I found myself isolated from the rest of the Movement. To avoid further bloodshed, I informed Ramón Santeliz Ruiz on the morning of 4 February that we were laying down our arms.

General Ochoa Antich told me that before you surrendered, you phoned him and proposed he lead the uprising 'to rid the country of corruption'. Is that true?
When did he tell you that?

I interviewed him in October 1992.[6]
Ochoa Antich is mistaken. He knew how jumpy and irritable the

---

6   See Ramonet, 'Derniers carnavals'.

atmosphere in the army had become. It was like a pressure cooker ready to explode. There were even rumours that he himself, with a group of officers, was going to attempt a coup.[7] He decided to send me two generals – two who were actually close to our Movement – to negotiate the terms of the surrender: Fernán Altuve Febres and Ramón Santeliz Ruiz were both friends of Arias Cárdenas. I took that to be a sign, a message. And when they took me to Fuerte Tiuna, Ochoa Antich even invited me to lunch, and we spent hours talking. I spoke about the situation in the country, the government, corruption, all the things he knew about already, and our duty as Bolivarian officers to put an end to this disgraceful situation. But I never suggested he take over.

Some historians have criticized you for staying in the Military Museum instead of actively helping to take the Miraflores Palace.
Yes, that's been said a lot. My enemies have made a meal of the subject. In reality, taking Miraflores was never my mission. Mine was to command and coordinate the uprising in Caracas and the rest of the country. It was all perfectly planned, down to the smallest detail. But Captain René Gimón's treachery turned our plans upside down. From 3 February, Army High Command began to disarm the battalions that were on the verge of rebelling. They took away the soldiers' guns, car batteries and tank radios, and confiscated their ammunition. There were military police all over the place. As a result the Ayala Armoured Battalion, which was crucial to the operation because it was to take the Miraflores Palace with infantry support, had no radios or ammunition. But even so, a group of our officers, in an act of suicidal audacity, took control of the battalion and attacked Miraflores. They did it with no ammunition and no contact with each other, nor with my central command base or my paratroopers near the Palace. Gimón's betrayal was decisive in Caracas. If it hadn't been for that, I'm sure our plan would have worked.

---

7   See Ángela Zago, *La rebelión de los ángeles*, Warp Editores, Caracas, 1992.

How many casualties were there?
It's estimated at about thirty-five fatalities, between soldiers, police and civilians. Among them were several much-loved *compañeros* from my battalion. Others were seriously injured. Lieutenant Freddy Rodríguez, for instance. I'd given him the job of taking the Navy headquarters, which was diagonally across from the Hospital de Clínicas in Caracas. He was shot six times and nearly died . . . He only survived, with the loss of three fingers, because he was wounded in front of the hospital and they operated right there and then. Anywhere else and he would have bled to death.

When you surrendered, was that the end of the rebellion?
No. Because as we didn't have any radio equipment I couldn't inform all of our officers. They arrested me and took me to Fuerte Tiuna. It was there that I learned fighting was still going on in Maracay, Valencia, Caracas, and that the generals were about to bomb our positions. I remonstrated with Ochoa Antich, saying it would be an unnecessary massacre. I proposed negotiating a surrender directly with my fellow officers. But Urdaneta had cut his phone lines, a sign he was ready to die there with his battalion . . . I couldn't speak to him.

That's when they suggested you spoke on television?
Yes. Admiral Rodríguez Citraro said, 'Why don't you go on television and ask all your men to surrender?' Naturally I accepted.

The public at large hadn't heard of you, had they?
Of course not. Not at all.

The Venezuelan people saw you for the first time when you went on television that day.
That's right. That's the day most people first heard of me.

There in Fuerte Tiuna.
Yes, in the headquarters of the Ministry of Defence. I was under arrest but my people were spread all over the country. Both the

government and I understood the bind we were in. As I said, the F-16 jets had orders to bomb the tank brigade in Valencia and the parachute brigade in Maracay. Those soldiers were dug in, surrounded on all sides, incommunicado . . . So I asked the group of generals, 'Let me surrender on behalf of my men. How can you bomb them now, if we've already surrendered?' And they said, 'Yes, but they're not surrendering!'

They were waiting for orders?
Of course, and that's where the idea of me talking to them came in. They gave me a phone and I asked for all the barracks phone numbers. But the commanders were obviously not sitting by the phone. In Valencia, for instance, they were out with their tanks. In Carabobo, a group of university students had gone to the barracks and the officers had given them weapons. They were all in the streets . . . They had seized a police station, some neighbourhoods had rebelled, several students had died, and far from being suppressed the revolt even looked like spreading to the shanty towns. Various anarchist groups began to join in spontaneously. I was very worried because people had already died, and it could all end in a massacre of unarmed civilians and a slaughter of our scattered, leaderless troops.

That's why you decided to give the order to surrender?
That's when the idea of me talking to our boys arose. I remember telling that admiral, 'Call Radio Apolo and let me send a message to my *compañeros*, the commanders out there.' Radio Apolo played popular Mexican and Venezuelan music, you heard it a lot in the barracks, in fact all over the centre of Valencia in those days. I don't know if it still exists. But the admiral replied, 'No, Chávez. We need something with a wider reach than Radio Apolo. Would you be capable of speaking to the whole country, asking your troops to surrender peacefully and calmly?' 'Of course!' I replied. So they called the television station. They took this decision without consulting Miraflores. Because if Carlos Andrés Pérez had been consulted . . .

He'd have refused.
Obviously. Crafty old politico he was . . . While those officers were
reacting to circumstances, Carlos Andrés had given orders not to let
me leave my supervised cell alive, or at least to kill me at some point
after I'd left. Some officers knew this and alerted me. Anyhow, that's
when I spoke to the people . . . Coming up to midday.

How long did your speech last?
About fifty seconds.

Totally improvised?
They wanted me to write it out so they could see what I was going
to say. I refused. To the deputy minister of defence, I said, 'If that's
how it is, don't call anybody. I've given you my word of honour. I've
surrendered, General, and what I'm going to say is a call to surrender.' 'Very well, but journalists are going to ask you questions.' 'I
won't answer questions,' I promised. Well, since it was in everybody's interest to wrap this up quickly, because blood was still being
shed, they agreed. Then I stuck my head round the door and saw
about a hundred television cameras. I never imagined I'd be speaking to so many cameras.

And on live television.
Yes, live, and with such a tension in the streets.

Had you never spoken on television before?
I had, remember, but it was an entertainment program, in a studio.
Never in such dramatic circumstances. This was a totally different
scenario. Addressing the whole country at a moment of tragedy.

Why on earth did they let you talk live?
The urgency of the situation. We all wanted to avoid bloodshed.
There was no time for more than one take. Every moment counted.
I insisted on coming out in my red beret and uniform . . . With
dignity. I didn't want to look beaten. I thought of General Noriega
when the Yankees invaded Panama and toppled him. They arrested

him and presented him to the media in his vest, demoralized, broken . . .

Your speech lasted less than a minute, but in that short space of time, you managed to assume the stature of a national saviour. Was the myth of Chávez born then?

A lot has been written about my television appearance that morning and about the improvised words I used.[8] Suddenly, all my long experience as a communicator, public speaker, master of ceremonies at fiestas, judge of beauty queens, etc., came in useful. I was also helped by my subconscious whispering to me. Because I remember coming out with my hands behind my back, and a voice inside me said, 'They'll think you're handcuffed.' I brought my hands forwards and held them like that for a while, then lowered them. Or when I was about to say 'civilian–military movement', I didn't, I said 'Bolivarian military movement'. I talked quite naturally. And I think that people – the whole country was watching TV! – appreciated it and sympathized. I assumed responsibility, publicly and personally, for both the rebellion and its failure. In this country, where political leaders have never accepted the slightest responsibility for the countless fiascos that have plagued Venezuela, that sincerity stood out.

However, to some degreee, the 'Chávez myth' was already under way by then in certain sectors: the Academy, junior officers, Elorza, some left-wing circles. That speech, in those

---

8   These are his words verbatim: 'First of all, I want to say good morning to all the people of Venezuela. This Bolivarian message is directed to all the courageous soldiers in the paratrooper regiment in Aragua and the tank regiment in Valencia. *Compañeros*: for now, unfortunately, the goals we had set ourselves were not achieved in the capital city. That is, those of us here in Caracas did not seize power. Where you are, you performed very well, but now is the time to reflect. New situations will arise and the country has to head once and for all towards a better future. So listen to what I have to say, listen to Commander Chávez who is sending you this message. Please reflect, lay down your arms, because the truth is that the objectives we set ourselves at a national level are no longer within our grasp. *Compañeros*, listen to this message of solidarity. I am grateful for your loyalty, for your courage, for your selfless generosity. Before the country and before you, I accept responsibility for this Bolivarian military movement. Thank you.'

circumstances, with the whole country watching, took the myth to a national level.

Some of your words sounded like a pledge, especially the famous 'for now'...
Yes, it gave people hope. Unconsciously, it meant we would be back.

When did you realize your speech had made you a popular figure?
Very soon afterwards. The first sign the people gave us was at Carnival, a few days later. The most popular Carnival costume was 'Chavito'. Children dressed in a uniform, a red beret and a toy gun. I was in jail watching television when suddenly I saw a journalist in the street talking to a kid dressed up as 'Chavito' at a bus stop with his mother. Live on TV, the journalist asked him, 'Who are you dressed up as?' And with a serious face, the little boy replied, 'You're silly, can't you see I'm Chávez?' The kid was very cheeky; being Chávez was not only the fancy dress, it was also the feisty attitude. So the journalist asked him, 'And where is Chávez?' and Little Chávez replied, 'Up there, in the trees.' Even women were dressing up as 'Chávez'. I also heard that, for the fiestas in Elorza that year, on St. Joseph's Day, 19 March, the town decided to put at the head of the Carnival procession a riderless white horse with red trappings, representing the 'great absent figure'. News began arriving from all corners of people joining the cause. Indescribable solidarity. The people's instinct . . . The people's response.

You didn't expect that kind of reaction?
To be perfectly honest, never. Because the people didn't know me. Suddenly my name began to be scrawled on billboards, on walls in the slums. Even though our uprising didn't achieve its goals, it helped rouse the people. And nine months later [27 November 1992], another uprising broke out, led this time by Admiral Grüber Odreman. Venezuela trembled once again. This showed that

patriotic members of the Armed Forces were still unhappy with the Venezuelan political class. The people came out onto the streets without fear. Their fear of repression had disappeared. The establishment, the old regime, or to use a French expression, *l'ancien régime*, was in tatters.

In August 1991, a few months before your 4 February 1992 rebellion, there had been a military coup in Moscow; it failed, but precipitated the collapse of the Soviet Union. Did you have those events in mind?

I remember them very well. On one occasion [26 September 2008], we were in Russia, meeting President Medvedev in Orenburg, near the border with Kazakhstan. Prime Minister Vladimir Putin insisted, as a friendly gesture, that we stop off in Moscow on our way home. We spent the whole night talking . . .

With Putin?

Yes. I told him, 'This is like my meetings with Fidel, no time limit, no rush . . .' We talked politics, economics, about the situation in the Caucasus. It was already dawn when I mentioned the history of the last twenty years. And I reminded him of exactly what you've just asked me.

About the military coup against Mikhail Gorbachev.

Yes. The coup against President Gorbachev took place in Moscow on 19 August 1991, while he was on holiday in the Crimea. Here, as the political command group . . . remember that I wasn't the head of the Bolivarian Movement, there was a directorate made up of Commander Arias Cárdenas, Commander Luis Reyes Reyes, Commander Castro Soteldo, Captain Ronald Blanco La Cruz and myself, a military command group with Major Alastre, and a civilian command group with Alí Rodríguez. So the movement was very collegiate. As Fidel says, 'Chávez wasn't a general, he didn't control the military institutions; the insurrection came from below.' Anyway, I remember us analysing with great interest the coup that had taken place in what was then still the Soviet Union.

Positively, or negatively?

At that time, in all honesty, we viewed it very favourably. It heart-
ened us. We knew the coup was staged by a group of officers who
opposed the break-up of the Soviet Union and a political course
that was bound to lead to the subordination of the Soviet Union to
US imperialism. I tackled this very sensitive subject with Putin,
choosing my words carefully but not mincing them either, because
of our growing friendship. Remember that Putin was right-hand
man to Boris Yeltsin, president of Russia at the time, the man who
took the decision to confront the coup from the top of a tank. In
three days he overturned that military pronunciamento. So, Yeltsin
emerged as a political figure and Gorbachev died a political death.

Subsequently [in August 1999], Yeltsin made Putin president of
the Russian government. Then, when he resigned [on 31 December
1999], he named Putin as his successor. Almost immediately afterwards [on 26 March 2000], Putin was elected president in democratic elections. So, Putin was in the front row for those events. I
told him that when the coup in Moscow happened, I had just taken
command of a parachute battalion in Maracay and was preparing
to organize our military rebellion.

But the leaders of the Moscow coup were arch-conservatives . . .

Well, the media campaign unleashed by the Western press persuaded
public opinion worldwide that the people who wanted to keep to
the socialist line and resist the collapse, or as Fidel puts it, the stab
in the back, of the Soviet Union, were 'conservatives'. The others
were, in contrast, 'progressives'. It was a massive media operation. I
remember admitting to Vladimir Putin that, from our point of
view, we were unhappy to see the Soviet Union disappear, just as
we'd regretted the defeat of the Sandinista government in the 1990
elections, or the fall of the Berlin Wall, and the domino collapse of
the so-called 'real socialist' governments of Eastern Europe.

But you told me you didn't yet identify yourselves as socialists?

That's true. We hadn't yet raised the flag of socialism. At the same
time, we were always inclined that way. We looked to Cuba and

Nicaragua as local examples, and, further away, to the Soviet Union as a potential ally. The defeat of Daniel Ortega's government hit us hard . . . Of course, the strength of our own movement, militarily speaking, lay in Bolivarianism. Our military, revolutionary, insurgent organization was not affected in itself by those international events. But in political terms, we were obviously affected by that 'end of socialism' atmosphere. Particularly considering the direction we wanted our new Venezuela foreign policy to take, looking for new horizons . . .

How was that period seen by your civilian partners?

After that traumatic August of 1991 in Moscow, we assessed the situation inside Venezuela. It continued to deteriorate through September, October and November. We were about to go ahead with the rebellion in December, when the Soviet Union began to disintegrate. That hit us hard, too. We suspended our uprising for other reasons, but for the Venezuelan civilian Left those events froze any attempt at insurrection. Our allies were paralyzed, even though they knew our military rebellion was imminent.

Did you feel the political parties were demoralized?

Yes, the whole global Left was in shock. During the second half of 1991, I saw the morale of our civilian comrades sinking. They were more devastated than we were; demoralized, dejected and depressed. And this accentuated internal divisions, which had negative consequences for 4 February.

What consequences?

At dawn on 4 February, when I began calling on the left-wing civilian groups who were supposed to be joining our rebellion, I got no reply. I stood looking out over the Miraflores Palace and Caracas from the terrace of the Military Museum, and I could see we were alone. We came out without the political Left, without popular mobilization. That's one of the reasons I decided to lay down our arms. The people who should have joined our action stayed at home, and the political leaders we had been talking to for years made no move. The few who wanted to, didn't know how. When I called on my troops to surrender and said, 'I accept responsibility for this movement', I remember clearly that I was going to add, 'I accept responsibility for this civilian–military movement'. But I took out the 'civilian', because that day there was only a military movement. None of those left-wing civilians came out to help the Bolivarian Movement, even though from the moment it was born, from the very first day, it was an authentic grass-roots, civilian–military, and revolutionary movement. However, I accept that it was a deeply demoralizing time for the Left.

Didn't all that – events in the Soviet Union, and the general retreat of the global Left – tempt you to abandon your idea of military insurrection?
No, because in the middle of all that – the end of the Soviet Union, demoralization of the Latin American Left, retreat of socialism, political turncoats, etc. – don't forget that I had just won the battle of Los Pinos against the Army High Command and graduated from the Staff College. This for me meant a moral and political victory. Besides which, members of our Movement began at the same time to be given positions commanding troops. That is, our insurgent organization was going in a totally opposite direction to political movements in general. It was growing stronger in the middle of a storm; it had a dynamic all its own, independent of what was happening around it.

How did Venezuelan society see it?
The people identified with our Movement, no doubt about it. And that's not always the case when the Armed Forces are involved, you know that. Especially in Latin America, where there have been so many repressive *'gorila'* experiences.

On that score, I remember one television news item from 4 February. That day a lot of footage was broadcast which I obviously didn't see, but recordings were brought into prison later. Our last bastion of resistance surrendered three blocks from the Miraflores Palace: one of the lieutenants I hadn't been able to contact was refusing to lay down his arms until he heard the order from me. He was commanding thirty or forty soldiers from my battalion, and they'd taken over a building and dug in. They were finally persuaded to give themselves up, and as they were coming out with lowered weapons, a lady standing on the corner shouted, 'But they're just kids!' And at the sight of those soldiers with red berets and armbands, surrendering with their heads held high, the group burst out into a spontaneous rendering of the national anthem: 'Glory to the brave people who shook off the yoke . . .'

In a gesture of solidarity . . .

We aimed a blow at the heart of the system, a moral blow. It set off a buzz, it was a wake-up call. A week later there was a night-time saucepan-banging demonstration, with the explicit refrain: 'Today's the 10th, the hour is ten, Carlos Andrés, it's time you went!'[9] Leaflets and graffiti started appearing – there were no mobile phones or Twitter in those days – just the grapevine, slogans passed on by word of mouth, from the poorest neighbourhoods to the richest. Drivers turned their headlights off and warning lights on, and banged on pots. In prison, we'd join the protests by whacking our cell doors so hard they nearly came off. Then, early one morning, they moved us to the prison in Yare [Miranda state]. Because the San Carlos prison where we were being held was in the centre of Caracas, and thousands of people were gathering outside, day and night, to show their support. It began to be said that there were two centres of power: Miraflores and San Carlos.

Prison made you even more popular.

Yes. 4 February was like a reveille: 'Bolívar awakes when the people awake,' wrote Pablo Neruda, and with him the idea of a *Patria*.[10] The masses were on the move, they started organizing, their

---

9   Translator's Note: Known as *cacerolazos*, from *cacerola*, Spanish for saucepan, banging pots in the streets is a favourite form of social protest in Latin America.

10   Paraphrase of Pablo Neruda, 'A Song for Bolívar', in *Residence on Earth*, trans. Donald D. Walsh, New Directions, New York, 1973.

consciousness grew, and a project developed. Over the following years, 1994, 1995, 1996, 1997, we began to rebuild an alliance of the Armed Forces, civil society organizations and left-wing parties, which led us to the unique electoral victory of 6 December 1998. Unique because everything was against us. The media was against Chávez, big business was against Chávez, Washington was against Chávez . . . Even the main opposition candidates united against me, and robbed us of many votes.[11] Thanks to the strength of the people, we overcame the obstacles, we ran roughshod over them, and they couldn't ignore us. I always told my voters, 'The only way they will recognize our victory is for us to win by a knockout.' And we won by a knockout.[12]

Despite your democratic electoral victories, some people still call you a golpista because you led the 4 February coup.
Yes, even today some call us *golpistas*. Some people are very confused ideologically, and start from the premise, 'They're soldiers, therefore they must be right-wing *gorilas*.' That's a mistake. We never considered forming a Military Junta. We never wanted a classic military coup, trampling over democratic rights and human rights. Never. We are anti-militarist and anti-*gorila*. We were never *golpistas*. We intervened on the side of the Venezuelan people, we were soldiers whose aim was to transform society.

It was sometimes referred to as a Nasser-style rebellion.[13] It was not, that wouldn't have made sense, but it *was* Nasserist in so far as we had a social, even socialist, platform: Pan-Americanist, i.e., Bolivarian, and anti-imperialist. We are patriotic revolutionaries.

---

11   A few weeks before the elections, the traditional parties in Venezuela – AD and Copei – withdrew support from their respective candidates (Irene Saéz for Copei and Luis Alfaro Ucero for AD) and threw themselves behind Henrique Salas Römer, hoping to prevent the expected victory of Hugo Chávez.

12   Hugo Chávez, candidate for the Movimiento Quinta República (MVR), won with 56.2 per cent of the votes. Henrique Salas Römer of Projecto Venezuela won 39.9 per cent.

13   Gamal Abdel Nasser (1918–1970), Egyptian colonel who took part in the coup d'état of 23 July 1953 which toppled King Farouk. As president he abolished the monarchy, proclaimed the Republic and sought to unify the Arab world.

'*Golpistas*' are army officers who help the oligarchy repress their own people; '*golpistas*' are those who tried to install a dictatorship in Venezuela on 11 April 2002; '*golpistas*' are those unpatriotic soldiers who kowtow to US imperialism. We are Bolivarians, revolutionaries, socialists, anti-imperialists. More and more so with each passing day.

14

The Fertile Prison

San Carlos barracks – Our popularity soars
'Two centres of command: Miraflores and San Carlos'
Lieutenants underground – Hubbub – The trial
In Yare – The conspiracy continues
Producing documents
Support from the *carapintadas* – (Implicit) message from Fidel
The *Blue Book* – National Forum – Constituent Assembly
Catholic progressives – 'How to Get Out of This Labyrinth'
What is revolution? – What is socialism? – Bolivarian socialism
Corruption yesterday and today – Rebellion of 17 November
Manipulation – 'Days in the wilderness'
Reading in Yare Prison – Fall of Carlos Andrés Pérez
Election of Rafael Caldera – Ministers from the MAS
A new revolutionary cycle? – Studying again
Transitional and constitutional processes

After 4 February, where did they imprison you?
To start with, in the San Carlos military barracks, an eighteenth-century colonial building in the centre of Caracas, near the National Pantheon. Then they moved us to the Yare prison, not far from Caracas, but in the state of Miranda.

Was the San Carlos barracks a prison?

Not really, but they used it every now and again for political detainees. When they locked us up, one wing was already occupied by a group of soldiers detained for minor offences, but no officers had been held there for a long time. And suddenly three hundred of us arrived.

Three hundred?

At least. They separated us according to rank. The captains, hundreds of them, had a wing to themselves. The same went for the lieutenants. The commanders were kept separate. The whole prison resounded with shouts, slogans, and at night, singing.

Were you mistreated?

They began interrogating us in the cellars of the Military Intelligence (DIM) building in Boleíta, a Caracas suburb. There was pressure and, yes, violence too. Some *compañeros* cracked, and tried to deny responsibility. Some lacked a solid ideological training, but most behaved with integrity and dignity. We gradually imposed our will, until we effectively took control. We wielded enormous influence, including moral influence, over our guards, who were also soldiers. One day, the colonel in charge of the prison sent for me. In his office, he said, 'Now, Chávez, keep this to yourself, but my wife and children are here, and want to meet you.' And out of a little room stepped his wife and children. They wanted my autograph and took photos with me [laughter]. I signed thousands of autographs and photographs while in prison.

So, your popularity grew while you were inside?

It soared. At first I had no idea. I was isolated, distraught, and wanted to die of shame. In fact, I felt as if I was already dead. It was a kind of death, the death of my military career, of barracks life, it was all over. My God! I thought of my *compañeros* who had died in combat on 4-F, and I regretted having led them into all that.[1] 'What

---

1 Translator's Note: 4-F is how the Bolivarian Movement referred to 4 February 1992.

have we done?' I asked myself over and over again. I was filled with doubt, terrible existential doubt. Until, after several days in solitary, a military chaplain – Father Torbes – came to my cell with a tiny copy of the Bible. As if to comfort me, he read me David's thirty-seventh psalm: 'The wicked have drawn out the sword, and have bent their bow, to cast down the poor and needy, and to slay such as be of upright conversation. Their sword shall enter into their own heart, and their bows shall be broken.'[2]

He marked the passage for me and covertly slipped the Bible into my hand. With his back to the security camera on the cell door, pretending to embrace me, he whispered in my ear, 'Cheer up, the people love you; you don't know what's going on outside; you've no idea, my son; in the street you're a national hero.' And from the pocket of his soutane he took out a fake banknote on which my face replaced Bolívar's, which was circulating everywhere. I'll never forget that priest. From him I learned the tremendous impact our action had had on the people. My resurrection began.

According to an opinion poll the day after, 5 February, 90 per cent of the people sympathized with your Movement . . .
The prison became the epicentre of a political whirlwind. I have here some original documents from that time: cartoons, songs, speeches . . . [He shows them to me.] Here's a book by two Cuban journalists: *Our Chávez.*[3] The title is taken from a prayer someone made up at that time, which went: '*Our Chávez, who art in prison . . .*' The media even talked about there being 'two centres of power in Venezuela', one in Miraflores, the other in San Carlos.

Why?
People came en masse, like a pilgrimage, bringing presents, food . . . With their peculiar nose or instinct for politics, they sensed that 4 February was not your standard military coup but something else,

---

2   Psalm 37:14–15.

3   Rosa Míriam Elizalde and Luis Báez, *Chávez nuestro*, Casa Editora Abril, Havana, 2004.

carried out by a generation of young officers who were truly representative of the people. With the result that San Carlos was permanently surrounded by crowds. The prison was a vortex from the outset, it turned into a centre of power, in a symbolic and in a real sense.

A few days later, the colonel sent for me again. He was a good man, who had these two massive dogs . . . He asked me to help him, 'Chávez, I've only six months to go before I retire. They sent me here, I wanted to have a quiet final year. Now I find myself involved in this hullabaloo.' 'How can I possibly help you?' I asked. 'This is a powder keg. Have you seen all those people outside?' There were thousands of them. They even made bonfires. The guards teargassed them but they came back. Thousands and thousands. The more force was used against them, the more numerous they became.

The authorities were obliged to grant open visiting hours. The prison got so busy that we struggled to get any private time with our families. People crowded into the cells. Some came with musical instruments, others with papers for autographing, or political messages. The first time my children came, I barely had a chance to hug them and sit them on my lap.

Did your family know in advance about 4 February?
Apparently, when someone told my father – he was retired from work and politics and had a little farm with pigs and four cows in Barinas – that I was involved in a military coup in Caracas, he said, 'No, it's impossible, my son Huguito wouldn't be mixed up in anything like that.'

And your mother?
My mother, on the other hand, when the neighbours told her, she walked up and down in tears, very upset. She understood straight away. Mothers are that perceptive. They know us better than we know ourselves. Apparently she said, 'I'm not surprised. Yes, Hugo's bound to be involved.' When she saw me on TV, like not only was I in it but I was one of the leaders, you can imagine . . . The whole

time I was in prison she was going on protest marches, and giving speeches all over the place.

How about your wife? Your children?

That was the painful part, my wife, my children, my home life. I was very much a homebody in spite of everything, I liked spending all the time I could with them. And of course they stood by me straight away. Although the kids were still young. I remember my boy Hugo, during one of his first prison visits, we went for a walk in the yard, and he said, 'Dad, my baseball friends say hi.' And then, as if reproaching me, 'You're a prisoner, where are the soldiers from your battalion? Why don't they rescue you?' How do you explain to a nine-year-old that there is no battalion – that my soldiers are prisoners too?

Were you still being paid?

We got our salary, sure. We were soldiers on active service, they had to pay us, and we kept our rights to social security, etc.

And back in the barracks, did the soldiers support you?

A lot. The moral impact of our action on the rank and file was enormously positive. We could count on the silence and solidarity of many *compañeros* who provided us with information, and gave disinformation to our enemies. They protected us in many ways.

For the first twenty days, we, the commanders, were kept in a very cold cellar, separated from each other in individual cells, and almost totally incommunicado. We ate on the floor, and slept on the floor as well. We were frozen, because they turned the air conditioning down to zero. The light was on the whole time, we didn't know what time it was, or if it was day or night. We lost all notion of time. We figured it out, more or less, by mealtimes. We had no news of anything. Except every now and again we'd get little notes.

Did they try to kill you?

Yes, on the president's orders. But a protective shell formed around me there and then. Because, let me assure you, no middle- or high-ranking officer intended to carry out that order. In fact, they protected me. I left the Historical Museum bent double and was put into a civilian car, driven by a general in uniform. It drove round in circles for a while. In front of us was a military jeep, simulating that I was inside, to confuse snipers with orders to kill me. What's more, I had my rifle. The general who arrested me said, 'Keep your rifle and pistol, because they might try to kill us all, me included.'

So, you were arrested but kept your rifle.
Yes, they left me my weapons. Because of the danger. I handed my rifle over when we got to the Ministry of Defence, the pistol and a hand grenade as well. Like I said, many soldiers protected us out of solidarity. And this continued to grow. Especially among the rank and file, and younger officers. Later on, certain officers came secretly to see us in prison. A colonel called Higinio Castro appeared on one occasion when I was in San Carlos: he was a much-respected officer, of African descent, a paratrooper. He said, 'Chávez, I want to talk to you, let's go into the toilet because there are cameras here.' We locked ourselves in the toilet and he put it to me, 'I want to unite the forces that have been dispersed. Another movement is on its way . . . We're taking up the struggle again.' He was offering me his services, even though he was a colonel, my senior. I gave him two or three names and he began to create a network. Because there were many committed officers and units who, for one reason or another, had not joined the 4-F rebellion. And they still thought something had to be done. On one occasion, a young lieutenant called Álvarez Bracamonte led his own mini-rebellion inside Fuerte Tiuna, capturing a command post and grabbing more than a hundred rifles and machine guns.

What did he intend to do?
He went underground with a group of civilians and soldiers. He left behind a message. He wasn't the only one . . . In Táchira, another officer attempted the same thing, but was caught. Yet another tried it in Bolívar. A 'lieutenant's rebellion' was in the making. Later we

discovered that because the commanders were separated from the captains, the captains were giving orders to lieutenants to leave their barracks with as many weapons as possible, and go underground. Apparently the order was coming out of San Carlos, yet we had not been consulted. So eventually we organized the Bolivarian Command Group, and began to put our house in order. Because that movement had been anarchic.

What happened to those lieutenants?
The first one, Raúl Álvarez Bracamonte, became famous, and eventually even one of our deputies. He was arrested several months after he rebelled, but he managed to send out video messages urging the people to mobilize. We published his messages in our prison journal which was called – what else? – *Por Ahora* [For Now]. That young man expressed himself very well. The news began, 'Lieutenant Álvarez Bracamonte speaks – To the courageous Venezuelan people'.

Did you ever think of escaping?
Not at that time. There would have been no point. But later on, yes, when we'd started mounting a new rebellion. We had soon begun cooking up a fresh conspiracy from inside. Messages were coming in: from the Air Force, which had not joined the 4-F; from the new generation of army officers, and from the Navy. An avalanche of offers to join us. That's when people started talking about the 'two centres of power'. We also renewed contact with multiple social movements and political parties, like La Causa R and the Movimiento al Socialismo (MAS), which had committed to 4-F but pulled out at the last minute. It didn't take much to re-establish contact, because some of their leaders knew our relatives, wives, brothers, friends . . .

Did any of the leaders visit you in prison?
Later on, when we were in Yare. Teodoro Petkoff came, even Enrique Ochoa Antich, the general's brother, and all the PCV leaders. Luis Miquilena was a frequent visitor. And Jorge Giordani, at

the time leader of the MAS and their expert on economic affairs.[4]
José Vicente Rangel got in touch with me, too.

Did José Vicente come to see you in prison?
He didn't come. He had a television programme. He sent me a
whole list of questions, managed to smuggle in a miniature camera
– in a priest's soutane! – and we recorded my answers. He edited the
interview so skilfully that it sounded as if the two of us were chatting inside my cell. But he couldn't broadcast it. It was censored.
We did two interviews, neither could be shown. So Rangel, with his
usual political nous, invited journalists to his home and showed
them the interview. It had a gigantic impact. I also got Laura
Sánchez in to interview me by passing her off as one of my cousins.
Laura was a journalist at *El Nacional*, and a great friend.

Were you still plotting?
We never stopped. As I said, the prison became the epicentre of a
new conspiracy and an important political and moral movement,
but as yet without a clear direction. More of a general hubbub. The
government knew. In the midst of this tornado came events like the
great blackout, I don't know how many minutes that lasted, and the
great *cacerolazo* of 10 March 1992.

Did all that agitation result in the order to transfer you?
Exactly. They took us to Yare to get us out of Caracas. They were
frightened of a new explosion. And they were right, it was about to
explode.

Was there no trial pending?
There was a trial, but we refused to go to court. We declared
ourselves political prisoners, who didn't recognize the jurisdiction
of the court.

---

4 In a conversation with the author (26 July 2013), Jorge Giordani denied ever
belonging to the MAS.

Inside Yare prison, were you still organized as the Bolivarian Movement?

Yes, of course. And openly now. In the end, I recall, the colonel in charge of San Carlos allowed commanders and captains to meet every Thursday in the barracks yard, so we reconstituted the Bolivarian Movement Command Group. I had requested it: 'Colonel, this movement has been going for twenty years. We're not just starting up.' And he agreed. It suited him, because the younger captains were more radical, and sometimes quite rude to him. We were more mature, so we respected the colonel personally. The captains and lieutenants insulted the guards, banged pots at them, and threw food into the yard. So I advised him to let us meet up with them: 'We're their chiefs. You may have three stars, but they won't acknowledge that. Understand, we've been their chiefs since they were cadets.' And, as an intelligent man, he agreed to us having contact. We met as a Command Group and got ourselves organized. We appointed an operations officer, an intelligence officer and a Bolivarian Movement committee, and began planning our legal strategy.

Did you have lawyers?

I didn't want any, but several turned up . . . Some we knew, others volunteered their services. One of them was Cilia Flores, she was very active.[5] I first met her in prison, she helped us a lot. None of them asked for money. Just as well, since we didn't have any. I agreed to work with them in the end, because many of our young soldiers had joined the rebellion without any basic training. Besides, there were about ten thousand soldiers in jail.

Ten thousand?

Well yes, the rebellion of 4 February1992 was the biggest in Venezuelan history, in terms of number of units, number of troops, geographic area covered, and political depth. The foot soldiers were

---

5   Cilia Flores, lawyer, was president of the National Assembly (2006–2011) and ombudsperson. She is married to the current Venezuelan president, Nicolás Maduro.

arrested and detained in their barracks, in Fuerte Tiuna, in gymnasiums, in stadiums . . .

Were they going to be prosecuted too?

Some of them, yes. But the majority were discharged after a few weeks.

Did the Army discharge them?

They humiliated them. I saw one photo, it really upset me. They were turfed out in their underpants, some didn't even have shoes on. They threw them into the street as 'traitors' – even though the responsibility lay with us, the officers, especially the commanders. When we saw this, our political command group started to deal with it. We gave a group of our lads the green light to go to court and fight their detention order, because that way they'd get properly released [not discharged].

How?

The truth was, the government couldn't keep three hundred officers in prison. It disrupted the Army. So they began to release us. One hundred and fifty – half of them, that is – got out after a few weeks, but they still had to go and fight the detention order. That's why we agreed to have lawyers to defend them. We had a whole legal team. The officers succeeded in fighting the detention orders, which were soon followed by release orders on the grounds of lack of direct responsibility.

Theoretically, that meant they were only obeying orders.

Yes. We defended that position and encouraged them. Many refused to leave, so we had to convince them, even order them, 'It's your mission to go back to the Army.' Some of them are generals today because they returned to their units. Those of us, however, who were deeply involved in our political project, stayed in prison. There was no question of us leaving. Not with the massive support we were receiving from the people.

I was in Caracas at that time, and everywhere I saw graffiti supporting you.
Yes, graffiti appeared almost immediately. Then came the jokes, and the fancy dress costumes. During carnival, little boys dressed up as paratroopers in fatigues and red berets, I told you . . . Furthermore, the most diverse movements – left and right – tried to make contact with us in San Carlos. The prison became a place of debate, reflection and spirituality. Never in my life have I written as much as I did in that cell, late at night and in the small hours.

Did you write for any particular magazine?
For several. I remember one article called 'Dirty war against the MBR-200' that I wrote for *El ojo del huracán* [The Eye of the Hurricane], a magazine published by Teodoro Petkoff. I also drafted fliers and leaflets for distribution in the street, and documents to send to Bolivarian groups around the country. All this material was sent out, but much got confiscated along the way.

Did you produce theoretical papers?
Yes, in-depth analyses and reports for our periodical *Por Ahora*, the one I told you about. We published an important document called, not coincidentally, 'What is to be done?' We wrote, 'Let us raise our banner with dignity and wait for new situations. For now, we will organize. Nothing comes free. Enough! *La Patria* calls us, we accept the challenge. Let us confront the "dirty war" being waged against the MBR-200.'

You smuggled those documents out of prison?
Relatives, friends, fellow officers – even some of our guards – took those messages out almost every week, to particular barracks or specific private individuals. They also brought documents in for us. One of our guards, Captain Ríos Vento, even joined the Movement. He was the one who locked our cells at night, but in fact he protected us and saw to it that nothing happened to us.

Later on, in Yare, I managed to record a good number of messages in my cell. It was forbidden, but David Ayala, for instance, a reporter for *Últimas Noticias*, secretly taped various conversations

with a mini tape recorder. I also taped a message for a pretty original propaganda operation. Copies of it were given to youngsters
travelling on long-distance buses. The trip from Caracas to Barinas,
for instance, takes between eight and ten hours, so the job of these
youngsters was to persuade the bus driver to play a Commander
Chávez message during the journey.

On the bus?

Yes, for the passengers. And it worked. The passengers applauded.
They arrested some of the youngsters, but people asked for copies.
A long-repressed energy was being unleashed. The people truly
woke up; their whole historical heritage galvanized them.

You mentioned the 'dirty war' against the MBR-200. What did it consist of?

More like 'dirty propaganda'. Because they were determined to
neutralize the MBR-200 as a force for change. But they had to
follow the instructions of the US political-marketing 'magician',
David Garth, who thought it was well-nigh impossible to rehabili-
tate the image of Carlos Andrés Pérez.[6] The only thing to do,
according to Garth, was to blacken the image of the Bolivarian
Movement. Their 'dirty war' took the offensive on several fronts,
and included accusing the MBR-200 of planning 'a classic coup to
establish a military dictatorship'. They published lists of people we
intended to take to the stadium and shoot. Lists that never existed,
but were published as 'authentic'. They said they'd found them in
our computers, among our 'secret files' . . . They spread those lies all
kinds of ways, through the press, radio and television: a disinformation campaign of massive scope that is still going on today.

How did you react?

We responded by affirming that the MBR-200 commanders
were united by a deep feeling of brotherhood; by the idea of

---

6   David Garth, well-known US political communications strategist. In 1978 he
directed Luis Herrera Campíns's successful presidential campaign.

liberating Venezuela from oppression; by the desire to make
Venezuela a free and sovereign country committed to Bolivarian
ideals; and by the wish to free our people from political sleaze
merchants and intriguers. We retorted with a robust defence of
our movement. And we put out plenty of counter-information
as well.

Like what?
To give you an example, we had recourse to popular culture –
Venezuelan music, llanero music. The people love it. We started
distributing the 'Corrido de Maisanta': 'Chávez is Maisanta's great-
grandson,' sang the llaneros. It gave us historical continuity. It put
our 4-F rebellion in the context of Venezuela's popular struggles.
Corridos like 'Letter to Comandante Chávez', by Cristóbal Jiménez,
started to appear.

Did you know him?
Cristóbal Jímenez? Very well. He's from the llanos and we got to
know each other there in fiestas and partying. After the rebellion,
he wrote and recorded that *corrido*. The words are lovely [he sings]:
'*Ay, mi Comandante Chávez*, thrown in jail / for his life's lucidity, for
Bolívar's dream.' And the end goes, 'In farewell, I ask God to bless
you / with this luminous phrase from Simón Bolívar: / he who
abandons everything for *la Patria* / loses nothing and gains all that
he devotes to her.'
    And another singer, Luis Lozada, who I also knew in Barinas but
is now dead, recorded a beautiful *joropo*: 'That fourth of February, a
hot early morning . . .'

Were those songs allowed?
Absolutely not, they were censored. But the people sang them and
everybody heard them in the street. They weren't allowed on the
radio, but who could stop the people singing them? And that was
much more effective than their press, radio and television campaign
against our Movement.

How did you actually create all those MBR-200 documents? It can't be easy to write collectively in prison.
We formed two command groups, the Yare group and the San Carlos group, after they separated us.

Oh! They didn't take you all to Yare?
No, they separated us. One early morning, using tear gas and batons, they got ten of us out of our cells in San Carlos [Hugo Chávez, Francisco Arias Cárdenas, Díaz Reyes, Ronald Blanco La Cruz, Duarte Mariño, Iván Freitas, Gerardo Márquez, Luis Valderrama, Pedro Emilio Alastre López] and sent us to Yare. Others stayed in San Carlos, and some went to Fuerte Tiuna.

We created those documents through thousands of hours of reflection and discussion . . . Whole nights spent talking until dawn. We set up working groups on various subjects. In Yare there were only ten of us, but we had four groups.

Could you meet? Weren't you held in individual cells?
No, we were in very small cells off a long corridor, and they weren't locked. We managed the corridor padlock ourselves. There was a tacit agreement between ourselves and the guards. During the night we had the key to that padlock, and the last one to go to bed locked up. So we actually locked ourselves in. With the key inside, eh? Until the events of November 1992, after which the rules changed.

Yare isn't a military prison, is it? It's a prison for common criminals.
Yes, it's for ordinary prisoners, the worst kind . . . But they put a wing aside for us, an *ad hoc* wing, as they say. That jail was quite an education.

Did you mix with the ordinary convicts?
We'd talk to them from a distance, from the yard. They were on the upper floors. We were on the ground floor. The block had four floors. So, sometimes I'd be sitting in my cell in front of the window,

and I'd see a little pot, or a tin, come down on the end of a string, with a message inside. Often a beautiful message.

Of support for you?
Full support. All of them! Those prisoners were on our side.

How many were there in that prison?
About two thousand.

Where is Yare?
In Valles del Tuy, about an hour from the centre of Caracas. It's very hot, they call it 'the little oven'.

It's for criminals from Caracas?
From all over the country. A tough place. But we had certain freedoms, our families, visitors. For us it was, I repeat, a real education. It was fighting in the trenches and going to school. It was fire and fire. It was a conspiracy centre and a political and military command centre. From there, Arias Cárdenas, Alastre López and I sent thousands of letters to far and wide. We began to dictate political lines. A lot of people came to the prison to ask, 'What shall we do? How shall we organize?' We shared out the work, there were so many letters. Messages to social movements, Bolivarian committees – illegal, persecuted committees. And we had *Por Ahora*, the journal I told you about.

Was that journal clandestine?
Of course, totally illegal. But clandestine printing presses sprang up all over the country. A huge effort was made, with no resources, no money. Later on we produced a document which posed an important question: 'How do we get out of this labyrinth?'

Did you get letters of support, from people wanting to join?
In vast quantities. Wanting to join us, support us, congratulate us, asking for information from us. Military Intelligence detected a lot of them, of course, they confiscated some, redirected others. But

many people, very courageously, wrote to us from all over the place. Women hid them down there, or in their bras, in food they'd cooked, in cakes ... Letters from children, men, women, everyone.

Were you able to speak to the people who wrote those letters?
Yes, I met almost all of them, and many – not all – joined the Movement.

And from abroad? Did you get a show of solidarity from Latin America? From any political group, or leader? Or wasn't the rebellion understood abroad?
It wasn't understood. If I remember correctly, during those months in prison, we didn't get a single message from left-wing movements. On the contrary, we got messages from the right wing. We even got invited to some meetings organized in Mexico by a movement we didn't know, founded by the American Lyndon LaRouche, on the far right.[7] They sent us some reports that seemed interesting, very well documented. I even asked my brother Adán to attend, and he went with some other people from here. On his return, he said, 'That's the extreme right.' We immediately cut off all relations.

We also got a message from Argentina, from the *carapintadas* military movement led by Colonel Alí Seineldín.[8] And the government here began to try to associate us with the far right. The mainstream press handled that very well for them. It began to say, 'Chávez is the Venezuelan *carapintada*', and the message spread from Buenos Aires to Washington. The result was that left-wing movements backed away from us ... All this happened in the general context of retreat, demoralization and division of the international Left we've already mentioned.

---

7   Lyndon H. LaRouche (1922–), US ideologue, ex-Trotskyist, founder of US Labor Party, a far-right grouping with international ramifications.

8   Mohamed Alí Seineldín (1933–2009), Argentine colonel who led several military uprisings against constitutional governments. His Nationalist–Peronist–Catholic forces were known as *carapintadas*, 'painted faces'.

And given that Carlos Andrés Pérez, a social democratic leader, enjoyed considerable international influence on the Left.

Yes, he had an excellent image on the international Left. So much so that, look, I brought these books to show you, I read them in jail, annotated and underlined [he shows us].

The same ones?

The ones that survived. Lots of others fell by the wayside, in house searches . . . But I wanted to show you this, look, it says here, 'Yare prison, July 1993'. It had just been published. The author is Tomás Borge, and between 18 and 20 April 1992 – my God![9] Only two months after the rebellion! – he conducts an interview with Fidel Castro in Havana.

I mention it because, in one of his questions, Tomás Borge recognizes the contribution of Carlos Andrés. He says, 'One of the political leaders who has done most for the continent's integration, stability of governance, and other features of Latin American democracies, is having a particularly hard time. I refer, of course, to Carlos Andrés Perez. What's your view on that?'

And Fidel replies, 'What has happened in Venezuela is unfortunate, but it precisely demonstrates the crisis that the shock treatment imposed by the US and the IMF will unleash on Latin America. What is happening in Venezuela is the clear result of the economic shock policy, of the measures and the theories, imposed by the US and the IMF. There you have the perfect example. Venezuela is the richest country in Latin America, Venezuela isn't a country that lives off sugar, Venezuela lives off oil, Venezuela earns $12 billion per year from its oil. Venezuela is a country with enormous energy resources, hydroelectric power as well as oil; a country with enormous mineral resources – iron, bauxite; it's a country blessed by nature. How can you explain the social explosions in Venezuela if not as proof of what we have been saying about the consequences of that economic policy in

---

9   Tomás Borge, *Un grano de maíz. Conversaciones con Fidel Castro*, Fondo de Cultura Económica, Mexico DF, 1992.

Latin America; proof that the situation in Latin American is growing unsustainable?'

When I read that, I jotted down here, 'Fidel is talking about "social explosions" in Venezuela, he's not talking about coups.' It made me think and, with the greatest caution, I asked myself, does Fidel know something?

Fidel analysed the situation the same way you all did, and expressed a certain implicit comprehension.
Of course, I was cautious because we didn't know each other. But it was clear that in his reply to Borge there was no criticism of our action, none at all. I remember clearly that when I read it in prison I said to Alastre López, the *compañero* closest to me, 'Does Fidel know something?' In any case, I took it, in Yare, as a message to us from Fidel. An indirect message, because don't forget that Fidel was on good terms with Carlos Andrés; he came when he took office, I saw him, he was three metres from me in the Palacio Blanco. Fidel might have defended Carlos Andrés, but how could he, knowing that Carlos Andrés was behind the US and the IMF's neoliberal package? Most importantly, Fidel – surely well informed at this stage – knew that our Movement was a left-wing movement.

I made a note at the bottom of the page: 'Fidel does not defend CAP, he explains the causes, he doesn't even name Carlos Andrés, despite being on good terms with him.' I read Borge's book in July, 1993 and – replying to your question – it could be the only indirect message we received from abroad from, let's say, the forces on the Left. Because, apart from our own people, I don't remember getting a single message from a left-wing movement.

And the Venezuelan Left? When did they begin to express their interest in the Movement?
Well, remember that before the rebellion there had been a series of contacts with several organizations, certain sectors. Immediately after 4-F, some tendencies, let's call them that, felt strengthened, especially La Causa R, perhaps the most solid movement, a small

cadre-based party that even had a few deputies – one of them was
Aristóbulo Istúriz – and made a lot of noise. As a party, they were
represented in Congress and had captured the governorship of
Bolívar state. They had a certain political space and had gained a
modicum of respect. It was one of the parties whose political leaders, almost all of them, had known about the preparations for the
rebellion a few years before.

So, within the Left – let's say, the left-wing parties – La Causa R,
or to be more precise, a group within La Causa R, had grown
stronger and from our early days in prison started to send us testi-
monials, contacts, messages, even expressions of support for our
families, and they also began preparing a lot of documents and
political actions.

How about the MAS? And the Communist Party?
Within the MAS, which was by now quite absorbed into the system,
some leaders were supportive and others weren't. They were divided.
As for the Communist Party, it was broadly in favour. But over and
above those parties, which were cadre-based structures, not mass
organizations, what was awakened was the people, and above all,
Bolivarianism.

You said Bolívar was there, in the people, but 'inactive', and that all it needed was to 'touch the fuse' for it to go off, didn't you?
And we touched that fuse on 4-F. Thus was unleashed the
Bolivarianism the Venezuelan people carry inside, in their hearts,
their souls, through the different cultural manifestations the people
have   at   their   disposal: murals,   fliers,   songs,   cartoons,
newspapers . . .

The rebellion speeded up the decomposition of the system. And Carlos Andrés was finally removed in May 1993, right?
Yes, it speeded up the decomposition. The so-called Pact of Punto
Fijo began to unravel and various solutions were on the cards, one
of which was the president's renunciation. Even before the rebellion, we had produced a document outlining some ideas: the *Blue*

Book. It began to circulate. Our main political demand was for a Constituent Assembly.

Where did that idea come from?

That had been proposed, before us, by the Frente Patriótico of Douglas Bravo, William Izarra and Manuel Quijada. They were the first to call for a Constituent Assembly. We took that idea up again, we introduced it into our policies, and in prison we began to examine the idea and develop it further. Those documents of ours are public, they're in the archives, in the publications library, etc. The idea took hold of the street, the people took up the cry, and the call for a Constituent Assembly became a popular imperative.

How did the government react to that proposition?

The system rejected it, and Carlos Andrés very skilfully appointed a so-called Consultative Council which comprised, among others, a Venezuelan historian who later, when Pérez fell, would act as interim president: Ramón J. Velásquez. The Consultative Council, in that post-rebellion political ferment, produced a document and proposals for the president. And one of them was precisely to call for a Constituent Assembly, and also to dismantle the IMF's economic policies. That is, they adopted our proposals.

Did they apply them?

Not one of those recommendations was accepted by the government. On the contrary, it actually rekindled the repression and political persecution. General repression on the streets and selective persecution of individuals.

Which gave you a reason to keep on plotting, didn't it?

Exactly. Because of the repression, the desire for insurrection grew. A group of leaders of different popular movements began, as they say, to knock on the barracks' door. Word began to reach the prison about a new uprising being prepared for July. In the Army barracks, new leaders were coming to the fore. In the Navy, Admiral Grüber Odremán. In the Air Force, General Visconti and officers Reyes

Reyes and Castro Soteldo. These last two were members of the
Bolivarian Movement, but they hadn't been arrested because the
Air Force had not, in the end, joined the 4-F uprising.

Did you have contacts in the Catholic Church?
We had close contact with a group of bishops. They were later
kicked out by the Catholic hierarchy. One of them was Mario
Moronta, archbishop of Caracas, left-wing without a doubt, a
progressive. After our victory in 1999, he was punished by being
sent to San Cristóbal, on the Colombian border. There were other
progressive priests too. They went out to talk to the people, to speak
in public and on TV. What's more, several of them came to visit us
in prison: Archbishop Mario Moronta; Father Arturo Sosa, a Jesuit,
Father Jesús Gazo, an elderly priest, also a Jesuit, a very courageous
man who ran a human rights organization. We also had support
from the Evangelical community.

Is the Evangelical community important?
In Venezuela it's important. And we have always been in favour of
freedom of worship. The Evangelical community supported us. But
we also sought support from many civil society organizations: the
trades unions; the university student movement which took to the
streets on 4-F; the neighbourhood organizations' movement;
professional bodies; colleges and academies; the business sector;
campesino organizations; indigenous communities, and scientific
bodies. We even had some friends in the Army High Command.

And among the intellectuals?
Well, actually, around the time our conspiracy started bubbling up
again, some other proposals were also emerging from the Central
University (UCV), from a group of intellectuals headed by my
good friend and tireless activist Francisco Mieres – now sadly passed
away – and including Adina Bastidas, who was to become vice president, and Yadira Córdoba, who was later rector of the Bolivarian
University. I must also mention another group of university professors, among them Jorge Giordani and Héctor Navarro, who were

responsible for the 'UCV to the Nation' document, containing proposals along very similar lines to our own. They asked if they could come to Yare and present them to us.

Is that how you met Giordani?

Yes, I met him then. They wouldn't let him in, because on the list of authorized people his name was spelt Giordano, not Giordani. As it didn't match exactly, the guard didn't let him pass. We had to convince him he was the same man; there was his photo, on his ID. But he had to wait outside for an hour.

Finally he got through. I greeted him, 'Ah, you're Jorge Giordani. I've read a lot of your work.' He was pleased. 'I know your books,' I said, 'they led me to Varsavsky.' And we began to talk. Giordani wrote a very good book, *Planning and the State*, with a vision very close to the one I had always intuited.[10] With his command of strategy and geopolitics, he had begun to develop the instruments of military planning. Giordani's views, his knowledge, our conversations, helped me a great deal in studying and developing policy proposals.

Did you prepare a programme?

Yes, in Yare, we published it in July 1992. It was a simple manifesto but with a clear programme, entitled 'Cómo salir de este laberinto' [How to Get Out of This Labyrinth]. It was a manifesto forged in the heat of debate, and published in a one-page broadsheet called *El Correo Bolivariano* [The Bolivarian Post]. Here's one that did the rounds in those days [he shows us], jealously guarded ever since by Military Intelligence. It bears the yellow, blue and red MBR-200 symbol. The manifesto made a series of proposals, and explained how we would achieve them. Among other things, we proposed convening a National Forum. Because our political objective was still to form a civilian–military front with other political sectors and other social forces. We soldiers weren't to act alone.

---

10   Jorge Giordani, *Planificación, Ideología y Estado. El caso de Venezuela*, Vadell Hnos. Editores, Caracas, 1986.

Were you inspired by classical Marxist texts?
Well, Marxism was the background canvas, but more concretely, in elaborating this document, I was helped by several books. Among them were these two [he shows us]: *National Projects*, by Oscar Varsavsky, an Argentine socialist thinker who lived in Venezuela for several years, I've mentioned him already; and this other one, *Planning Situations* by Carlos Matus [1931–98], a Chilean economist, also a socialist, one of Salvador Allende's ministers, who lived in Venezuela for a long time and died here.[11]

During my time in prison I did a lot of studying, especially about things like that – national projects, social objectives, strategic planning. I'd already read up on these subjects when I did my postgraduate degree in political science at Simón Bolívar University.

What were you proposing?
We were trying to put forward new ideas. There were thousands of ideas circulating on the streets, including proposals for a new rebellion, but we knew that politically that was difficult. It would only be possible with a very strong grass-roots movement, but the risk of violence was enormous and we felt it was our responsibility to advance non-violent proposals. We wanted a peaceful solution.

That's why we were looking for ways of generating concrete actions that would in turn stimulate other political sectors capable of becoming authentic mechanisms of change. In the two books I mentioned, I found some of the answers we were looking for and we set them out in our manifesto 'How to Get Out of This Labyrinth'.

That's where you talk about the National Forum and the Constituent Assembly?
That's right. That document said the following; allow me to read some extracts.

---

11   Carlos Matus, *Planificación de situaciones*, Fondo de Cultura Económica, Mexico DF, 1980.

The MBR-200 proposes to the nation, as a peaceful solution,

1. A National Forum made up of diverse social, political and economic sectors of the nation.

2. A 'liberating' referendum, so called because the act itself would untie the moorings currently holding the country back, and open a channel of rapid and constructive evolution towards wider participation by the Venezuelan people, giving them a higher profile in government and making them the protagonists.

This popular consultation would simultaneously address the following aspects:

a. Withdrawal of the presidential mandate;

b. Delegation to the National Forum, from the National Congress, of a constitutional faculty that would authorize it to elect an emergency government instead of a provisional president, and then call elections for a National Assembly;

c. Appointment of an emergency government – a Bolivarian patriotic junta – within a lapse of time no greater than five days following approval of the referendum;

d. Immediately after being appointed, this emergency government will be sworn in by the National Forum and will begin carrying out its functions in lieu of the president of the republic;

e. Thirty days after embarking upon its functions as an emergency government, the members of the National Constituent Assembly will be elected by direct and secret universal suffrage, and will take their seats within a lapse of time no greater than fifteen days following their election;

f. The National Constituent Assembly will assume the functions of the National Congress, and will be tasked with drawing up a new Constitution, the single instrument under whose legitimate guidance the entire nation will begin to build a new and definitive model of society.

We were setting out our programme within that time frame. Obviously, we knew that, from the institutional point of view, what

Varsavsky calls 'institutional viability' was practically impossible. But we put forward these ideas because we wanted to speed up a solution.

Why did you have to speed it up?
We were very concerned about the nature of the rebellion that was being planned. We'd been informed that right-wing forces were preparing a classic Pinochet-style coup, with the threat, perhaps, of civil war.

Is that why you were thinking of a transitional government?
Yes, we proposed a transitional government, the product of a civilian–military alliance, and we published the basic programme of that government. We believed the National Forum should set out the short-term measures required to generate a new situation in which the 'balance of phenomena' – this is a very Matus terminology – would allow for an evolutionary transition towards later stages of profound structural transformation. The aim would be to implement a model of development that would lead to a new society based on creativity and solidarity.

All told, we produced three important documents [in prison] which essentially set out our vision for Venezuela: the *Blue Book*, the Simón Bolívar National Project, and 'How to Get Out of This Labyrinth'.

Did you explain the economic model you wanted to implement?
We said – and this can be seen in the documents I mentioned – that we had to [he reads] 'establish the foundations for, and set in motion, a new model of development that would replace the current system of economic and social domination'. We insisted on the need to completely revise 'the economic package' [of Carlos Andrés Pérez] and adopt a range of measures aimed at drastically reducing the levels of poverty among the vast majority of the population. To do this we must put in place a series of simple, viable and consistent projects in the following areas:

'1. Reduce the cost of living to a tolerable minimum threshold;

'2. Increase productive employment through self-build housing, ecological projects, reforestation, provision of basic services, agriculture, etc.;

'3. Reach an adequate level of self-sufficiency and food security, through the creation on a national and regional level of a simplified and functional system of production, circulation, distribution, and consumption of basic goods and staples.'

You were suggesting what was to become known the Misión Mercal?[12]
Indeed. I can't forget how much hunger there was. Hunger, malnutrition, those are terrible things. We also proposed 'developing a national programme of cooperatives and self-management within a subsystem of new specific economic methods aimed at creating a model of economic solidarity'. And we insisted that there had to be a 'significant reduction in the fiscal deficit, through a thorough reform of the tax system which would achieve a fair redistribution of income and a rational reduction in public spending'.

I notice there's no talk of socialism . . .
No, in fact, the word 'socialism' doesn't appear at all. You have to take into account the global context. And even us, when we asked for the 'reduction in public spending', we'd got sucked in by what was the current dominant thinking, even in left-wing circles. It was a contamination . . . Not surprising in a bunch of prisoners drafting documents. But, anyway, there was the strategic bit: the Constituent Assembly. And the important bit: to develop a process of transition which would lead to a far-reaching programme of popular education designed to include the population in the planning, preparation and implementation

---

12 *La Misión Mercal* (Mercal Mission, or Food Market) is one of the social programmes launched by the Bolivarian government. Officially created on 24 April 2003, it is aimed at the food distribution sector. The programme consists of providing stores and supermarkets with basic foodstuffs at low prices, accessible to the poorest sectors of the population. These foodstuffs are subsidised and there is no middleman, so they are between 30 and 45 per cent cheaper than those from other distribution chains.

of the various projects governing the transition. The aim was to revise the letter of intent signed with international financial organisms for payment of the external debt. In short, we were proposing a real revolution.

How do you conceive of revolution?

I think a revolution should be something very practical. One of the mistakes made by many attempts at revolution in the past was to get bogged down in theory. People gave too much weight to elaborating the theory, and not enough to the practical dimension. And I think a revolution needs to work hard at the dialectical, theoretical aspect, of course, but also at the praxis. What's more, I believe that the praxis is without a doubt what makes a true revolution. It's the 'transformative praxis' that changes a reality. At least that's been our experience here, in Venezuela, since 1999.

What is socialism, for you?

Rómulo Gallegos famously wrote: 'Llanura venezolana, toda horizontes como la esperanza, toda caminos como la voluntad' [Venezuelan llanos, made of horizons, like hope, made of paths, like resolve]. For me, socialism is like the Venezuelan plains: an endless horizon, an endless path, like our will, our resolve, our determination. And I add, our socialism must be our own invention.

In what sense?

In the sense that, as history shows us, there are many socialisms, and Venezuela or Venezuelan society has its own unique features. We don't want to apply dogmas conceived for other situations, in other contexts. What we are inventing – here and now – is a way of bringing two things together: on the one hand a new type of socialism, on the other a rapidly mutating Venezuelan society. A way of matching them up dialectically so that they modify each other reciprocally. That double transformation, which is under way, is what we call the Bolivarian Revolution.

On that point, I'd like to know what relationship you are estab-
lishing between the Bolivarian Revolution, socialism and
national independence? Because you also talk a lot about
'national' character and the importance of the Armed Forces.

Let me try and relate those three concepts. On the road to development, there comes a time when countries find themselves at a cross-
roads and have to choose between two paths: capitalism and socialism. They are the only paths that exist. We have chosen socialism.
But, as I already said, there are many varieties of socialism, and we
don't want to copy any socialist model, we want to invent our own.
I'm not a theoretician, I'm not Lenin, or Marx, or Mariátegui. But
I like studying, reading, thinking, and I've begun to develop some
ideas of my own, inspired by great Venezuelan, Latin American,
and global intellectuals. For example, Simón Bolívar, a great pre-
socialist thinker; Simón Rodríguez who wrote that wonderful work
Treatise on Social Lights and Virtues, where he criticizes capitalism,
speculators, and sets out ideas that are fundamental to a socialist
project in South America; or the Brazilian José Ignacio Abreu e
Lima, another prodigious socialist.[13] And obviously Christ, the true
Christ, the revolutionary, the greatest socialist of all.

Christ's message is socialist?

Authentic Christianity is one of the major sources of socialist morality. Socialist values are summed up in one of Christ's command-
ments: 'Love thy neighbour as thyself. Love one another.' Socialism's
supreme value is love. Capitalism is synonymous with ambition,
egoism; that's why brothers can hate each other, they stop being
brothers because one exploits the other. In capitalism, human
beings are regarded as objects or products. The motto of capitalism
is 'Each man for himself!' Whereas the socialist motto would be 'All
for one. United like brothers.' Love against hate. The socialist ethic
should determine the way the new revolutionary citizen behaves.
We have to transform the human spirit. 'Without transforming the

---

13   José Ignacio Abreu e Lima (1794–1869), a Brazilian general who played an active
part beside Simón Bolívar in the Independence Wars in Greater Colombia.

spirit,' said Trotsky, 'man cannot transform himself.' It's the only way to become the 'new man' that Che Guevara called for; twenty-first-century socialist man, or of course woman. In fact, there can be no revolution if we are not able to transform the spirit. All the rest is secondary, no matter how important. That's why I conceive socialism to be, above all, moral. It can't be just an economic model, it would lose its soul.

And the social?

Well, of course, there is also 'social socialism', if you'll excuse the redundancy, based on the struggle for equality, for a 'society of equals', the luminous concept of pure socialism coined by Bolívar at Angostura. All the missions we have launched – the figure has risen to thirty in these past few years – represent the essence of social socialism. Their main aim is to raise the people out of poverty and bring about equality, not only in the eyes of the law, but also in practice. This has allowed us to build a social shield which protects the most vulnerable and helps them out of extreme poverty.

So you see Bolivarian socialism as having two dimensions: moral and social.

No, there are more dimensions. As well as moral and social, our socialism has other components: especially, obviously, the economic and political. Economic socialism is nationalization of the strategic sectors of the economy; development of coopera-tives; participation of workers at all levels of organization and management of enterprises, state banks, etc. Where does political socialism lie? In democracy. Not bourgeois or liberal democracy, but the 'participative and protagonistic' democracy defined by our Constitution.

Are there other components?

Yes, our socialism also has a territorial dimension. We talk about 'geographic socialism' because there are territorial injustices in Venezuela, inequalities in development depending on the region.

And we need a more radical, dynamic, transformative vision of our geography. Territory is not something static; we have to imagine a territorial socialism.

And finally, in my view, our socialism also has a military component: military socialism. The Armed Forces participate in building the national project, alongside the people; that is, not only underwriting the national project but effectively building it hand in hand with the people, in a close civilian–military partnership. It's the only way national independence – the third concept – is possible. It was never possible within the framework of dependent capitalism, the only capitalism Venezuela has ever seen. We were condemned to the indignity of being a dominated, dependent, corrupt country: a colony. That's all over now.

And corruption?

We have always combatted it with the utmost severity. During our years in Yare, we elaborated a concrete plan to bring the corrupt to book, eliminate corruption, and restore ethical behaviour in all aspects of life.

I keep a close eye on the people who work with me, on ministers, institutions, state banks, etc. They may have their faults, and there may be the odd disgraceful case, but I can guarantee that corruption has declined, there's no comparison.

With the previous level of corruption?

Absolutely, there's no possible comparison. Look, right here in the Miraflores Palace there used to be a courtyard called 'the Japanese suite', it was famous. All kinds of fiestas, business deals, champagne, whisky, women . . . It was Sodom and Gomorra. Don't forget I worked here for the last few months of 1988 and most of 1989, I had access to everything, I watched and listened, I had an internal network of military officers and civilians. Until I was forced out of here, accused of plotting to kill Carlos Andrés, I've already told you . . . Corruption reached to the very summit of the state, I can assure you.

It seems, however, that there is still quite of lot of corruption in the Customs.

Customs . . . Probably still some corruption there but the military run it now, and there's much less likely to be corruption among army officers. Although, yes, there's the Baduel case, and others that are still being investigated.[14] In the past, though, corruption in the military was a matter of arms deals commissions. That's all under control now.

Going back to your years in prison, 1992–1994; you talked before about the 'threat of civil war'. Did that danger really exist?

Of course it existed. We were convinced that if the Bolivarian military and the grass-roots organizations didn't join forces, and if minority oligarchic interests continued to dominate, the process of violent social conflict would be unstoppable, and would result in a terrible spiral that could effectively plunge the country into a bloody civil war. That's how we explained it then to the press and in various texts we published. We warned them that new uprisings were coming.

Were you aware of the preparations for the 27 November [1992] rebellion?

That second rebellion was inevitable from the moment that a blind and senseless government refused to undertake the necessary reforms. And not just the government, for behind it stood the United States and its military mission, giving orders to our Military High Command. And there too stood the rancid oligarchy, which obviously didn't want any reforms at all, had no wish for a Constituent Assembly or any structural economic changes. They did not even look at the programme we proposed.

---

14   Raúl Isaías Baduel (1955–), one of the four founders with Hugo Chávez of the MBR-200. He was commander in chief of the Venezuelan Army from January 2004 to July 2006, and minister of defence from June 2006 to July 2007. On 7 May 2010 a Caracas court sentenced him to seven years and eleven months for 'for the undue appropriation of 30 million bolívars and 3.9 million dollars' during his term as a minister.

Because that petty-yankee oligarchy – as I now call it – controlled our international reserves, the Central Bank, the state banks, the huge weapons purchases, all the import deals . . . Yet little by little, almost all the rest of the country began to demand changes. Even the government's own party [Acción Democrática], maybe because of its instinct for survival, began to talk of the need to revise the IMF's package of shock measures. But Carlos Andrés didn't want to do it, he couldn't do it, his hands were tied.

By the international financial institutions?
Yes, the IMF, the World Bank, the Venezuelan business class. They refused to backtrack on privatization, wage freezes, deregulation of the price of petrol, energy, food, etc. That attitude, that blindness, made the movement that led to the second rebellion inevitable. We started to feel the cracks internally.

Within the Bolivarian Movement?
Yes, a group of *compañeros* – I'm not mentioning any names – maintained that what we'd done by force of arms was done, and that there was no point in a second rebellion. We had very respectful debates, but outside influences were at work.

What influences?
Left-wing groups infiltrating the prisons via the families of certain officers or via direct contact with others. They were only thinking of the next gubernatorial elections, the next presidential ones. A new uprising didn't suit them at all. They hadn't wanted the 4 February rebellion, let alone a second armed movement. They wanted to ride the wave to the next electoral process and, well, take their seats . . .

But did you know precise details of what was being prepared?
Yes, we always knew. The majority of *compañeros* in Yare prison supported a second rebellion. We appointed a liaison man to communicate with the *compañeros* in San Carlos, Commanders Joel

Acosta, Jesús Urdaneta, etc; Captains Ronald Blanco La Cruz, Edgar Hernández Behrens, etc; Lieutenant Diosdado Cabello and all the others.

The liaison did his work with that uniformed group, and with some civilians as well, members of the MBR-200 who had contacts with political organizations. That's how we learned that a new rebellion would erupt, in principle, in July. It was even called the '5 July Movement', Venezuelan Independence Day.

Who was leading it?
The new leaders were higher-ranking than we were; admirals, generals . . . And they began acting hierarchically, without taking into account the political variables and the collective imagination. They didn't understand that Commanders Arias, Urdaneta, Chávez, etc., were not just lieutenant colonels; we were also a political reference point for the people.

Did that cause problems?
Obviously. Because it was divisive. A group of army officers – lieutenants, captains – decided not to join that movement, and pulled out.

Why?
Because in a meeting in Caracas with senior officers, some subalterns asked, 'What do we do with the commanders who are prisoners in Yare?' And a senior officer, a right-wing infiltrator, replied in a very clumsy, disrespectful way: 'A prisoner's first name is Prisoner and his surname is Padlock.' They didn't like that. Our boys – who were starting to call themselves 'Chavistas' – decided to pull out and try to create a separate movement.

And another, third group appeared, who were very radical – or rather, their ideas were far removed from ours – and wanted to kill the president. They had the plan ready: they were going to fire a rocket at Carlos Andrés Pérez on 5 July. They were decent officers, but their mindset was anarchic. Fortunately we put an end to that madness.

The new uprising was planned for July. Why was it postponed until November?

At first it was July. Admiral Grüber Odremán, with his prestige and seniority, was gradually taking over the 5 July Movement. But the commander of the operation for the Air Force was General Visconti Osorio, and we knew him. Our officer friends in there were Luis Reyes Reyes and Castro Soteldo, they were permanently in touch with us. Preparations for the rebellion dragged on, July passed, August passed, September passed and at one time we thought it wasn't going to happen.

Finally, in October, things took off again. Navy units joined, political groups joined, civilian groups joined, including Bandera Roja [Red Flag], despite my warning it might cause trouble because the group was so infiltrated.

Did you have information about that?

Yes, we knew it was infiltrated. So, for us, it was no surprise to discover on 27 November that government forces were ready and waiting for the uprising. I remember how days earlier my son Hugo came running into my cell, it was a Thursday . . . 27 November, what day of the week was that?

Friday.

Well, the previous day, then, my son Hugo, who was ten, came to visit me. They searched family members very carefully. He dodged the search and came running towards my cell with a guard in hot pursuit. I grabbed Hugo, shielded him and said to the guard, 'Don't you touch my son!' The guard went away and I took Hugo into my cell. The kid took an object out of his trousers: 'Look what they've sent you!' It was a small radio, a transmitter, to communicate with on a particular frequency. He also gave me a note: '27 at dawn, 5 a.m.' Luis Reyes Reyes sent it. So we were sure that was the day. We had the information. I told the others. But we couldn't do anything, we didn't have a single weapon, nothing.

They didn't think about getting you out?
Yes, a rescue was planned. A group of civilians and soldiers was
going to attack the Yare prison and rescue us. They planned to take
us to Caracas in a helicopter to join the rebellion. On one of the
mornings leading up to the uprising, I was studying the plan. I
looked out at the yard and thought, 'Getting us out of here will be
hard.' Because the National Guard had reinforced the area around
the prison, right up to some nearby hills, and surrounded it with
minefields. Extreme security. Dangerous tension.

It sounds like mission impossible. Were you afraid?
At one particular moment that morning I sighed deeply and told
myself, 'Afraid? Of what? What will be will be.' From that moment,
I've never been afraid of death. My physical integrity? Of no interest. The important thing was the cause, our mission, saving the
country, helping the people, social justice.

And what happened? Why didn't they rescue you?
On the night of 26 to 27 November 1992, we didn't sleep. I was on
a folding chair. We were dressed in fatigues, we weren't armed but we
were on the lookout and ready, from five in the morning, with the
radio on. Five o'clock passed, five-thirty . . . We were getting anxious.
Nothing happened. It was almost six when news began to filter out
on the radio: 'Troop movements have been seen around La Carlota
airport; some military vehicles; the government says there are no
problems . . .' We said, 'It's underway!' But then, astounded, we
heard the following: 'Commander Hugo Chávez is on television
talking to the nation.' And on came the voice, the audio.

How weird!
Shameless manipulation. It was an old video.

How did they do it?
I'll tell you. In the prison we had a clandestine recording system
with a miniature camera. We sent out a lot of recorded messages.
And once – through my then wife, Nancy – I sent a recorded

message to a journalist in the Dominican Republic, in which I appeared, in uniform of course, with the MBR-200 flag behind me. The tape was banned. What's more, the Dominican government protested strongly to Venezuela, because on the tape I was addressing Dominican soldiers, invoking the name of Colonel Caamaño, and telling them that in Venezuela a new insurrection was coming and that we were supporting it. And I called on the soldiers' commitment, etc. It was a video in favour of the new insurrection, in support, so that people abroad would know . . .

I recorded that video in June, and in July there was no insurrection, as I told you, not until November. So I recognized it immediately. I was more surprised than anyone. I said to Arias Cárdenas, 'Hey, why is that video on?' But anyway, it was aired and repeated, over and over again. At first people thought it was live. Then a group of young civilians came on television – one of them became famous as the 'man in the pink shirt' – using very aggressive, threatening language, inciting the people to get knives, guns . . . Practically calling for civil war.

They were making you responsible?
Right, that was used in the worst possible way by the government to destroy me, physically and morally.

So tell me, meanwhile, did the attack on Yare prison happen or not?
Yes, the attack on Yare happened. The mortar and grenade attack began a few minutes later. It was a serious battle. But they didn't manage to rescue us. I remember them ramming one *compañero*'s face against the fence, he lost an eye. Midway through the morning, our people withdrew, they couldn't get inside. We heard it all on the radio. By the afternoon, we learned the rebellion had failed. The leaders surrendered.

They negotiated exile in Peru, didn't they?
Yes, General Visconti with a hundred men. Luis Reyes escorted Visconti's Hercules in his F-16 fighter plane because President

Pérez had given orders to shoot the insurgents down. So, Luis and other pilots escorted the Hercules to Iquitos, in the Peruvian Amazon, on the frontier with Brazil. Then they came back and surrendered too. The rebellion was mostly by the Air Force, with one or two Navy units. The Army hardly participated. The masses didn't come out into the streets either. Only a few small political groups, more cadres than masses. Then the manipulation of the situation started.

In what way?
In the sense that I got blamed for the disaster. And for the deaths, because there were many more deaths than on 4 February. Rebel planes fired missiles, even bombed the Miraflores Palace. And people began to say the defeat was my fault. Even some of our own prisoners in Yare were saying it. Victims of the video manipulation. They said I'd planned a coup within the coup. Even though I wrote, explained, sent letters . . . It was no use, they weren't having any of it. Because the admirals and generals, in their gala uniforms, had also secretly recorded a message to the country. That was the one that should have been broadcast.

And not yours.
And not mine. Not either of mine, I should say, because in fact there were two.

How do you mean, two?
One of the great unanswered questions about the 27 November events is the following: why were two videos with my messages broadcast, instead of the recording made by Admirals Grüber and Cabrera, General Visconti and other senior Army and National Guard officers? These said the video they'd recorded was to be the key to success. That wasn't true either, but anyway.

Broadcasting their video was crucial to explaining 27-N?
Yes, because they represented the four components of the Armed Forces – Army, Navy, Air Force and National Guard – and each of

the senior officers made separate speeches. But it wasn't broadcast. Chávez appeared instead [laughter].

Where did those videos of you come from?

The first we recorded as a test, but we stopped because there was a fly circling around me. It gave rise to lots of jokes about 'Chávez's fly' and 'Chávez's corpse' . . . [laughter]. The second, shorter, video they made from the one I told you about, the one we'd made for the Dominican Republic, even before we'd established contact with the group directing the 27-N operations. When the MBR-200 was still thinking about leading a new uprising itself.

Who was responsible for broadcasting those videos?

At first we thought it might have been military intelligence infiltration by the DIM or the DISIP. But I later found out the truth: certain soldiers, infiltrated by Bandera Roja, decided to broadcast my videos precisely because the senior officers who were leading the 27-N rebellion did not recognize Bolivarianism. It was intended to create political tensions. They made the decision after they'd taken over Channel 8. When they took control of the airwaves, they managed to link up all the TV stations, because they had the engineers, plus inside support. Then those shits decided to play my videos.

That group behaved totally irresponsibly, not to say criminally. Not only did they kill a policeman at Channel 8, they also executed people at La Carlota airport. A truly fascist attitude. And they accused me of all that! In the press, on television . . .

There was also another accusation. They blamed me for having diverted land troops towards Yare to liberate us. They said the central command didn't have enough land support because their reinforcements had gone to liberate us first, giving priority to the attack on Yare. This accusation kept being repeated. And it's not at all what happened. What happened was that the Army officers didn't trust the overall command structure, and disobeying its orders, decided to go to Yare. They attacked it with a group of university students. The truth was, the 27-N central command didn't want to see me get out, but those soldiers did. We had no idea about this clash of interests. And they accused me!

Exactly what responsibility did you have in 27-N?

Look, I told you, it's obvious I was linked to 27-N. It was impossible for me not to be. And that's what I claimed in a document I published, entitled *La verdad que conocemos* [The Truth We Know]. I want to stress one thing: the MBR-200 did not participate in the strategic decision-making process; we weren't in on the general plan of action. Nevertheless, we wanted to keep faith with our commitment. That's why, even when the movement was betrayed on the night of Thursday, 26 November, which meant all the land units were immobilized, some of our men went out to fight, and several died. Others ended up in prison, and a large group went underground. So, the accusations against me were totally unfair. A group of my own *compañeros* even sent me some terrible letters. For the first time, I felt unjustly accused of something that for me was very serious – disloyalty – and of being the sole cause of a defeat for which I was not responsible. But that was the line: get rid of Chávez at all costs, Chávez the 'ambitious', the 'self-promoter', the 'caudillo'.

So, if I understand correctly, you're telling me that not only the government but also part of the Left and even your own compañeros *lent themselves to this stigmatization, in order to ruin your reputation and destroy you morally.*

Exactly. The movement that led the 27-N rebellion was divided. It was an amalgam of forces that had only come together at that juncture, for that purpose. It lacked a clear political direction. The officers in command were not very strong, nor was there the kind of structure we had for 4 February. In other words, there were pro-Chávez and anti-Chávez forces; the Left and the Right; moderates, and extremists both Left and Right; and lastly the infiltrators. And one of the missions of that last group was to destroy me morally. I'm not blaming anybody, it was the product of the circumstances.

How did you react?

Faced with the magnitude of the doubts of some of my good friends and *compañeros*, and the way the facts had been manipulated, I withdrew into my cell. I hardly went out. I just studied, wrote and meditated with Major Alastre López; like the good *compañero* he had always been, he stayed with me. And, well, I waited for news of the exit of Carlos Andrés Pérez. Deep inside, I began to prepare myself for future responsibilities. I started to think about having to leave there one day, when all the doubts would be resolved.

Inside the prison, there was tremendous frustration. It was clear there would be no more rebellions, and hopes of being freed from Yare in the short term were dashed. Although that wasn't what worried me particularly. I concentrated on philosophy and meditation. They were my days in the wilderness, and the wilderness was good for me personally because I took refuge in books.

Do you remember any of the books you read?

Some of them had a profound effect on me. For example, one which set out the findings of the South Commission, a commission presided over by Julius Nyerere.[15] Of course, when it was published in 1991 [Spanish edition], the Soviet Union was collapsing and the so-called Third World was fading out. So those findings remained in aspic. But it's a very good book, and I always carry it with me even now. I reread and take notes. Twenty years on, its extraordinary proposals are more valid than ever. It's what inspired my *Sur* [South] theme, which I used for Telesur, Banco del Sur, Petrosur . . .

I also read, at that same time, Fidel Castro's *History Will Absolve Me*, the famous defence he made at his trial after the attack on the Moncada barracks on 26 July 1953.

Those books were useful in my search for a practical knowledge, suited to the times we were living in. From my point of view, that

---

15 *The Challenge to the South*, Report of the South Commission, OUP, Oxford, 1990; Julius K. Nyerere (1922–1999), one of the main leaders of the struggle for African independence. President of Tanzania from 1964 to 1985.

'prison of dignity' was essential; it was an obligatory transit camp I had to pass through. It was also an oven.

An oven?
Where our revolution really started to heat up. And do you know what other book helped me to understand that?

Which?
This one! [He shows it to me.] Nietzsche's *Thus Spake Zarathustra*. This copy kept me company in my cell. General Pérez Arcay sent it to me in September 1993. And look which sentence I've under-lined: 'The noble man wants to create new things and new virtue. But the other hangs on to the old and tries to perpetuate it.'

Were you allowed all sorts of books?
Yes. There were no restrictions at all until 27 November. After that, they took everything away. The lot! Even the pencils! My cell in Yare had been like an office, I'd had a typewriter, a small library and a filing case, the sort that looks like a paper accordion. I kept my things very tidy. I even had a secretary, Major Alastre López. A very cultured young man, well-read, studious, organized; more than a few of our documents are written by him. He helped me answer letters, and stood by me during those dark days when I felt more alone than at any point in my whole life. It was a tough time, I had nothing to read and nowhere to write. Because I'd been writing a diary in my cell, I wrote poems, I even painted pictures.

Is that where you painted your portrait of Ezequiel Zamora?
No, I did that painting of Zamora in 1991, shortly before the 4-F rebellion. It was inspired by a portrait of Bolívar. And I added a caption: 'Land and free men, general elections, horror to the oligar-chy'. I'm not very good at frontal faces, that's why I mostly paint profiles. I'm useless. I've tried to paint Fidel but so far without success. I couldn't get him how I wanted him. It's a gift that's hang-ing fire . . . In prison I painted a nocturnal scene; it's called *Moon of Yare*. But after they stripped our cells, I couldn't even paint.

They took everything?
About a hundred guards burst in, threw a whole load of tear gas down our very narrow corridor, beat us up and dragged us along the floor. Alastre almost died asphyxiated. They took all our papers. Just as well that, fearing they would search our cells, I'd burned many compromising documents the previous night. Carlos Andrés Pérez even ordered the guard to take our uniforms. 'Hand over your uniform!' one colonel shouted at me. I categorically refused. I said, 'You'll have to kill me to get it off.' I had a tube beside me. I picked it up, and warned him, 'You'll have to shoot me! Because I'm going to hit you with this, Colonel. We have dignity here.' They didn't know what to do, none of them dared tackle us outright to get our uniforms off. They sent some generals, and they finally had to give in: 'Alright, keep your uniform.' They asked for our red berets. I didn't accept that either: 'I'm not handing it over.' So, I left the cell with my uniform on, the same one I had on during the rebellion. I've got it hanging up over there as a keepsake.

How long did those reading and writing restrictions last?
Until January 1993. Then they began to be more lenient. Because Carlos Andrés was on his way out . . .

When did he finally go?
Well, he'd survived two military uprisings: ours of 4 February 1992, and the other of 27 November that same year, which was ferocious. Like I said, they bombed buildings of the major institutions, took control of key barracks, and captured the television channels. Carlos Andrés responded by stepping up the repression, which together with his disastrous ultra-liberal shock programme, made him the most unpopular president ever. He hid from his electorate. His own Acción Democrática party did their political sums and decided to withdraw their support. Right there, in Congress, they accused him of corruption. And he left office in June 1993.[16] In reality, it was an agreement.

---

16   The historian Ramón J. Velásquez took over the presidency until the end of the original mandate in January 1994.

An agreement?

Yes, the system got rid of Pérez to lower the tension. It was an agreement with his own party, because he refused to resign and they threw him out. They were looking for a pretext and they uncovered the trail of a thousand incidents of corruption: in particular, money that Pérez had sent to Violeta Chamorro of Nicaragua.[17] So they found him guilty of corruption and sentenced him to just two years, no more, and he didn't go to prison, he just stayed at home.

I interviewed him there in 1995, in his imposing residence in the hills of East Caracas, and he was on fine form.[18]

In such fine form that he stood for election again. The day I took office [January 1999], Carlos Andrés was in the front row as senator-elect. He won a seat in the Senate of the last Congress before it disappeared with the Constituent Assembly. He was senator for a year. And he stood for the Constituent Assembly as well.

While you were president?

Yes. In reality, the dominant political class threw Pérez out to try and reduce the pressure. He was no longer any use to the political and financial elites, so they simply decided to drop him and let him fall into the abyss of history for evermore. It was all manipulated. They sacrificed Pérez to preserve the system. Among other things, they said they had saved democracy. I remember the then attorney general, Ramón Escobar Salom – whom Rómulo Betancourt, who could be biting, once called 'a little tub of shit' – used to introduce himself as a 'hero of democracy', because he was the one who had convicted Pérez. When in fact it was a stitch-up among themselves, and the attorney general was part of the chorus. Pérez went back home with all his political rights intact. He was rich and maintained his share of power. He kept on governing through the many

---

17   Violeta Barrios de Chamorro (1929–), president of Nicaragua from 1990 to 1996.

18   See Ramonet, 'Le Venezuela vers la guerre sociale?'

people he had in key positions. The public knew all this. They were turbulent, nauseating times. As I said, a possible coup d'état from the Right was mooted, to be carried out by the Army High Command who were toying with the idea of a 'saviour coup', given the situation in the country.

What did you do when they dismissed Carlos Andrés?
When Carlos Andrés fell, we put out a press release saying that this wasn't the solution. That the system had simply shucked off a burden that no longer served any purpose, it had got rid of a dead weight. But the structural problems of the system were still there.

They appointed Ramón J. Velásquez, a much respected figure, you told me.
Yes, undeniably a venerable character. He arrived to take the helm, or at least to paddle the boat along, until the elections of 1993 which Rafael Caldera won.

I met Caldera during his first months as president. He had read some of my books and invited me to a Communications conference in Caracas, which he himself chaired. He described himself as an opponent of* pensée unique *and was critical of ultraliberalism. That discourse surprised me somewhat, coming from the former leader of the Christian Democrats.
Yes, very surprising, but he'd evolved. Caldera was politically dead. And he came back to life on 4-F when, with considerable cunning, he made a great speech in Congress justifying our rebellion. It contained the famous sentence, 'It's difficult to ask the people to sacrifice themselves for freedom and democracy, when they consider freedom and democracy incapable of feeding them or preventing the exorbitant rise in the cost of living; and when the government has been incapable of eliminating the disease of corruption.'

He then left the party he had founded, Copei, and allied himself with the Movimiento al Socialismo (MAS). He later gave ministerial posts to some of the most emblematic leaders of MAS, notably Teodoro Petkoff, who played a very important role in Caldera's cabinet: as planning minister he promoted a package of ultra-liberal counter-reforms. Pompeyo Márquez, ex-communist and founder of MAS, was also a minister in that government. Jorge Giordani, on the other hand, refused to be a part of it.

You had asked people to abstain in those elections, hadn't you?
The Bolivarian Movement was split over those elections. One group supported Caldera. Myself and another group were implacable. We said, 'This isn't the solution.' And more than asking people not to vote, we distanced ourselves from Caldera without denouncing his programme. But abstention won, at 40 per cent, when it was usually 20–25 per cent. Caldera only got 30 per cent of the vote. In fact, none of the candidates came out with a clear majority. The difference between Caldera and the others was minimal. Claudio Fermín, of AD, got 23.6 per cent; Oswaldo Álvarez Paz, of Copei, got 22.7 per cent; and Andrés Velásquez, of La Causa R, got 21.9 per cent. Winning by so small a margin, Caldera did not have a majority in Congress and his government was shackled, at the expense of alliances.

Do you think that what really allowed Caldera to win the elections was having 'understood' the 4 February rebellion?
I don't have the slightest doubt. That attitude brought him the extra votes he needed for victory. Because Caldera rode our wave and our discourse. So did Aristóbulo Istúriz and La Causa R. Above all, Aristóbulo. But Andrés Velásquez as a candidate, and La Causa R as a party, also managed to get the people to associate them with us. They manipulated them with a video, some speeches . . . I had a few run-ins with some of them almost immediately, because I didn't like this attempted manipulation. It was never open warfare, however, because we saw them as allies.

But you told me they didn't join in the 4 February rebellion?
That's right. But we still saw them as allies, despite their pretty irresponsible decision to back out of the rebellion without even telling us. Only Alí Rodríguez turned up, saying, 'Well, I'm here, even if my party decided not to come with me.' From then on I started

withholding information, so they didn't know about our action until it actually happened on 4 February. They learned of it at the same time as everybody else. André Velásquez, who was governor of the state of Bolívar and one of the most important leaders of La Causa R, came straight out with a statement to the press, calling us 'a bunch of petty dictators'. What a jerk! And he nearly betrayed us, because knowing that we were preparing an uprising, he told Carlos Andrés there was going to be a 'coup d'état'. The president asked him who was organizing it, and he said, 'Some commanders.' Carlos Andrés shrugged it off: 'Oh, not to worry, then. They'll forget it when they're promoted to general.' He thought all soldiers were corrupt.

Which wasn't altogether untrue . . .
Maybe not, but he didn't understand that a new generation was arriving on the scene, which wanted to wipe away that image and be worthy of the example set by Simón Bolívar.

And do you think the people instinctively understood that?
Yes, I told you, the people's instinct. Because the image of those military officers was abhorrent. But the general public understood that 4 February had unleashed a real cyclone. A moral, ethical, and also political, cyclone of faith and hope; it was almost religious in some way. Even mythical. There was talk of the 'Chávez myth'. I refused to be a myth! I still refuse.

But a Chávez myth really was created. The 'saviour' of the people, to a certain extent.
Yes, there was a sort of mythical, messianic, element. It reflected a whole tradition of caudillos, after all. But anyway, more to the point, 4-F was the awakening of the 'expansive, explosive forces', as another good book that accompanied me in prison put it. Written by a Venezuelan philosopher, Isaac J. Pardo, with a prologue by García Bacca, *Fire beneath the Water: The Invention of Utopia*, a marvellous book.[19]

---

19   Isaac J. Pardo, *Fuego bajo el agua. La invención de la utopía*, Fundación Biblioteca Ayacucho, Caracas, 1990.

That event was so mighty, it unleashed an energy that's defined the direction of Venezuela all these years. And what's more, over and above my person and the role I'm playing, I'm absolutely certain – and I hope I'm right and it will be a force for good – that for many years to come, the presidents who follow me will also be a product of that event. Because it was an event that blew lids off, that opened doors, that revealed new horizons.

The years have passed – a decade already! – and that date is still a watershed. Because it marked the beginning of a new historical cycle, not only in contemporary Venezuelan history, but in the history of progressive movements in Latin America and around the globe. What's more, dare I say it, on that day a new revolutionary era began.

What happened in those last months in Yare prison?

After the exit of Carlos Andrés, I got them to let me finish my Master's in Political Science. You may remember that I still had my thesis to do; I'd been prevented from finishing it as a punishment. So, I applied in writing to the Ministry of Defence. With the help of friends, lawyers and university professors, I managed to get the rector of the University to endorse my application, on grounds of the right to study.

The new interim president, Ramón Velásquez, finally gave me permission. I chose Jorge Giordani as my supervisor. He accepted, and came to the prison every Thursday afternoon from two to three. He's like an Englishman, you tell him a time and he arrives on the dot. A highly disciplined man, a great *compañero*, a great friend.

Did he teach you one to one?

No, other *compañeros* came, we had a sort of school. We began working on the theme of transition politics. I remember reading a lot of books by the Hungarian economist István Mészáros.[20]

---

20   István Mészáros (1930–), Hungarian Marxist philosopher and professor of social sciences, a disciple of Georg Lukács. He fled Hungary in 1956 after the Budapest uprising against the Soviet invasion. Author of, among many other books, *Beyond Capital: Toward a Theory of Transition* (1995). Professor Emeritus at Sussex University, UK.

Giordani and he knew each other, and I realized there was some professional rivalry between them. Because, with all due respect, he made some comments about Mészáros's ideas [on transition] that I didn't agree with. Giordani helped me to work in a more organized, disciplined way. I spent my days at the typewriter composing my thesis. He guided me, and brought me material.

They allowed him to carry documents back and forth without any problem?
No. They searched everything, in and out. I once asked him to take stuff out for me, but he said, 'Commander, you know they're watching me. I mustn't carry any papers . . .'

So, he didn't take any documents out, except for occasional manuscripts I asked him to put on his computer. And he sent a paper I'd written to István Mészáros, who was about to publish his *Beyond Capital*, about the theory of transition. If you look in that book, around page eight hundred and something, he quotes from the MBR-200 proposal for Venezuela.

Why didn't you present your thesis?
Something happened, I don't remember exactly what it was . . . They stopped Giordani coming, I think it was because of some statements I'd made. Since I was a soldier, they kept reminding me, in writing, of the Army rule prohibiting me from making public statements. I wrote to the minister of defence and the military chiefs, saying, 'I'm a prisoner, what more can you do to me? So I consider myself free to say whatever I wish.' [Laughter.]

They couldn't punish you any further.
Sometimes they stopped my visits. On one occasion I went three months without a visit, I didn't see my wife or my children, nobody. When they banned Giordani, it was because of a clash I had with the High Command. They stopped him coming. They searched my study-cell, and removed everything I had. My books, and the manuscript of my thesis that never appeared.

Had you got very far?

Pretty far, I'd written a lot of pages and had defined a general approach to transition. When they took it, we were just working on the topic of the Constituent Assembly. Giordani was helping me find material on different models of Assembly. That's how I got my hands on Toni Negri's book, *Constituent Power and the Modern State*.[21] He takes a pretty hard position, but his approach to constituent power is very good. And we were starting to go over Rousseau's theses again, and the same with Bolívar and the Congress of Angostura, the foundational power of the Republic.

You finally left prison in March 1994.

Yes. Rafael Caldera recognized his political debt to us, and when he began his mandate [January 1994], he ordered the release of the soldiers involved in the two 1992 rebellions. Right at the end, the last month, they took me to Caracas Military Hospital, for a political task.

What task?

Help convince several *compañeros* who had doubts about leaving jail. Some of them didn't want to be released in such circumstances. They said it to me too: 'It's best if you stay in prison, because you're a symbol.' They didn't understand that we had to go out and join the fray. I talked it over with those *compañeros*, one by one. One even got angry and called me a traitor, because I was negotiating. I told him, 'I'm not negotiating anything, but we have to weigh things up. Do we want to stay here? Till when? Or do we leave with our heads held high?' In the end, they were all persuaded. I was freed on the night before Easter Sunday, on 26 March 1994.

What lesson did you learn from those years in prison?

We can divide that stay in the 'prison of dignity' – two years and a few months – into several stages, and all of them were characterized,

---

21   Antonio Negri, *Insurgencies: Constituent Power and the Modern State* (1992), University of Minnesota Press, Minneapolis, 1999.

from beginning to end, by a huge intellectual effort, by studying. I learned more in prison than I'd learned in the whole of my previous life. Not only on the scientific knowledge front, but also about my own ability to face what lay ahead.

15

The Victorious Campaign

When you were released, did you carry on in the military?
No, that was one of the conditions of my release: I had to resign from the Army. The government insisted.

But I remember a photo on the day you left prison, and you were in uniform . . .
No, it wasn't a military uniform, it was a beige *liqui-liqui*. I began

to wear the *liqui-liqui*, which is our national costume, but when it's beige or green it looks like a uniform. I had four *liqui-liquis*, blue, green, beige and black: a gift from friends in Maracay who knew an amazing tailor who made stylish *liqui-liquis* of good material to measure. And I wore short boots; the whole thing was like a uniform. I'd worked it out. At public events, I was 'in uniform': t-shirt, *liqui-liqui* and red beret. I started wearing a tie when I became a presidential candidate in 1998, my advisers recommended it. Ridiculous really.

Did the government plan your release from prison so there wouldn't be a crowd waiting outside?

Exactly. It was delayed until midday on 26 March 1994, the Saturday before Easter, when everybody was on holiday. The government did it deliberately so my release would attract the least possible media attention. I had this crazy plan: go to the furthest point in the savannah and set off from there on a long march to Caracas. My friends persuaded me it might not be the best thing to do.

So how did you leave prison?

I was transferred from Yare to the Military Hospital for my last fifteen days because of an eye infection. I waited there to be released. I made two demands of the emissaries who negotiated the conditions of my release. First, I wanted to go to the Military Academy in uniform before signing the army discharge forms. They accepted. I went alone, no media or anything, accompanied by General Raúl Salazar. Second, I wanted to be the last to leave. All of us who were left were released. Them first, me the day after. When it was my turn, they came for me in a military pick-up truck. It was like a bit of me died. I asked to be left alone for a moment in the Academy parade ground, a magical place. I walked around, meditated at the foot of Bolívar's statue, and wept at the thought of my military career ending, aware that a phase of my life was over. I finally signed the discharge form, took off my uniform and put on the *liqui-liqui*. They drove me to the exit, I got out of the pick-up at the

checkpoint, and said goodbye to my military *compañeros*. I walked
out of Fuerte Tiuna, a free man at last.

Do you remember how that first contact with freedom felt?

I remember it perfectly. It was traumatic. In front of the main gate
at Fuerte Tiuna there was an amazingly huge crowd. I couldn't
move, it was pandemonium, an avalanche of people, a tremendous commotion. It was all filmed, you should see the pictures.
And masses of journalists were waiting for me as well. They'd put
up a table for me to give a press conference . . . It was impossible.
The crowd climbed over the table, motorbikes broke the cables,
people wanted to touch me, embrace me. They ripped my *liqui-
liqui*. In the middle of this confusion I got into a van someone
provided, but the crowd tore a door off. I was carried away on
their shoulders.

From there I went to do an interview with José Vicente Rangel at
Televén. He'd invited me to record a special programme to be
broadcast that same evening. I was with Adán, Cilia [Flores], the
Otaiza brothers [Juan Carlos and Eliécer], Nicolás [Maduro] and
others. But we couldn't get into the TV station, there was such a
crush on all sides. We finally fought our way in; I changed into
another *liqui-liqui*, did the interview, and went back out into the
street.

You went to the Pantheon that same day, didn't you?

No. I went to the Pantheon the following morning, on Palm
Sunday. I also gave a press conference on the balcony of the
Atheneum. There were people everywhere, even up in the trees. The
previous evening some journalists had managed to ask me a couple
of questions, and I remember the Sunday headlines: 'Where is the
Commander going? To power!'

They weren't wrong.

They had asked, 'Aren't you going to Miraflores?' And I replied
without thinking, it just came out: 'There's nothing for me to do in
Miraflores for now, first I'm going to the catacombs with the

people.' And we went around Caracas for three days on a massive march with hundreds of flags. We went to the east, the west, Petare, Los Teques, El Valle, everywhere.

Then what did you do?
I travelled around Venezuela from end to end. Thanks to the political work we'd done in prison, by the time I came out the MBR-200 movement had organized groups all over the country. I aimed to strengthen it further, and set up MBR-200 branches in every state, town, municipality . . . forming a national command centre, with regional command groups.

What was your objective?
I wanted to confront Rafael Caldera's government, establish myself firmly as the opposition. That was my strategy. Other *compañeros*, even within the MBR-200, decided to ally with the government with an eye on the next elections. Not me. I was always convinced that we had to hold firm to the idea of the Constituent Assembly and form a strong opposition.

Did various tendencies coexist within the MBR-200?
There were all sorts. In those days the Movement was a heterogeneous amalgam of groups, lines and tendencies: former guerrillas; retired soldiers of various inclinations; right-wing groups; extremists on the Left and Right. The only common denominator was the desire for rapid change, and a predisposition to nationalism. For the rest, there was no real cohesion or concrete ideology. So, my first task on leaving prison was to give the Movement structure and cohesion by reinvigorating political discussion and activism in the branches. And we unveiled a Bolivarian watchword: 'Hope in the Streets'.

Nice phrase.
We had lots of them. For instance, 'The people are Bolivarian and will triumph' and, also, simply, 'Power to the People'. We even composed songs. The idea was to encourage optimism, create a

desire for change, and flood the country with hope – but based on a concrete political programme.

Another stage of my life began. I travelled the length and breadth of Venezuela: in an old jeep, on foot, sleeping on floors, walking country paths, mountains, rivers, villages. I did whistle-stop tours from city to city. By 1997, there wasn't a state in Venezuela that didn't have a MBR-200 command group. We spread the Movement everywhere, helped by youngsters who began taking on organizational roles. Nicolás Maduro,[1] Elías Jaua,[2] Rafael Isea,[3] Jesús Aguilarte Gámez,[4] for example, came through that process. And also my bodyguards, Lieutenants Otaiza and Calatayud, and Sergeant Venero, with a couple of old pistols. They were just youngsters then; I was forty and they were barely twenty-five.

We had a platform [laughter], a small cart on wheels, very pretty, we'd decorate it with flowers and banana leaves. As soon as we'd set ourselves up, people would appear out of nowhere, on foot, on horseback. I'd talk anywhere, speeches in the main squares, press conferences, live radio . . . Day after day, without fail, all through 1994, 1995, 1996 . . .

You reactivated the 'Chávez myth'.

We've already talked about that, and I'll try and clarify my thoughts on the subject. I'll start by saying I don't believe – I've never believed – in the 'Chávez myth', and I'm sure the Venezuelan people have never seen me in that way. The support I have received from ordinary people is, in my opinion, absolutely rational. It's not the result of who knows what collective irrational beliefs. People know what

---

1   Nicolás Maduro (1962–), minister of foreign affairs from 8 August 2006 to 13 October 2012, then vice president. After Hugo Chávez died on 5 March 2013, he was appointed acting president, before winning the presidential elections of 14 April 2013.

2   Elías Jaua (1969–), PhD in sociology and Chávez's minister of agriculture, becoming vice president from 10 January 2010 to 13 October 2012. Appointed minister of foreign affairs in January 2013.

3   Rafael Isea (1968–), Military Academy graduate, governor of the state of Aragua since 5 December 2008.

4   Jesús Aguilarte Gámez (1959–2012), governor of Apure state from 2004 to 2011. He was murdered in Maracay on 2 April 2012.

they want, or to put it another way, they certainly know what they don't want. I talk to people about politics straightforwardly, using concrete, precise arguments. And I respect them. I'm not a 'social charmer', nor a 'magician' who bewitches people with trickery and artifice.

Nevertheless, you're often called a 'populist'.
Yes, it's one of the kinder descriptions my adversaries use [laughter]. But I'm more of the opinion, and I've said this many times, that certain journalists and intellectuals, distorting the collective reality, have harped on that and also on the myth thing – which amounts to the same – as a way of extinguishing the flame of rebellion that burns in the national soul. They despise the people. They think they 'don't understand', that they 'don't know', like an 'eternal child', a dependent minor, waiting for someone to lead them by the hand. They think that because the people go along with the arguments I make, they must be stupid and I'm a demagogue, a 'populist' as they call it . . .

So, there was never a 'Chávez myth'?
I'm not a myth. My adversaries might have liked me to be. I'm a reality. And I'm a more and more concrete reality every day. On the other hand, let me remind you that Aristotle said, 'Myths always have a kernel of truth'. Ethnologists know this very well, as the great Claude Lévi-Strauss demonstrated in *Tristes Tropiques*, and the Brazilian Darcy Ribeiro – advisor to Velasco Alvarado in Peru and Salvador Allende in Chile, who also lived for a time in Venezuela – in his book *The Civilization Process*.[5]

That kernel of truth in the collective mind of Venezuelan society, in the years from 1992 to 1998, lay in the revival of hope. The people began to reclaim their right to dream and, what's more, their

---

5   Claude Lévi-Strauss, *Tristes Tropiques* (1955), trans. J. & D. Weightman, Jonathan Cape, London, 1973; Darcy Ribeiro (1922–1997), Brazilian anthropologist. *The Civilization Process*, trans. Betty Meggers, Smithsonian Institution Press, Washington, 1968.

duty to fight for that dream. In short, the idea of a political utopia became part of the national psyche again. That is, the collective imagination began to envisage a new country, with more justice and equality, and less corruption. And that's precisely the point at which utopia can be confused with myth. But it's a myth that can't be concretely personified; a myth that is the expression of a collective hope.

And at the time, you nourished that hope?

That was my mission. To give substance, in the psyche of the Venezuelan people, to the prodigious invention of a possible country. I had to create a tangible utopia; in other words, create the collective myth of a future that was achievable. The 'myth of Chávez' the person had to die for the 'myth of a new Venezuela', a collective Venezuela, to emerge. And so that everything could be transformed, like in the fable.

What fable?

The fable of Daphnis, related by Theocritus in his *Idylls*.[6] Daphnis was a demi-god, a shepherd on Mount Etna, who died tormented by love of Venus, for having dared profane the delights of the goddess Aphrodite. As he lies dying, Daphnis exclaims, 'Since Daphnis dies, let everything be transformed. Let pine trees grow pears, and stags chase hounds . . .' I thought the same; the important thing was for everything to be transformed by the death of the 'Chávez myth'. Venezuela was 'upside down', as Eduardo Galeano would say, and needed putting back on its feet.[7]

That's where your idea of the 'possible utopia' came from.

Yes, I thought of Victor Hugo, when he said, 'Today's utopia is tomorrow's reality'. And quite simply I proposed reviving the

---

6   Theocritus (310–260 BC), Greek poet, born in Sicily, founder of bucolic or pastoral poetry.

7   Eduardo Galeano, *Upside Down: A Primer for the Looking-Glass World* (1998), trans. Mark Fried, St Martin's Press, New York, 2001.

'Bolivarian utopia', which, like a Latin American phoenix, has been here for almost two centuries, reborn every now and again only to be buried once more. We decided to rescue it once and for all.

In political language, the idea of utopia is generally associated with 'impossible fantasies' or 'dangerous experiments'. In those particular years people were talking of 'the spectacular decline of the Soviet utopia'. In such circumstances, was it wise to use the word 'utopia'? Weren't you afraid it would be wrongly interpreted?

Well, I was talking about my kind of utopia. And you could just as well point to the 'spectacular decline of the neoliberal utopia'. Especially in Latin America, in the 1980s and 1990s, or in the US and Europe from 2008. The definition we gave that term was, let's say, an 'anticipatory project', implying the announcement of a concrete programme of transformation. What's more, we subjected the project to discussion, comparison, and citizens' debate. For us, it was inconceivable that a 'programme for transforming the country' could be elaborated by one single person, a 'great leader', a 'saviour', alone and isolated in his office. No, it could only come from a broad-based discussion, from the 'collective intellect' of the people themselves.

When you came out of prison, Carlos Andrés Pérez was no longer president, and Rafael Caldera's new government was also proposing to transform Venezuela; to eradicate corruption with the help, indeed, of left-wing ministers, from the MAS, to be precise. Didn't this new context complicate things for you?

Yes, because under Caldera, the country appeared to be headed for relative stability. But it was a false, superficial stability. The departure of Pérez worked like a safety valve, and tension visibly dropped. Caldera had cleverly distanced himself from Copei, a party compromised by the decomposition of the two-party system, and had established his own organization – Convergencia – with which he was elected president.

He then courted, with some success, sectors of the population that would identify him and his programme with what we were representing. On one occasion, in the midst of the 1993 electoral campaign, Dr Caldera went to Barinas and sought out my mother. Through her, he sent a message telling me not to attack him – because I'd already said some harsh things – and that my insistence on a Constituent Assembly was not the way forward. Some of my *compañeros*, both in Yare and San Carlos, were backing Caldera and even went as far as to say that Caldera's victory at the polls meant the 4 February uprising had been a success.

As far as you were concerned, that was false.

More than false, it was fraud and even theft of some of our ideas. But anyway, that's the way the country was going. Caldera's discourse was nationalist and, initially, slightly critical of the IMF. He was a conservative, of course, right-wing, but he knew how to make significant alliances. The Communist Party supported him, so did the MAS.

Did you find that strange?

It was a curious alliance, a product of the decline of the left-wing parties, their lack of unity, and erosion of their support. They should have made a real left-wing alliance, and thrown their weight behind Andrés Velásquez, one of the leaders of La Causa R, with whom I had already locked horns.

La Causa R had come to Yare to ask for support. I had a meeting with Velásquez and several of his colleagues. I remember sitting at a table in the middle of a sun-drenched yard, so we couldn't be tape-recorded. Some of our military *compañeros* had agreed to be included in the lists of parliamentary candidates, some for La Causa R, others for MAS. The parties were competing to see who could get a commander or a captain from among the 4-F or 27-N prisoners to stand for them.

I told Velásquez I had already had a manifesto, called 'How to Get Out of This Labyrinth', that was in the public domain. I also said I belonged to a movement – the MBR-200 – and our aim was to strengthen that strategic project. And we were going to ask people not to vote, because the elections were a swindle.

How did Andrés Velásquez take that?
It wasn't what he was expecting. We had a polite argument. I held firm to my position. A large group of us stood our ground, and before the presidential elections we published a document in which we denounced the attempt to defraud the people and appropriate their victories.

Which didn't prevent Caldera winning.
Yes, that's right, though by a small margin and on a very low turn-out. So, by December 1993, we had a new president-elect. Suddenly there was no more talk of the coup being cooked up in the Army High Command. More than one general had wanted to take advantage of the moment by staging a coup, especially Vice-Admiral and Minister of Defence Radamés Muñoz León, a right-winger representing a whole strand within the military.

That particular phase was over. Caldera came to power and you were released. It was a huge change, wasn't it?
Yes, but what I mean to say is that I didn't want to be manipulated, or tamed. Because, in the end, that whole system we'd been denouncing was still the same. Obviously Rafael Caldera was a long way from having the same corrupt image as Carlos Andrés Pérez. In the collective imagination he was a conservative, right-wing, but undeniably an honourable and honest man.

That's why it bothered him and his followers that we MBR-200 members remained critical. I remember when Caldera took power, a great deal of pressure was put on me not only to accept the dismissal of court proceedings they were offering all the officers who'd been in jail – which in the end we did accept – but also to go to the palace and visit the president. Even the night before I left, Caldera's very son – I think he's called Andrés – came to the Military Hospital on his father's behalf to say the president wanted to say hello and thank me. I said, 'He has nothing to thank me for, and I have nothing to thank him for.'

You didn't want to let yourself be seduced.
I didn't think it was appropriate. Before leaving prison, I had warned the people, quite clearly, not to let themselves be bamboozled. So, for me, it was also quite clear that I shouldn't go to Miraflores.

What was Caldera thinking when he decided to release you?
As an old political fox, he had a good nose. That's what led him to say what he did on 4 February, when, in Congress as senator for life, he expressed a certain solidarity with our movement. That same political sixth sense meant he did not want to confront us. This was not only the right thing politically, but clever. The first few days after my release was a kind of honeymoon. I was inundated with offers . . . In reality, however, they were offering me a gilded bridge into a trap.

During his campaign, Caldera had pledged to release the military prisoners and bring peace to the country. He took power in February 1994, and we were out at the end of March. It happened relatively fast. But for the people who supported our cause, it was unbearably slow. Don't forget that, in Caracas, there was continual mass mobilization in favour of the imprisoned officers, by the associations of families of political prisoners, groups of lawyers, student organizations, and all sorts of people demanding our freedom and respect for electoral promises. Caldera barely had a moment to breathe. The day he took office, he went to the Pantheon to lay flowers on Bolívar's tomb. And when he came out, the crowd in the street chanted in unison, 'Free Chávez!' The pressure was enormous, and as the days went by it got stronger and stronger. He had no choice but to set us free as soon as possible.

And you then set off to cover every corner of Venezuela, as you said, in order to strengthen the MBR-200 everywhere.
Yes, and I must tell you about the battle I waged alongside a group of *compañeros* in order to keep organizing and developing the MBR-200 project.

What battle?

A battle to inject new life into our Movement and set our own political agenda. Because, what with the uprising of 27 November and everything that represented, some people tried to distort the image of the MBR-200 or to simply deny it was an original movement. Even several of our own *compañeros* said, 'Well, the MBR-200 did what it had to do, now its time has passed.' I said no, I was afraid that the energy unleashed would all be for nothing, gone with the wind, divided, confused, manipulated . . . And I stood my ground: 'No, the Movement has barely been incubated; on the contrary, now is the time to develop it!'

Some *compañeros* agreed with me, and we began to send letters to Bolivarian groups set up around the country, the Bolivarian circles. Alastre López was my assistant. We produced documents and launched an ambitious mobilization plan to keep the MBR-200 in the critical vanguard against the system. This plan moved forward, they organized a lot of Bolivarian assemblies. It wasn't easy because our Movement was persecuted.

Persecuted?

Our adversaries played all kinds of tricks to delegitimize our project. Military Intelligence drafted hostile reports: 'On his country-wide tours, Chávez calls for insurrection.' Enemies on the right called me 'violent', 'extremist', 'communist', etc. And the Left accused me of being on the extreme right. The objective of all of them was to liquidate me, politically and morally. They wanted me to melt into the landscape and fade away. They did everything in their power to make me disappear.

They wanted to spread fear.

That campaign had an effect. Sure, it terrified a lot of people. Even friends of ours thought the word 'revolutionary' was scary, that we should change the Movement's name, call it something else. So a good friend, General García Barrios, suggested – and I accepted – we create the Bolivarian Association 200, to stop certain people feeling nervous. But in the end this name didn't stick, the people preferred the Revolutionary Bolivarian Movement-200.

What were you living off? Your pension?
Yes, I had an [army] pension. It all went to the children, in Barinas. I'd separated from Nancy and felt miserable without my kids. At the same time I was enjoying a great love affair with Marisabel, who was to be my second wife.[8] In those days I lived in about a hundred houses; I'd lug my boxes of books from here to there, from house to house.

Did the MBR-200 have any financial resources?
Well, we raised what we could. But we didn't have any resources. Absolutely nothing! Not even mobile phones. We were four people and a truck we called the 'Black Donkey', an old Toyota I'd been given, a gas guzzler that leaked oil. Going from town to town in it, I'd always ask, 'How much petrol do we have?' And the answer would determine the venue of our next meeting. But we had the support of the Venezuelan people. Food was never a problem; we had more invitations to eat than we could cope with. By the time we'd been going two or three years, we were receiving more substantial help. We had a savings account, people made donations and suchlike.

You were very isolated . . .
Well, relatively, because a huge mass of people supported us [laughter]. *'Un mar de pueblo'*, a 'people-sea', Fidel called it. I couldn't walk down a street in Venezuela without being mobbed by affection, support, love . . . There was always a bed or a hammock to sleep in, food, petrol, even cars to borrow.

All that effort went into consolidating the unique political character of the MBR-200?
Exactly. To build our self-confidence and reinforce the MBR-200 internally. I was absolutely convinced we needed our own political organization, with its own ideological profile.

---

8   Marisabel Rodríguez (1964–), journalist and radio announcer. Chávez and Marisabel got married in 1997 and had a daughter, Rosinés, the youngest of his four children (the others are Rosa Virginia, María Gabriela and Hugo Rafael). They divorced in 2004, after a two-year separation.

Why?

Because otherwise we'd end up as thousands of splinter groups. We'd be chopped up in a blender. That's why I was being attacked on all sides, from the PCV to La Causa R, from right-wing groups to left-wing groups. Not to mention the far Left.

Who did the far Left consist of?

Some minuscule little groups: the Coordinadora Nacional Revolucionaria [Revolutionary National Coordinator]; Tercer Camino [Third Way]; Bandera Roja [Red Flag]; Insurgencia Popular [People's Insurgency]; Desobediencia Civil [Civil Disobedience]; Junta Patriótica [Patriotic Junta] . . . They could all have fitted in one bus. Anyway, when I came out of prison I was determined not to fall into the trap of making false alliances, but to extend the unique political nature of the Bolivarian Movement.

Bolivarianism didn't fit into traditional political boxes?

Not at all. That's why members of our own central command group began to use different language. For them, the name Bolívar, or the Simón Bolívar National Project, was no longer the main slogan. 'No,' they'd say, 'this is something else now.' It also stemmed from infiltrators from the right wing of the military, whose aim was to deflect our Movement away from the left-wing military tendency. Guess who turned out to be one of their supporters and financial backers?

Who?

Lyndon LaRouche! Yes sir, Lyndon LaRouche himself, who even formed a political party in Venezuela; Alejandro Peña Esclusa is still about somewhere, sounding off.[9] And at the other extreme, taking advantage of the naivety of many of our military cadres, our

---

9   Alejandro Peña Esclusa (1954–), founder of the *Partido Laboral Venezolano* (PLV) [Venezuelan Labour Party], a local branch of LaRouche's US Labor Party, and of the organization Fuerza Solidaria [Solidary Force]. An ultra-conservative Catholic, he supported the coup of April 2002 against President Chávez. He was arrested in July 2010 for 'links with Salvadorean terrorism', and freed on probation a year later.

Movement was also infiltrated by friends of Gabriel Puerta Aponte and Bandera Roja, who tried to infiltrate the 4-F rebellion and assassinate me.

The aim of all these groups was to destroy the growing grassroots popular movement and my leadership of it. That infiltration caused confusion and dispersal, of people and cadres. They wanted to redirect our movement away from Bolivarianism and make it more irresponsible and violent, in order to discredit it. It was quite a plan.

Did you do something to dismantle that plan?
Yes, like I said. While I was in prison, I called for the organization of Bolivarian committees throughout Venezuela. I introduced discipline by insisting we keep our political orientation true to the ideas of Bolívar, Robinson [Rodríguez] and Zamora. I knew we represented a perfectly valid alternative way of bringing about the profound changes Venezuelans were demanding. That's why I also encouraged people to set up regional Bolivarian assemblies whose mission would be to prepare a National Bolivarian Assembly. Despite the difficult times spent in prison, I fought to establish our rigorous political line as I had always done.

What was that line? The ideas defined in the document 'How to Get Out of This Labyrinth'?
Not only that. We also had the Simón Bolívar National Project, in which we defined the basic elements, concepts and categories that we would subsequently develop, in 1999, in the process of creating a new Constitution. It unleashed a big debate. We talked, for example, about the new powers we wanted to propose – Electoral Power and Moral Power – and we described the new system of government we would put in place: participative and protagonistic democracy.

When you came out of prison, you chaired this big debate yourself?
Yes, because it was hugely important. I set out the three options before us. One, take power militarily; two, take power legally via a

political route; three, abandon the struggle altogether. Because when we came out of prison many *compañeros* lost heart, they went to work for the government or created their own projects, and many just clung to their families.

Did I understand you to say you hadn't completely given up the idea of taking power by another military rebellion?

In the early years, 1994, 1995 and 1996, I always retained the possibility of armed action. It's true. We had a few weapons, and people prepared to undertake a new insurrection. At the time, I thought – and I wrote it in one of our manifestos – that the existing Election Law and the Political Parties Law were mechanisms of domination that suppressed the sovereignty of the people and the spirit of democracy.

That is, you questioned the democratic nature of the Venezuelan Republic?

Absolutely. Our 4-F rebellion destroyed the myth of Venezuela as 'the most solid democracy in Latin America'. It was a false theoretical construct that strove to depict that regime as a permanently established system. We denounced the fact that, on the basis of this false premise and sheltering behind a corrupt state, immense fortunes had been made – reducing, by the same token, large swathes of the population to extreme poverty. We talked of the urgent need for a 'new democratic practice'. We understood this to be a process propelled by diverse liberated forces, the main one being our MBR-200.

There was one particular sophism we wanted to refute: many Latin American governments preached 'popular' participation as a basic component of 'democratic politics'. In the Simón Bolívar National Project, we rejected the notion of popular participation as a charitable concession limited to the most trivial issues, excluding the working classes from taking decisions about fundamental aspects of their livelihoods, development and well-being.

We proposed the people govern themselves directly though Community Councils, People's Power, and Communes – three bodies we intended to create, and did create after 1999. In this way, we changed the very concept of democracy, which stopped being solely representative and became, as well as participative, fully protagonistic.

In any case, given your severe critique of the Venezuelan democratic system, you weren't at that time thinking of participating in any electoral process, were you?
It's true I wasn't planning to do it at that particular point. Later on, we debated it, and I changed my mind. But back then I was still a soldier, at least in my heart. And the only process to which I was devoted body and soul was the 'profound transformation of the appalling structures that crush the nation', as we wrote in one manifesto, in which we also expressed the following warning: 'If the dominant classes do not loosen their grip, the Bolivarian Armed Forces and the Venezuelan people will once more sing with the hurricane of the Army Hymn.'

But as you were no longer in the Army, I guess you couldn't count on units of the Armed Forces, as was the case on 4-F and 27-N.
Of course not. Although I still had all my military contacts, obviously. Remember that I had spent over twenty years organizing, developing networks, making connections, conspiring. That can't be undone in a day. I was still providing my friends in the Armed Forces with political analysis, via contacts, documents, secret meetings . . . I made it my business to keep strengthening the most revolutionary cadres within the military. Among other things, this helped me, later on, to neutralize the 1998 coup that certain senior officers planned when it looked like we were winning the elections. It also helped on 11 April 2002, when some *golpistas* tried to topple me. And this solid bulwark of resistance will keep helping me fight off any resurgence of latent right-wing military groups, always being egged on from outside.

What's more, I have to confess that, when I left prison, I also initiated a strategy to reintegrate certain officers, friends, members of the MBR-200, into the Army. I invented a scenario. I made them write declarations, which we had verbally agreed beforehand, in which they officially stated they had distanced themselves from me. They declared, 'I want no more dealings with the MBR-200.' In many cases this strategy worked, and we got them back into the Army.

Like MBR-200 'moles' . . . But anyway, you were saying that your main political objective, at that time, was to create a Bolivarian ideological critical mass, to become more important nationwide. Hence your travels all over Venezuela.
Yes, that's why I travelled through Venezuela with three or four friends; I've already mentioned Rafael Isea, Nicolás Maduro . . . But it was compatible with my strategy towards the military. Remember that I'd always favoured joint civilian–military action. I didn't neglect either of the two fronts. So, I did five whistle-stop trips through the whole country. The first began on 29 March 1994, a mere five days after I was released, and finished at the end of June. It was the 'hundred day tour'. I could see a great longing for revolution in the eyes of the people. The poor were not demanding victory at the polls, their greatest hope was for a social revolution. Social and Bolivarian. This helped me keep true to my convictions, defending them all over the country, creating Bolivarian committees in every nook and cranny – but they had to be made up of compatriots with no links to any other political organizations.

Why did you demand that?
Because La Causa R, the MAS and the Communist Party were campaigning as well . . . And they all wanted to steal our cadres.

They were your rivals on the Left.
Well, I didn't regard them as enemies. But I always thought the MBR-200 should be a separate movement with its own Bolivarian profile, its own ideology, its own platform, its own projects . . . And history proved me right, because look what happened along the way. Those so-called left-wing parties – the MAS, La Causa R, the

Communist Party, and later on, Podemos [We Can], Patria Para Todos [*Patria* for All] – didn't understand a thing. All they had, regrettably, was electoral opportunism. And they were out to demolish me any way they could . . .

You mean they criticized you so that the MBR cadres would leave you and join them, is that right?
More or less. They said anything and everything. The secretary general of the Communist Party said, when I came out of prison, 'The presence of "Caudillo Chávez" damages the people's movement.' He objected to me joining the marches and demonstrations. On one occasion, May Day, those left-wing parties organized a march, followed by an event in the Parque Central. None of them invited me. I was invited by a workers' association, however. And I went. I arrived, and sat down – not on the platform with the other leaders, but among the workers. All eyes turned towards me. I tried to listen to the speeches, but could hear a murmur going round the crowd, it got louder and louder. The speaker finished and handed the mic to another. Suddenly an angry shout rose from the crowd: 'Aren't you going to salute the presence of Commander Chávez?' Silence from the party leaders, then eventually they felt obliged: 'We'd like to welcome . . .!' Huge ovation. I wasn't going to speak, but the pressure from the people was tremendous. Someone went up to the platform, took the mic from the speakers and brought it to me: 'Commander, salute the workers!' That was how it was.

And internationally, the political Left boycotted me too. In 1995, during the São Paulo Social Forum, held in San Salvador, they refused to let me speak.[10] Quite disgraceful! I was hurt. They didn't understand a thing. They didn't see what was coming, what is happening now. The tremendous strength of the social movements: Evo Morales in Bolivia, Rafael Correa in Ecuador.

---

10   Organized initially in 1990 by the Brazilian Workers' Party in São Paulo, this annual Forum is a focus for left-wing parties and social movements of Latin America.

Well, you weren't very complimentary to them yourself, were you?

It was clear to me that with the existing political parties – and I say this with all due respect to their memory, their members and the leaders I'd worked with since 1978, like Alfredo Maneiro, Douglas Bravo, Andrés Velásquez and Pablo Medina – it would have been impossible to bring down the system, whether by armed struggle or peaceful protest. Don't forget that this was the most difficult period the Left had seen in its one-hundred-year-old history. The Soviet Union had disappeared. The light of utopia had been extinguished, and the rout of the Left had begun. This was chronicled at the time by Jorge Castañeda in his book *Utopia Unarmed*, on the abdication of the Left and its farewell to arms.[11] Fidel alone remained true to his beliefs. He was the bulwark defending socialism! Rafael Caldera, meanwhile, went to the First Summit of the Americas in Miami to support Bill Clinton and deliver up Venezuela to the FTAA.[12] And, despite this betrayal, he was backed by the PCV, the MAS, the MEP, and some of the most important leaders of the 'Left' like Teodoro Petkoff and Pompeyo Márquez, who were ministers. What kind of Left was that? The people were in despair, confused, without direction or leaders . . .

How do you explain it?

I think they were trying to transform the system from inside. We opposed that 'entryism', because they didn't have enough internal political structure to resist the seductions and trickery inherent in the system. Our idea was to channel the power of the people towards an anti-system objective: the Constituent Assembly. Some of those left-wing leaders thought that was a dead end. They said, 'Careful, Chávez, you'll end up being the Pied Piper of Hamelin leading the

---

11   Jorge G. Castañeda, *Utopia Unarmed: The Latin American Left after the Cold War*, Alfred A. Knopf, New York, 1993.

12   Free Trade Area of the Americas, intended as the extension of NAFTA (North American Free Trade Agreement between US, Canada and Mexico, 1994) to the rest of Latin America, barring Cuba.

people over a cliff.' And where were they leading the people? To Caldera and the same old system! Into the abyss!

But still, changing things from the inside is what a lot of honourable and honest left-wingers aspired to do – including revolutionaries who came down from the hills, surrendered their guns and formed political parties, and some went as far as to sit in Congress.

And did they manage to change the system?
Of course not [laughter]. They were changed themselves. They were absorbed into the system. They ventured into the swamp and the system engulfed them and transformed them. I remember one good friend, José Rafael Núñez Tenorio, the first serious Venezuelan intellectual to come out in favour of the Bolivarian Movement, author of over thirty books, former guerrilla, former political prisoner . . . anyway, at one point, when intellectuals were all steering clear of me, he broke the ice and stated, 'I support the project embodied by Chávez.' And he explained why, in a very good speech he gave in the Aula Magna of Caracas University.

Unfortunately he died soon afterwards and I, of course, went to his funeral. And there, as we were lowering the coffin, his grown-up son said, 'Chávez, don't forget what my father said, "You take power, don't let power take you."' I've never forgotten that lesson. That's why I remained convinced that we had to create our own power base, with the people as its foundation, with our own Bolivarian revolutionary cadres, and our own political analyses.

Apart from the ideas expressed in the Simón Bolívar National Project and 'How to get out of this labryinth', what other analyses did you perform?
We had regular weekly workshops where we outlined and discussed our projects. And that's how we created our Strategic Map.

What was that?
The Strategic Map was a political diagram, the result of a lot of academic research by many *compañeros*. I can draw it from memory [he draws it]. In the centre is the MBR-200, then come its potential

allies. First, among the left-wing parties and groups. Then comes the 'Ind', which could have meant 'Independents' but actually meant 'Indescribable', that is, the military factor we couldn't mention. Besides these national allies, there were international ones. That's how we built up the scenario of political actors. It allowed us to navigate the map.

Then we set out the 'mobilizing projects', examples of which were the people's constituent process; defence of the quality of life; defence of national sovereignty; Latin American integration . . . For each one we designed a range of political strategies or 'generators'. For example, defence of the quality of life had two 'generators', housing and employment. National sovereignty involved border strategies and the Armed Forces. Do you see? For the people's constituent process, we began to organize pro-constituent committees which spread the idea of a new Constitution all over the country. We began to 'warm up the generators' from below, so that the project came from the grass roots, from the people. To explain this all over Venezuela, I took on the role of schoolteacher. I'd hold meetings, ranging from small groups of *campesinos* to university students and lecturers. Sometimes I'd talk to serving military officers – clandestinely in the early mornings at a ranch, or in somebody's house – or I'd explain to retired officers where our project was going.

Did you have concrete objectives?

Of course, our Strategic Map had objectives and strategies for attaining them. For example, we'd draw an arrow with 'transition project' on it, pointing towards a circle, the Simón Bolívar National Project, say. This was our internal programming framework, and was directly linked to the 'trigger' of the transitional process, which was the Constituent Assembly; and the Assembly itself was only a transitional stage. We actually conceived a very dynamic, dialectical model; like permanent revolution, you might say. Still ongoing today, because we're still building a new political model, a new social model, a new economic model . . . This hasn't finished.

Did the social movements appear on your Strategic Map?
No, they didn't. We only put political parties on it. The fact is the
social movements were in disarray, and the unions were fighting
among themselves. We were in touch with some of them. I remember the one that contacted us most, and we reciprocated, were the
people from *La Chispa* [The Spark], a Trotskyite weekly. We lost
track of them later . . . There were also student movements. But, I
repeat, the Left had been crushed. At one stage, we did appoint a
coordinator for social movements, and I attended lots of meetings
with left-wing political groups, popular movements, etc. Until one
day I exploded: 'I'm tired of these meetings, I'm off to the streets.'
Interminable discussions leading to zero social action. I decided I'd
had enough.

Very sterile?
Yes, too sterile. It was an old custom here, 'arguing over the sex of
angels' as someone said. It went nowhere. Zero action.

How was the outside world represented on the Strategic Map?
Various arrows linked our Movement to the rest of the world. First
priority went to Latin America and the Caribbean. Then, the third
world: Africa, the Arab world, Asia, China. Especially countries we
thought we could make progressive alliances with.

The Map served as a compass, did it?
Yes, it was our navigational chart, it set each different course of
political action. Jorge Giordani guided that ship. And it added
up to a fiendishly busy diary for me. Nevertheless I didn't
improvise, I didn't go round giving random talks just to see
what might come of it. No, I went around with that chart in
my head, as you said, like a compass. I knew where I wanted
to go . . . And, among other things, I wanted to create a
continent-wide structure for our Bolivarian Movement in Latin
America. A continental movement with Latin American integration as its goal. And going on to link Latin America with the
rest of the world.

With that geostrategic vision in mind, we began to organize our Movement internally. We created all kinds of working groups for different political tasks. We organized tours, activities and events to try and reach the people in different ways, so that we could break the media embargo, which naturally had already started. For example, I would call a press conference, only three or four journalists would come, and hardly any would publish anything. We began looking for political allies for each of our themes, and didn't find any, of course. The leaders of the different parties were all busy campaigning for their own mayoral candidates, or other political offices. I repeat, it was the total degeneration of proper politics. We realized those parties didn't have policies to fight for housing, employment, wages, food, education, health. I asked myself, 'But who's defending the people? Where are the political parties to defend the people?' They didn't exist. We were terribly alone.

Well, you still had allies in the Armed Forces, didn't you?
Correct. We maintained a permanent dialogue with the 'Independents', as we called them, meaning the military factor, organized groups inside the Army, Air Force, Navy and National Guard. Some contacts were with officers of the High Command, others were medium-level officers. It was strenuous work, because it required extreme precautions. For security purposes, I'd go in disguise. Sometimes I dressed up as a hippie, I even wore this wig with a green streak (laughter), or a false moustache that Freddy Bernal got for me.[13] They never got wind of a single meeting.

At that stage, were you still wondering whether to choose the political path to power or the military path again?
Yes, as I mentioned, we didn't discard any form of struggle. But I must say, in all honesty, a lot of people wanted to take up arms

---

13 Freddy Bernal (1962–), a police studies specialist, one of the leaders of the Fifth Republic Movement, and member of the Constituent Assembly. In April 2002 he led one of the main popular fronts opposing the coup against Chávez. He was mayor of the Libertador municipality in Caracas from 2000 to 2008.

again – in the barracks, but especially in the streets. I used to go into very poor neighbourhoods, and to the countryside where there was extreme hardship, and the people would urge us to act. Once, in a mining camp, I remember many workers saying, 'Chávez, where are the guns? Don't turn into just another politician. Bring us guns, Chávez, to put an end to this.'

In 1995 there were gubernatorial elections, weren't there?

Yes, that's why I said the parties had their eyes fixed on political posts. The PCV was supporting Rafael Caldera, the MEP was in Caldera's government, so was the MAS. La Causa R was not, but they wanted to put up joint candidates with us for Congress. Governors and mayors, too. It was clear what their aim was, they wanted our MBR-200 cadres. So we fell out with La Causa R. And also, needless to say, with Bandera Roja. With the result that the 'internal allies' category on our Strategic Map began to look pretty thin. We only maintained contact with certain individuals. We called for active abstention. Our slogan was 'For now . . . for no one. Constituent Assembly now!' Many left-wing leaders – in particular Andrés Velásquez and Pablo Medina of La Causa R – accused me of hindering the country's political development with my attitude. But at the same time they were trying to recruit me. I was deluged with offers to stand for governor, in Aragua, Barinas, Lara . . . Even Caldera's inner circle put out feelers for me to join the government. They obviously didn't know me . . . [laughter].

Did they make you any specific offers?

Sure. They proposed sending me abroad to do a postgraduate degree. They also offered me an embassy or a consulate in Europe. In fact, they let one of my former *compañeros*, Jesús Urdaneta, choose where he wanted to go. He consulted his brother-in-law, who worked in the Foreign Ministry, and he advised, 'Our consulate in Vigo is one of the nicest in Europe.' So off he went. He spent five years as consul in Vigo, in beautiful Galicia. A couple of years later, on a visit to Spain, I went to Vigo to see him, in that lovely bay, those islands, that sea . . .

Your friend Francisco Arias Cárdenas also agreed to stand for governor of a state, didn't he?

Yes. And he wasn't the only one. Because many *compañeros* left jail with nothing. Most of them didn't have a house, or a pension. The only soldiers with pensions were those of us who'd served for ten years or more . . . So I can't criticize them. More than a few accepted those offers. Hundreds, I'd say. I was the exception, with four or five others. Some took jobs in the Seniat – Customs and Revenue – or went on courses. And others worked in social action programmes, like the PAMI [Mother and Infant Nutrition Programme]. Arias Cárdenas was president of PAMI, for instance.

Finally he, one of the historic commanders of the MBR-200, stood as La Causa R candidate for governor of Zulia state. And he won. When he came out of prison, he had joined La Causa R, which contributed to divisions in our Movement. The leaders of La Causa R applauded his stance: Arias was a true leader, an intelligent man, whereas I was 'crazy' and 'irresponsible'. They said I repre-sented 'messianic leadership', and called it 'political regression prej-udicial to the progress of the masses' [laughter].

You deplored the fact that the Venezuelan Left was supporting Caldera.

Rafael Caldera was a member of Opus Dei, the Catholic Right at its most putrid. And the Venezuelan 'Left' supported him, aban-doning their historic principles. No one mentioned Marx. No one mentioned the State, they only invoked the Market. As I said, the FTAA was being launched. On 9 to 11 December 1994, Caldera went to Miami and met Bill Clinton during the Summit of the Americas, and he had the cheek to declare, 'Now we are truly carry-ing out Bolívar's dream.' A few days later, on 13 to 15 December, I happened to be in Havana, on my first trip to Cuba, and from there I shot back, 'As a counterbalance, we are holding a Summit of Rebels.' Just Fidel and me, the two of us, alone! Yes, and to cap it all [laughter] I was a mere ex-con. The Venezuelan Left never forgave me for that irreverent attitude.

How do you explain their constant criticism of you?

Various reasons no doubt. Some I've already mentioned. Perhaps also because I wasn't an intellectual on their terms, or because I hadn't studied in the best universities, like they had, or because I was a soldier. When I realized what their attitude was, I thought, 'I'm not going to waste my time trying to gain their individual trust. My objective is to make a direct commitment to the people.' Besides, I sensed the people felt the same way. When I came out of prison and saw that human tide, I understood where my commitment lay. To assume the leadership the people were demanding of me. Those leaders never accepted my leadership, out of jealousy or for whatever reason.

Arias Cárdenas once told me that, while he had an excellent relationship with you, there was something he had not grasped. He had thought you two were like Don Quixote and Sancho Panza – with himself as Don Quixote. Until he finally realized that in fact it was the other way around. You were Don Quixote and he was only Sancho Panza.

Yes, I think many people got it wrong. There was a kind of superiority complex, an arrogance, a vanity. They thought, 'How can this guy be the leader? He's barely forty. He'll have to submit.' And for a time, I accepted that, with humility I have to say. This is what happened. A few months after I left prison, a pro-Constituent Assembly front was formed. Who were the coordinators? Intellectuals like Manuel Quijada and Luis Miquilena, high-ranking officers like Grüber Odremán and Visconti Osorio – leaders of the 27-N – and myself. But at press conferences and meetings with other politicians, it was always them who took the floor. Since I respected them all very much, I never thought, 'I'm going to push myself forward.' No, I said to myself, 'I'm going to accept it humbly.'

But then what happened? Whenever we organized a public event, the people would begin to shout, 'Let Chávez speak! Let Chávez speak!' It was an irresistible force . . . So the others finally left the group, and I took over, as I had to. It was written. Not in a magic book, but in the consciousness of the people. In truth, the people

– and it's hard for me to say this – sensed that they had found a leader, they felt it. What I've been trying to do, since 1999, is to fulfil that commitment. I must try to do it all my life.

Have you always had this singular idea of your leadership? A leader who stands outside all the politicking, in direct contact with the citizens?

It happened gradually. I was pretty much on my own. With some very loyal aides, of course, like Rafael Isea or Nicolás Maduro. And I also had a group of advisers, but in the background. They were not political heavyweights, they didn't want to be; their ambition was to help create the project. So let's say that between this leader and the masses, there were no intermediaries: no parties – our organization was just getting off the ground – no intellectuals, nothing. Just Chávez and the people.

You mentioned before that there was debate within the MBR-200 over which path to take, whether or not to take part in the elections.

Yes, there was debate [in 1993 and 1994] and we decided not to. Our analysis of the situation would change in 1997, and then we decided to compete in the presidential elections of 1998. But at that point, 1994, we launched our campaign for 'active abstention'. A case was brought against me for that: they called it 'incitement to commit an offence'.

Is the vote compulsory in Venezuela?

It was in those days. I had to go to court twice. I told the lady judge, 'I'm not calling on people not to vote. I'm calling for a referendum for a Constituent Assembly, a much more democratic process.' I've already told you our slogan: 'For now . . . for no one. Constituent Assembly now!' In the 1994 local elections, abstention was very high, 70 per cent, and in many places as high as 80 per cent. We made the most of it by launching a series of debates around the meaning of abstaining in elections, partisanship in politics, and our alternative proposal for a Constituent Assembly. We tried to spread our ideas via the mass media, but the main newspapers and TV channels were already boycotting us. That made us all the keener to get down to the grass roots: we collected signatures on every corner, organized speaking tours, events, meetings, workshops, committees for the defence of housing, employment and education . . . We also made great strides on the question of national sovereignty, a subject of great importance for our military faction. And our Strategic Map was slowly being coloured in on an international level. We formed our first foreign alliances.

In 1994 you began to travel abroad. What was your aim? To form those alliances?
We didn't want to remain isolated internationally. Furthermore, what kind of Bolivarians would we be if we didn't seek closer ties with the rest of Latin America? In 1994, in Venezuela, I was reluctant to get involved in the political framework of a system that we wanted to bring down. But my group and I were always thinking about how to organize an integrated continental-wide Bolivarian movement. We had in mind starting with nationalist military officers, active and retired, all over Latin America. The other important objective was to study the different constitutional processes, starting with the Colombian.

And listen to this. One day when I was in Yare prison, a Venezuelan general appeared. He had taken a very brave stand as president of the military court that found Orlando Bosch and Luis Posada Carriles guilty of the 6 November 1976 bombing of the Cuban airliner. The terrorists subsequently escaped from prison, and the general's son was killed as an act of revenge.

His name was Elio García Barrios, an honest, highly educated man, a doctor of law, a lawyer, now retired from the Army. He came to Yare prison to see me. We hadn't met personally before, but I knew who he was. He placed himself at the service of our Bolivarian Command Group. He put on the armband, and declared, 'I come as a soldier.' A respected man, known throughout Venezuela, he became friends with my parents and began giving speeches up and down the country in support of our cause.

He came to Yare again and we sat in the yard, under a little tree, to talk. He said, 'Look, Chávez, they've threatened me for doing what I'm doing. In case something happens to me, I'm giving you a list of military officers from various Latin American countries who are members of the Organization of Military Officers for Democracy in Latin America and the Caribbean, the OMIDELAC.' And he told me about this group of progressive left-wing military officers. He gave me the list, country by country.

There weren't any in Argentina, only one old general who was already dead; in Uruguay, Captain Gerónimo Cardoso; in Santiago, Chile, Captain Raúl Vergara, soldier and economist, who had worked in Salvador Allende's government as adviser – in the Ministry of Finance – to General Alberto Bachelet, father of President Michelle Bachelet. In Colombia, Major Bermúdez Rossi, and so on . . .

Did this open doors for you in Latin America?
Not really, because I realized these were *compañeros* from another era. The OMIDELAC didn't really exist anymore, they didn't meet . . . But it was the only information I had, and I was going to use it.

Did you have any problems travelling abroad? You hadn't lost any of your civil rights?
No, none. That wasn't a problem.

And you obviously didn't go abroad in your uniform, did you?
No. In civvies, absolutely. Well, the green or beige *liqui-liqui* I told you about. And I wore the red beret at public events, but without any military insignia. I was always very respectful of the military.

What country did you visit first?
My first invitation came from Colombia. From Gustavo Petro and José Cuesta, former parliamentarians who used to belong to the M-19 guerrilla group and ran the Simón Rodríguez Foundation. That was in July 1994. I celebrated my fortieth birthday on 28 July in Colombia.

Do you remember any details of that visit?
Perfectly. That group only sent me the ticket, they didn't have funds
for a hotel, nor did I. So they put me up in a great big house belonging to the Jesuits, in Bogotá naturally, headquarters of the Young
Workers of Colombia (JTC), an organization linked to the
Communist Party. It housed a lot of people, Afro-Colombians from
the Pacific Coast, some girls from somewhere or other, groups
coming and going. We ate together, slept in bunk beds, took collective showers; it was terribly cold at night. Pretty much like a
barracks. We stayed there for three nights.

The government gave me a bodyguard. I remember that, on the
second day, that security officer, a lieutenant, said, 'Commander, I
don't think you should be in this position, you're a soldier. You're
not safe.' He sort of felt sorry for me.

Were you able to meet any political figures?
Yes, I asked them to arrange meetings with the three co-presidents
of the 1991 Colombian Constituent Assembly. And I met Antonio
Navarro Wolff, a former M-19 guerrilla chief; Álvaro Gómez
Hurtado, of the Conservative Party; and Horacio Serpa, of the
Liberal Party.[14]

The meeting with Antonio Navarro was at his home. I remember
him saying, 'Comandante, if you manage to install a Constituent
Assembly in Venezuela, don't make the mistakes we made . . .' There
was a vase of flowers on the table. 'What we did was tweak it, try to
fix it, hide the cracks in the vase, make it look pretty. You must take
a hammer and break it.' Because the M-19 disappeared: the
Constituent Assembly swallowed it up.

I met Álvaro Gómez Hurtado in his house as well, in the library.
When I sat down, he asked me, 'How is Venezuela, Commander?'
And before I could speak, he answered his own question: 'Ah, no,
you've already been here for two days. To know what's going on in

---

14 Álvaro Gómez Hurtado (1919–1995), son of Laureano Gómez who was president from 1950 to 1953. Lawyer and leader of the Conservative Party, three times presidential candidate. Assassinated on 2 November 1995 in Bogotá.

Venezuela, you need your ear to the radio all the time, things change by the minute.' He knew very well what was going on here. A right-wing intellectual, he died riddled by bullets in Bogotá.

As for Horacio Serpa, he was campaign manager for Ernesto Samper, who shortly afterwards won the elections [7 August 1994], beating César Gaviria. Serpa became interior minister a few weeks later. He received me in Samper's campaign headquarters.

Did you meet any military officers?

Yes, I met some retired officers. A colonel, Guillermo Lora Ramírez, who had been discharged from the Army for blowing the whistle on some corrupt generals in La Guajira. I also met several Navy men, and others from the Army. They brought me a book called *The Formation of the Moral Movement in the new Colombia*, and said, 'Commander, there's a lot of admiration for you and your Movement here. We are Bolivarians, not Santanderists.[15] We're in touch with soldiers on active service.'

That group of soldiers invited me to swear an oath on the Campo de Boyacá, where the Battle of Boyacá took place.[16] We drove out there. It made me miss the plane home to Caracas, because an accident on the road back caused a huge traffic jam. I'd wanted to be home that night, it was my birthday and my children were waiting for me. But I was forced to stay. I spent my birthday in that JTC house, with guitars, beers and a cake, among the youngsters and lefties. And at breakfast I met Senator Manuel Cepeda Vargas [1930–1994], general secretary of the Colombian Communist Party, whom they nicknamed 'the last Mohican in Colombia', the last great communist leader. A few days later, [9 August 1994] he was killed in the street in Bogotá.

---

15 Francisco de Paula Santander (1792–1840), Colombian lawyer and soldier who fought the Spanish alongside Simón Bolívar. Left to govern Gran Colombia while Bolívar battled on towards Peru, his legalistic scruples brought the two men into increasing conflict.

16 One of Simón Bolívar's major victories in the South American Wars of Independence, 7 August 1819.

Did you give any lectures?

I was invited to the Javeriana University and gave a talk. I remember a young man standing up and saying, 'You can't be a career soldier.' I replied, 'Of course I am, I studied at a Military School.' So he said, 'No one in the Colombian military would say what you just did.' I replied: 'I'm sure some would, you just don't know it.' I was convinced that was true. Because before our 4 February 1992 rebellion, the left-wing movements in Venezuela used to say the same thing, 'All the military are sold out to the oligarchy.' Yet we were taking action, albeit clandestinely. How could patriots among the Colombian military go round openly declaring their solidarity with the people? 'There must be some,' I told the young man. 'It's impossible for there not to be.'

I spoke at another college as well. We held an informal workshop with hundreds of lecturers, academics and artists, chaired by Gustavo Petro, a brilliant intellectual, much admired in Colombia. He was very young then.

Were you in touch with the media?

I was invited to the newspaper *El Tiempo*.[17] I remember going into that majestic building with one of the sons of the Santos family, owners of the newspaper. He said, 'Commander, presidents are made here.' 'Or unmade,' I remarked. All the big cheeses were there to meet me.

I also went on television. I did an interview on RCN where I faced five top media experts chaired by a well-known Colombian journalist, Juan Gossaín. They asked me question after question about Venezuela and current affairs.

Did you visit the place where Gaitán was killed?[18]

Yes, we went there, it was very emotional, it's such a busy street. We laid flowers. We also went to what had been Gaitán's

---

17   *El Tiempo*, founded in 1911, is the largest circulation newspaper in Colombia. Its major shareholders are the Santos family. Juan Manuel Santos was elected president in 2010.

18   Jorge Eliécer Gaitán was killed on Friday 9 April 1948, when he was coming out of his law office in the Agustín Nieto building on the corner of 14th and Jiménez, Bogotá.

residence and the garden where he is buried. He was buried standing up.

Standing up?

Yes. Didn't you know? Gaitán is buried upright. There's a rosebush on his grave. I met his daughter Gloria Gaitán there. There were a lot of people wearing red berets. I also visited Quinta Bolívar, where the Liberator lived with Manuelita Sáenz when he was in Bogotá. When word got around that I was there, hundreds of locals turned up spontaneously.

That trip made a big impact, it was very important. The red light was beginning to shine in Colombia . . . So much so that they were already planning how to extinguish that flame. The following month they accused me of being with the Colombian guerrillas.

Meanwhile, you visited other countries, starting with Panama, if I'm not mistaken.

Yes, my visit to Panama began on 15 September of that same year, 1994. Conditions [for change] existed there too. When I arrived, the press went straight on the attack: 'Chávez has arrived and is mounting a coup against *El Toro* Balladares.'[19] I'd been invited by some military officers, and I found the memory of Omar Torrijos more alive than ever.

But hadn't the Defence Forces been dismantled after the US invasion in 1989?

Yes, they were former military officers but big followers of Torrijos. I visited Colonel Delgado who was under house arrest for an attempted uprising. He was Torrijos's cousin, a wealthy guy, with an extremely luxurious house. Things went much better for me in Panama than in other countries; my visit generated a whole host of contacts. I went on radio and television, did press conferences and

---

19   Ernesto Pérez Balladares (1949–), nicknamed 'the Bull', president of Panama from 1994 to 1999.

visited the Casa Azul, where so much happened.[20] The hotel where I was staying was invaded by young army officers, Torrijos followers. They came because I'd said, controversially, in a television interview, 'Panama must one day get its Defence Force back.' That statement spread like wildfire. Former captains, lieutenants, etc., all descended on my hotel, I found about forty of them in the lobby. It was packed! I greeted all of them, and made a note of all their names.

They too gave me a bodyguard: 'We've designated Lieutenant Martirio Herrera as your security chief.' Martirio slept in the corridor, outside my hotel room. I kept saying, 'Come on in, kid, use this sofa.' But he said, 'No sir, my mission is to guard you; I'll sleep here.'

What selfless devotion!

I had very emotional experiences in Panama. I remember, on that same television programme, the interview was very polemical. They were two interviewers, one attacked me very strongly, and the other's attack wasn't so bad [laughter]. That's where I talked about the Battalion 2000 . . .

Battalion 2000?

It was an elite battalion. I said, 'I'm a Battalion 2000 soldier.' To be honest, it was only symbolically true. A Panamanian *compañero* who graduated from the Military Academy in Caracas, Antonio Gómez Ortega – I think I told you about him – had invited me to Panama in 1988 and I visited after I came back from Guatemala, before the gringo invasion. I stayed at his house. I remember we talked a great deal, we visited several barracks, and I got to know a lot of officers and signed up as an honorary member of the Battalion 2000. You could tell that conflict with the US was

---

20   Casa Azul (Blue House). Che Guevara spent time there in 1953. Graham Greene, Pablo Neruda and Gabriel García Márquez wrote there. Omar Torrijos formed the Panamanian Brigade 'Victoriano Lorenzo' there, which fought on the southern front in Nicaragua. It was in that house that the three Nicaraguan revolutionary factions decided to unite in 1979.

imminent, the atmosphere was supercharged. And a year later came the invasion of 20 December 1989. I'll never forget it. 'Operation Just Cause' they called it . . . How dare they . . . I was a prisoner in Maturín on that day, because a few days earlier they'd pulled me out of Caracas – I told you – accused of wanting to kill President Pérez. On a prison television I watched the bombing, the invasion . . .

Did you remind Panamanians of those events?
Yes, I talked about all that. I proclaimed myself a soldier of the Battalion 2000. And I confessed that when the gringos invaded Panama, that night I cried like a baby in my cell . . . They bombed the neighbourhood of Chorrillo. We went to see it. Three thousand people died there! It was the first time they'd used those stealth bombers [F-117A Nighthawks]. I spoke out forcefully against the gringos, against the invasion.

Early in 1994, the Zapatista National Liberation Army (EZLN) appeared in Chiapas, Mexico. Did you have any contact with that movement? Any relationship with Subcomandante Marcos?
No, never. It's a rather strange movement. Although I've read some very original texts by Subcomandante Marcos, and also the book of interviews he did with you, I've never really understood that movement, to be honest.[21] Well, we've never had any contact. No, from Panama, we went almost straight to Argentina where I arrived on 20 September.

How did that happen? Who invited you?
Through a retired Venezuelan army colonel, Luis Alfonso Dávila García, who later became our foreign minister. His sister was married to an Argentine businessman who had lived in Caracas for many years, and was probably following my progress. He knew

---

21 Ignacio Ramonet, *Marcos, la dignidad rebelde. Conversaciones con Ignacio Ramonet*, Capital Intelectual, Buenos Aires, 2001. (First published by Ediciones Cybermonde, Valencia, 2001.)

businessmen in Argentina and they were the ones who invited me. I was surprised. 'What use is this?' I wondered. But, anyway, we were looking for entry points and accepted. So we went to stay in Buenos Aires. And the local press, again, received us with violent attacks. The headlines said: 'The Venezuelan *carapintada* has landed' [laughter]. We spent two days there. Argentina was asleep, the Argentine people were in cold storage. You couldn't detect a glimmer of protest in that society. Those were the days of Carlos Menem.[22]

Do you go with Norberto Ceresole on that trip?[23]
No, in fact that's when I met Ceresole. It wasn't him who invited us. I met him through some retired military men, who had been *carapintadas* but had moved away from that group. They were on the progressive wing of the *carapintadas*, the right-wing movement linked to Lyndon LaRouche. Ceresole was a very able man . . . An historian, author of I don't know how many books on security and defence. He conceived a plan for Latin American integration via the Orinoco, the Amazon and the River Plate. I was fond of Ceresole. But he was never an adviser of mine, let alone a mentor. He held some very outlandish views, some of which I share, others I don't, and others are beyond the pale.

He also had some blatantly anti-Semitic ideas.
Absolutely. I'm telling you, totally unacceptable. I have never shared them.

---

22   Carlos Saúl Menem (1930–), president of Argentina 1989–1995 and 1995–1999. During his mandate, Argentina accepted the Washington Consensus and was subject to extreme neoliberal policies which led to a huge crisis.

23   Norberto Rafael Ceresole (1943–2003), Argentine sociologist and political scientist, author of numerous essays. He influenced many Latin American military leaders. He championed an authoritarian, 'post-democratic' Peronism, based on the 'caudillo–army–people' triptych and on 'revolutionary nationalism'. He swung from a certain Left to the extreme Right. His radical critiques of 'liberal democracy' led him to defend very controversial theses, such as the 'Jewish plot' and the 'Jewish financial mafia' in his book *La Conquista del Imperio norteamericano*, Al-Andalus, Madrid, 1998.

But given your relationship with Ceresole, some people have tried to accuse you of anti-Semitism as well.

A repugnant accusation. I've been accused of everything, absolutely everything! But that is one of the most sickening. It's been made several times. There have been various campaigns against me on that score. But let me tell you that I have very good relations with the Jewish community in Venezuela and its representatives in the CAIV [Confederation of Venezuelan Jewish Associations]. It's a patriotic and supportive community, an integral part of this cultural, religious and ethnic melting pot that makes up the Venezuelan nation. On various occasions, it has come out to refute these mendacious campaigns.[24] And I thank them for that.

I take this opportunity to repeat that I have the greatest respect for the Jewish people, one of the most unjustly discriminated against in history. The genocide the Nazis carried out between 1939 and 1945 is totally horrific. That desire to destroy European Jews, the extermination camps . . . Auschwitz . . . certain concepts of political reason died there. Anti-Semitism is an unacceptable, repugnant crime. No discussion. I've always maintained that.

How did you and Ceresole part company?

Well, besides the above disagreement, he started saying that Chávez was his 'creation'. Such vanity . . . That put a coolness between us. He left Venezuela and returned to Buenos Aires even before I took office for the first time, in February 1999. I think he went to Spain after that, he lived in Madrid for a while, and died.

Who did you meet on that first trip to Buenos Aires?

Like I said, the only 'politician' I met was Ceresole, the rest were businessmen. And a journalist, Stella Calloni. Norberto ran a centre for Latin American geopolitical studies called Argentina and the World, from a very modest place in the San Telmo area. I gave a lecture to a group of students, intellectuals and people on the Left.

---

24   President Chávez met with the World Jewish Congress on 2 February 2009. At the meeting, Chávez vowed to combat anti-Semitism throughout Latin America.

And come to think of it, it was also where I met Che's younger brother, Juan Martín Guevara. Then we went for a drink and talked politics with Ceresole's team and a group of soldiers, who were more like police than soldiers – a special elite corps of coastguards on the River Plate – who had joined Colonel Alí Seineldín in an uprising called the Albatros Rebellion [on 3 December 1990]. By then, however, they had left the *carapintada* movement.

Another officer turned up, a veteran of the Malvinas war, Commodore Horacio Richardeli. We all went to visit the Malvinas cemetery, well, a replica on the outskirts of Buenos Aires of the one on the islands, for the Argentine soldiers who died there. There was a mass and some people thought I was the priest because I was wearing a dark *liqui-liqui* . . . 'Ah, the priest's arrived!' [Laughter] 'No, I'm not the priest!'

Then, with Richardeli and some Peronist workers from a movement called the 'Eva Perón Movement', we went to a big hangar in a poor neighbourhood, where loads of people, workers and unemployed, had organized an Argentine barbecue.

Despite the hostility of the media, did you give any interviews?
Yes, I went to a radio station in Buenos Aires. I remember an old man rang in. He said, 'You remind me of someone – Juan Domingo Perón.' And he began to cry. And since I stayed at the radio station for an hour and a half, he came to see me there. He had known Perón; he got very emotional. Someone said, I remember, 'Careful, that old fellow's had a heart operation.' He said to me with tears in his eyes, 'It's years since I've heard the kind of things you are saying. Talk to the people!'

Did that move you?
A lot. To that group of young Argentines I met, I talked about Bolívar, his ideas, the need for a new Amphictyonic Congress; about continental integration and unity. And we managed to create a local coordinating committee to work on ideas for the preparatory meeting of the 1996 Panama Amphictyonic Congress. It was to take place later in the year, in Santa Marta, Colombia, in December

1994.[25] That meeting and the Amphictyonic Congress itself was one of the reasons for my trips abroad.

How long did you stay in Buenos Aires?
Two days. We did all that in two days. We didn't sleep. And we got some things, some contacts, set up.

From there you went to Uruguay?
Yes, we crossed over to Uruguay to see Gerónimo Cardozo, of the OMIDELAC. He worked in the Montevideo town hall. Tabaré Vázquez was mayor at the time.[26] And General Liber Seregni was then presidential candidate for the Frente Amplio [Broad Front]. When I arrived, the press reacted in the usual vein: 'The Venezuelan *golpista* has come to advise Seregni.' We didn't know each other, we hadn't had even been in touch, and they were in the middle of the electoral campaign, so Seregni and I didn't meet. I only talked to Cardozo and walked around Montevideo a bit, and from there we went on to Santiago de Chile.

What did you do in Santiago?
In Santiago, there was no one to coordinate anything for us. I had very few contacts. Just that member of OMIDELAC, Captain Raúl Vergara, who was an economist. We also met up with several social movements. Small groups, tiny. I remember one conversation I had with a Mapuche leader.

How was your trip to Cuba in December 1994 organized?
I'd been in contact with the Cuban ambassador, Germán Sánchez Otero, a few clandestine meetings, everything secret.[27] And then one day, 30 July to be precise, on my return from Colombia, we

---

25 Simón Bolívar died in the Finca San Pedro Alejandrino, Santa Marta, on 17 December 1830.

26 Tabaré Vázquez (1940–), former mayor of Montevideo, leader of the Frente Amplio (coalition of left-wing parties) and Uruguayan president from 2005 to 2010.

27 See Rosa Miriam Elizalde and Luis Báez, *El Encuentro*, Oficina de Publicaciones del Consejo de Estado, Havana, pp. 56–62.

called a press conference in the Caracas Atheneum. We went into a room, and someone told me a Cuban was giving a lecture on Bolívar upstairs. I finished early, because since the press was boycotting me hardly any journalists came . . . So I went to say hello to the Cuban speaker, who turned out to be the City of Havana historian, Eusebio Leal. We introduced ourselves, and exchanged details. That was how an invitation arrived: the Casa Simón Rodríguez in Havana invited me to give a lecture on Bolívar on 17 December. They sent me the ticket, as I couldn't afford it.

But I couldn't make the 17th, because the efforts we'd made on the international front had borne their first fruits. I told the ambassador the 17th was impossible, as we'd already arranged a preparatory meeting on that day for what we were beginning to call the Bolivarian Amphictyonic Congress.

Did they accept to change the date?
Yes, they brought it forward. And we left for Havana on 13 December. We went on a Venezuelan commercial flight, chatting to a group of Cubans and some Venezuelans. When the plane landed I remember hearing an announcement that the plane was taxiing and would not be stopping at the passenger terminal but at the 'protocol' terminal. I'd no idea what that meant. It was my first time in Cuba. I felt the plane coming to a halt; I grabbed my hand luggage, my suit carrier. Rafael Isea, my aide at the time, was with me. Another announcement: 'Passenger Hugo Chávez, please make your way to the door . . .' I looked out of the window and saw television lights. It was night-time, I imagined a television or radio crew was waiting. That's the most I was expecting.

You never thought Fidel could be waiting there in person?
Never. Of course, I'd told the ambassador, 'I'd like to say hello to the comandante.' But he just said, 'I'll let Havana know.' That was all. So when I reached the door of the plane, I saw Angelito, the Cuban head of protocol, and he said, 'They're waiting for you . . .' 'Who?' 'The *comandante en jefe*.' I couldn't believe it, I wasn't prepared for this, nobody had told me. 'It can't be!' I never thought

Fidel himself would be waiting by the plane. And when I looked out . . . There was Fidel, standing at the foot of the steps. I gave my briefcase to Isea. I went down the steps, and well, that first unforgettable embrace. The 'embrace of death', my enemies called it.

Did Fidel explain why he received you like that?

No, actually he didn't. I didn't ask him either. Imagine how honoured I felt. In the University, I said, 'I don't deserve this honour, this reception; I hope one day I will deserve it.' Looking back, I think some things were obvious, don't you? Remember what I read about Fidel's response to Tomás Borge in the days following 4-F. That same year 1992, when we were in prison, he must surely have read some reports of our prison manifestos. And then, by December 1994, we had already been out mobilizing in the streets for eight months, and he must have got some more concrete information about what was going on, and what our platform was. Not to mention his nose for politics, developed over so many years, with the experience of having seen so many movements and so many events in Latin America.

Besides which, don't you think Fidel was sending signals?

Absolutely. By receiving me like that, with his constant shows of affection, his words in the University, his presence in the Casa Bolívar, I think Fidel was sending several messages.[28]

First, to Rafael Caldera, who a month earlier had received two anti-Castro leaders from Miami, Jorge Mas Canosa and Armando Valladares, at the Miraflores Palace. And who a couple of days earlier, in Miami, during the first Heads of State of the Americas Summit – to which Fidel was not invited – had violently attacked Cuba and called for 'regime change'.

The second message, in my view, was aimed at the Latin American Left and was, for me, very important. Although he has never said so, I'm sure that Fidel, when he began to adopt me, wanted to

---

28   For a detailed description of that visit by Hugo Chávez to Cuba, see Elizalde and Báez, *El Encuentro*.

bestow on me a kind of recognition, and send a signal to the Left. Fidel's embrace demolished, once and for all, the accusation that I was a '*carapintada*', a '*golpista*', a fascist ... That was, without a doubt, what Fidel wanted to do.

It was important, because your image, at an international level, was more related to the military Right. Politically speaking, no one really knew what you were. All the 'Bolivarian' stuff didn't mean anything to many people on the international Left.
I recognize that there were reasons to doubt us, and especially me personally. Perhaps Fidel himself had doubts. I recall that, from the first moment we sat down to talk, he was scrutinizing me. And he kept it up during all the activities we took part in. For example, he arrived unannounced at the Casa Simón Bolívar, where I was giving a lecture. Nobody knew he was coming. He just appeared, and sat down in the front row. I felt his eagle eye, the look of someone who was examining every word. The same in Havana University; his eyes didn't leave my face while he was taking notes. I felt as if I was being examined, sized up.

Daniel Ortega was there too.
Yes, Daniel was there by chance. He was spending a few days in Cuba for some medical tests, and Fidel sent for him the day after my arrival. After the Casa Simón Bolívar event, Fidel took me to his car and invited Daniel as well. The three of us drove in that black Mercedes round Havana, a city where you didn't see any cars, the only one was Fidel's, it was like a ghost ...

It was during the 'special period'.[29]
Yes, you didn't see a single car. I saw skeletons of buses drawn by horses or tractors, with people inside ... There was no fuel. Frequent

---

29   Name they give in Cuba to the ten years [1992–2002] that followed the fall of the Soviet Union and the European socialist camp with which Cuba did 80 per cent of its trade. That loss, added to the continuing trade embargo imposed by the US in 1961, caused serious shortages.

blackouts: the electricity was only on for a few hours a day. Neighbourhoods took it in turns, one night on, one night off. A lot of lifts weren't working. Rationing was strict . . . A difficult time. But that people showed extraordinary dignity.

Where did Fidel take you?

To various places. The night I arrived, we went to the Palace of the Revolution where we had our first conversations. I also remember going to the Military Academy of the Revolutionary Armed Forces. They gave me a medal and we went to visit a tank battalion. After that we had lunch at the Palace, and then went to the Casa Bolívar in the historic centre of Havana where, as well as Daniel Ortega, Carlos Lage and Ricardo Alarcón were present.[30] And at 8 p.m., in the Aula Magna, Fidel pronounced that phrase [he takes a book and reads],

'Let people call it what they will. We, as everyone knows, call it socialism. But if I'm told, that's Bolivarianism, I'll say, I totally agree. If I'm told, that's Marti-ism, I'll say, I agree. And what's more, if I'm told, that is called Christianity, I'll say, I totally agree!'[31]

That day was frenetic. Fidel came to everything. But it didn't end there. After our intervention in the Aula Magna of the University, at midnight, he took me to see the Venezuelan ambassador [Gonzalo García Bustillos] in Havana. He had to do it discreetly, because relations between Caldera and Fidel were pretty tense at the time . . . But the ambassador was a good friend of Cuba. Then Fidel took me to the residence where I was staying. I remember him going in and opening the fridge, saying, 'Let's see what there is to eat around here.' We hadn't eaten. He took out some cheese, asked for a knife, cut it, and we sat down to eat. He asked, 'Do you drink wine? A glass of wine every now and again is good for cholesterol.' We drank a toast. I could see that his reputation for being indefatigable and insomniac was not exaggerated.

---

30 Carlos Lage (1951–), vice president of the Cuban State Council (equivalent to prime minister) from 1993 to 2009; Ricardo Alarcón (1937–), president of the Cuban National Assembly from 1993 to 2013.

31 Elizalde and Báez, *El Encuentro*, p. 56.

Did that meeting with Fidel facilitate contacts with the Left in Latin America? Did the idea of your going to San Salvador for the São Paulo Social Forum come up then?

Yes. Fidel and I evaluated the international situation. When I explained the ideas that were moving me towards holding an Amphictyonic Congress in Panama in 1996, he, very cautiously, supported the idea of that Bolivarian Congress, and even sent a delegate to the preparatory meeting in Santa Marta. But he also mentioned other existing mechanisms. That's when he told me about the São Paulo Social Forum, which I didn't know about. He gave me a lot of information.

How did you get on in the São Paulo Forum?

That was the following year, 1995. I've told you a little about it already. Fidel told me they were convening the Forum's meeting in El Salvador. Probably through him, or anyhow through Cuba, we got an invitation, and then we were in touch ourselves. So we were able to attend the Forum in San Salvador. Shafik Handal looked after us very attentively.[32]

I met Lula there. We didn't sit down and talk or anything, but we shook hands. And I met a lot of other left-wing Latin American leaders – Dominicans, Mexicans from the PRD [Democratic Revolutionary Party], Panamanians, Brazilians . . . Let's say it was a sort of debutante presentation, a coming-out among the Latin American Left. Of course, there was still that situation I told you about. Several delegations categorically refused to let me speak. I wasn't allowed to speak. Despite Fidel's backing.

Coming back to your stay in Cuba, how long did you spend in Havana?

Not long, only two intense, unforgettable days. I arrived on 13 December and left on the 15th. When I said goodbye to Fidel, at

---

32   Shafik Jorge Handal (1930–2006), former secretary general of the Salvadorean Communist Party, was one of the five leaders of the revolutionary war of the Farabundo Martí Liberation Front (FMLN) in El Salvador from 1981 to 1992.

José Martí International Airport, next to the plane, I put on my red beret and gave him a military salute. Me in my green *liqui-liqui*, and him in his legendary olive green uniform. The scene was filmed, the images of that salute are there. It caused a tremendous commotion in Caracas.

Why?
Because some television 'analysts' showed the footage in slow motion and explained, 'Look, Chávez shakes hands and so does Fidel. But if you run the images on, you see that Fidel lowers his hand first, and Chávez holds his there for longer. It's the code for subordination!' They presented me as a lackey, at the orders of Fidel, at the service of Cuba. I laughed about it. But it was worrying, too, because it was a very aggressive campaign. It's still going on!

Then you went to Santa Marta, to the preliminary meeting of the Bolivarian Amphictyonic Congress.
We didn't have money for a ticket. We went in a pick-up truck, a journey of twelve hours to Maracaibo. And from Maracaibo, still in the truck, across the whole of La Guajira to Santa Marta, Colombia. We arrived, but couldn't afford a hotel. The Colombian delegation was already there, and they didn't have a cent either, they'd assumed we would pay for rooms. I apologized. In the end we all went to sleep at the home of someone's journalist friend, in her big house on the outskirts of Santa Marta; eight of us slept in a hammock and a camp bed. Ceresole came from Argentina, Fidel sent José Luis Joa, head of their Office for Latin American Affairs. And a Panamanian came too.

Only four delegations? Not very many, was it?
Well, it was starting to take shape. The embryo of what would be our Strategic Map. That was all destroyed by the counter-offensive by the US, allied governments, intelligence services. I remember that in Santa Marta we held our meeting modestly in some place we found; we did a radio interview, talking about Santa Marta, Bolívar, etc. On 17 December, we wanted to go into San Pedro Alejandrino

[the estate where Bolívar died], where there were official commem-
orations taking place. We weren't allowed in. But the next day, the
18th, ten times more people came to our do than to the official
events. The crowd was so big, it couldn't all fit in that patio. We did
just the same as them: national anthem, band, floral tributes,
speeches. Colonel Augusto Guillermo Lora, who had formed a
Bolivarian movement in Colombia, gave a speech. At the end, I
urged them, 'You who are left-wing soldiers, join us.'

So, on balance, you thought that year 1994 ended up positive for the MBR-200.

In 1994 we made good progress, both at home and abroad. A
Bolivarian Movement was already well-established over almost all
of Venezuela, and a few tentative international steps, which were
royally capped with the visit to Cuba and the meeting in Santa
Marta of the coordinating committee for the Panamanian Bolivarian
Amphictyonic Congress in 1996.

That's perhaps why the offensive against you also intensified?

Of course. Two months later came Colombian president Ernesto
Samper's accusation that I was in league with the guerrillas. It had
international repercussions. It was the missile launched against the
response to our Amphictyonic Congress, and the hopes it was raising. In Colombia, for instance, various left-wing groups had
suggested the idea of doing a horseback ride along the route the
Liberators took, from Boyacá to Carabobo. The groups comprised
military, civilian and ex-guerrilla people: this was new. Similar to
what was happening here in Venezuela, with the extension of the
civilian–military confluence. That's why they fired that missile at
me. It hit me below the belt. The accusation caused a lot of anxiety
in Colombia. All our efforts had been for nothing. There were no
more meetings.

What were they accusing you of exactly?

A guerrilla group had killed some Venezuelan soldiers on the border
between Venezuela and Colombia. And the Colombian president

Ernesto Samper sent a report to Caracas accusing me of commanding the attack. Commanding it, not supporting it! Actually commanding Colombian guerrillas . . .

And what was that accusation based on?
On a report fabricated by the intelligence services out of forged documents and false evidence. Years later, when I was already president, Ernesto Samper came to see me in Caracas. I received him and didn't even mention the subject. He was the one who brought it up, and I said, 'There's no need. I know what happened.' But he insisted, 'No, allow me to explain, President. They completely fooled me, they presented me with documents, photos, videos, etc.' He thought the accusation was true and sent the report to Rafael Caldera.

They demonized you.
Yes, those days in 1995 set off a general offensive. They accused me of everything under the sun. The media siege cranked up, amid pressure and manipulations. In Argentina, for example, I was reported to be preparing a coup with Seineldín. In Panama the same, that I was preparing a coup and was in touch with Noriega – though he was in jail in Florida! Here in Caracas, our tiny office was ransacked about five times [laughter]. One day a journalist phoned from London to ask me, 'You're in Caracas, aren't you?' 'Yes'. He spoke Spanish, more or less. I don't remember which newspaper or radio it was. He said, 'I don't understand. Are you clandestine?' 'No, sir, I'm in my office in downtown Caracas.' And then he told me, 'It's just that we have a cable here saying you're bringing thousands of weapons down the Orinoco, supported by Fidel, to liberate the south of Venezuela.' I was astonished. All this stuff was circulating. I had a plan to liberate the Orinoco and the south of Venezuela, to unite with Arauca and Apure, and form the Gran Colombia guerrilla front. The media made all these claims. You can see them in the newspaper library.

***Strangely enough those attacks intensified after your visit to
Cuba, didn't they?***

Yes. Everything intensified after that greeting from Fidel at Havana
airport on 13 December. When they published the photo of the
embrace, the newspaper headline was 'The Kiss of Death'. A friend
who worked in Miraflores told me he'd heard a minister say, 'Chávez
is fucked now. Fidel killed him.' That whole day they were broadcasting images of my visit to Cuba, part of my speech and part of
Fidel's . . . and the embrace. They did it to destroy me. They repeated
over and over again, 'Chávez has shown his true colours, he went to
subordinate himself to the tyrant, the communist . . .' They
demonized Fidel, a 'troglodyte', a 'dictator'. 'See? Chávez is going
backwards. What can this *golpista* offer us? Now he's a communist,
just when communism has disappeared.' Remember this was 1994,
the Soviet Union had imploded. They never understood the
psychology of the people, and never will.

***But they were worried about the Chávez–Fidel connection, and
understood all the political potential it implied.***

Absolutely. And in fact, it was after my visit to Cuba that they
began to worry we might really create an international movement.
And this scared them stiff. However, I must say that I've always
been quite lucky. Because someone warned me, 'The Colombians
are going to accuse you of something serious, we don't know what
exactly.' So when the headlines and television got going with
'Chávez Kills Venezuelan Soldiers', I knew immediately it was a
shot aimed at the heart.

They wanted to destroy you.

Of course. Shoot me through the heart. We met to evaluate what
was going on and I decided, 'I'm going to Bogotá.' Everyone was
against it: 'Are you crazy, they'll arrest you, they'll kill you.'

It was risky.

But I went with a *compañero*. We got in touch with our Colombian
friends from the Amphictyonic Congress, the retired officers, and

they met me at the airport. My arrival passed almost unnoticed, because we hadn't booked tickets and turned up at Maiquetía airport at the last moment.

Anyway, we arrived, our friends took us to a hotel, and arranged for me to go on TV early next morning. Hardly anybody knew I was in Colombia. At seven in the morning, I went on Juan Gossaín's television show. He knew me already. He began by asking me, live on air, 'So, what are you here for, Colonel Chávez?' In Colombia they call me 'colonel'. I replied, 'I've come to defend my military honour. Either I stay in Colombia, in jail, or dead, or I return to Venezuela with my honour restored. One of the two.'

'Why do you say that?'

'Because the president of this country has accused me of commanding the attack that killed those soldiers in Cararabo.'

'And you're innocent?'

'I'm innocent. Here I am, Señor Presidente, let the intelligence services come and get me. I'm in such and such a hotel. I am unarmed.'

I don't know how Gossaín did it, but a few minutes later they had Ernesto Samper on screen, live, arriving at a meeting. A journalist went up to him: 'President, you have accused Colonel Chávez of being the author of the Cararabo massacre.' Samper confirmed: 'Yes, we have proof that Colonel Chávez is with the ELN and the FARC; they attacked that post, killed those soldiers and cut their tongues out . . .' Then the journalist said, 'We have Colonel Chávez live, in the studio. He came to Bogotá and wants to talk to you. Will you see him?' Samper went green, then purple, and all he managed to say was, 'No, no, I can't see him, it might damage relations with the Venezuelan government. Thank you very much.' And off he went.

You were watching this live?

Yes, I was in the studio with Gossaín and I saw it live on the screen. My Colombian friends had got me a prestigious lawyer, a man of the Left, very respected in Colombia, Ernesto Amésquita, who subsequently came to live in Venezuela because they threatened to kill him for having defended left-wing causes. With him, the retired officers from the Colombian Moral Movement, and a swarm of journalists behind us, we went to the Ministry of Defence.

What for?

Those same Colombian *compañeros* had advised me to do it. The night we arrived, in the hotel, one of the retired officers began phoning serving officers, and even managed to speak to the Army commander in chief: 'General, Colonel Chávez is here. He's being unjustly accused of a serious crime in Cararabo, he wishes to talk . . .' The general wouldn't speak to me on the phone. But my friends had contacts in the Ministry of Defence and insisted we go.

We arrived, identified ourselves, went in, and an admiral intro-duced himself as the head of public relations: 'The minister cannot receive you. What can I do for you?' 'Señor Almirante, I have come to deliver this document, requesting, as an army officer, clarifica-tion of this matter. I have been unjustly accused of a terrible mili-tary action. These are my lawyer's recommendations. The Colombian Constitution stipulates that you respond to my petition.'

Is that in the Colombian Constitution?

Yes, and now it's also in ours. And I have to say, they actually responded. A month later, I received a missive from the Colombian Ministry of Defence telling me that there was no serious evidence.

They recognized the accusation was false.

They had no choice. I moved heaven and earth. I went from the Ministry of Defence to the Military Appeal Court and talked to its president, 'Colonel, I have come to ask you to bring a case for me: this is the *notitia criminis*. I am accused of participating in an ambush and of killing fourteen Venezuelan soldiers. I demand a trial.' I appealed to the minister publicly, held a press conference, asked journalists to let President Samper know in which hotel to find me, at what time I was leaving the following day, and that I was at his complete disposal until then.

The intelligence services immediately went to work distributing defamatory leaflets in the streets, slandering me, repeating the worst accusations. A real lynching. Incitement to crime, to someone taking a shot at me.

What did you do?

Well, I'd fulfilled my mission, which was to publicly repudiate these false accusations in the media and before the Colombian justice system. I aimed to leave the following day. I arrived at Bogotá airport, and I was summoned to the office of the DAS (Colombian intelligence services). A rather nervous bureaucrat said, 'We need a declaration from you.'

I had an envelope in my wallet with a four- or five-line resumé of what was in the Samper Report. A journalist friend in Bogotá had somehow obtained a copy of the Report from a senior official and dictated it over the phone to another friend in Caracas, who copied the main points on the first bit of paper he found: an envelope from the Eurobuilding Hotel. I remember cutting out the bit with the hotel name so as not to compromise anybody. Then, when the bureaucrat began to question me, I took out this paper and said, 'Tell your boss to recommend to President Samper, who did not want to receive me, that he should extricate himself from this mess, because someone's put their foot in it. And also tell him that I've seen the "secret report" where it states that on such and such a date I was with "Gabino".'

He was astonished I knew about that. I gave him all the details, he took notes. 'Tell your boss that I can prove that, on that date, I was at a public event with thousands of witnesses.' I had checked my diary against the report. 'Very well, thank you very much,' he said. And as I told you, a month later I received an official document acknowledging that the report was erroneous.

But the damage had been done.

Yes, the damage was enormous. From then on the accusations came thick and fast … Arms trafficking, drug trafficking, money laundering, guerrillas, etc. Wherever I went, whichever country I visited, they connected me in some way with those accusations. The press talked about the 'Venezuelan *golpista*', the '*carapintada*', 'Noriega's friend', the 'drug trafficker', 'Gabino's comrade who kills Venezuelan soldiers', 'Fidel's subordinate' . . . They dealt a hard blow. Cleverly managed. And for me it was a test of fire.

After those trips abroad, did you keep giving speeches inside Venezuela?

We didn't stop. 1994, 1995 and 1996 were three years of building support. The Strategic Map became clearer, we defined strategic priorities, and undertook a new round of intensive speaking tours in the interior. The activity was frenetic: organizing the Bolivarian Movement into a major political player; making alliances at home and abroad; establishing political programmes and trying to ignite generators in the light of those programmes. Both in the shanty towns and in the countryside, I stressed the evils of machismo, the way it negated half of humanity. I repeated that liberating women also liberated us men.

Of course, our intense activity was a way of fanning the bonfires, so to speak, that were blazing all over the country. We had gigantic rallies. I used to say, 'My God! Where have all these people come from?'

Weren't people afraid of the government?

No, the people had lost their fear. There was a lot of popular enthusiasm. All the while the credibility of the traditional political parties, Right and Left alike, decreased in direct proportion to the increased credibility of our discourse, our project, our message. This was one of the factors that influenced the decision we were later to take to stand in the elections. Other factors were influential as well, particularly the failure of Caldera's government. Because if Caldera had been successful, it would have had a negative effect on what we were proposing. But what we'd been saying all along proved to be true.

At that time, were you still not participating in any elections?
Right. We didn't participate ourselves, nor did we support candidates from any other party. But the social indicators were deteriorating. The political crisis was getting worse. The government did nothing to alleviate hunger and poverty, quite the opposite. It bailed out the bankers who had stolen $8 billion. A figure which, for Venezuela, was equal to – I don't have the data to hand, but approximately 20 per cent of GDP. This further increased the poverty, inequality and unemployment. Inflation rose over 100 per cent a year, while wages increased 0 per cent.

In 1994, there was a serious banking crisis.
Yes. The Banco Latino collapsed and other important banks went broke. The bolívar plunged. Inflation shot up, to over 70 per cent in twelve months! Caldera announced the privatization of state enterprises. So I began accusing him of following in the footsteps of Carlos Andrés Pérez. I said, 'Caldera should dissolve Congress and call for a Constituent Assembly.' Not that I expected him to do so, but that was our political line, and we thought the crisis demanded that solution.

In his first year, Caldera had criticized the IMF . . .
He was a neoliberal who, at one stage, criticized neoliberalism. But he was very lukewarm about it. He tried to take some measures appropriate to a sovereign government, but then caved in. He caved in to the IMF, he caved in to the criollo oligarchy, and to the international financial oligarchy. He then announced the 'Venezuela Agenda'. This economic programme turned out to be the same as the one the IMF tried to implement here in 1989. That is, he was following in the footsteps of Carlos Andrés Pérez.

That fresh collapse of the banking system offered you a wonderful political opportunity, didn't it?
Absolutely. Because it meant the political class had completely surrendered. Many honest people on the Left had supported

Caldera in the belief that at least he was going to create a nationalist government, and make an effort to turn the country in another direction. And initially, as we said, he did try. But he gave in quickly when he realized he couldn't.

We told him, 'Dissolve Congress, call a Constituent Assembly, or call a referendum without dissolving Congress.' I didn't have to dissolve Congress in 1999, I simply called a referendum. They said they couldn't call a referendum; the law didn't allow it. I explained – to the people, not to them – that Article 3 of the then Constitution states, 'Sovereignty resides with the people who exercise it by suffrage through the public institutions . . .' On that legal basis, they needed to draft a Law with ten articles and call a referendum, or give the president the authority to call a referendum, and see what the sovereign people wanted. I explained it in a thousand different ways.

I soon realized Caldera was not going to do it. On the contrary, he launched the *Agenda Venezuela*, went begging to the IMF, etc. He got back on board the same old ship . . . So I said to myself, 'Caldera's sunk', and so he was, he was a spectacular failure.

And that's when you first thought of becoming a presidential candidate?

Yes, it was one of the factors that made me decide to stand. But there was something else as well: the question of military action. As I told you, for all those years I'd kept in touch with our military cadres in the Army. They were under a lot of surveillance and some had been sent to posts on the border. Discussing and analysing the options with them, I came to the conclusion that a new military movement was not feasible. We were not strong enough and we could no longer count on the element of surprise. We had been infiltrated to the core by the DIM. They had even got inside my aunts' house, taking photos . . . One of my own drivers, Francisco, was an informer . . .

We could have created various guerrilla fronts, for sure, because lots of ordinary people were willing to go. It wouldn't have been difficult. But the time for that had passed, guerrilla movements had failed everywhere. Besides, Venezuela happens to be a predominantly urban country.

So, from 1997 onwards I was quite clear in my mind that it was not possible – not in the short term – to successfully launch a new military operation of the 4-F type, or a civilian–military one like the 17-N. I was sure the armed struggle was not viable at that time.

How much popular support did you have then?

According to official surveys, when asked if they wanted Chávez as a leader, only 10 per cent said yes. However, having toured towns and cities, I saw for myself that the impact of 4-F was still being felt and had solid support throughout the country.

But you couldn't quantify that support?

No. That's why, when the time for the presidential elections of 1998 was getting close, one of the things we did to help us take a decision was to carry out our own survey, which was actually much more than a survey. We prepared a big consultation, all over the country, quite unlike the traditional format used in opinion polling – something that would have scientific value.

What sort of consultation?

More than polling, it was measuring. We asked for help from university professors, especially sociologists. We designed a measurement system, trying to make it as objective as possible. We organized workshops. The university students who would be doing the measuring didn't know it was for the Bolivarian Movement. Neither did they know what the aim of the measurement exercise was. They weren't volunteers, nor did they necessarily sympathize with us and, since by that time we had some resources, they got paid.

One hundred thousand questionnaires were filled in, representing a larger respondent base than most polls. I revised the technical details of the measuring process myself, to make sure we didn't score an own goal. We needed to know the objective truth. Among the many questions that were asked, the two that interested us most were: 1. 'Do you think Commander Hugo Chávez should be a candidate for president of the Republic?' And 2. 'Would you vote for him?'

What were the results?

To the first question, over 70 per cent said yes. And to the second, 55 per cent said yes. Surprising because, in December of 1998, we won the elections with 56.2 per cent! That is, very close to the result given by our poll done in 1997. Pretty scientific, wouldn't you say? This was the defining factor that persuaded us to go for the elections.

At that stage, was all the MBR-200 in agreement about going for the elections? It meant a Copernican change of direction, didn't it?

Yes, absolutely. There was no unanimity in the Movement. I remember one night, in Maracaibo, when I proposed we discuss the subject . . . They all stood up, I don't remember anybody supporting me. I'm talking about regional cadres. In the national leadership, support and opposition were more or less evenly spread. But in the majority of regions it was considered a betrayal of the Movement and the people.

That's understandable, when you'd made non-participation in elections the emblematic stance of the Movement?

Sure. We'd spent several years calling for boycott of the vote, and demanding a new Constituent Assembly . . . We were known for two military rebellions, one call to abstain in the presidential elections, another to abstain in the gubernatorial elections, and constantly denouncing the impotence of party politics. So I went from state to state trying to convince them. I set out my arguments, I reasoned: 'Listen, this is a step towards the Constituent Assembly.' Even then I couldn't convince them. Our Movement was born out of debate, of course, with different tendencies, there was freedom of opinion.

The first time I talked of the possibility of standing for election was in Cumaná. And when we arrived, my own bodyguards, with their pistols or old rifles from the guerrilla war, came to see me, like eight of them. They said, 'Comandante, we love you dearly, but don't count on us for any elections.'

Many *compañeros* accused me of betraying the MBR-200, of getting carried away by electoralism. They believed the system would swallow us up. I felt as I were in the dock. Those were bitter days because, after having created the MBR-200 and having helped establish it throughout the country, I saw the Movement turning more radically against participation in elections. Very prestigious voices spoke up against the vote. That tendency asserted more and more loudly that to stand for election was to betray the people, sink the Movement, and dash people's hopes.

There was a meeting in San Cristóbal, where the verdict was even worse for me. I was tired, bruised and disheartened. I told myself, 'OK, then, if that's how it is, I'll withdraw.'

Did you seriously consider it?
Very seriously. I remember that at the end of that meeting in San Cristóbal, very late at night, I talked to two of the Movement's founders, Iris Varela and *El Gocho* Zambrano. She was a lawyer and one of my fiercest opponents on this subject, even though she was very fond of me. She and Zambrano were a couple at the time. She had a car, and when the meeting ended, I asked them to please take me to my father's farm. Barinas was about three hours away. They agreed. I lay down in the back seat, I was tired out, soul-weary. I asked myself, 'What have we created? What do these people want? Another military uprising? What with? What for?' There wasn't the slightest chance of success. And I couldn't make them see it!

Did that depress you?
I was above all immensely tired. Overwhelmed with exhaustion. I needed a solitude cure. I spend a week there meditating, walking by the river. I was alone, like Jesus in the wilderness . . . I wouldn't let anyone come with me: 'Just leave me alone!'

At the end of that week, a commission came to find me. I put it to them, 'What are we to do? I'm not going to impose on you. You don't want us to stand in the elections, so I have to mull it over, think what to do. Because I can't go along with your idea of a new armed uprising: I think it's madness, I don't want to lead people to their deaths, like I did on 4 February 1992, or to prison. What's the point? We'd be letting rip just to show what brave rebels we are.'

I had to be loyal to them. Because I wasn't about to say, 'OK, you don't want to follow me, so I'm joining up with La Causa R. No, these were my people. I was duty-bound to keep trying to convince them.

So, you found the heart to throw yourself back into the debate.
Yes, during that week of solitude and meditation, I came to the conclusion that my analysis was the correct one. A voice inside me told me to fulfil my duty and accept that mission. I decided that I had to lead the country if I wanted to change it. And my first task was to persuade my *compañeros*. I returned to the fray. I'm not one of those people who give up at the first hurdle.

It's what one calls character.
Heraclitus said, 'A man's character is his destiny.'

I thought you were going to quote The Path of the Warrior . . .[33]
Ah! The 'Oracle' . . . Well, I could have. For example, in that little book there's an aphorism that says something like, 'Now is the moment to stop taking action. Leave the whirlwind of life and make space for meditation. Seek solitude. Only then will you be able to see clearly. Repose, rest, meditate. Then see and take action.' It was apt in that situation. But I don't remember if I'd read the book by then . . .

---

33   Lucas Estrella Schultz, *The Path of the Warrior: Consult the Oracle for Everyday Guidance on Your Life Journey*, St. Martin's Press, 1998.

That book became very famous; you quoted it a lot in the 1998 presidential campaign. How did you come across it?

It fell into my hands by chance. I think it was a present from my [second] wife Marisabel. It's a short little book, like a breviary, some ninety pages, divided into forty chapters, full of aphorisms and homilies, infused with a philosophy that combines reflection and action. I liked it enormously. Some of those sayings, like the one I just quoted, summed up exactly what I wanted to express. Yes, I did quote it a lot in my 1998 electoral campaign. And the book actually became a best-seller. Amazing! And heaven knows how many pirate versions also came out. In any case, it helped us win. And I'm reading it again, with a view to my strategy for the presidential elections of October 2012.

Is that a warning to the opposition?

Absolutely. It's a warning to my adversaries, but also to ourselves. Because the bourgeoisie and their allies – at home and abroad – will never leave us in peace. And that's normal in democratic rivalry. We have to get used, therefore, to living in a state of permanent struggle, in permanent conflict, in permanent revolution. And what does the 'Oracle' tell us about that? 'Warrior, when the battle ends, don't sheath your sword. Why? Tomorrow is another battle.' I say the same, the road ahead is full of battles. But in each of those battles we'll be victorious.

Going back to what we were talking about before, you were telling me you decided to 'return to the fray' and convince your friends in the MBR-200 of the need to take part in elections.

Yes, I put my boots on again, and called a MBR-200 National Congress to debate the matter for several days. The debates were hard-fought. I reminded them that sometimes, if you don't want politics to be worse than it is, you have to act – even if it means selling your soul to the devil, as Max Weber said.

Ultimately, the decision was to hold a general consultation. Some, Domingo Alberto Rangel senior and other cadres, didn't accept the decision and left. Still, what mattered to us, over and above the feelings of the cadres, was the opinion of the people. We did that survey, those questionnaires I told you about, and obtained those encouraging results. And in the end, in Valencia, on 19 April 1997, two resolutions were taken: one was to create a political electoral instrument, and the second was to launch my pre-candidacy.

The 'political electoral instrument' was the Movimiento Vª República, wasn't it?

Correct. We decided to create a party called Movimiento Vª República [Fifth Republic Movement], and defined its bases, its programme and the candidate list.

Why did you change your name?

Because the Political Parties Law did not allow the name Bolívar to be used for a party. So, early one morning, searching my brain for acronyms, I came up with Movimiento Vª República which at least kept the sound, a link between 'MBR' and 'MVR'.

Some people maintain that, historically, the Fifth Republic is incorrect. What do you say to that?

Yes, some people talk about the Third Republic, for instance . . . Depends how you see it. There are different ways of dividing the periods. Which is mine? We place the First Republic in 1811, no doubts there, first Constitution, first Republic. Then came what official history calls the Second Republic. It was born in 1813, after the *Campaña Admirable*. Bolívar became leader, crossed the Andes from Nueva Granada, and in a meteoric campaign known as 'Admirable', entered Caracas in August of 1813. He formed a government and installed the Second Republic.

But in the following year, 1814, that Republic fell when the Spaniards retook Caracas. Until 1817, when Bolívar liberated Isla Margarita, installed his government, and the Third Republic began to be born. It was not definitively established until 1819, with the Angostura Congress and the Constitution of Gran Colombia. From our point of view, it's the Third Great Republic, or the original Bolivarian Republic. That Republic fell with the death of Bolívar [17 December 1830].

Then came the Fourth Republic, which was anti-Bolivarian and oligarchic, and lasted throughout the nineteenth and twentieth centuries. Some historians dispute that, because there was a Constituent Assembly in 1947, and many other Constitutions. But, in reality, the fact of changing a Constitution does not necessarily imply a change of Republic. For instance, the Republic that was born in 1830 with Páez as president is, in my opinion, the same as the one Rafael Caldera presided over 160 years later. There were some changes, of course, elected governments, governments after coups d'états, governments from direct elections, governments from indirect elections . . . But the Republic was the same, a regime where the interests of a minority held sway, and with forms of government that were in many cases openly dictatorial and in other cases disguised as democratic. In any case, that's the explanation I put forwards, which finally convinced the others.

After that you launched your electoral campaign.
Well, I still went through a period of grave doubt, after those times I was so harshly criticized I thought I'd die. Once I'd got back on my feet, I still thought, 'And what if Domingo Alberto Rangel was right?' What if it proves impossible, by taking the electoral path, to make the changes only a revolution can? What then? I once more began to wonder whether if that happened, we wouldn't have to resort to arms again . . .

I had these serious doubts. In the end I told myself, 'OK, but first let's give it a go.' And that's what we did. And how! We organized it all very methodically, we studied every detail. We took the advice of Marcus Aurelius: 'The secret of every victory lies in the organization of the impossible.'[34]

During the campaign, apparently you wanted to go to Miami and the US refused you a visa. Is that true?
Absolutely. It was a blunder on their part. It happened, I think, in April 1998 when the Venezuelan–American Chamber of Commerce

---

34   Roman emperor nicknamed 'The Wise' (121–180), author of *Meditations*.

in Florida invited me to explain my views to local businessmen. I planned to go on to New York, where other businessmen, and even bankers, had invited me. But Washington denied me a visa. A US State Department spokesperson [Jeffrey Davidow, aide to the secretary of state and former ambassador to Venezuela] said, 'Commander Chávez has no right to a visa because he attempted to overthrow a democratic government.' Such scruples! These people have spent their lives toppling democratic governments and welcoming Latin American dictators and terrorists to their shores. Of course, they were 'theirs' . . .

Anyway, it didn't stop us winning the elections in 1998. We took power in February 1999 and showed that the electoral and democratic path was viable. And I believe it is still viable. We see it in what has happened – and is still happening – all over Latin America, in Bolivia, Brazil, Ecuador, Argentina, Uruguay, Paraguay, Nicaragua, Peru . . .

When did the Movimiento V República join the Polo Patriótico [Patriotic Pole] election alliance?

When we created the MVR and decided to run for election, the parties on the Left had no option but to recognize our leadership and our manifesto. There was no alternative. Our campaign with me as candidate was in its infancy when the Communist Party left the government and announced it was backing me, without even being asked. We're not sectarian, or vain, and we accepted their support.

Then, a few months later, La Causa R, the MAS and the MEP did the same. So it occurred to me to talk up a Patriotic Alliance – an alliance that would be strategic as well as tactical. But I think those parties, without exception, were only looking for political space, government posts, through either the regional or the national elections.

That reminds me, I'd just been elected president when the leaders of the MAS arrived to demand two ministries: 'We've come to ask for two ministries, Mr President, it's our due, it's only fair.' 'I'm sorry,' I said, 'I'm not doling out posts here. I thank you kindly, but off you go and tell your party this government is not going to be a "broad church" like in the old days of AD–Copei.'

Then, when I began to form my first government and designate ministers, of course I weighed up the talents of many of the cadres from those parties and appointed them. Not because they were from the MAS, the PCV or the PPT, but for their intrinsic qualities.

I'll tell you something. Right here at this very table, many nights, especially around election time for Congress, the Constituent Assembly, and then for the National Assembly, I always acted generously with the people from those parties when it came to drawing up the lists. I always told my *compañeros*, 'We'll give more posts to the Communist Party, or the PPT, etc., because they have good cadres. We're going to do away with any idea of MVR hegemony.' We were the party with the most votes, but with the least sectarianism. That was the Polo Patriótico, and with that alliance we won the December 1998 elections.[35]

Churchill said that victory has a hundred fathers, and defeat none. Did those parties latch onto you because they scented victory?
No doubt. In fact, they were leaving one government for the next . . . But they weren't the only ones. By the end of the campaign, when it was obvious who would win, the oligarchs, who are very clever, also began to change their attitude. Some of the staunchest representatives of that Venezuelan oligarchy, that *ancien régime*, even wrote in a newspaper that, since they couldn't beat the beast – the beast was me – they would have to tame him. So they started circling around me. I remember, the day after our election victory I was invited on to a television channel owned by members of that same putrid and very powerful oligarchy, and you can't imagine the adulation and obsequiousness with which they treated me on that programme. I cringed for them, it was embarrassing.

---

35   The results were Hugo Chávez (MVR), 56.2 per cent; Henrique Salas Römer (Proyecto Venezuela), 39.9 per cent; Irene Sáez (IRENE), 2.8 per cent.

When I took office, on 2 February 1999, I came here to the Miraflores Palace that first night and Alberto Fujimori, Carlos Menem and the Prince of Asturias were waiting. José Luis Rodríguez *El Puma* – imagine that! – came to sing me a song.[36] And above all, the oligarchy appeared, singing my praises. I was surrounded by a full quota of oligarchs. They wanted to consume me, like vampires. They all showed up, the Cisneroses, the Azpurúas, the super-rich, the bourgeoisie . . . I was beside myself. I had campaigned thinking of the poor, those who have nothing, and are the heart and soul of Venezuela. And now the people, the long-ignored people, were barely represented – well, except for the chauffeurs, bodyguards, waiters, etc. Fidel Castro popped his head into that plush salon, and asked me ironically, 'Is this the Fifth Republic?' And left.

Well, and we're also leaving. 'For now', as you would say, let's leave this conversation, this visit to your early life, your struggles and your ideas. Let me thank you for the great amount of time you have been kind enough to devote to me, and congratulate you on your good state of health.

Thank you, Ramonet, for your questions, your critiques, your interest . . . and your stamina, because I talk a lot and you've stood it with great patience. Although you'd already trained hard with our friend Fidel.[37] As for my health, I can say that I feel very strong, in very good spirits, very optimistic and very confident. Because we have set in motion a renaissance in our country. Venezuela will once again enjoy dignity, greatness, glory. It is raising the banners of hope of its people. And I assure you we will continue advancing, in freedom and democracy, towards a fairer, more inclusive, society. Venezuela was one of the most unequal countries in the world, and is on its way to becoming one of the least unequal.

I'd like to take my leave with this phrase of Bolívar, repeating the oath I took all those years ago: 'My arm will not rest nor my soul

---

36   José Luis Rodríguez (1943–), famous singer, member of the Latin American jet set, resident of Miami, friend of Carlos Andrés Pérez.

37   See Ramonet, *Fidel Castro: My Life.*

repose until we see Venezuela truly be as we dream of it: with dignity, prosperity and glory.'

One last thing, to tell you that I hope this is only the beginning. Next time we will have to complete the tour, round the other half of your life.
For now, let's take a breather. If the occasion presents itself, if you keep up your interest, if my activities permit and if God grants me life, I promise we will go on talking about all these matters that concern us so much.

Thank you, President.

Acknowledgements and Further Reading

Authoring a book of conversations with a man of Hugo Chávez's calibre has proven to be a difficult enterprise. Before beginning, I had to spend months studying Venezuela in the years 1950 to 1990, a period when the country was generally not making international headlines. In addition to extensive reading, I consulted with many people without whom I would have been quite unprepared for the interviews that followed.

I would like to express my gratitude to all those who gave me their support. It is impossible to name them all here, but it would be unfair not to mention, first and foremost, the on-going assistance, logistical help and intellectual capital provided to me, from the first moment, by my friend Maximilien Arveláiz, special advisor to President Chávez for international affairs and the dedicatee of this book. He motivated me to undertake this project, provided new ideas, asked useful questions, accompanied me to all my meetings with Hugo Chávez, and encouraged me when difficulties accumulated. Finally, Maximilien reread and corrected the manuscript in its final stage. His cooperation and support is so important that I consider him a co-author. But I remain solely responsible for all its errors and shortcomings.

I would also like to thank the family of Hugo Chávez, particularly his brother Adán and his parents, Hugo de los Reyes and

Elena. All three were kind and patient enough to give me long hours of interviews to evoke the little-known aspects of his childhood, adolescence and youth. I also wish to express my gratitude to his two eldest daughters, Rosa Virginia and Maria Gabriela; both attended several working sessions and Chávez entrusted them with the delicate task of finding and collecting documents from his 'first life' on which the president relied to recall many aspects of his past.

President Nicolás Maduro strongly encouraged me to write this book and, despite his multiple occupations, has never hesitated to help me by recounting his time with Chávez, especially the 'epopee of Chávez' – between the time of his release from prison in 1994 and his first election victory in 1998 – when Maduro was alongside him on the front line.

I cannot fail to mention the huge contribution of my friend Temir Porras, who is very knowledgeable about the Venezuelan political system and whose advice and analysis were essential. Nor would this project have been possible without Teresa Maniglia's help. She is the living memory of the Venezuelan revolutionary process; she filmed everything, recorded everything. Her archives are the chronicle of the Bolivarian Revolution to which she devoted her body and soul with an infinite talent and an unshakable will. I also thank the team and Teresa's employees who performed a tremendous task in transcribing these conversations.

I must also express my appreciation for the members of the armed forces who knew Lieutenant Colonel Hugo Chávez well and whose stories and observations helped me understand military life in Venezuela: Jesse Chacón, Antonio Morales, Francisco Arias Cárdenas, Luis Reyes Reyes, Pedro E. Alastre, Jesús Rafael Suárez Chourio, Jorge Jaspe, Ladera Juan Carlos, Julio Marciales, Kenny Diaz Rosario and Rhôny Pedrosa. I would like to give a very special mention to young and Juan Escalona, Chávez's last aide.

I am indebted to the many personalities who were kind enough to explain various subtle aspects of Venezuelan politics, in particular Bexhi Segura, Farruco Sesto, Alí Rodríguez, Roy Chaderton, José Vicente Rangel, Aristóbulo Istúriz, Rafael Ramírez, Gustavo Vizcaino, Michel Mujica, Ramón Gordils, Bernardo Álvarez, Jesús

Pérez, Arévalo Méndez, Pedro Calzadilla, Carmen Bohórquez, Luis Britto García, Ernesto Villegas, Blanca Eekhout, Patricia Villegas, Marayira Chirinos, Andrés Izarra, Farid Fernández, Carlos Ron, Thierry Deronne, Tatiana Tello, Ilia Calderón, Elba Martínez, Eleazar Díaz Rangel, Tarek Saab, Marta Harnecker, Maryclén Stelling and Neila Nahir.

My friends Bernard Cassen, Ramón Chao and Christophe Ventura shared with me daily the long months of writing and editing, as well as my doubts and uncertainties. They were the first readers of the manuscript; their many comments and corrections have greatly improved the text. I want to express my deepest gratitude.

These acknowledgments would not be complete if I did not mention the many friends and specialists of Latin American geopolitics and Venezuelan society: Íñigo Errejón, Raúl Morodo, Roberto Viciano, Luis Hernandez, Monica Bruckmann, François Houtart, Atilio Borón, Sarah Testard, Maurice Lemoine, Renaud Lambert, Salim Lamrani, John Ortiz, Pascual Serrano, Hernando Calvo Ospina, Franck Gaudichaut, Romain Mingus, Jean-Marc Laforet, Claude Kalifa, Fernando Sulichin, José Ibañez, Cerezal Manuel and Jorge Elías.

With regard to this edition in English, I would like to express my heartfelt thanks to my translator, Ann Wright, who painstakingly managed to capture the nuances of Chávez's idiolect. Appreciation and admiration are due also to my old friend Richard Gott, who was close to Chávez as well as an ardent student of the Venezuelan Revolution. He brought a personal touch while overseeing the translation.

In the introductory text I have already had occasion to express my debt to President Hugo Chávez. Obviously, without his contribution this book would not exist. From the moment he agreed to leave a historical testimony, Chávez never hesitated to devote his time and confidence with great generosity. Indeed, I cannot fully express my gratitude to him and my greatest regret is that death prevented him from seeing a detailed account of his early life finally published.

Further Reading

Chávez
CHÁVEZ FRÍAS, Hugo et al., *The Bolivarian Revolution at the ONU,* Collection of notes for debate, Ministry of Popular Power, for Communication and Information, Caracas, 2009.

Biographies
JONES, Bart, *Hugo! The Hugo Chávez Story from Mud Hut to Perpetual Revolution,* Steerforth Press, Hanover, (New Hampshire), 2007.
GOTT, Richard, *In the Shadow of the Liberator: Hugo Chávez and the Transformation of Venezuela,* Verso, London, 2000. Translated by Temir Porras.

On Hugo Chávez and the Bolivarian Revolution
GOLINGER Eva, *The Chávez Code: Cracking US Intervention in Venezuela,* Olive Branch Press, Northampton, Massachusetts, 2006.
_____, *Bush Versus Chávez: Washington's War on Venezuela,* Monthly Review Press, New York, 2007.
GOTT, Richard (photographs by Georges Bartoli), *Hugo Chávez: The Bolivarian Revolution in Venezuela,* Verso, London, 2005.
KOZLOFF, Nikolas, *Hugo Chávez: Oil, Politics, and the Challenge to the US,* Palgrave Macmillan, New York, 2007.
ROWAN, Michael and SCHOEN, Douglas, *The Threat Closer to Home: Hugo Chávez and the War against America,* Free Press, New York, 2007.

General
ALI, Tariq, *Pirates of the Caribbean: The Axis of Hope,* Verso, London, 2006.
BRAVO, Douglas, *Douglas Bravo Speaks: Interview with the Venezuelan Guerrilla Leader,* Pathfinder Press, Atlanta, 1970.
DI JOHN, Jonathan, *From Windfall to Curse? Oil and Industrialisation in Venezuela, 1920 to the Present,* Pennsylvania State University Press, University Park, 2009.